The Divine Dixie Deva's
Supper Time in the South

by

Kathryn Pierce-McAllister

Enjoy this book of recipes, stories and traditional values.
— *Kathryn*

The Divine Dixie Deva's Supper Time in the South

LCCN: 2007905172
ISBN: 9780977198306

Thank you to the following people; if you didn't help edit, you inspired me: LaDonna, Barb, Debbe, Vanessa, Hanna, Sally, Susan, Pam, Noel, Linda, April and Shelley.
-KPM

Edited and proofed by Ardith Bradshaw, Barb Burnett, Susan Hyde & LaDonna Robinson

Copyright ©2007 by Kathryn Pierce-McAllister
The Divine Dixie Deva, LLC
For additional copies: www.dixiedeva.com

Graphic Design by Carrie Treder

Thank you to my beautiful children, Jade and Seth, and my incredible husband, Greg. I couldn't have done this without you.
-CT

All rights reserved. No part of this book may be reproduced without written permission from the publisher, except by a reviewer who may quote passages or reproduce illustrations in a review with appropriate credits; nor may any part of this book be reproduced, stored in a retrieval system, or transmitted in any form by any means—electronic, mechanical, photocopying, recording, or other—without written permission from the publisher

WIMMER
COOKBOOKS

A CONSOLIDATED GRAPHICS COMPANY

Printed in USA   800.548.2537 wimmerco.com

Dedication and In Loving Memory

When someone meets me, it does not take them long before they know my dear passed Grandmother, "Mama Gillis." Her given name was Ruthie Lee. She was my soul and inspiration. After reading my cookbook, you will see that she had a strong influence on me as well as anyone that had ever met her. Everyone that knew Mama Gillis came to know her Southern charm as well as her Southern cuisine. If ever there was a Southern cook, this "Lady" fit the bill. Just ask any of the "ole timers" that lived in a rural town of Leesburg, Georgia. Folks came from miles around to sample, or rather take home, at least half of one of her different fourteen layer cakes.

Mama Gillis was a hardworking woman that had a drive in her that would make "today's" most successful woman cringe. She invented the word multi-task.

There were several priorities in her life: God, her grandbabies, her children and Olen. Olen was my Grandfather who we called "Papa" and the funniest person ever. Tall and stately with beautiful blue eyes that had a hint of mischief in them, that was my Papa. He had a wit about him that would keep you in stitches. I loved staying up at night when he was barbequing a hog in the pit while Mama Gillis and I were grinding up hog's head for Brunswick Stew. That is "real" Brunswick stew. Please do not give me Brunswick Stew with chicken. What an insult to Brunswick Stew.

There was not a day that I did not see Mama Gillis literally on her knees in her kitchen praying. I would come running in –"Mama Gillis, Mama Gillis—I have something to tell you." She would immediately stand up from her bowed position and I would apologize for interrupting her. She always told me she could get back on her knees and pray.

I can still remember their phone number. That number will stay with me forever. I would call Mama Gillis at least twice a day and one of those calls would be to ask her how to make something. Her detail in telling you a recipe was immaculate. Always, always have your loved ones give you their recipes for future generations.

Mama Gillis gave me Faith, Encouragement, and Unconditional Love. She was a strong advocate on women succeeding in life.

This cookbook is not only a book of recipes, but Life Happenings of two of the most cherished individuals in my life. This book belongs to you, Mama Gillis and Papa.

Ruthie Lee Gillis

Mama Gillis and Papa

Here are some stories that I hope you will enjoy of my life at Mama Gillis' and Papa's house.

Keep in mind while you are reading this that Mama Gillis' given name was Ruthie and Papa's name was Olen.

While Papa was shelling butterbeans and peas and watching Lawrence Welk, I would sit up with Mama Gillis late at night in her brick red colored kitchen, while she was cooking and canning. Not only was I amazed as to what she would create in the food category, she was quite the handicraft individual.

She always had time. How did she always have time? Beats me. She had a 5-acre garden laden with vegetables that she worked. If you rode down Leslie Highway in Leesburg, Georgia, you would see a little figure of a woman with a bonnet sitting in the middle of a garden. She would literally sit down and slide on the ground to work her vegetables. You see, Mama Gillis wore a brace on her back—her back was broken. Those same bonnets are hanging in my kitchen today and I have her wood-cook stove, as well. She made me a bonnet that I had to wear, for she never wanted sun to reach my fair complexion. I would play with my two sisters under the Oak Tree, which is still there.

She helped supply the area grocery stores as well as the larger stores, Harvey's and Piggly Wiggly with her vegetable produce.

Mama Gillis instilled in me that time was love. In other words, that no matter how long it took to bake a cake or two for the neighbors, this was giving of herself. There was no such thing as, "I don't have time". There was not a selfish bone in her body.

At lunch we always had at least two or three meats and fresh fried chicken. English peas with dumplings, butterbeans, squash, and stewed tomatoes along with rice, creamed potatoes, corn bread and biscuits graced the kitchen table.

She always had a big pan of rice. This was mainly for my uncle. He was my favorite uncle and I was always told I got my red hair from him. He had two patches of rice on his plate. He would take Mama Gillis' stewed tomatoes and put them on top of one patch of rice and then he would put her wonderful butterbeans seasoned with ham hock on top of the other.

The fresh field corn that had been scraped off the cob which Mama Gillis called "roast nears" was cooked in a cast iron skillet, I could eat cold.

Not to mention all of the pies and the wonderful muffins with caramel icing which she would put a cherry on top.

Her cakes made history. Please! No one made cakes like my Mama Gillis. Fourteen-layer cakes with cooked icing between the layers and drooling over the tops and sides of the cakes. Every kind you can imagine. To name a few- Chocolate, Coconut, Banana, Banana Walnut, Chocolate Coconut and Black Walnut. The local postmaster would make a "bee" line to the house for a half of one of her cakes. Mama Gillis would always cut him a huge hunk of cake to take with him on the route.

Papa & Mama Gillis courting

As far as Papa was concerned, he was something else. As I said earlier, he had a true wit about him. He always chewed "Bull of the Woods" chewing tobacco. He always picked at us and played practical jokes.

I will never forget we went to feed the cows at the farm and me and my sisters were in the back of his pick-up truck. He would intentionally speed up the truck and spit his tobacco out of his window and guess who would get splashed in the face with "Bull of the Woods". Ick!

Papa always used the phrase, "If you don't shell, you don't eat". That meant whoever did not shell peas and butterbeans did not eat. Now you know that Mama Gillis was not going to let her dear Grandbabies starve. In fact, she would make a check every so often in the den to make sure that Papa was still shelling peas. Oh, we shelled our share of peas or what we thought was our share. Papa never thought so. He grumbled and grunted the whole time thinking that we were getting out of work. No sooner than Papa would get through with a pan of peas, here comes Mama Gillis with another pan heaping full of peas for him to shell. "Olen, I have a few more for you to shell", she would say. He would be grumbling something under his breath. I'm sure that grumbling was a censored word.

During the summer and pea shelling time, we would "put in" to Mama Gillis to go to the Leesburg swimming pool. She would get someone from the farm to take her Grandbabies to the swimming pool. Anything to keep from shelling. This is where I learned to swim. My sister taught me. And this is where I first heard the new release on the jukebox, "I'm Henry the Eighth I Am, I Am" by Herman's Hermits.

Back to the Lawrence Welk Show. Mama Gillis had a vision that her three granddaughters would be "The Lennon Sisters." We had to watch Lawrence Welk every Saturday night while we were shelling peas and butterbeans... We were at the age that The Lawrence Welk Show wasn't to our liking. "Soul Train" was more to our liking. Of course, my oldest sister would be Janet Lennon, and there was a Kathy Lennon and we know who that would be and I don't know who my baby sister would be in the "The Lennon Family", but Mama Gillis knew.

Mama Gillis would sit at her antique piano or her pump organ and play songs while we sang and danced. I'm afraid we disappointed her with this dream of hers for us being an ensemble somewhat like "The Lennon Sisters". I don't think The Lennon Sisters "cut the fool" or caused a "ruckus" like Papa said we did.

Mama Gillis played music by ear. She would sit on that round piano stool and buddy would it rock and roll. The kind of music she played was from one extreme to the other. The religious hymns were beautiful, but she could have also played the music for Miss Kitty in the "Long Branch" (not that she would have.) She was just that talented. I have a tape of songs that she sang to Papa before he passed.

At night time, we all slept in one room. Now the house was huge and had several bedrooms. However, it was special that we were all together in one room. Papa did not think so, though.

After you read on down you will know why.

Papa was in one bed and Mama Gillis and all of us three Grandbabies were in the other. About the time Papa was sound asleep we started begging Mama Gillis if she would tell us about the story of "Epamanondous". This is a story of a little boy that was sent on errands by his mother. You may remember it. Well, Papa was just a fussing. Naturally, he had heard it a zillion times. He kept saying "Ruthie, by God I can't sleep with all of this racket. I wish to gosh (only he didn't say gosh) they would go back to their Mama and Daddy."

"Now Olen, these are our Grandbabies and they are precious."

"Good God. I'm going to precious them if they don't shut up."

Well, this just got us going that much more. We had so much fun poking fun at Papa and irritating him for we knew that Mama Gillis would stand by her Grandbabies, regardless. We also knew that he didn't mean a thing that he said about us.

After the story, we all wanted something to drink and Mama Gillis would bring us orange juice. She made it in a little boiler (Southern term for saucepan) with slushy ice water from an ice tray that had not frozen completely and on those hot, sultry nights in Leesburg, Georgia, it was wonderful.

Later that night after Papa would be sound asleep, one of us would want his feather pillow. Mama Gillis would reach over and snatch it from under his head without batting an eye.

He always threatened that he was going to call Mama and Daddy to come and get us, but we knew Mama Gillis wouldn't let him. Lord, he put up with some stuff.

A souvenir of Mama & Papa's 50th Wedding Anniversary

He always said we were the "meanest youngins" he had ever seen. We knew he didn't mean it. Or did he? Now that I'm grown, I'm wondering it myself.

I was the only Grandbaby that Papa ever chastised, or for a better word, corrected. Now when I say corrected, that doesn't mean beat, either. Nowadays, it has gone to the extreme when a parent spanks a child. I sassed Papa, he went and got his buggy whip, I ran from him and slid under Mama Gillis' bed, and he pulled me out and tanned my legs. Boy, did they sting. Mostly, he hit the bed post to make a whole lot of noise to scare me. You know what, he didn't hurt me. It taught me not to sass at him anymore. I loved him, though, oh my gosh. Was he something! By the way, if you are wondering where Mama Gillis was when Papa cracked the buggy whip on me, she had to have been in the garden and not in the house. Ain't no way, he would have done that with Mama Gillis in the house.

He would sit under the pecan tree and shell peas and tell jokes. He would always predict what was going to happen in the future. As a staunch Democrat, Papa always shared with me his views on the government. By the way, a whole lot of different happenings have come to pass just as Papa predicted. I only wish he were here to say, I told you so.

There are so many theories of being "rich". Well, I was "rich", in the fact that my grandparents were my playmates, parents, and most of all my best friends. Well, you may have heard the old saying, "I wouldn't take a 'purty' for it." This was a Mama Gillis phrase. Well, I wouldn't have taken a "purty" for the life I shared with them.

These are just a few happenings that occurred during my life with Mama Gillis and Papa. They were special. If someone to this day, handed me a million dollars for my memories of Papa and Mama Gillis, ain't no way buddy would I take the money for my life with them.

My thanks go to my mother and father for allowing me the time with my Mama Gillis and Papa.

Kathryn Pierce-McAllister
"The Divine Dixie Deva"

Testimonials

Kathryn McAllister is a delight when she shares her recipes on ABC 12 News This Morning. Mid-Michigan has come to know her as a woman who dishes up homemade comfort, based on the kitchen connection and the love she shared with her grandmother, Mama Gillis. It's not only the taste that makes her recipes outstanding, but the presentation, and the family history that goes into each dish or dessert.

Kathryn has a recipe for every occasion, and a story to go with it. She'll share a number of those stories in this cookbook, and you'll see what a profound impact her grandmother had on her life and her passion for putting a wonderful meal on the table.

Karen Gatlin
ABC 12 News
Flint, Michigan

I was eating breakfast at the counter at Zora's restaurant in Flint, Michigan, one December Saturday when I heard this high-pitched voiced. I had to put my fork down and look to see if this was the reincarnated Patsy Cline sitting a few stools away.

If I were a Georgia native, I surely would have recognized the accent as belonging to someone from south Georgia. Natives would immediately know that person is from Doughtery County. I asked this red-haired charmer where she hailed from. She said, "A'hm from Albany, which is just about two hours miles south of Macon, if y'all know where that is."

Anyway, we got to talking and I learned that this Southern lady had come to Flint with just as much culinary talent and far more folklore than Paula Deen, the Food Network celebrity. I would put my money on Kathryn McAllister in an Iron Chef cook-off with Paula Deen, who also is from Albany. I don't know how one town could contain the both of them.

Anyway, I let my eggs get cold after Kathryn told me she had judged in the Memphis in May barbecue contest, arguably the biggest such event in the world. I said, if you ever go there and judge again, let me know and I will go and tag along with you. Well, it happened in 2005 and I have to tell you it was a great experience.

A couple of years ago, I was privileged to be a guest of Kathryn and Lee for a Christmas dinner. I did promise to write an article about it for The Flint Journal, but I don't think that would have made any difference as far as the unbelievable array of food is concerned. If you saw it, you would have thought she had three people helping her cook. But it was just her. This is a rare and special individual, if I do say so.

This book is the realization of a dream Kathryn has had for a long time. All of us who know her share her joy in completing it. Anyone who takes the time to go through the book will appreciate the powerful bond she had-and still has with Mama Gillis. The next step is to prepare some of their favorite recipes. This way, you will be guests at that big dinner table in Albany.

Ron Krueger
The Flint Journal, www.flintjournal.com

How does one begin to describe the Divine **Dixie** Deva, Mrs. Kathryn McAllister? I can start with her sweet down to earth southern accent, but what about that awesome personality she possesses? Oh wait a minute! Her cooking! Did I mention she is the best cook this side of the mason Dixie line? Get it? **Dixie**..... Now let's get serious folks this woman can cook like no other. I was delighted and honored to be part of this gathering of her Mama Gillis's recipes and of course her own delicious recipes. I was fortunate enough to have been invited on more than one occasion to sit at her dinner table. As a matter of fact, I may have inadvertently invited myself a time or two! Shhhh! Let's keep that a secret, anyway. I can attest that any dish that she prepares has a little bit of Mama Gillis and a whole lot of the deva! She puts her heart and soul into every dish she makes. I must say though I would love to have her at my house nightly. Who wouldn't like to eat like that all the time? Her husband is one lucky fellow. Now for a few of my favorites: I love the asparagus casserole; I hope it made the book! And her holiday cranberry raisin pie! Sweet potato's from heaven or somewhere real close and her pecan pie... I could go on and on. Well how about you see for yourself? You should try all her recipes and pick your favorites; those were just a few of mine. I'm getting ready to go there now to bake cookies for Christmas with the children and as always we will have a splendid time and fill our palates with the best from the Deva!!!

Karen Smith
Director, YOUR Magazine

Kathryn McAllister's stories of the South are as delicious as her southern-style cooking. From her grandmother, affectionately known as "Mama Gillis," Kathryn learned the value of hard work, trusting in God, and how to find her way around the kitchen.

With Southern charm, old-fashioned hearty meals, and her flare for storytelling, Kathryn McAllister will teach you how to make meal time memorable at your house.

Kathryn's mission is to get the family back to gathering around a hearty meal for dinner each night, knitting the memories that will keep each one warm long after their parents or grandparents are gone. Following her recipes will help you create dinners no one will forget.

Julia Zaher
Co-host
The My Mom and Me Show

𝒦athryn, from our first encounter to our last at the Big Pig Jig in Vienna, you have always impressed me with your fair and unbiased evaluations of a teams performance, regardless of your friendships you may have with the participants. But, your love for BBQing and your desire to learn more while cultivating relationships with the teams is what truly makes me glad to call you my friend. Best of luck to ya, sweety.

Myron Mixon
Chief Cook of Jack's Old South Competition Bar-B-Que Team & Three-time Grand Champion at the World Championship in Memphis in May

Myron Mixon at the Big Pig Jig in Vienna, Georgia.
See Myron's Rib Recipe on page 474.

Acknowledgements

To my "Yankee" husband:
You have given me encouragement, drive and supported me in my every little "whim," and have never burst my many bubbles. You always tell me, if it makes you happy, do it. You even say I look beautiful without my mascara. And most of all, thank you Lee, for allowing me to have my four "babies," Duke, Belle, Rebel and Baby Bubba, (Lab puppies).

Thanks for the kiss under the Magnolia tree and calling me, "Your Lady".

I love you. Kathryn

To my wonderful children, Jeff and Mandy:
Thank you for keeping the secret of "Supper Time in the South". I am so proud and blessed to have such talented, responsible individuals for my children.

I love you both. Mama

To my two sisters who I love:
Even though, when we would play hide-and-go-seek you would ultimately find my hiding place and sit on top of the toy box so that I could not get out. Possibly hoping that I would suffocate? Who knows? There were only three air holes and you would put your feet over them. Of course, this was the only place I could ever think of hiding. It was not easy being the middle child.

I love you both. Kathy

To my Mama:
I can never thank you enough for the qualities that you have instilled in me. You also gave me drive, ambition and perseverance. When we were little girls, you would stay up late at nights sewing all three of us girls beautiful clothes, even though I would sash-shay all over town bare-footed to your disgust. You always made sure we had a clean and beautiful home. But just to let you know, not everyone in this world has a mother that looks like a "movie star". I hope you like, "The Divine Dixie Deva's Supper Time in the South".

Love to you Mama-Kathy

To my Daddy:
Daddy, you always remarked, "You have a roof over your head, clothes on your back and food in your belly". Yes, we did and we could not have had all of that if you had not worked three jobs.

On many occasions, I was allowed to stay up and watch the television show, "Thriller", with Alfred Hitchcock. And on those same occasions, I would wake up screaming and hollering, afraid that the "boogie bear" was going to get me. Of course, I was told "who would have me?" At any rate, thank you Daddy, for coming to my rescue when I would wake everyone up in the house screaming and hollering because I was scared to death. I'm sorry that on one of those screaming frenzies, you ran into the closed door when coming to my rescue. For everyone's information that was the last time I watched "Thriller".

I thank you for always making me feel safe. Thanks for being my Daddy.

I love you, Gerb.

About the Author

"Diva" versus "Deva"? "Prima Donna" or "good in spirit"?

I'll choose "good in spirit" any ole day. Kathryn Pierce-McAllister, being the proud mother of two children and four Labrador pups, clearly exemplifies the true meaning of "good in spirit".

I am a Southwest Georgia born and bred redhead that grew up with her Grandmother's influence in the kitchen, working in the garden, canning the bounty on her wood cook stove, and learning to make dress patterns out of grocery bags. She preserved the past and created the future for her granddaughter with her traditional values. I was probably no doubt born a "century too late."

I worked for an old-time aristocratic family at a Southern plantation estate as a house coordinator—planning menus, preparing hors d'oeuvres, making specialty desserts for them and their guests.

As a certified judge for the famous "Memphis in May" cook-offs, I have judged cook-offs for 20 plus years. I have judged wild game cook-offs and have been selected as a final cook-off judge several times.

I express my passion of cooking through live demonstrations, when I am featured on the local ABC-affiliate station for different holidays during the year.

My recipes are featured in *Your Magazine* on a monthly basis, which is published here in Michigan.

Being featured on a live radio talk show here in Michigan, sharing recipes and telling my "tall tales," growing up in Southwest Georgia is a favorite of mine also.

I met my "Yankee" husband in my hometown and he lured me to the North where I had the "hugest culture shock." I made the "gutsiest" move to marry the man of my dreams, and I have found that it doesn't matter where you live, there are wonderful people everywhere.

My nickname is "Gerb." My daddy calls me "Gerb." Stories have it that when I was a baby, my parents had to buy Gerber baby food by the case. If the truth be known, I still slip several jars in my grocery buggy even today.

Daddy use to say, "Gerb, don't go and load up when you get to Ruthie's (which is Mama Gillis') house." He was so afraid I would grow up looking like a blimp.

There are only certain times that my father chose to call me by "Kathy," and I knew he wasn't thrilled at something I had done. Anyone in Albany, Georgia, who knows my father, knows who "Gerb" is.

I have used my "Southern Lingo" in this book for I am indeed a true Southern Belle.

So folks, bring your family back to the supper table.

Kathryn Pierce-McAllister
The Divine Dixie Deva

Introduction to my Readers and Cookers

When I think of home-cooking, I think of good ole butterbeans with pieces of ham in there, homemade mashed potatoes with plenty of butter and cream in them and fresh creamed corn right off of the cob. Southern Fried Chicken, Cubed Steak 'n' Gravy so tender that you could cut it with a fork, homemade biscuits with Mayhaw Jelly and last but not least, homemade cakes and pies gracing the table. This is nothing in the world but sharing of ones' self.

What better way to give of one's self than to prepare a meal for family or friends. This is love.

This is what I was taught to do. My grandmother, Ruthie Lee Gillis, and my mother, set this tradition and example for me to follow.

This book has taken me years to complete. As you will read, I have dedicated this book to Mama Gillis and Papa, my grandparents. Mama Gillis knew at least two years before her passing that I was going to write a cookbook and dedicate it to her. I had so hoped that I would have finished it before that time. She left me drawings of her "doodling," which are little pictures that she drew, which was her way of relaxing. Mama Gillis wrote verses and songs from her heart which was a true gift to me and I hope it will be to you.

My mother has always said that I should write a book about my life. Well, even though this is a cookbook, it is about my life. This cookbook is a conglomeration of Family, Memories, Adventurous Trips and of course, Cooking.

Not all of the stories relate to Mama Gillis and Papa. But you can rest assured that Mama Gillis knew most of the stories.

When I come across a recipe from "ump-teen" thousand years ago, if it reminds me of an event, I have written a little story that comes to mind. I so hope you will enjoy it.

When I was growing up, we never had "between" meals, our meals were satisfying. We never had to run to the nearest fast food joint for a meal that wasn't going to stick with you. Now, you might be thinking—well, back then both parents were not working.

WRONG—my mother worked full-time.

Remember Home Economics? I'm sure you have heard of it. We learned to plan menus and purchase our ingredients by the menus. I have always followed this method and not only does this help you plan nutritional meals; it saves you "lots of dough" as in dollars, and time. There is less waste, also.

We have compromised our health for convenience.

Schools back then had balanced lunches. What happened? Later on down the road schools started having soft drinks and candy machines in them. You hardly ever heard of a child that had juvenile diabetes when I was in school. Now it is more prevalent.

America, I am glad to see that we are finally taking notice of nutrition.

I want to thank you for selecting "Supper Time in the South."

Thanking you again,

Kathryn Pierce-McAllister
"The Divine Dixie Deva"

Sketch by Ruthie Lee Gillis

Table of Contents

The Divine Dixie Deva's Glossary of Southern Terminology	25
Something to Nibble On	29
Something to Swig On	59
Breads	81
Desserts	111
Cakes, Frostings, Icings & Fillings	131
Remedy	178
Cookies	179
Pies, Cobblers & Crunchers	201
Something Sweet to Eat	231
Breakfast	249
Meats, Main Dishes, Skillets & Casseroles	261
All Kinds of Salads	307
Soups, Sandwiches, Spreads & Relishes	331
Sides & Vegetables	355
Syrups, Sauces, Toppings, Glazes & Gravies	401
Jams, Jellies, Preserves & Pickles	421
Wild Cooking, Fishing & BBQ	445
The Grand Finale!	475
Resources	479

The Divine Dixie Deva's Glossary of Southern Terminology

Boiler – If I have slipped up and said the word boiler, I mean a pot or saucepan. I have never called a pot a pot. It is in my vocabulary to call it a boiler.

Crispy – the browned bits of seasoned flour left floating in the skillet after frying a chicken or some such food item; NOT TO BE DISCARDED but incorporated into a mess of milk gravy.
"Pour that grease up through the strainer but be sure to save those crispies (plural)."

Crud – means something nasty that needs to be gotten rid of; may be as complicated as an illness or as minor as something on the bottom of one's shoe.
"Those tomatoes will be good as soon as we wash the crud off of them."

Dinner – the noontime meal of the day; mistakenly referred to as lunch by those north of the Mason Dixon line.
"They go to the diner to eat dinner every day at lunchtime."

Doom's day – the end of time, as we know it.
"Lordy, we'll have enough squash this summer to last til doom's day."

Dose – bigger than a dash or a smidgen.
"Go on and put a dose of black pepper in there, too."

Light bread – sliced white bread usually from the store; not wheat and not cornbread. Typically, in the South when you have pulled pork sandwiches, the restaurants serve light bread with it in lieu of buns.
"Pass me some of that light bread. I want to make a baloney sandwich."

Mess – enough of one food item for a single meal; maybe anything from turnip greens to freshly caught fish.
"Come on over and eat with us. Bubba caught a whole mess of catfish today."

Ole timey or **Old timey** – vintage or old-fashioned.
"Well, would you just look at this old timey recipe I found?"

Pick at – to aggravate or to play fun at.
"We would pick at Papa."

Puny – feeling poorly.
"Mama took to her bed…she was a feeling a little puny."

Purty – means a reward, possibly a million dollars.
"I wouldn't give a purty for all the sushi in Japan."

Put in – to beg or get our way.
"I put in for banana puddin' for dessert – sure hope mama makes it!"

Pick at – to aggravate or to play fun at.
"We would pick at Papa."

Put up – in the cooking terminology, it means to preserve food as in canning or freezing.
"I can't go with you tonight; I've got a bushel of green beans to put up."

Put up – could also refer to a whole different meaning as in having to "deal" with certain individuals.
"Papa had to put-up with us young-en's."

Skeeters – mosquitoes.
"Needs no further explanation!"

Smidgen – a small amount.
"Just put a smidgen more salt in the soup and it'll be fine."

Sop – to overly clean one's plate, often using a food item such as bread to absorb every bite.
"She took that cornbread and sopped up (past tense) every drop of those greens."
"I like to use cane syrup to sop my biscuits with."

Supper – last of three major meals of the day; mistakenly referred to as dinner by those north of the Mason Dixon line.
"Y'all get in here and eat your supper while it's hot!"

Sweet milk – white milk, which may or may not be from the store. It could mean fresh from the cows. Mama Gillis would always ask us to pick her up a gallon of sweet milk.
"Pass me a jug of that sweet milk."

Swig – to take a large drink of.
"He came in from the field and took a big ole swig of sweet tea."

Tin foil – aluminum foil.
"Wrap what's left of that pie up in tin foil and we'll have it for supper."

To boot – means in addition to.
"They paid him twenty dollars and gave him a frying chicken, to boot."

Ump-teenth – an almost unending number of times.
"I have told those kids for the ump-teenth time to stop slamming that back door!"

Wad – a generous amount of a food product that is traditionally used in smaller amounts, such as butter on grits or sugar in tea.
"She put a wad of that grape jelly on her biscuit this morning."

"Yes, siree, bob tail" – affirmative; in case one had any doubt remaining about the situation.
"Is it hot down here? Yes, siree bob tail, it sure is!"

Something to Nibble On

Bonnet made by Ruthie Lee Gillis. She used this bonnet while gardening.

*O*f course, when you think of New Year's, you think of parties, food, decorations, and noise makers. This story comes to mind when New Year's Eve rolls around.

I was probably about 7 or 8 years old at the time, and on New Year's Eve at Mama Gillis' house, my sister and I, "put in" to have a New Year's Eve party, with just us being the only attendees. That meant we could stay up extra late to bring in the New Year, making a whole lot of extra noise with our homemade noise makers, dressing up in our homemade costumes and eating snacks.

All of this to say, our ultimate goal could have been was to consciously irritate Papa, which was a "hoot" for us. I can't ever remember "asking him," if we could stay up late to do this. We knew the answer would have been a big "no." But, Mama Gillis never said "no," and she could have also wanted to "pick" at him; so we knew she would let us go about our business to plan the big "hoopla."

On a few New Year's Eve nights while Papa was sleeping downstairs, we would skate upstairs, whooping and hollering and bringing in the New Year, knowing that Papa's bed was directly under the room where we were.

But boy, did we learn our lesson this one year!

On a New Year's Eve, we went upstairs, where Mama Gillis stored a lot of "stuff." That "stuff," consisted of boxes and boxes of old pie tins, dresses, hats and you name it, anything that anyone could imagine making costumes with. We were looking for items to make noise makers to bring in the New Year also, anything we could probably use our imagination and make New Year's hats and costumes. We mentioned to Papa that we were going upstairs to make noise makers for our party. You can imagine that the "racket" us girls could make would be enough noise. Papa always remarked that we didn't need to make noise makers for we were all the noise makers anyone could ever want.

So here I was, upstairs looking in all of the boxes for treasures. All of a sudden, I looked up and I saw this tall creature with red fire in his eyes. This monster looking creature had eyes that were blinking red on and off, constantly. He had a flannel shirt, blue jeans and a straw hat to boot.

I started hollering, crying for Mama Gillis and couldn't get down the stairs quick enough. As I was flying down the stairs, I did not notice that Papa was in hysterics laughing. I noticed for some reason that Mama Gillis seemed a little unconcerned and was still in the kitchen cooking. However, when I got in the kitchen, Mama Gillis was quite sympathetic, but she had a smirk on her face and a twinkle in her eye. I don't even remember how my sister reacted; I didn't care, for all I could think of was to get out of those upstairs.

Papa had mentioned to our Uncle that we were going to have our annual New Year's Eve party and was looking for noise makers, costumes, and decorations.

With the guidance of Papa, (you notice that I did not put any of the blame toward Mama Gillis) come to find out my Uncle had rigged up a plan to get us down from the upstairs by dressing up like a monster by doing the following:

He had gotten a gourd of Mama Gillis's, in which she had cut out two eyes, a nose and mouth. My Uncle had put a trouble light in the center of the gourd. He had put the gourd in front of his face while the blinking red light would go on and off. My Uncle had pulled the flannel shirt up over him and placed a straw hat on top of the gourd making this creature extra tall. Quite the creativity he bestowed. That was the very last time that we ever went back upstairs looking for noise makers and New Years decorations.

Jezebel Cheese Ball

1	(8-ounce) package cream cheese, softened
1	cup Cheddar cheese, grated
1	cup extra sharp cheese, grated
1	cup Pepper Jack cheese with jalapeños, grated
¼	teaspoon onion salt
¼	teaspoon garlic salt
2	tablespoons Miracle Whip salad dressing
1	tablespoon Worcestershire sauce
½	cup pecans, chopped*

Chopped nuts are to roll cheese ball in.*

Combine all of your ingredients except for the nuts. Blend well. Form into ball and refrigerate overnight. Roll into nuts and serve with crackers

Holiday Cheese Ball

2	(8-ounce) packages cream cheese, softened
2	cups (8-ounce) Cheddar cheese, shredded
1	tablespoon pimento, chopped
1	tablespoon green or red pepper, chopped
1	tablespoon onion, minced
2	teaspoons Worcestershire sauce
1	teaspoon lemon juice
	Dash of seasoning salt
	Dash of red pepper
1	cup pecans, chopped
	Assorted crackers

Combine all of the ingredients, except for the pecans. Chill for at least one hour, shape into a ball and then roll into pecans. Serve with assorted crackers.

Kathryn's Favorite Cheese Ring

4	cups sharp cheese, grated
1	cup pecans, finely chopped
1	cup mayonnaise
1	small onion, grated
	Dash of cayenne pepper to taste
	Paprika
	Strawberry or raspberry preserves

Mix all of the ingredients together except for the preserves and paprika. Shape into a ring or place into a greased 5 or 6-cup ring mold. Chill overnight, unmold, and fill in the center, either raspberry or strawberry preserves. Sprinkle paprika around the cheese ring for color. Serve with assorted crackers. *I could eat the whole thing.*

Kicker Cheese Ring

1	(12-ounce) block sharp cheese, grated
1	(10-ounce) package cream cheese
4	tablespoons mayonnaise
1	(2.25-ounce) jar dried beef, chipped up with scissors
1	cup nuts, optional
1	teaspoon hot sauce, optional
1	tablespoon garlic, minced
1	teaspoon Worcestershire sauce
1	tablespoon onion, minced
	Assorted crackers

In a large bowl, cream all of the cheeses together and then combine all other ingredients. Prepare a mold or pan by lightly greasing with oil and press the mixture in it. Cover and put in fridge 4 hours or more. Serve with assorted crackers.

Note: If you would rather have cheese logs, prepare the recipe as you would the Kicker Cheese Ring, but put in the fridge for at least one hour to chill. Chilling the mixture will firm up the mixture enough so you may divide the mixture up into two logs. Roll the cheese logs into 1 cup additional crushed pecans. Serve with crackers.

Pecan Cheese Ball

1	(8-ounce) package cream cheese, softened
1	teaspoon garlic salt
1	tablespoon Worcestershire sauce
1½	cups pecans, chopped (divided use)
	Assorted crackers

In a medium sized bowl, mix the cream cheese, garlic salt and Worcestershire sauce until well blended. Add 1 cup of the pecans, mixing well and shape into a ball. Roll the ball in the remaining ½-cup of pecans. Refrigerate. Serve with assorted crackers.

Cheesy Apple Spread

1	(8-ounce) package cream cheese, softened
2	cups sharp cheese, shredded
1	medium-size tart apple, unpeeled, cored and chopped
½	cup walnuts, chopped
⅓	cup Miracle Whip
	Pinch of nutmeg
	Apple slices (dip in lemon juice to keep them from discoloring)
	Fresh pear slices
	Assorted crackers
	Parsley or mint sprigs for garnish

Using a medium-size mixing bowl beat the cream cheese until very creamy, folding in the sharp cheese and mixing until smooth. Blend in the apple, walnuts, Miracle Whip and nutmeg. Pour into a small serving bowl and arrange apple and fresh pear slices and crackers around the serving bowl.

Hint

When I have coat, jacket, or vest buttons that come off; sew them back on with unwaxed dental floss. The floss is very strong and will stay on until doom's day.

Orange Cheese Spread

2	(8-ounce) packages cream cheese, softened
½	cup confectioners' sugar
2	tablespoons orange peel, grated
2	tablespoons Grand Marnier
2	tablespoons frozen orange concentrate
	Dash of mace
	Sprinkle with nutmeg

Beat the cream cheese, adding the rest of the ingredients, except for the nutmeg. Cover and put in the fridge until ready to serve.

For a unique container, scoop out a large navel orange and pour spread into the orange shell. Sprinkle with nutmeg. Serve with gingersnap cookies.

Spicy Cheese Loaf

2	(8-ounce) packages cream cheese, softened
4	cups sharp cheese, grated
1	(10-ounce) can Rotel diced tomatoes and green chiles, drained
2	small bunches of spring onions, chopped
3	(2.25-ounce) jars dried beef, chopped
1	(16-ounce) container sour cream, use just enough to make the mixture creamy
1	large loaf French bread*

In a large bowl, mix all the ingredients with the exception of the French bread and sour cream. Then lastly add the sour cream, using just enough sour cream to make the mixture creamy. Hollow out the bread and save the inside of the bread to toast for use later in the recipe. Fill the cavity of the loaf bread with mixture and bake in 350 degree oven for 20 to 25 minutes until completely heated.

*Toast the bread that you hollowed out. You may use this to spread the mixture on. A great way to toast this and add a little extra flavor and calories, is to pour butter on the bread before you toast it. This will be delicious with the mixture on it.

*You may also use assorted crackers with this recipe.

Ole Timey Cheese Straws

What would a Southern Tea or Wedding shower be without the Ole Timey Cheese Straws to grace the table?

- 2 (8-ounce) packages sharp Cheddar cheese, shredded
- 2 sticks oleo margarine (not butter)
- 3 cups self-rising flour
- ½ teaspoon red pepper *(You might want to start at ¼ teaspoon and taste. I use ½ teaspoon.)*

After shredding the cheese, set the cheese and oleo margarine out overnight and let them soften. Combine flour, red pepper, cheese and oleo together. Pack into a cookie press or cookie gun.* Place on an ungreased cookie sheet and bake at a preheated 350 degree oven 12 to 15 minutes. You need to watch them while cooking, they will brown quickly. Cool before storing in tins. You may freeze these.

*The term "Cheese Straws", comes from using the tip on the cookie press that shoots out flat, ribbed dough, that ultimately when cooked would look like a flat, narrow wafer. We, "Southerners", call that the "Cheese Straws".

You can make this cookie into any shape, you so desired. Whichever, shape works for you. Try this version for a little different twist.

For a Sweet and Cheesy Twist:
Take the dough and roll into small balls. Flatten with fork. You may have to dip your fork in flour to keep dough from sticking to the fork. Cook according to the above directions. When cool, but not cold, take some confectioners' sugar and roll the cheese straws in the sugar very carefully. You will find this is a very different taste, sweet and cheesy, but great. A little different variation.

Cheese Crackers

This is a different recipe using oatmeal. You will love it.

2	cups grated sharp Cheddar cheese *(You can tell I love sharp cheese.)*
½	cup butter, softened
¼	cup water
1	cup all-purpose flour
¼	teaspoon salt
1	cup uncooked oatmeal, quick or old-fashioned

Beat cheese, butter, and water until well blended. Add flour and salt. Mix well. Stir in uncooked oatmeal, mixing until well blended. Shape dough into a roll. Wrap the roll with wax paper and refrigerate for at least 4 hours. When ready to cook, take out of refrigerator and let stand for about 15 minutes to soften before cutting. Cut into ¼-inch thick slices. If dough begins to stick as you flatten with tines of the fork, dip the fork in a little flour. Bake on a lightly greased cookie sheet in a preheated 400 degree oven for 10 to 12 minutes until lightly golden brown. Immediately remove from cookie sheet.

Yields: 6 dozen

Rice Crispy Cheese Wafers
By Mrs. Edna Lane Higgins

1	pound sharp cheese, grated
2	sticks butter, softened
3	cups all-purpose flour
4	cups rice cereal
¼	teaspoon red pepper
½	teaspoon salt

Combine all of the ingredients. Knead with your hand and make small balls. Flatten and bake at 350-degrees for about 10 minutes, just until delicate brown.

Apple Cheese Crescents

Makes 32 crescents

2	medium sized apples, finely chopped
½	teaspoon cinnamon
1	cup Cheddar cheese, shredded *(Try using my favorite cheese, sharp)*
2	(8-ounce) can refrigerated crescent rolls

Preheat oven to 375-degrees.
Combine the apples, cinnamon and cheese. Separate the crescent dough along the perforations and cut each triangle in half lengthwise. Place a small amount of apple mixture on the wide end of each triangle and roll up into the crescent shape. Place on a greased cookie sheet and bake for 15 to 20 minutes.

Peanut Butter Cheese Ball

If you have a house full of company for the Holidays and you feel that the kids need to have their own cheese ball; this is the one to make for them. The big kids will like it, too.

This would make a wonderful after school surprise treat, in addition to being very nutritious.

2	(8-ounce) package cream cheese, softened
1	(12-ounce) jar creamy peanut butter
¾	cup confectioners' sugar, sifted
1	teaspoon cinnamon
1	cup honey roasted peanuts, crushed
	Apple or pear slices (dipped in lemon juice)
	Assorted crackers

Combine the cream cheese, peanut butter, confectioners' sugar and cinnamon in a large bowl. Mix well and shape into a ball. Place crushed peanuts in a bowl and roll the cheese ball in the peanuts. Wrap the cheese ball in wax paper and chill. Just before serving, set the ball out to reach room temperature. Serve with apple or pear slices and crackers.

Corned Beef Balls

1	can corned beef
1	(8-ounce) package cream cheese, softened
3	tablespoons lemon juice
2	cups sharp cheese, grated
¼	cup sweet pickle relish
½	teaspoon Worcestershire sauce
1½	teaspoons prepared mustard
1	teaspoon horseradish
1	cup pecans or walnuts, chopped fine
	Parsley, if desired to garnish

Combine all ingredients except for the nuts in a large bowl. Form into small balls and roll the balls onto the nuts. You may garnish with several sprigs of parsley. You may spread this on crackers. I like to use Wheat Thins.

Smoked Fish Spread

1	(8-ounce) package cream cheese, softened
1½	cups flaked smoked salmon or mullet.* Remove skin and bones before flaking.
½	teaspoon curry powder
¼	teaspoon salt
¼	teaspoon pepper
	A few grains of red pepper to taste
	Sprinkle with paprika

Combine cream cheese, fish, curry, salt and peppers in a bowl and mix well with hand mixer until blended and smooth. Chill and spread onto crackers or cocktail square bread. You may use with raw vegetables.

After moving to the North, I found that mullet does not exist here in the North. Folks here did not even know what mullet was. I love mullet. I had to settle using the salmon which is a wonderful substitute. On the other hand, I did not know what smelt was either when I moved up here.

Salmon Log

1	pound can salmon
1	tablespoon lemon juice
2	teaspoons onion, grated
1	teaspoon prepared horseradish
¼	teaspoon garlic salt
¼	teaspoon liquid smoke
1	(8-ounce) package cream cheese, softened
½	cup finely, chopped pecans
	Assorted crackers

Drain and debone salmon. Combine salmon with lemon juice, onion, horseradish, garlic salt, and liquid smoke. Mix in cream cheese. Mix real good. Chill several hours for flavors to blend. Shape into a log roll and roll in chopped nuts. Chill well and enjoy with crackers.

Note: In lieu of shaping into a log roll, you could just spread the mixture into celery sticks for a healthy treat.

A Man's Man Appetizer

2	cans smoked oysters
4	tablespoons onions, chopped
4	dashes hot sauce
2	tablespoons lemon juice
1	teaspoon Worcestershire sauce
¼	teaspoon garlic salt
1	loaf cocktail square bread
	Parmesan cheese

Mash undrained oysters. Add all of the ingredients except the Parmesan cheese, and of course saving the bread to spread this wonderful concoction on.

Toast one side of bread, then flip the untoasted side of the bread over and spread with a scant tablespoon of the oyster mixture. Sprinkle with Parmesan cheese. Toast under the broiler for just a few minutes.

Remember, how much you put in a spoonful on that bread will determine how many appetizers you will have. Serve hot and oh my gosh!!!

Baked Oysters

1	dozen oysters (cleaned, drained and returned to the half shell)
12	dashes Worcestershire sauce
12	dashes hot sauce
	Salt and pepper to taste
4	slices bacon, partially cooked
12	tablespoons or ¾-cup chili sauce
4	tablespoons Parmesan cheese (more or less)

For each oyster, add 1 dash of Worcestershire sauce, 1 dash of hot sauce and season with salt and pepper. Cut bacon in enough pieces to top each oyster. Top the oyster with the piece of bacon, 1 tablespoon of chili sauce and then top with the Parmesan cheese. Bake in a preheated 350-degree oven for 10 to 15 minutes or until oysters begins to curl. This is scrumptious. You can tell I love oysters!

Shrimp Spread

Approximately 2 cups of Spread.

1	(4.5-ounce) can shrimp, finely chopped
1	tablespoon horseradish or to suit taste
⅓	cup chili sauce
½	cup celery, minced
½	cup mayonnaise
	Assortment of crackers

Combine all of the ingredients, except the crackers. Mix well. Chill until serving time. Spread on crackers.

Marinated Shrimp

5	pounds shrimp, cooked, peeled, deveined and chilled
½	cup catsup
½	cup chili sauce
1	cup tartar sauce
1	cup mayonnaise
3	onions, chopped fine
	Salt to taste
	Pepper to taste
	Dried parsley flakes to sprinkle

Assorted crackers or cocktail square bread

Mix all of the ingredients together, except for the dried parsley flakes. Add salt and pepper to taste. Cover and refrigerate at least 2 hours for flavors to blend. Place a shrimp on an assortment of crackers or cocktail square bread with a little dash of dried parsley flakes to garnish. Great for parties.

Yields: 25 ample sized servings

Deviled Eggs with Shrimp

8	hard-boiled eggs, peeled
2	tablespoons Miracle Whip salad dressing
1	cup shrimp, cooked, deveined and shredded
2	tablespoons celery, minced
2	tablespoons sweet pickle relish
	Salt and pepper to taste
	Paprika

Slice eggs in half lengthwise and remove yolks. Mash yolks with Miracle Whip; blend in shrimp, celery, pickle relish, salt and pepper. Spoon mixture carefully into egg whites. Sprinkle with paprika. You may substitute celery salt in lieu of regular salt.

Party Shrimp Mold

1	(8-ounce) package cream cheese, softened
2	(1-ounce) envelopes unflavored gelatin, softened in cold water
½	cup cold water
1	cup good quality mayonnaise
1	tablespoon lemon juice
2	tablespoons onion, grated
1	tablespoon dried parsley flakes
1	teaspoon seasoned salt
1	teaspoon Worcestershire sauce
2	teaspoons Durkee's Famous Sauce
	Dash of cayenne pepper to taste
	Paprika to sprinkle for garnish
3	cups shrimp, boiled, deveined, and chopped *(Be sure to drain all water out of the shrimp really well. Use paper toweling and squeeze out the excess moisture.)
	Assorted crackers

Beat the cream cheese until creamy and set aside. After softening the gelatin in the cold water, place the gelatin in a small saucepan over low heat, stirring the gelatin until completely dissolved. Mix the gelatin mixture, mayonnaise, lemon juice and all other ingredients, except for the shrimp and paprika. Lastly, fold in the chopped shrimp, mixing well. Pour into a well-greased (spray with baking spray) 1-quart mold. Chill overnight. Unmold and sprinkle with paprika and serve with assorted crackers.

* You may want to purchase additional shrimp so you may have them around the Shrimp Mold. I used a ring mold and place shrimp sauce in the middle of the shrimp mold.

Crabmeat and Spinach Appetizer

4	green onions, chopped
½	cup butter, melted
	Garlic salt to taste
	Black pepper to taste
1	(6-ounce) can crabmeat
1	(10-ounce) package frozen spinach, cooked and drained*
	Cocktail Rye square bread
	Parmesan cheese to sprinkle

Sauté the onions in butter. Add garlic salt and black pepper. You may want to add a little table salt to taste. Fold in the crabmeat and spinach. Top the mixture on the rye squares and sprinkle with Parmesan cheese. Broil until heated.

*To drain the spinach, I take paper toweling and squeeze excess moisture out.

Deviled Ham Balls

1	(8-ounce) package cream cheese, softened
1	(4.5-ounce) can deviled ham
1	cup nuts, chopped

Put cream cheese and deviled ham in a food processor or by hand. Mix well. Remove and chill in refrigerator until firm enough to handle. Shape into balls and roll in chopped nuts. Serve on toothpicks.

Hint

Save your butter wrapper papers. Why? I use them to grease baking dishes and cookie sheets. There is just enough butter left on the wrappers when you take them off of the butter to do the job. And another thing—your hands do not get greasy. Store any extra wrappers in the freezer in a zip-top bag.

Chicken Wings with Wing Ding Sauce

3	pounds chicken wings, removing the wing tips and discard
	Salt and pepper to season
3	tablespoons olive oil
1	clove of garlic, minced
⅓	cup soy sauce
¼	cup dry sherry
2	tablespoons catsup
1	tablespoon apple cider vinegar
1	cup honey

Preheat oven to 350-degrees. Season the wings with salt and pepper. In a 2-gallon zip-top bag, combine all of the ingredients. Place as many chicken wings in the bag as you can and "douse" the wings. Place the sauced wings on a foil lined baking dish. Bake for 50 to 60 minutes until chicken is tender and completely cooked. Turn chicken periodically while cooking.

After the chicken wings have cooked and you want that extra kick to them; try the following simple recipe for a dipping sauce. This is an optional choice.

Sauce:

¼	cup butter, melted
1	(15-ounce) can tomato sauce
	Several splashes hot sauce

In a small saucepan, combine all of the ingredients, heating until a simmer.

For a variation, try this dressing!

Ranch dressing:

2	packets Ranch dressing
2	(16-ounce) containers sour cream

Mix contents of packets with the sour cream. Whisk till completely mixed and chill. Dip away and enjoy!

Chicken Salad Puffs

Puffs:
½	cup butter
1	cup boiling water
1	cup all-purpose flour
¼	teaspoon salt
4	eggs
1	cup Swiss cheese, grated

Filling:
3	cups cooked chicken, chopped fine
¼	cup celery, minced
1	(4-ounce) jar pimento, chopped
2	(3-ounce) packages cream cheese, softened
¼	cup Miracle Whip salad dressing or mayonnaise
½	cup pecans, finely chopped

Preheat oven to 425-degrees. Melt butter in the boiling water. Add flour and salt; stir vigorously. Cook and stir till mixture forms a ball that doesn't separate. This takes about 2 minutes. Remove from the heat and cool slightly. Add eggs, one at a time and beat well after each addition until smooth. Stir in cheese. Drop dough onto greased baking sheet, using about 1 level teaspoon for each puff. Bake for about 20 minutes. Remove puffs from oven and cool and split.

Yields: 6 dozen

For the filling:
Combine the filling ingredients and fill each puff with 2 tablespoons of chicken salad mixture.

Note: You may add a little curry powder in this filling—be careful—it's overwhelming.

Sausage Bites

¼	cup sharp cheese, grated
¼	cup butter, softened
¾	cup all-purpose flour
½	teaspoon paprika
¼	teaspoon salt
5	brown and serve sausage links

In a medium size bowl, blend cheese with butter, stir in flour, paprika, and salt. Stir ingredients until dough is well blended. Set aside.

Brown sausage in the skillet. Blot the sausage with paper toweling and cut each link into four pieces. Wrap just enough of the dough around each piece of sausage to cover completely. Bake on an ungreased baking sheet at 400-degrees 10 to 15 minutes until golden brown. For those of you that like green olives, substitute green olives for the sausage. You may want to double this recipe.

Yields: 4 to 6 servings

Sausage Stuffed Mushrooms

30-35	fresh whole mushrooms
1	pound of your favorite brand roll sausage, cooked and drained
¼	cup fresh bread crumbs
1	cup mozzarella cheese, grated
	Butter

Clean and remove the stems from the mushrooms. Chop the stems and set aside. Fry the sausage and crumble the meat as it cooks and drain the grease. Combine the bread crumbs, cheese and add one cup of the stems. Stir. Fill the caps of the mushrooms with the sausage mixture. Top each of the mushroom caps with a pat of butter. Bake at 300-degrees for 10 minutes. If you have leftover sausage mixture, freeze this to use again for more mushrooms.

Scotch Eggs

I had always wondered what these tasted like until I went to an opening of a restaurant and they served these and oh my gosh-they are well worth the effort. I could make a meal off of these. I love making these. Men love these while watching the games on TV.

1	pound your favorite bulk sausage, hot or mild
1	dozen hard-boiled eggs, shelled
2	eggs, beaten
⅔	cup fine dry bread crumbs*
	Vegetable oil for deep frying

Preheat the oil for deep-frying to 375-degrees. Divide the sausage into 12 equal portions. Shape each portions of sausage into a patty and wrap completely around the boiled egg.* I wet my hands with cold water, thus making the wrap easier. Seal the sausage completely around the egg. Dip the sausage wrapped egg in the beaten eggs and then roll in the bread crumbs until completely coated. Cook the sausage coated eggs 8 to 10 minutes until golden brown and heated throughout. Serve hot or gold. Delicious with a Honey Mustard dipping sauce or just by itself.

*Here is a trick that I like to use when a recipe calls for fine, dry bread crumbs. Buy a bag of croutons, flavored or plain, pour the croutons in a food processor. Give a twirl in the processor and obtain wonderful bread crumbs perfect for breading. I use the garlic croutons in this recipe which gives a delightful taste for this appetizer.

Hint

Ammonia is the one of the best dirt chasers. When I go to the grocery store, I always get at least 1 jug of ammonia. I pour ½-cup in my washer along with soap powder. It cuts perspiration odors and boosts your cleaning. DO NOT add it along with your bleach. Remember certain chemicals don't mix—and these two together create poisonous gasses.

Swedish Meatballs

What would a cookbook be without an ole faithful recipe of the reliable Swedish Meatball? Of course, use this for appetizers or just as the recipe depicts, you can use it for the main course.

1	pound ground chuck or round
½	pound ground pork
½	cup onions, minced
¾	cup fresh bread crumbs
1	egg, slightly beaten
½	cup half-and-half or evaporated milk
1	teaspoon salt
¼	teaspoon ginger
	Dash of nutmeg
	Dash of pepper
2	teaspoons Worcestershire sauce
¼	cup Crisco oil or bacon grease
¼	cup all-purpose flour
1	teaspoon paprika
4	beef bouillon cubes
2	cups boiling water
1	(8-ounce) container sour cream
	Dried parsley flakes or fresh parsley to garnish

Mix all the meat, onion, bread crumbs, egg, milk, salt, ginger, nutmeg, and pepper and Worcestershire sauce. Mix these ingredients well and chill for about 2 hours for flavors to blend. Shape into small balls.

In a skillet, brown meatballs in the hot bacon grease or oil. Cook on medium heat until meatballs are nice and brown. Remove the meatballs from the oil, draining on paper towels, and set aside. Stir in the all-purpose flour and paprika into the drippings, stirring constantly. Add 2 cups boiling water to the bouillon cubes and stir this into the flour mixture. Return meatballs back to skillet and simmer 30 to 35 minutes. Remove from heat and stir in the sour cream and sprinkle with the dried parsley flakes or fresh parsley to garnish. This would be a great dish to use in a chafing dish. Serve with noodles, rice or for appetizers.

Peanut Butter Pork Balls

¼	cup crunchy peanut butter
2	tablespoons butter, melted
½	cup water
2	cups packaged herb seasoned stuffing
1	egg, slightly beaten
½	pound bulk pork sausage, hot or mild, uncooked
¼	cup roasted peanuts, chopped
1	pound of sliced bacon, not the thick sliced kind

Mix peanut butter, butter, water and stuffing. Stir in egg, sausage and peanuts, mixing well. Chill for about an hour. Shape into small balls. Cut bacon slices into thirds. Wrap a piece of bacon around the stuffing ball and secure with a toothpick. Place on a cookie sheet.

Bake in a preheated 375-degree oven 30 to 35 minutes. Halfway through the cooking turn the balls over. After 35 minutes, check to make sure there is no pink left in the sausage. Drain on paper towels. Serve hot. These maybe frozen.

Porky Balls with Dipping Sauce

1	pound favorite brand pork sausage
1	egg, beaten
3	slices bread, torn into pieces
4	tablespoons butter

Dipping Sauce:
¾	cup chili sauce
¼	cup light brown sugar, firmly packed
2	tablespoons soy sauce
2	tablespoons white vinegar

Combine in a medium-sized bowl sausage, egg, and bread. Melt butter in a skillet on medium high while forming sausage mixture into small balls. Cook sausage balls until brown; drain on paper towels. Serve Porky Balls with the Dipping Sauce. In a saucepan, cook chili sauce, brown sugar, soy sauce and vinegar, stirring until hot.

Herb Dip

2	cups buttermilk
2	cups mayonnaise
1	tablespoon seasoning salt
½	tablespoon garlic powder
2	tablespoons onion, minced
1	teaspoon black pepper

Mix all ingredients in a medium sized bowl, by hand or blender, blending well. Put in the fridge overnight to blend flavors. Use as a dip for potato chips or vegetables. Also tastes great on your favorite salad. Refrigerate leftovers.

Riblet Nibblers

3	pounds spareribs
¼	cup molasses
¼	cup prepared mustard
3	tablespoons lemon juice
3	tablespoons soy sauce
3	tablespoons Worcestershire sauce
¼	teaspoon cayenne pepper

First cut the rack of spareribs into 3 lengthwise strips. Then cut each rib into separate ribs by themselves. Spray a 9 x 13-inch baking pan with baking spray. Place the ribs in the baking pan. Blend together all of the remaining ingredients and brush the ribs with only half of the sauce. Bake in a 350-degree oven for 1¼ hours. After cooking, pour off any grease, cover the pan with aluminum foil and cook for another 30 to 40 minutes. Take the aluminum foil off and glaze with the remaining sauce. Let sit for 10 minutes before serving. You may serve in a chafing dish.

Sassy Saucy Ham Spread

3	cups ham, finely chopped
1	(8-ounce) package cream cheese, softened
1/3	cup hot mango chutney
1¼	teaspoons hot sauce
1	cup pecans, chopped (divided use)
	Pimento strips
	Parsley

Combine ham, cream cheese, chutney and hot sauce. A food processor works wonders for this recipe. Mix well. Stir in ⅔-cup pecans. Reserve the other ⅓-cup for garnish. Line a 4-cup mold with plastic wrap.* Pack ham mixture into this. Refrigerate for several hours. Turn onto serving platter. Remove plastic wrap. Press the remaining pecans on tops and sides of loaf.

*I use a deep square pan for the mold, so that when I use the pimento strips, I place the pimento strips around the Ham Loaf like ribbons on a square gift box. I also use the pimento strips to make a make-shift bow on top with a sprig of parsley on top.

You may also make this Ham Loaf into a Ham Log. Serve with crackers, Wheat Thins are my favorite with this. This is very, very tasty.

Spiced Pecans

2	tablespoons butter, melted
2	cups pecan halves
1	teaspoon salt
2	teaspoons soy sauce
	A few dashes of Tabasco sauce

Melt butter in saucepan, adding pecans, and stir to coat well. Add salt, soy sauce and Tabasco sauce, blending well. Spread in a cookie sheet and toast in a 300-degree oven for 30 minutes, stirring with a fork occasionally.

Yields: 2 cups

Baby Pizzas

I was in 4-H and received this recipe, "ump-teen ages" ago, using canned biscuits. Perfect for an after school snack.

1	container canned biscuits
1	small can of your favorite pizza sauce
1	cup mozzarella cheese, grated

Preheat oven to 400-degrees. Roll the canned biscuits to ¼-inch thick circles. Place on a lightly oiled baking sheet. Pinch up the sides of each biscuit all around. Add 1 tablespoon of your favorite pizza sauce. Sprinkle grated cheese on top. Bake at 400-degrees until pizzas are light brown and crispy looking and the cheese is melted.

Variations:
Use any one of the following or several for toppings.
- Parmesan cheese
- Sliced olives
- ½-pound hamburger meat cooked and drained
- Pepperoni sausage
- Sliced mushrooms

Edna Lane's Baby Quiches

Quiche Shell:
½   cup butter, softened
1   (3-ounce) package cream cheese
1   cup all-purpose flour

Cream butter and cream cheese together. Work in the flour by hand. Chill until firm, about 2 hours. Roll small pieces of the dough into little balls; mash them in small muffin tins. Do not bake shells prior to filling them with quiche mixture.

Yields: 24 quiche shells

Filling:
1   egg, beaten
½   cup evaporated milk
¼   teaspoon salt
1   cup ham, chopped fine or several slices of cooked bacon, drained and crumbled. You may also use leftover sausage or bacon.
1   tablespoon dried, minced onion
1   cup Swiss cheese, grated
    Dash of paprika

Mix all of the ingredients for the filling, except for the cheese and paprika. Mash a small amount of cheese into the bottom of each the quiche shells. Add 1 tablespoon of quiche mixture into the shell. Sprinkle paprika on each of the quiches for color. Bake at 350-degrees for 30 minutes.

Sweet and Glazy Peanuts

2   cups sugar
1   cup water
4   cups raw shelled peanuts

Dissolve the sugar and water in a heavy skillet over medium heat. Add 4 cups raw, shelled peanuts and continue to cook and stir until the peanuts are glazed over about 20 minutes. You need to stir constantly until the liquid crystallizes on the peanuts. Spread evenly onto a greased cookie sheet and bake in a 325-degree oven for 15 minutes.

Nacho Waffle Bites

¼	cup butter, softened
½	teaspoon chili powder
½	teaspoon garlic salt
1	package frozen jumbo waffles
1	cup sharp cheese, grated
1	(4-ounce) can green chiles, chopped and drained

Preheat oven to 400-degrees. Cream butter, adding chili powder and garlic salt. Spread on the waffles. Cut each waffle square into 4 squares. Bake on an ungreased cookie sheet for 10 minutes at 400-degrees until crisp. Combine the cheese and chilies in a small bowl, sprinkling the cheese and chilies mixture on the top of each waffle piece. Bake again until the cheese melts. This appetizer needs to be served hot.

Apple Nut Biscuit Treat

You always have apples left in your fruit bowl, and if you have some canned biscuits, here's a way to put them to use.

Roll of canned biscuits
Apples
Walnuts or pecans
Raisins
Honey
½ stick butter, melted
Powdered sugar

Peel and chop apples. Chop raisins and walnuts together. Roll refrigerated biscuits till they are ¼-inch thick. Brush the biscuits with butter. Make a paste of apples, nuts and honey. Use enough honey to make a paste to hold the mixture of apples and nuts together. Place a teaspoon of the mixture in the center of the biscuit. Fold over and seal the edges Bake at 375-degrees for about 15 minutes till golden brown. Roll in powdered sugar, if desired.

Cute Coconut Toasties

8	slices white bread
¼	cup butter
½	cup brown sugar
½	flaked coconut
	Cookie cutters

Cut bread into a variety of shapes with a cookie cutter. Cream butter with the brown sugar. Spread over the bread and sprinkle with coconut. Place on cookie sheet and broil until the coconut is light brown and toasty. What an easy appetizer and cheap!

Remedy:
Southern Concoction

Have you ever felt that you could not pick your head up off of the bed; you are barking like a dog and your head feels as heavy as a brick?

This "Southern Concoction," was given to me by a true "Southern Lady." She lived to be 97 years old. Are we missing something?

Take a fifth of liquor, Bourbon to be exact. Fill up the fifth with peppermint candy canes or peppermint sticks. Now, don't pour out the liquor. Put the candy canes in the bottle along with the liquor. Put as many candy canes in the fifth as they will hold. Put the top back on it. Shake it several times.

Take the concoction and sit it beside your bed. Go to bed and wrap yourself up with the covers. Every now and then shake up the bottle and sip on this concoction

I'll bet my red hair you will feel better by morning one way or the other.

Note: And you wondered what to do with those Candy Canes left over from Christmas!

Tipsy Grapes

1	pound of seedless green or dark grapes. *(I like to use some of both.)*
½	fifth of crème de menthe
1	(1-pound) box confectioners' sugar, sifted

Place grapes and crème de menthe in a 1 or 2 gallon zip-top bag. Marinate them with the crème de menthe by turning the bag over and over. Remove marinade and drain on paper towels. Get a cookie sheet and layer paper towels on the cookie sheet. Spread one half of the confectioners' sugar on the paper towel and roll the drained grapes in it. When they are dry, repeat this procedure again with the sugar. I continued this until I know the grapes are coated well. Refrigerate the grapes until serving time. They may be frozen. This not only makes a wonderful appetizer, but add this to a beautiful tray of assorted fruits and cheese. I display the grapes along with one of my Baked Hams, Beef Tenderloins or Leg of Lamb as a garnish, also. I served these at an event and I wasn't paying any attention as to who was eating them. I overheard a parent talking about how much her child loved these. So, steer the toddlers' little fingers away from these. They are sweet and delicious and they love them. Boy, I bet that child slept good that night. What could I say? It was too late to tell her the grapes were soused.

Lemon Curd Tassies

You can make this as part of your menu for a Shower or Tea. You may fill with chicken or ham salad fillings or fill with those delightful sweet pie fillings.

Pastry:
This is the basic recipe for the pastry. Double the recipe for the Lemon Curd. I wanted you to have this recipe for any other filling you desired.

½	cup butter, softened
1	(3-ounce) package cream cheese, softened
1	cup all-purpose flour

Blend the butter and cream cheese together until smooth. Add the flour and roll into a ball. Chill for 1 hour and shape into 24 small balls pressing into 1-inch muffin tins. Bake at 450-degrees until lightly brown.

For Lemon Curd Tassies, you want to bake the tassie pastry prior to filling the pastry.

Lemon Curd Filling:
Makes about 2½ cups of filling.

5	eggs
½	cup butter
1	cup granulated sugar
2	tablespoons lemon peel, grated from about 3 lemons
½	cup lemon juice
	Sweetened whipping cream

Beat the eggs in a small mixing bowl until thick about 5 minutes. In a medium saucepan, melt the butter, stirring in the sugar, lemon peel and juice on medium heat. Blend in the eggs, a small amount at a time, stirring constantly just until mixture thickens and boils. Cover with wax paper to prevent a skin from forming on the lemon curd while cooling. Chill several hours or overnight.

Fill the tassie shells with the cooled filling and dollop with sweetened whipping cream. If you like garnish top with a sliver of lemon peel on each Tassie.

Something to Swig On

Mama Gillis' ice water cooler

*B*efore I get to the beverage recipes, I have a couple of stories to share with you.

Mama Gillis' kitchen cabinet was equipped with every extract imaginable. Mama Gillis kept McCormick's Extract Company in business. My sister and I would climb up on the counter top and sample the flavorings in the cabinet. How did we know they were 53% alcohol! We would not stop at just one flavor, either.

Get a load of this beverage. My oldest sister should be a comedian and in show business. She will keep you in stitches laughing and so very dramatic.

I have always loved pineapple juice. When I was a little girl, I would always look in the refrigerator for leftover pineapple juice to drink. After my mother would make something with pineapple, she would always put the leftover pineapple juice in a cup.

My sister wanted to be her dramatic self and to be real funny one day. She went running to the refrigerator and said "Oh, here is some pineapple juice in this cup. I'm going to drink this leftover pineapple juice and you can't have any." Well, I came running to the refrigerator, full speed and pushed her out of the way. I grabbed the cup from her and took a big swallow. UGH! Little did I know that this was egg whites instead of pineapple juice! How's that for a beverage!

I love a good punch recipe.

Note: You do not have to have an event to have punch. Save your empty gallon-sized milk jugs and make punch in them. Freeze it and you will have a quick beverage. Especially in the summer when it's hot.

Yellow Fruit Punch

1	(3-ounce) package lemon Jell-O
1	cup sugar
2	cups boiling water
2	cups cold water
2	(6-ounce) can frozen concentrate lemonade
1	(46-ounce) can pineapple juice
1	(2-liter) bottle of ginger ale or lemon lime carbonated drink

Dissolve the flavored gelatin and sugar with the boiling water. Add all other ingredients, except for the ginger ale or carbonated drink. You might want to add a little more sugar to taste. Mix well and now add the carbonated drink. Delicious.

Yields: 1 gallon

Note: If you wanted green punch-you would want to use lime flavored gelatin; red punch, use raspberry, cherry or strawberry flavored gelatin. You get the point.

Don't forget to make the ice ring or ice mold when you are making punch for a party, picnic or wedding. It takes a few minutes and you will get even more compliments. Doesn't everyone like to get compliments?

Kool-Aid Fruit Punch

1½	cups reconstituted lemon juice
3	packages strawberry Kool-aid, unsweetened
3	packages cherry Kool-aid, unsweetened
1	(46-ounce) can pineapple juice
1	(64-ounce) bottle apple juice
5	pound bag granulated sugar
3	gallons water

Mix the entire ingredients together well and add the 3 gallons of water.

Note: I always boil just enough of the water to dissolve the sugar and then add all the rest of the ingredients, stirring to dissolve.

Ice Ring

1 or 2 pineapple slices canned, drained
1 lime, thinly sliced with the skin on
1 lemon, thinly sliced with the skin on
Red and green maraschino cherries, about 6

Note: Use your imagination with different fruits that are in season-such as strawberries, melon balls, etc. In lieu of water in making the ice ring, you can use different juices, such as pineapple juice, cranberry juice, etc. I like to dilute the juices when I fill the ice ring. Choose a 1½-quart mold that will fit into your punch bowl. While I'm preparing my punch, I put the mold in the freezer to chill out. Then take the mold out and rinse the inside of the mold with cold water and return to the freezer until a thin coating of ice forms. Arrange as much fruit as possible in the mold. Gently pour enough water to just cover the fruit. Freeze until firm. Now gently, trying not to disturb the fruit and pour in more water until you fill the mold completely. Freeze overnight. When you are ready to use the mold, pour cold water over the mold, to loosen.

You may add sprigs of mint in the punch for added color.

Mocha Punch

Very similar to Mocha Eggnog Punch, but just without the eggnog.

1 quart strong coffee
  Sugar to taste
1 quart milk
1 teaspoon vanilla extract
1 pint vanilla ice cream
1 pint chocolate ice cream
  Sweetened whipping cream for dollops to garnish with.

Sweeten coffee with sugar to taste; chill. Add milk and vanilla extract; pour into punch bowl. Chop up ice cream and add to coffee mixture. Stir briskly before serving.

Mocha Eggnog Punch

Perfect for a Holiday party! Since one of the ingredients is coffee, while you are brewing the coffee for the party, just make a little more for the punch. My guests loved it!

1	quart premium coffee ice cream (My favorite)
1	quart premium vanilla ice cream
1	quart commercially prepared eggnog
2½	cups hot brewed coffee*
½	cup Hershey's chocolate syrup
1	half-pint whipping cream whipped with 4 tablespoons powdered sugar
	Ground nutmeg

*You may substitute ½-cup of coffee liqueur in the place of the ½-cup of the coffee.

Scoop both kinds of ice cream into the punch bowl. Add the eggnog, coffee, and chocolate syrup. Stir slowly, just until the ice cream starts to melt. Serve in mugs and dollop with the sweetened whipping cream and sprinkle with nutmeg. Serve immediately. If you have doubts about what to fix at your next Holiday party, this is it! It is sure to be a hit. It is at my parties!

Strawberry Lemon Punch

3	(6-ounce) cans frozen lemonade concentrate, diluted according to directions on the can
1	(10-ounce) package sweetened frozen strawberries, thawed*
1	(2-liter bottle) ginger ale

Pour into punch bowl the lemonade and add the strawberries. Mix. Just before serving, add the ginger ale. You may not need to add the whole bottle of the ginger ale.

*If fresh berries are used, you will want 1½-cups fresh berries, sweetened with ½-cup sugar. Let stand for 30 minutes.

Use the ice ring recipe with this recipe. Lemon, limes and fresh mint leaves will be beautiful with it.

Bridal Shower Punch

This next recipe is a staple to serve for a Bridal Showers, and Tea Parties in the South. Try sipping on this on a hot, sultry summer afternoon.

2	cartons of any flavor sherbet
2	(2-liter) bottles ginger ale

Scoop the sherbet in a punch bowl. Then pour the ginger ale over the sherbet. Depending on how thick you want the punch depends on how much ginger ale. Your preference. Wonderful. Add a sprig of mint to this. Delicious!

Note: Ahead of time, if you like, make small scoops of sherbet and freeze them.

Wouldn't this punch be pretty with orange and lime sherbet balls mixed together in a punch bowl? For 12 servings, allow 1-pint of sherbet to 1-quart of ginger ale.

Lime Orange Freeze Drink

1	(1-ounce) package lemon lime Kool-Aid or powdered fruit flavored beverage
1½	cups granulated sugar
8	cups cold water
1	pint orange sherbet
	Crushed ice, optional

Combine the powdered fruit flavored drink or Kool-aid with the sugar and water. Stir until the sugar is dissolved. Chill several hours until ice cold. Place in 8-ounce glasses, adding the crushed ice. Top each glass with orange sherbet. Serve at once.

Yields: 8 (8-ounce servings)

Rainbow Punch

While I'm still talking about the using sherbet in punch drinks, here is a beautiful punch drink that can be served at bridal showers, baby showers, and weddings. The pastel colors are beautiful. Double or triple recipe to suit desired quantity.

Note: This is a recipe that needs to be prepared on the spot and not before the occasion.

1	pint raspberry sherbet
1	pint lime sherbet
1	pint lemon sherbet
3	pints vanilla ice cream
1	(46-ounce) can pineapple juice
1	(28-ounce) bottle ginger ale, chilled
	Mint sprigs for garnish

Scoop balls of all kinds of the sherbet and ice cream into the punch bowl. Carefully, pour the pineapple juice. Last of all; carefully pour the ginger ale over the sherbet and ice cream balls. This is absolutely delicious and gorgeous in color.

This makes about 25 cups of punch. If it looks like you are running out, just add more pineapple juice and ginger ale.

Eggnog

1	dozen eggs, separated
1½	cups granulated sugar
4	cups whole milk
1	cup whipping cream, whipped
½	teaspoon mace
1	teaspoon vanilla extract
1	teaspoon rum flavoring
½	teaspoon nutmeg

Sweetened whipping cream in the aerosol can for dollops on top of individual servings

Note: If you want Spirited eggnog, add ¼-cup rum and ¼-cup brandy

Beat egg yolks until thick and smooth. Combine egg yolks and sugar in top of double boiler over hot water. Stir in milk gradually. Cook, stirring constantly, until mixture coats a spoon. Remove from heat and chill a couple of hours or overnight.

Beat egg whites until stiff peaks. Fold egg whites and whipped cream into chilled egg yolk mixture. Fold in the mace. Stir in flavorings or spirits. Sprinkle with nutmeg. Makes about 20 servings

*Make sure you rinse the beaters after beating the whipping cream, prior to beating the egg whites. The egg whites will not beat to their capacity if any residue is left on.

Peppermint Eggnog

Prepare the morning before your party or night before.

For my Peppermint eggnog, use my eggnog recipe. Leave out the rum, nutmeg, mace flavorings and spices.

Pour at least 4 tablespoons of peppermint flavoring in it. If it is not pepperminty enough, keep adding more, 1 tablespoon at a time. Don't get too frisky with that flavoring. The flavors are going to blend together. Add the vanilla extract also. If you like spirits in your eggnog and want a Peppermint flavor with a kick, try putting Peppermint Schnapps in your eggnog.

This is a delightful twist to eggnog and beautiful, yet tasty. At serving time, pour the nog in the punch bowl. I hang candy canes around my antique Tom & Jerry Punch Bowl. I put dollops of sweetened whipped cream in the punch bowl along with crushed peppermint candy.

Then for the individual servings, I put a dollop of sweetened whipping cream with crushed peppermint candy on top of the whipping cream. I also find the smaller candy canes and put one of these on the outside of the punch cup. Very pretty.

Garnishes:
Crushed peppermint candy for garnish and extra flavor
Sweetened whipping cream in aerosol or 1 cup whipping cream sweetened with 4 tablespoons powdered sugar.
Large and small peppermint candy canes

Apple Cider Nog

2	eggs, beaten
½	cup granulated sugar
1	apple juice or cider
½	teaspoon cinnamon
	Pinch of nutmeg
	Pinch of mace
3	cups milk, scalded
1	cup whipping cream, whipped with 4 tablespoons powdered sugar
	Whole cinnamon stick for garnish

Combine the eggs, sugar, cider or apple juice and spices. Add the scalded milk gradually. Heat on medium, stirring constantly. Serve hot or cold. Pour into mugs and top with a dollop of sweetened whipping cream, sprinkle with additional cinnamon or nutmeg and have a whole stick of cinnamon in the mug for stirring and garnish. So much comfort with this drink.

Party Punch

2	quarts strong tea, unsweetened
2	cups sugar
2	quarts water
1	quart pineapple juice
1	quart orange juice
2	cups lemon juice
2	cups apricot nectar
1	Liter of ginger ale
	Dash of salt
	Oranges, thinly sliced
	Mint sprigs

Following the package directions, brew enough tea to make 2-quarts. Place the brewed tea in the refrigerator overnight. Boil just enough water to dissolve the 2 cups of sugar. After sugar is dissolved, add the remaining water. Add the brewed tea and combine all of the juices, the sugar syrup, dash of salt and ginger ale. Place ice or ice ring in punch bowl. Pour punch over the ice ring or ice. Garnish with the orange slices and mint sprigs.

Sparkling Fruit Punch

1	quart orange sherbet
4	cups apple juice, chilled
4	cups orange juice, chilled
1	(2-liter) bottle ginger ale, chilled
	Mint sprigs

Make small balls of sherbet and freeze them. When you are ready to serve the punch; combine all other ingredients in your punch bowl. Lastly, add the sherbet and mint sprigs.

Yields: 20 servings

Steaming Hot Cocoa

How many times do we in this busy world, prepare the home-made version of hot chocolate? You cannot beat this. If you have never tried it, try it one time. You will not go back. Promise!

1	cup cocoa
1	cup sugar
¼	teaspoon salt
1	teaspoon vanilla extract
8	cups milk
	Marshmallows big or small

In a large saucepan, combine the cocoa, sugar, salt and vanilla extract. Gradually, add 1 cup of milk, stirring constantly until smooth. Stir in the remainder of the milk. Cook over medium heat until heated thoroughly, stirring often. Do not boil. Serve with marshmallows floating in each cup or mug.

Yields: 8 (1 cup) servings

Hawaiian Slurp Drink

When making this recipe, sit on the porch during the summer time and slurp away.

1	(8-ounce) can crushed pineapple in juice, undrained
¼	cup chopped maraschino cherries, juice and all
½	cup mashed bananas
2	pints vanilla ice cream
1	quart orange soda, chilled
6	Tall glasses

Place 2 tablespoons pineapple, 2 teaspoons cherries and 1 tablespoon of mashed banana in each of the 6 tall glasses. Scoop 6 balls of vanilla ice cream and place 1 ball in each glass; stir until you have blended the fruit with the ice cream. Fill the glasses almost to the top with orange soda. Then add 1 more scoop of vanilla ice cream in each of the 6 glasses. Serve immediately.

Yields: 6 servings

Almond Fruit Punch

1	(6-ounce) package flavored gelatin, any flavor
1	(46-ounce) can pineapple juice
1	(46-ounce) can grapefruit juice
½	small bottle almond extract
2	cups sugar
3	cups water
1	(2-liter) bottle ginger ale
	Any flavor sherbet, if desired.

Make flavored gelatin as per directions on box and add the rest of the ingredients, except for the ginger ale and sherbet. Mix thoroughly. Add ginger ale and scoops of sherbet when ready to serve.

Cheap and Easy Kool-Aid Punch

Kool-Aid, Kool-Aid tastes great!

4	unsweetened packets of Kool-Aid, any flavor
2	(46-ounce) cans pineapple juice
6	quarts water
4	cups sugar
2	(28-ounce) bottles ginger ale

Mix all ingredients except ginger ale. Chill. Add cold ginger ale, just before serving. This is cheap and good. This will serve at least 50 people depending upon size of cups.

Vanilla Milk

Years ago when we were little bitty things, my mother would make us a wonderful milk beverage. How many of you have heard of Vanilla Milk? I'm sure you have, but have forgotten about it. Now folks are getting filthy rich over different milk drinks. Too bad, we didn't have one of those expensive machines to make the milk foam. Boy Howdy! It took years for someone to think of something that simple. We would just blow in the straw to make foam bubbles and get in trouble for being rude. Here's my version, a wonderful twist to get your kids back to drinking there milk. Simple.

1	glass ice cold milk
2	teaspoons sugar (You may want it sweeter)
½	teaspoon vanilla extract

Mix and enjoy. It was so good.

Fruity Health Shake

3	medium bananas, frozen*
2	cups cold milk
1	medium apple (the apple needs to be cold)
	Peel, quarter and seed the apple.
1	teaspoon sugar (You might need to add more sugar to taste)
1	teaspoon vanilla extract

*Freeze the bananas ahead of time by peeling them and placing in a plastic bag. Freeze for at least 8 hours.

Pour milk in the blender and add the apple. Add sugar and vanilla. Cut bananas into thirds and place them in the blender. Turn on the blender to low and then turn to a higher speed until smooth and thick. Serve immediately in cold glasses. Very refreshing!

Note: You might need to try honey in lieu of sugar in this recipe.

Good Morning Shake

1	cup plain yogurt
½	cup milk
2	tablespoons honey
1	cup of sliced fruit (bananas, strawberries, peaches, or pineapple)
	I've never tried blueberries. Wonder how that would taste?

Add all the ingredients in the blender. Cover the blender and pulse for 1 to 2 minutes. Pour into 2 glasses. This is a low calorie drink. If you are really watching your calories try it with low fat yogurt and low fat milk.

Banana Milk Shake

Here is another shake to try on kids to get them to drink more milk. A nutritious quick shake. I have always kept a box of non-fat dry milk on the shelf to add a little pick me up in a milk based drink.

3	medium-sized ripe bananas, peeled (to make 1½-cups mashed)
3	cups very cold milk
½	cup non-fat dry milk
	Dash of almond or vanilla extract
3	scoops vanilla ice cream *(optional, but who is going to leave this ingredient out)*

Slice bananas in blender and pulse to mash. Add milk and extracts; lastly, fold in the scoops of ice cream.

Maple Milkshake

4	cups cold milk
¾	cup maple syrup
1	pint vanilla ice cream

Mix the milk and maple syrup in a blender. Pour into chilled glasses and top with scoops of vanilla ice cream.

Honey Bee Banana Booster

3	ripe bananas
3	cups cold milk
4	tablespoons honey
1	teaspoon vanilla extract

Peel and slice bananas. Place the bananas in the blender with milk. Add the honey and vanilla extract. Blend just until frothy. Pour into glasses and enjoy.

Chocolate Mint Milkshake

2	squares unsweetened chocolate
1	cup water
½	cup granulated sugar
1	teaspoon vanilla extract
½	teaspoon peppermint flavoring
	Pinch of salt
4	cups cold milk
1	pint vanilla ice cream*
	York Peppermint Patties for garnish
	Dollops of whipping cream (aerosol)

In a small saucepan, melt the chocolate over low heat. Add the water and sugar to the chocolate, stirring over low heat until thickened about 5 minutes. Place the saucepan in the fridge to chill. After chilling pour the chocolate mixture, vanilla, peppermint flavoring, salt, milk, and scoops of ice cream in the blender. Blend until frothy and pour into tall, chilled glasses. Garnish each glass with a dollop of whipping cream and top that with a York Peppermint Patty.

*Top with additional ice cream, if desired.

Hint

Do you like the small round chocolate peppermint patty candy? I do. If you want to frost sugar cookies easily, just place one of these mint patties on top of the sugar cookies and return it back to the oven for a minute to soften the chocolate. Take the cookies out of the oven and spread the melted chocolate over the top of the cookies. You may have to chill the cookies to solidify the chocolate once again.

Georgia Peach Brain Freeze

This is an alcoholic drink. You might really want to just sit on the porch for this one. The title of this recipe tells it all.

- 1 cup peach ice cream
- ¼ cup rum
- 3 tablespoons powdered sugar
- 4 peaches, sliced and unpeeled
- Cracked ice

In your blender, combine the ice cream, rum, sugar and peaches. Process until smooth and frothy. Add enough of the cracked ice to about 1-inch of the top of the blender. Blend.

Non-Alcoholic Georgia Peach Brain Freeze

Note: If you prefer a non-alcoholic drink, follow the recipe above, omitting the rum of course, but substitute 1 tablespoon of almond extract or rum extract.

Southern Sea Breeze Smoothie

¼	cup crème de menthe
¼	cup lemon or lime juice
¼	cup commercial sweetened lime juice *(you will find this in the cocktail makings in your supermarket)*
1	pint vanilla ice cream
1	quart lemon-lime beverage (Sprite, *etc.*) or ginger ale *(I prefer lemon-lime beverage)*
	Lime and lemon slice
	Sprigs of mint
4	Tall slender glasses would be ideal with this recipe. If you don't have them, use what you have.

Combine the crème de menthe and juices. Mix well. Spoon ½-cup of the vanilla ice cream into each of the 4 glasses. Pour 1 cup of lemon-lime beverage into each of these glasses over the ice cream. Garnish with lemon, lime and mint sprigs. This is beautiful to have a pitcher already prepared with this wonderful concoction. Just picture your picnic table adorned with this beverage.

Melon Breeze

Note: Use a beautiful cut glass pitcher to display this drink.

Use the same recipe of Southern Sea Breeze Smoothie, omitting the ice cream. Fill your pitcher and tall glasses with scoops of assorted melon balls such as, honeydew, watermelon and cantaloupe. Mix the crème de menthe and juices together, combining well. Pour the juices into the pitcher. Fill tall glasses with this beverage and garnish with lemon, lime and mint sprigs. Enjoy!

Strawberry Lemonade

Simple and easy.

1	(12-ounce) can frozen lemonade
½	pint fresh strawberries, washed, hulled (Save a few out for garnishing)
1	(10-ounce) frozen strawberries
	Fresh mint sprigs

Prepare the lemonade according to package directions. Put strawberries in blender. Pour all ingredients into a pretty glass pitcher. Garnish with a couple of whole strawberries and a sprig of mint.

Cranberry Lemon Supreme

2	cups sweetened cranberry juice, chilled
1	pint lemon sherbet
1½	cups cold milk
	Lemon slices and sprigs of mint for garnish

Put all ingredients in the blender. Blend on high until it reaches the consistency you like. Pour in tall, chilled glasses. This recipe will make 4 good size drinks. Garnish with lemon slices and sprigs of mint.

Hot Cranberry Punch

2	(12-ounce) bags fresh cranberries
2	cups water
2/3	cups brown sugar, firmly packed
1/2	teaspoon ground cinnamon
1/4	teaspoon ground allspice
1/4	teaspoon ground cloves
1/8	teaspoon ground nutmeg
	Pinch of salt
1 1/2	cups water
2 1/4	cups unsweetened pineapple juice

Sort and wash cranberries. Bring 2 cups of water to a boil in a medium saucepan, adding the cranberries. Cook for 5 minutes or until the skins burst. Pour cranberries into a strainer lined with cheesecloth and squeeze the cranberries collecting the puree. Discard the pulp. Combine all of the sugar, spices, salt and water in a medium sized saucepan. Bring to a boil. Add cranberry puree and pineapple juice. Return to the heat and simmer for 5 minutes. Serve hot with a cinnamon stick.

Yields: 1½ quarts

Hot Lemon Spiced Tea

This will really perk you up if you are having the blues or feel "puny".

1	quart boiling water
2	large family size tea bags
1/2	cup honey
2	tablespoon lemon juice, fresh or bottled
1/4	teaspoon allspice
1/4	teaspoon nutmeg
	Lemon slices cut in half

Heat water into a kettle to a boiling point and pour the boiling water over the tea bags that are placed in a medium sized saucepan. Cover and let steep for 5 minutes. Remove the tea bags, by picking them up and squeeze them the remainder of tea out (There is always tea left in there.) Discard the tea bags and add the other ingredients, stirring until the honey dissolves. Stir over low heat until the tea is well heated. Serve with lemon slices.

Orange Lemonade

Syrup:
- 1 cup fresh orange juice (about 3-4 oranges)
- 1 cup fresh lemons (about 6-7 lemons)
- 2 cups sugar
- 2½ cups water
- Mint sprigs (10-15)

Mixer:
- 1 (32-ounce) bottle ginger ale
- Water and ice cubes
- Additional Mint sprigs to garnish

In a large saucepan, combine all ingredients, including the mint sprigs except for the ginger ale and water. Bring to a boil and continue to stir until all of the sugar dissolves. Cover the saucepan and let is steep for about 30 minutes. Strain the syrup into a pitcher and put in the fridge. To serve this beverage, pour an equal amount of syrup, water, ice and topping it off with ginger ale. Garnish with sprigs of mint.

Yields: 15 servings

A Swig of Sweet Tea

My mother always made the best Sweet Tea. I would always tell her I wanted a "swig" of her sweet tea. I literally meant that I want to sip out of her tea glass. I guess it probably tasted like any other Southerner's sweet tea, but it was my mother's, so it was sweeter.

Here is a recipe of my Sweet Tea. Since I have been here in the North, I have found very few Northerners who like Sweet Tea. They say it's more like Sugar Water. Oh, Well. It's what you are use to. I can not get use to unsweetened tea. No way, no how. Ugh!

6	tea bags (not the real big ones)
1-1½	cups granulated sugar
	Lemon wedges, if desired
	Sprigs of mint
	Half gallon pitcher

Fill up a medium sized saucepan of water and boil. Set off the stove and place the tea bags in the boiling water and steep for 15 to 20 minutes. Measure at first 1 cup of sugar in the tea pitcher. Pour the hot tea mixture on top of the sugar, stirring to melt. Now pour just enough water on top of the tea bags and squeeze the tea bags (to get the goodie out of the tea bags). Pour this in the tea pitcher. Stir. You will need to add enough water to fill the pitcher. Taste to see if you need to add more sugar. Naturally, I always add a little more. Add lemon wedges and sprigs of mint, if desired.

Breads

sketch by Ruthie Lee Gillis

Quick Bread Sticks

I got this recipe in my Home Economics class. I will not go into how long ago that was. I took every Home Economics class there ever was and then some. I have a hunch our country will get back to basics and I hope they will incorporate these classes back in the school systems. When you see this recipe, you will note that they are canned biscuits. If you have leftover bread dough, this will work. This was before I learned to make them from scratch.

The kids would love to help with this. Look at the recipe. Lots of different kinds of seeds they can sprinkle. This would be perfect for that favorite spaghetti, lasagna or manicotti recipe. Make a double batch using each kind of the seeds.

1	can of biscuits
4	tablespoons of butter
	Garlic salt
	Sesame, caraway, and poppy seeds

Roll each biscuit between your hands into a stick. Place biscuits in an 8-inch square pan in which you have prepared with 2 tablespoons of melted butter. After placing the bread sticks in the pan, pour the remaining 2 tablespoons of butter over the biscuits. Sprinkle with sesame, caraway or poppy seeds or garlic salt. Bake in a preheated oven at 450-degrees until toasty brown.

Hot Dog Bun Bread Sticks

Do you ever have leftover hot dog buns that go to waste?
- Hot dog buns
- Melted butter
- Parmesan Cheese in the can or
- Garlic powder

Cut hot dog buns in quarters lengthwise. Brush melted butter on the buns. Sprinkle Parmesan cheese or garlic powder on the buns. Bake the buns in a slow oven at 200-degrees for 1 hour. The concept of cooking the buns for this long is to dry them out. The bread sticks are crunchy and delicious with soup or spaghetti.

Corn Bread Sticks

1	cup sifted all-purpose flour
¾	cup corn meal
2	teaspoons baking powder
¾	teaspoons salt
2	tablespoons sugar
1	egg, beaten
¾	cup milk
¼	melted shortening (This is where your bacon grease comes in)

Sift flour, corn meal, baking power, salt and sugar together. Add egg, milk and shortening or melted bacon grease. Stir until blended. **Do not over mix.**

You may make muffins with this recipe as well as corn sticks. For muffins, spoon batter into greased muffin tins, fill ⅔-full. Bake in a 425-degree oven for 25 minutes, or until lightly brown.

For corn sticks, I put about 1 teaspoon shortening or bacon grease in the slots of the corn stick pan. I always heat my greased cast iron corn stick pan till it is smoking in a 450-degree oven while preparing this recipe. Fill the corn stick slots till ¾-full. Bake for about 20 minutes or until brown.

Cracklin' Sticks

Have the butter ready to smear on this!!

2	cups self-rising corn meal
1	cup coarsely crushed cracklings or ready-to-eat pork rinds
1	tablespoon sugar
¼	teaspoon garlic powder
2	eggs, beaten
1-1¼	cup milk
¼	cup melted shortening, bacon grease, or oil

Preheat oven to 425-degrees. Stir together corn meal, cracklings or pork rind, sugar and garlic powder in mixing bowl. Blend together eggs, 1 cup milk and shortening. Add liquid all at once and stir just until moisten. If batter is not thick enough, add a little more milk. Fill greased corn stick pans. Bake 20 to 25 minutes until golden brown.

Crackling Bread

3	cups cornmeal
1	teaspoon salt
3	teaspoons baking powder
1	cup milk to make stiff dough
1	cup broken cracklings

Preheat oven to 425-degrees. Sift cornmeal, salt and baking powder together. Add milk and cracklings and pour into a well greased baking pan. Bake 20 to 25 minutes.

Poppy Seed Yeast Bread

1	package dry yeast
1¼	cups warm water (105 to 115-degrees)
¼	cup shortening
2	tablespoons sugar
1	teaspoon salt
2⅔	all-purpose flour, divided use
1-2	tablespoons poppy seed
1	stick butter, melted

Combine the yeast and warm water in a large bowl. Add the shortening, sugar, salt and 2 cups of the flour. Beat for 3 minutes at low speed of electric mixer, scraping bowl occasionally. Cease using the mixer and stir by hand the remaining ⅔-cup of flour.

Cover the dough and let it rise until double in bulk.

Stir dough down and spread evenly into a greased 13 x 9 x 2-inch baking pan. Sprinkle the poppy seeds over the top. Cover and let rise again until doubled in bulk about 40 minutes. Drizzle the melted butter on top. Bake at 375-degrees for 30 minutes. Cut into squares.

Loaf Bread

Indulging in the aroma when you bake this bread is one thing; but be sure to have a nice slice slathered in butter, while still warm.

2	packages dry yeast
2	cups warm water (105 to 115-degrees)
½	cup granulated sugar
1	tablespoon salt
2	eggs, slightly beaten
¼	cup vegetable oil
6-6 ½	cups unbleached flour, divided use
	Vegetable oil
	Melted butter

In a large bowl, dissolve the yeast in the water. Let stand 5 minutes, adding the sugar, salt, eggs, ¼-cup vegetable oil and only 3 cups of the flour. Mix well and gradually stir in the remaining flour. Turn the dough out onto a floured surface and knead until smooth and elastic about 8 minutes. Place the dough into a greased bowl, turning the dough to grease the top. Cover and let the dough rise in a warm place (85-degrees), away from drafts for 1½ to 2 hours until doubles in bulk.

Punch the dough down, dividing in half and place on a floured surface. Roll each half into a rectangle about 18 x 9-inch rectangle. Beginning at the narrow end, roll the dough up and pinch the seams and ends together to seal. Place the loaves seam side down in 2 well-greased 9 x 5 x 3-inch loaf pans.

Cover the loaf pans and let rise again until double in bulk. Brush with melted butter and bake on the lower rack at 375-degrees for 30 to 35 minutes or until the loaves sound hollow when tapping them on top. Remove the loaves from the pans and brush again with the melted butter. Makes 2 loaves.

Cranberry Glazed Rolls

This is another recipe that was demonstrated when I was in Home Economics class a zillion years ago. I have always loved it and is quite different. Great for the Thanksgiving Dinner or Christmas Dinner!

¼	cup nuts, chopped
½	cup Jellied Cranberry Sauce
¼	cup brown sugar
6-8	Brown 'n' Serve Rolls

Preheat oven to 400-degrees. Grease muffin tins or custard cups. Sprinkle a few chopped nuts into each of the tins or cups. Combine cranberry sauce that has been crushed with a fork and brown sugar. Put a tablespoon of the mixture in each muffin cup. Then turn the brown 'n' serve rolls upside down and press into each muffin cup. Bake at 400-degrees for 12 to 15 minutes. Let cool for 4 to 5 minutes. Invert pans and gently remove rolls. They have the wonderful Praline and Cranberry glaze on top of them.

Hint

A hint for greasing cake pans, biscuit pans, etc.

1	cup solid shortening
1	cup cooking oil
1	cup all-purpose flour

Beat ingredients together. Store in a covered plastic container and put in the fridge. Keeps forever.

Quick 'n' Easy Buttermilk Rolls

¼	cup warm water
1	package active dry yeast
¾	cup lukewarm buttermilk
¼	teaspoon baking soda
1	tablespoon sugar
1	teaspoon salt
3	tablespoons butter, softened
2½	cups all-purpose flour, divided use
	Additional flour
½	stick of butter melted to brush on the tops of the rolls prior to cooking

Dissolve the yeast in the warm water. Add the remaining ingredients, using only 2 cups of the flour. Slowly incorporate the other ½-cup of flour. Turn the dough onto a lightly floured surface. I use a clean tea towel on my counter. Knead dough until smooth and elastic. Grease a cookie sheet with Crisco, butter makes the bottom brown too much. Shape into rolls and place on cookie sheet; let rise until double in bulk. Melt butter and brush on top of rolls prior to baking.

Preheat oven to 400-degrees. Bake for 15 to 20 minutes until lightly brown. Makes approximately 2 dozen.

Sour Cream Biscuits

2	cups self-rising flour
4	tablespoons Crisco shortening
⅔	cup sour cream
¾	cup of milk (Enough milk to make spooning consistency)

While preparing batter for biscuits-preheat the oven to 450-degrees. Cut in your shortening with a fork or pastry blender until your flour and shortening is mixed. Then add the other ingredients and mix well. Do not over mix. Drop the dough using a tablespoon in a greased muffin tin. These bake for about 8 to 10 minutes. These are excellent to toast the next day if you have any left over. I just split them in half and smear butter on both sides and put them under the broiler until they are good and toasty.

Angel Biscuits

This recipe makes a lot of biscuits. When I have a lot of company, this is the recipe to I like to use. You can cut the recipe down for smaller amounts.

Men and homemade biscuits, there is something there! If you want to make your husband or significant other totally fall in love with you all over again- make him biscuits every morning. This dough will keep in the fridge in a covered container for several days, and you can take a little bit of the dough out a little at a time to make him biscuits.

2	packages dry yeast
¼	cup warm water
5	cups self-rising flour
1	teaspoon soda
¼	cup sugar
1	cup Crisco
2	cups buttermilk

Additional ½-stick of butter, melted to brush on top of rolls prior to cooking

Dissolve the yeast in warm water and set aside. In a large bowl, sift together the flour, soda, and sugar and using a pastry blender, cut the Crisco into the dough until it resembles little peas. Add the yeast mixture and buttermilk. Mix gently, but well. Shape into biscuits or I like to use biscuit cutters. Grease a cookie sheet with Crisco. I have found if you grease it with butter, it burns the bottoms of the biscuits. I like to place the biscuits close together. Bake at 400-degrees until brown.

Mama Gillis use to makes us "Hoe Cakes". It was biscuit dough cooked in a buttered fry pan or "spida" on top of the stove. This was an ole-fashioned biscuit. I would take my butter and syrup and mix it together and "sop". You can use this recipe to do the same thing. My! Oh! My!

Mama Gillis's Buttermilk Biscuits

Years ago, I watched Mama Gillis make biscuits over and over. Of course, she never had a recipe. After watching her for years, I have learned to make them without a recipe, also. This recipe is as near to Mama Gillis's Buttermilk Biscuits as you can get. Try it. I hope you like it.

¼ cup plus 1 tablespoon shortening *(I like to use Crisco, but lard is better if you can get it)*
2 cups self-rising flour
¾ cup buttermilk
Butter to top the biscuits *(You may melt it to coat the tops)*

Preheat oven to 400-degrees. Cut the shortening into the flour until it resembles like coarse meal. Add buttermilk, stirring just until dry ingredients are moist. Turn dough onto lightly floured surface. Knead the dough about 10 times. *See note on biscuit tip below.

I roll my biscuit dough out about ½-inch thickness and cut with a floured 2-inch cutter. Mama Gillis would pull her dough off (about the size of golf balls) and squash them into biscuits. Her grand-daughter never mastered that or actually I really want that memory of her little hands making biscuits.

Grease a cast iron skillet (spida) or baking pan with Crisco or lard and place biscuits touching each other. Brush the tops of the uncooked biscuits with melted butter. Bake for 15 to 18 minutes until brown. The reason that I want the biscuits to touch each other is to keep the edges from getting too crisp and crusty. I like my biscuits to be thick and have soft sides.

Biscuit Tip: When you roll your dough out or when you knead your dough, you do not want to use too much flour. This will make a dry and tough biscuit. You just have to practice. Once you get the feel of making biscuits you will keep it. Kinda like driving.

Mini Cheese Biscuits

¾	cup plus 2 tablespoons all-purpose flour
2	teaspoons baking powder
¼	teaspoon baking soda
¼	teaspoon salt
	Pinch of cayenne pepper
1	(4-ounce) cup extra sharp Cheddar cheese
2	tablespoons cold Crisco shortening
6	tablespoons buttermilk

Preheat oven to 450-degrees. In a medium bowl sift together flour, baking powder, baking soda, salt and pepper. Using a pastry cutter, cut in the cheese and shortening with the dry ingredients until mixture resembles coarse meal.

Make a well in the center of the dough and pour in the buttermilk. Toss gently with a fork, just until moistened. The dough is real sticky. Turn dough out onto floured surface and knead gently with floured hands. Do not work too much flour into the biscuits. Pat the dough to ½-inch thick. Dip a 1½-inch cookie cutter in flour and cut out biscuits. Bake in an ungreased baking sheet for 12 to 15 minutes. These are best served warmed. This recipe would go great with chili or would make a wonderful appetizer. Try strawberry preserves with this biscuit.

Hot and Spicy Biscuits

Everyone has gone to this very familiar seafood restaurant and has had biscuits similar to these. This recipe is as near to those biscuits as you can get.

2¾	cups all-purpose baking mix (Very few of my recipes have a mix.)
½	teaspoon crushed red pepper
¾	teaspoon garlic powder
1	cup milk
1	cup sharp cheese, grated
2	tablespoons butter, melted
	Paprika

Preheat oven to 450-degrees. Combine baking mix, red pepper and the garlic powder. With a fork, stir in the milk and cheese until mixture forms soft dough. Drop dough by tablespoons on a greased cookie sheet and brush melted butter on tops of biscuits. Then sprinkle with paprika.

Bake for 10 to 12 minutes until golden brown.

Yields: 12 biscuits

Hot Chili Cornbread

This is wonderful for those cold nights here in Michigan with a hearty bowl of chili. Brr!

1	cup unsifted all-purpose flour
⅔	cup yellow corn meal
¼	cup sugar
½	teaspoon baking powder
½	teaspoon baking soda
½	teaspoon salt
1	cup buttermilk, warmed enough to take the chill off
1	stick butter, melted
1	large egg
1	cup frozen whole kernel corn *(you may use fresh right off the cob)*
½	cup sweet green pepper, finely chopped
1	tablespoon canned green chiles, chopped

Preheat oven to 350-degrees. Grease a 9-inch round baking pan. If you have a cast iron skillet, this is prefect. I put a glob of bacon grease in the cast iron skillet and have it heating while preparing this recipe.

In a large bowl, combine flour, cornmeal, sugar, baking powder, baking soda, and salt. In a small bowl, combine the warmed buttermilk, butter, and egg. Stir milk mixture into cornmeal mixture just until combined. Gently fold in corn, chopped pepper, and chiles. Spoon up the batter into the pan and bake 40 to 45 minutes or until center springs back when lightly touched. Cool in pan 15 minutes. Remove from pan.

Yields: 4 servings

Hush Puppies

1½	cup plain *(not self-rising)* cornmeal
¾	cup self-rising flour
¼	teaspoon baking soda
¾	cup onion, chopped *(If you want to you may use just ½-cup of onion)*
½	teaspoon salt
2	tablespoons sugar
2	eggs
¼	teaspoon black pepper
	Buttermilk—Enough to make a stiff batter (about 1 cup)

Combine all ingredients in a large bowl. Stir just until mixed. Drop by teaspoonfuls into hot deep oil. Oil should be (370-degrees). Turn once to brown. Drain onto paper towels.

You will not attend a Fish Fry in the South without having hush puppies and Cheese Grits.

Yields: 2 dozen

Sweet Breads
Pecan Caramel Muffins

⅓	cup brown sugar
4	tablespoons butter, softened
	Pecan halves
1	cup sifted all-purpose flour
¼	cup granulated sugar
3	tablespoons baking powder
½	teaspoon salt
¼	cup shortening
1	cup oatmeal, quick or old-fashioned, uncooked
1	egg, beaten
1	cup milk

Preheat oven to 425-degrees. Prepare the muffin tin by greasing the muffin cup. Mix the brown sugar and butter. Using your fingers, mash about a heaping tablespoon of sugar mixture into each muffin tin. Place a pecan half in the middle of this mixture. This will make a strudel like topping.

Sift flour, granulated sugar, baking powder, and salt. Cut in the shortening. Blend in the oatmeal. Stir in the egg and milk, stirring just until blended. Fill muffin tins ⅔-full and bake for approximately 20 minutes. Turn out onto a cake rack immediately. Delicious with coffee!

Yields: 12-15 servings

Cherry Surprise Muffins

1	cup pecans, finely chopped
½	cup light brown sugar, firmly packed
¼	cup granulated sugar
1	stick butter
2	egg yolks, well beaten
1	teaspoon vanilla extract
½	teaspoon almond flavoring
1	cup cake flour, sifted
¼	teaspoon baking powder
2	egg whites, stiffly beaten
48	maraschino cherries, drained and blotted on paper towels
2	cups powdered sugar, sifted

Preheat oven to 350-degrees. Prepare the tiny muffin tins by greasing well with Crisco or lining them with the small baking cups.

Sprinkle a very small amount of pecans in the bottom of each muffin tin cup.

Cream butter and sugar until light and fluffy. Add the egg yolks, vanilla and almond flavoring, beating well. Sift the flour and baking powder together. Blend well into the batter. Now fold in the stiffly beaten egg whites. Drop 1 teaspoon of batter on top of the pecans into each of the 48 muffin tins. Press a whole cherry into the center of the batter of each muffin. Bake at 350-degrees for 10 to 12 minutes. Empty powdered sugar in a large zip-top bag and place warm muffins in the bag, shaking gently only a few muffins at a time.

Yields: 48 muffins

Raisin Bran Muffins

1¼	cups all-purpose flour
½	cup sugar
1	tablespoon baking powder
½	teaspoon salt
2½	cups wheat Bran Flakes cereal
1¼	cups milk
1	egg
⅓	cup vegetable oil
¾	raisins

Preheat oven to 400-degrees. Prepare muffin tins by greasing cup cake liners. Combine the flour, sugar, baking powder and salt in a small bowl and set aside. Combine the cereal and milk in a mixing bowl, stir and let sit for 5 minutes. Add the egg and oil to this mixture, beating well. Add the flour mixture and raisins to the batter, stirring just until moistened. Fill the muffin tins ⅔-full. Bake at 400-degrees for 30 minutes or until golden brown in color.

Yields: 15 muffins

Coconut Muffins

1¾	cup all-purpose flour, sifted
½	cup granulated sugar
1	tablespoon baking powder
1	teaspoon salt
1	egg, beaten
1	cup milk
¼	cup vegetable oil
1	(3.5-ounce) can of coconut

Preheat the oven to 400-degrees. Sift the flour, sugar, baking powder and salt together. Set aside. In a medium sized bowl, combine egg, milk and oil. Add the dry ingredients, stirring just until moistened. Fold in the coconut.

Grease the muffin tins and fill ⅔ with the batter. Bake for 15 to 10 minutes. Remove from tins and serve hot. Delicious with hot chocolate or hot tea.

Yields: 1 dozen

Pineapple Muffins

1	(8.5-ounce) can crushed pineapple, drained and reserve for use in recipe
¾	cup milk
1	egg, slightly beaten
1½	teaspoon orange rind, grated
2	cups all-purpose flour, sifted
¼	cup granulated sugar
1	tablespoon baking powder
¼	teaspoon salt
¼	teaspoon ground nutmeg
¼	cup butter, melted

Preheat the oven to 400-degrees. Add enough milk to the drained pineapple juice to make 1 cup. Combine this mixture with the egg and orange rind.

In a separate bowl, sift together the flour, sugar, baking powder, salt and nutmeg. Blend the milk mixture into the dry ingredients. Add the melted butter and stir just until blended. Stir in the crushed pineapple.

Butter muffin tin or line them with cupcake papers. Fill the tins ⅔-full of batter. Bake for 20 minutes until golden brown and toothpick tests clean. Cool slightly and remove from pan. You may add a very light powdered sugar icing or glaze on the tops if desired.

Glaze (optional):

⅔	cup confectioners' sugar, sifted
1	tablespoon warm evaporated milk
¼	teaspoon vanilla extract

Mix all ingredients together and drizzle on the tops of the muffins.

Yields: 1 dozen

Zucchini Carrot Muffins

You will love these muffins. They are great to make up a batch or two. Freeze them in those zip-top gallon bags and take out what you want for work in the morning.

1½	cups all-purpose flour
1	tablespoon baking powder
½	teaspoon salt
1½	teaspoon pumpkin pie spice
2	eggs
½	cup brown sugar, packed
¾	cup milk
¼	cup vegetable oil
¼	cup raisins (preferably golden)
½	cup carrots, grated
½	cup zucchini, grated
½	cup walnuts, chopped

Preheat you oven at 375-degrees. Prepare your muffin tins by greasing them or lining them with the cupcake papers. Combine the dry ingredients of flour, baking powder, salt and pumpkin pie spice in a large mixing bowl.

In another mixing bowl, blend the eggs and brown sugar. Beat in the milk, vegetable oil.

Fold in the carrots and zucchini, raisins and walnuts. Now add this mixture to the dry ingredients and mix just until blended. Spoon into the muffin tins. Bake 15 to 20 minutes or until toothpick tests clean. Delicious!

Blueberry Muffins

1	cup uncooked oatmeal, quick cooking kind
1	cup buttermilk
1	cup all-purpose flour
¼	cup sugar
1	tablespoon baking powder
¼	teaspoon salt
	Pinch of cinnamon
1	egg, beaten
¼	cup oil
1	cup blueberries

Preheat the oven to 425-degrees. Grease the muffin tins or line them with cup cake papers. Combine the oatmeal and buttermilk. Let this stand 5 minutes. Combine the flour, sugar, baking powder, salt and cinnamon in a large bowl. Add the egg and oil to the oatmeal mixture. Stir just until moistened. Fold in the blueberries. Spoon batter into the muffin tins, filling ⅔-full of batter.

Note: You may bake the cupcake now for 20 minutes or you may make a simple topping on them consisting of cinnamon and sugar. If you decide to put the topping on the muffins, do not bake them first. Sprinkle the topping on and then bake them. See below.

Topping:
2	tablespoons sugar
½	teaspoon cinnamon

Combine these two ingredients and sprinkle on the batter. Bake as directed in the recipe for 20 minutes or until toothpick shows clean.

Yields: 16 cupcakes

Orange Nut Muffins

¼	cup shortening
¼	cup granulated sugar
1	egg, beaten
1	orange rind, grated
½	cup seedless raisins, chopped
2	cups all-purpose flour
4	teaspoons baking powder
½	teaspoon salt
¾	cup milk

Preheat oven to 425-degrees. Cream shortening. Add the sugar blending until light and fluffy. Add beaten egg. Beat well. Add the orange rind and raisins, mixing thoroughly. Sift together the dry ingredients. Add dry ingredients to batter alternately with milk, beginning and ending with the dry ingredients. Stir just until the ingredients are moistened. Prepare muffin tins by greasing them with oil or simply lining them with cupcake liners. Fill ⅔-full of batter and bake for 20 to 30 minutes.

Apple Carrot Muffins

If you have just a little Raisin Bran cereal left in your cupboard and 2 apples, you can make these healthy muffins.

1¾	cup Raisin Bran cereal
1¼	cup all-purpose flour
¾	cup granulated sugar
1¼	teaspoon baking soda
1	teaspoon cinnamon
¼	teaspoon salt
1	egg
¾	cup buttermilk
¼	cup cooking oil
¾	cup apple, peeled and chopped*
¾	cup carrots, grated*
¼	cup walnuts or pecans, chopped*

Preheat oven to 400-degrees. In a large bowl combine the first 6 ingredients and set aside. In a small bowl beat the egg, buttermilk, and oil. Stir this mixture into the dry ingredients, just until moistened. Fold in the apple, carrots and nuts. Line muffins tins with cupcake liners or grease them good. Fill muffin tins ¾-full. Bake at 400-degrees for 20 minutes. Cool muffins before removing from pan.

Yields: 1 dozen

*Before assembling the muffins-the first thing I would do is to prepare my apples, carrots, and nuts, by simply getting our food processor and "go to town" by chopping. You can do this at one "whack" by throwing everything in together.

Banana Walnut Bread

1½	cups sugar
½	cup butter, softened
2	eggs
4	ripe bananas, mashed
1	teaspoon vanilla extract
1	teaspoon baking soda
⅓	cup buttermilk
1½	cups all-purpose flour
1	cup walnuts or pecans, finely chopped
	Powdered sugar to sprinkle

Preheat oven to 350-degrees. In a large bowl cream the sugar and butter together, adding the eggs one at a time. Beat well after adding each egg. Now add the mashed bananas and beat until the batter is smooth. Add the vanilla extract. Measure the all-purpose flour and set aside. Measure the buttermilk in a cup and add the baking soda. Give it a little stir. Add the buttermilk mixture to the banana mixture while incorporating the flour. Stir just until blended. Now fold in the nuts. Pour into a prepared 9 x 5-inch loaf pan and bake for 1 hour until toothpick tests clean. Cool in pan 10 minutes and then dump onto cake rack. Sprinkle with powdered sugar, if desired.

Homemade Cinnamon Sweet Rolls

In school, we had the best Cinnamon Sweet Rolls. I remember this as if it was yesterday; I would always look down the table and see if someone left some of theirs and I would sweet talk them out of it. My sweet talk wasn't as sweet as the cinnamon rolls, though. I was always out of luck.

This would be a wonderful and inexpensive gift for friends or neighbors at Christmas time. Wouldn't it be nice to have a pan of Homemade Sweet Cinnamon Rolls on Christmas morning? Have the kids help you with this recipe, too.

2	packages granulated yeast
½	cup lukewarm water
¾	cup Crisco shortening
¾	cup sugar
1	teaspoon salt
3	eggs, beaten well
¼	teaspoon nutmeg
¼	teaspoon cinnamon
¼	teaspoon mace
1½	cups milk, scalded and cooled
8-9	cups all-purpose flour, sifted
	Melted butter to spread
	Extra brown sugar to sprinkle and

Cinnamon Topping:

4	tablespoons butter
1	cup brown sugar, firmly packed
1	cup pecans, ground (optional)
1	cup raisins (optional)
	Powdered Sugar Drizzle (see recipe on page 104)

Dissolve the yeast in the lukewarm water. Cream together the shortening and sugar. Add salt, eggs, nutmeg, cinnamon, mace and lukewarm milk. *The bottom of the milk pan will be easy to touch when lukewarm. Blend these ingredients together and thoroughly. Beat until smooth. Gradually add 3 cups of flour to start. Beat until smooth.

Add the remaining flour, as much as needed to make dough that is easily handled. Turn the dough out on a lightly floured board. Knead until smooth and the dough is elastic. Place the dough in a lightly oiled bowl. Brush with melted butter. Cover with a cloth. Place the bowl over very hot, not boiling water. Let rise until the dough is doubled in bulk, approximately 1½ to 2 hours.

* To test to see if doubled in bulk, just insert a finger in the dough. If the finger imprint stays it is doubled.

Now turn out on a lightly floured board again and knead very gently. Roll the dough into a rectangle ¼-inch thick. Spread with melted butter. Sprinkle on top of the butter the extra brown sugar.

Doesn't this sound yummy right now? I have already pinched and eaten pieces of the dough a dozen times by now.

Roll the dough like a jelly roll. Cut into ¾-inch slices.

For the cinnamon topping:
Cream together the 4 tablespoons of butter and the 1 cup of brown sugar. Place the butter and brown sugar mixture in the round baking dish. If you are using raisins, pecans or both, now is the time to place them on top of the brown sugar and butter mixture in the baking dish.

Place this mixture in a 9-inch round baking dish. Brush more melted butter on the tops and sides of the rolls. Put the rolls cut side down. Cover with cloth and let rise in a warm place until double in bulk again. This time it will take approximately 45 minutes. Bake in a 350-degree oven for 30 minutes. Turn upside down and now ice with the wonderful Powdered Sugar Drizzle.

Powdered Sugar Drizzle

1 cup powdered sugar, sifted
   Enough evaporated milk for spreading consistency

Combine the powdered sugar and milk to give a good spreading consistency.
Spread over the Sweet Rolls. This is wonderful.

Apple Date Nut Bread

I make this recipe every Christmas and have for at least 20 years. This is indeed the moistest bread you have ever had. The reason is that you soak the dates in the apple juice.
Freezes well, too.

2 cups apple juice
2 cups dates, chopped and pitted
2 cups sugar
⅔ cup butter, softened
2 eggs
3 cups sifted all-purpose flour
2 teaspoon baking soda
   Pinch of salt
1 teaspoon vanilla
2 cups pecans or walnuts, chopped

Preheat oven to 275-degrees. Bring the apple juice to a boil and pour over the dates. Set aside. Cream the butter and sugar together. Add the eggs and mix thoroughly. Sift together flour, soda, and salt and add this to the creamed mixture alternately with the date mixture. Add the vanilla and nuts. Grease and flour 2 loaf pans and divide the dough equally between them. Bake in the oven for 1 hour and 45 minutes. After cooling about 30 minutes or so, wrap bread in plastic wrap and then Reynolds wrap. I use a tea towel in lieu of the Reynolds wrap.

Apple Bread

2	cups sugar
1	cup oil
3	eggs
3	cups all-purpose flour
1	teaspoon salt
1	teaspoon baking soda
1	teaspoon cinnamon
2	cups baking apples, peeled and chopped
1	cup pecans, chopped
2	teaspoons vanilla extract

Preheat oven to 325-degrees. Prepare 2 loaf pans by spraying them with baking spray. In a large bowl, beat together sugar, oil, and eggs with an electric mixer. Sift dry ingredients in a separate bowl. Add the dry ingredients to the batter and stir only until just blended. Then stir in the apples, vanilla and pecans. Pour batter into prepared loaf pans. Bake for 1 hour until toothpick shows clean.

Apple Coffee Tea Bread

1½	cups self-rising flour
½	cup sugar
1	egg, beaten
½	cup milk
3	tablespoons cooking oil

Sift together the flour and sugar. Blend together the egg, milk and oil. Add the liquid all at once to the flour mixture and stir just until smooth. Pour this mixture into a greased 9-inch round cake pan.

For topping:

½	cup brown sugar, firmly packed
2	tablespoons self-rising flour
½	teaspoon cinnamon
¼	teaspoon mace
¼	cup pecans, ground (optional)
2	tablespoons butter, softened
2	medium unpeeled apples, cut into eighths

Combine the brown sugar, flour, cinnamon, mace, and nuts. Cut in the butter until the mixture resembles coarse crumbs. Sprinkle this mixture over the cake batter. Top with the apple slices. Bake the bread in a preheated oven for 25 to 30 minutes at 400-degrees.

My four babies, Duke, Rebel and Belle

and Baby Bubba

Carrot Bread

1½	cup all-purpose flour
1	teaspoon baking soda
¼	teaspoon salt
1	teaspoon cinnamon
1	cup granulated sugar
½	cup oil
½	cup buttermilk
2	eggs
1	cup carrots, grated
½	cup pecans, chopped
1	teaspoon vanilla extract

Preheat oven to 350-degrees. In a small mixing bowl, combine the flour, baking soda, salt, and cinnamon. Set aside. In a large mixing bowl, combine the sugar, oil, buttermilk and eggs. Beat this mixture for one minute at medium speed. Now add the flour mixture, mixing at low speed just until moistened. Fold in the carrots, pecans and vanilla extract. Grease and flour a loaf pan. Spoon batter into the loaf pan and bake for 55 to 60 minutes until toothpick tests clean. Cool for 10 minutes in pan and then dump onto wire rack to finish cooling.

Hint

This is a trick I learned being a General Manager of a hotel from my wonderful housekeepers. After you purchase your trash can liners, take them out of the original box that they came in and store the new, unused trash can liners in the bottom of your trash can, right under the trash can liner that is on the trash can. That way when you empty the weekly trash your trash bags will be at your finger tips. This also saves on a little extra storage space.

No Knead Raisin Bread

1	cup milk
6	tablespoons sugar, divided use
1	teaspoon salt
¼	cup shortening
1	(.25-ounce) package of yeast
½	cup lukewarm water (115-degrees)
3	eggs, well beaten
1	cup raisins, dark or golden
4	cups all-purpose flour
½	teaspoon cinnamon

In a medium saucepan, heat milk to 120-degrees. After heating the milk, pour the milk in a large bowl with 3 tablespoons sugar, salt and shortening. Stir the ingredients to dissolve the sugar and to melt shortening.

Soften the yeast in water and add this to the milk mixture. Stir in the raisins and the eggs.

Add the flour one cup at a time, mixing thoroughly after each addition. Beat the batter well. Cover and let rise in a warm place for 1 hour or until double in bulk. Stir dough down, getting all of the air bubbles out. Pour into 2 greased 9-inch layer pans. Combine the remaining sugar and cinnamon and sprinkle this mixture over the tops of the loaves. Cover and let rise again for 1 hour until double in bulk.

Preheat oven to 400-degrees. Bake for 30 minutes. Cool 5 minutes and turn out onto wire rack. When bread is cool wrap in tea towel with ribbon. Makes 2 loaves.

If you like, you may make a powdered sugar drizzle to top the loaves. *(See recipe on page 104.)*

Zucchini Tea Bread

3	eggs
1	cup cooking oil
2	cups granulated sugar
1	teaspoon vanilla extract
2	cups raw zucchini, peeled, grated and drained
1	teaspoon soda
¼	teaspoon baking powder
3	cups all-purpose flour
1	teaspoon salt
3½	teaspoons cinnamon
1	cup nuts, chopped

Preheat the oven to 325-degrees. Prepare two loaf pans by greasing and lining with wax paper. Beat the eggs until foamy. Add the oil, sugar and vanilla, mixing well. Stir in the grated zucchini. Sift the remaining dry ingredients and add to the batter, stirring just until blended. Fold in the nuts. Pour into two greased loaf pans and bake at 325-degrees for one hour or until toothpick tests clean.

Pumpkin Bread

3	cups granulated sugar
1	cup vegetable oil
4	eggs, beaten
1	pound can pumpkin
3½	cups all-purpose flour
2	teaspoon soda
2	teaspoon salt
½	teaspoon ground cloves
1	teaspoon each cinnamon, allspice, nutmeg
⅔	cup water

Preheat oven to 350-degrees. Mix sugar, oil, and eggs together. Add pumpkin. Then add dry ingredients, and water, stirring just until mixed. Do not beat. Pour batter into 2 greased and floured 9 x 5-inch loaf pans. Bake for 1 hour.

Desserts

I've got several recipes that I would like to share with you that are not cakes, pies or candies. They are just good ole desserts that are easy to prepare and you can take to different functions. They are pudding desserts, ice cream desserts with candy bars in them, etc.

Chocolate Pudding Torte

This recipe I made for my children long time ago when they were little bitty things. It is cheap, good and quick to make. I always doubled it.

1	(3.75-ounce) box instant vanilla pudding
1	(3.75-ounce) box instant chocolate pudding
1	package whole graham crackers
	Milk as directed on boxes of pudding mix
1	small carton Cool Whip
2	tablespoons dry cocoa, sifted

Lay the whole graham crackers flat in the bottom of a Pyrex or glass dish 9 x 9-inch. Mix vanilla pudding as directed on box of pudding mix. Pour over graham crackers. Top vanilla pudding with another layer of graham crackers. Mix chocolate pudding as directed on box of pudding mix. Pour chocolate pudding over second layer of graham crackers. Empty Cool Whip bowl into a bowl and add sifted cocoa. Spoon this mixture over the top of chocolate pudding. Spread evenly. Chill overnight. Cut into squares. I hope this dessert will become a regular, like it was at my home when my children were growing up.

Banana Pudding
The ole timey way

I have never been to a church home-coming down South that someone didn't bring the original version of the Banana Pudding.

1	11-ounce box vanilla wafers
3-4	bananas, sliced*
4	eggs, separated (reserve the whites for the meringue)
1	cup granulated sugar, divided use
3	tablespoon corn starch
2	cups milk
1	teaspoon vanilla extract
	Pinch of salt (for the meringue)
¼	teaspoon cream of tartar (for the meringue)

Preheat oven to 375-degrees.

Filling:
In a medium sized saucepan, beat the egg yolks and add ¾-cup sugar, corn starch and milk. Combine the ingredients real well. Stir over medium heat until thickened. Remove from the heat and add the vanilla extract, stirring real well.

In a 2-quart baking dish, place a layer of vanilla wafers, followed by a layer of bananas, followed by a layer of the hot filling. Top again with the vanilla wafers, bananas and finally a layer of hot filling. Top with the meringue. Set aside while you prepare the meringue.

Beat 4 egg whites in a deep mixing bowl on high speed. Add the remaining ¼-cup sugar a tablespoon at a time, pinch of salt and the cream of tartar, continuing to beat until stiff peaks form.

Pile the meringue on top of the hot filling sealing the filling well all around the casserole dish. Place in a preheat oven at 375-degrees for 8 to 10 minutes or until the meringue is lightly brown.

Note: I like to sprinkle a very small amount of lemon juice on my bananas to keep them from turning dark. There's a lot of people that don't mind their bananas to turn dark, but I'm not one of those people.

Pineapple Pudding

Mama Gillis made this all of the time. It was just as good to me as the Banana Pudding.

Prepare the Pineapple Pudding just like the Banana Pudding, only leaving out the Bananas and adding 1 (20-ounce) can of crushed pineapple, well drained.

For the cookie part—I know you have seen the Coconut Washboard cookies in the grocery store for like $.99. Use them in the Pineapple Pudding in lieu of the Vanilla Wafers as in the Banana Pudding. The coconut cookies, pudding, the pineapple, and don't forget the meringue is delicious. Try it. Bake the Pineapple Pudding just like you did the Banana Pudding. This sure does bring back memories for me.

Baked Apples

Don't forget if you have apples laying around, turn them into a delightful light dessert.

6	medium-sized apples, cored and peeled ⅓ of the way down
	Water or apple juice
½	cup light brown sugar
2	teaspoons cinnamon
	Dash of cloves
3	tablespoons butter, melted
¼	cup raisins, optional
¼	cup nuts, optional

Preheat oven at 400-degrees. Place prepared apples in a greased shallow baking dish. Add enough water or apple juice to cover the bottom of the dish. Combine the remaining ingredients about 1 tablespoon of the mixture into the cavity of each apple. Baste often with the juices in the pan. Bake 40 minutes or until tender. Top with sweetened whipping cream, if desired.

Peach Custard Dessert

1½	cups all-purpose flour
½	teaspoon salt
½	cup butter, softened
1	(1-lb, 14-ounce) can sliced peaches, well-drained and reserving ½-cup syrup
½	cup sugar
½	teaspoon cinnamon
1	egg, slightly beaten
1	cup evaporated milk
1	teaspoon almond extract

Preheat oven to 375-degrees and prepare an 8-inch square pan by greasing well with butter. Combine in a 1½-quart bowl, the flour, salt and butter. Using a pastry blender, mix until the mixture looks like little peas. Using your hands or the back of a spoon, press mixture firmly on the bottom and halfway up the sides of the square pan. Place peach slices on the crust in the pan. Mix the sugar and cinnamon together, sprinkling over the peaches. Bake in a 375-degree oven for 20 minutes.

While the peaches and crust are cooking, mix the reserved peach syrup, egg, evaporated milk and almond extract together. After the peaches and crust have cooked, pour the egg and milk mixture over the peaches. Bake another 30 minutes or until the custard is somewhat firm. The center of the custard will not be firm as the sides but it will become firm as it cools. Serve warm or cold with sweetened whipping cream. Serves 9.

Banana Split Dessert Cake

By Mrs. Sally Duquette

This recipe was given as a contribution from a true "Northern Lady". She was my first real genuine friend here in Michigan.

Crust:
- 1½ cup graham cracker crumbs
- ½ cup butter, softened (divided use)
- 1 cup powdered sugar
- 1 egg
- 4 bananas cut in half lengthwise
- 1 (8-ounce) can crushed pineapple, drained and reserving ¼-cup liquid
- 1 (8-ounce) package cream cheese, softened
- ½ cup nuts, chopped

In a small bowl, combine the crumbs and ¼-cup butter, mixing well. Press in the bottom of a 9 x 9-inch baking pan. Bake in a 350-degree oven for 10 minutes. Cool 5 minutes.

Combine the sugar, egg, ¼-cup butter, beating until smooth. Spread sugar mixture over the cooled crust. Now layer the bananas over the sugar mixture and sprinkle the pineapple over the bananas. In a small bowl, combine the reserve pineapple juice with the cream cheese, beating until smooth, Spread over the pineapple. Top with chopped nuts. Refrigerate several hours or overnight.

Optional choice: Drizzle chocolate syrup over the entire desert before cutting.

Yields: 12 squares

Coffee Chiffon Dessert

I made this for my son, and he loved it. I sometimes made this for him for his birthday in lieu of a birthday cake. It is light and airy and makes a wonderful dessert.

2	envelopes unflavored gelatin
2	cups whole milk
1	cup light cream (half-and-half)
2	generous tablespoons instant coffee
5	eggs, separate the yolks from the whites
1	cup sugar (divided use)
½	teaspoon salt

Heat the gelatin, milk, cream and coffee. Beat the egg yolks until thick and add ½-cup of the sugar gradually in a separate bowl. (Save the other ½-cup for the egg whites.) Add the egg mixture gradually to the hot coffee mixture and cook till the custard coats a spoon. Remove from heat and chill until syrupy. Meanwhile, beat egg whites with the salt until stiff peaks, but not dry. Gradually beat in the remaining ½-cup sugar. Fold this into the custard mixture and pour into a greased 2-quart mold. Chill until set and unmold. Garnish with grated chocolate.

Yields: 8 Servings

Strawberry Surprise

Crust:
1	cup all-purpose flour
½	cup pecans, chopped
1	stick butter, melted
¼	cup brown sugar, firmly packed

Mix the above ingredients, stirring until well mixed. Pour and pat into a 9 x 11-inch square baking dish. Place in a 350-degree oven and bake for 20 minutes.

Filling:
1½	cups of sliced fresh strawberries or 1 (10-ounce) frozen package of strawberries, thawed *(Save a few strawberries for garnishing)*
1	cup granulated sugar
2	tablespoons lemon juice
2	egg whites
½	pint heavy cream, whipped

For dollops to garnish:
½	pint of heavy cream whipped with ¼-cup of powdered sugar.

Combine the strawberries, sugar, lemon juice and egg whites in a large and deep mixing bowl. Beat at high speed for 15 to 20 minutes at high speed until mixture is light and fluffy. Fold the ½-pint whipped cream into this mixture. Pour the strawberry mixture into the cooled crust. Freeze and cut into squares.

Garnish with a dollop of sweetened whipping cream and a strawberry.

Easy Egg Custard

When I was expecting my son, I ate custard every night. This is not a false-hood. I always said that was why he was so sweet, pretty and healthy when he was a baby. Now he's handsome. I wish I could eat it now every night, but I would look like a "blimp." This is a very nutritious dessert that takes practically no time to prepare. Fix this when you hit the door in the evening and it will be done and cooling while you fix the main meal.

- 4 eggs, beaten
- 2/3 cup sugar
- 1 teaspoon vanilla extract
- 2 cups whole milk (scalded) or 1 cup evaporated milk and 1 cup water
- Few sprinkles of nutmeg or mace

Beat the eggs well, adding the sugar, vanilla. Add the milk gradually and beat well. You do not want the hot milk to cook the eggs, pour into custard cups. Sprinkle with nutmeg or mace. In a 13 x 9-inch baking dish. Pour water into the bottom and set the filled custard cups in it. Bake at 350-degrees for 30 minutes or until a knife is inserted in the middle of one of the custards and it shows clean.

Homemade Ice Cream

Now, I hope everyone has had real ice cream. I still use a hand crank believe it or not. I think the camaraderie of sitting in my rocking chairs on my front porch taking turns turning the crank makes it all the better. I remember sitting on top of the churn while Papa and Mama Gillis was turning the crank years ago.

My sisters and I would fight over who was going to get the "dasher" of the ice cream churn. I always won. Of course, they would argue that one.

In making homemade ice cream the term "ripen" means after the ice cream has frozen, let the ice cream sit a spell and harden and those wonderful ingredients will blend and mellow throughout. That is awful hard to do for we always would just open the churn right up and start scooping it out. That's okay, too. But if you have the will power to just let the churn sit wrapped up with towels or old newspapers to keep the cold air in or even put the churn in your home freezer while you are eating supper for about one hour, you will have the best ice cream you could ever wish for.

Lemon Ice Cream

1¼	cups lemon juice
2	tablespoons lemon rind
4	cups sugar
5	cups whipping cream
4	cups half-and-half
	Mint sprigs

Combine the lemon juice, lemon rind and sugar. Stir until the sugar dissolves. Stir in the whipping cream and half and half. Pour this mixture into your ice cream freezer. This recipe will make 1 gallon churn. Freeze according to your manufacturer's directions. Pack the freezer with additional ice and salt to let ripen and let stand 1 hour before serving. Garnish with mint sprigs, and, if you like, add some lemon curls.

Homemade Peach Ice Cream
"The Ultimate"

I have tried several versions of Peach Ice Cream and this recipe is just like it reads "The Ultimate". The nectar makes it.

6	eggs, beaten real good until frothy
2	cups granulated sugar
2	tablespoons vanilla extract
1	(12-ounce) bottle peach or apricot nectar* If you can't find peach nectar, just use the apricot. You cannot tell the difference.
2	large cans evaporated milk
2	cups peaches (4 or 5 peaches), peeled and seeded
½	cup granulated sugar to add to puree
	Whole milk, enough to fill churn to the fill line

Gradually add the sugar while beating the eggs. Beat well. Add 2 tablespoons vanilla extract to the egg and sugar mixture. Add the peach or apricot nectar to this mixture and mix well. Mix the evaporated milk and peach pureed with the above mixture. Pour the mixture into the churn and fill up to the fill line with whole milk. Freeze according to the direction of your ice cream churn.

Note: I use my blender or food processor on this recipe to mix the ingredients. It eliminates the splatters.

Butter Pecan Ice Cream

½ cup pecans, chopped
2 tablespoons butter, melted
4 eggs
2½ cups sugar
1 (14-ounce) can sweetened condensed milk
1 (3.75-ounce) package butterscotch instant pudding mix
 Approximately 6 cups whole milk
 1-gallon ice cream freezer

Melt butter in small skillet and add pecans, sautéing them until golden brown. Cool. Beat eggs with mixer until frothy, gradually stirring in the sugar, beating until thick. Stir in the condensed milk and pudding mix. Pour mixture into the ice cream freezer and add enough milk to reach the fill line of the freezer. Freeze according to the freezer's manufacturer's instructions. Let the ice cream ripen 1 hour.

Yields: 1 gallon ice cream

Chocolate Ice Cream

This recipe reminds me of the "junket" ice cream mix.

4 large eggs, slightly beaten
1 cup sugar
1½ quarts whole milk (divided use)
1 (3.4-ounce) package chocolate flavored instant pudding mix
1 (16-ounce) can chocolate syrup
1 (14-ounce) can sweetened condensed milk
1 tablespoon vanilla extract

Combine the eggs, sugar and 2 cups of the milk in a large saucepan, mixing well. Cook on medium heat, stirring constantly until temperature reaches 160-degrees about 5 minutes. Remove from the heat and stir in the remaining milk, pudding mix, and the remaining ingredients. Put in the fridge to chill for at least 1 hour or more. Pour ingredients into a 1-gallon ice cream freezer and process according to manufacturer's directions. Let ripen for at least 1 hour before serving.

Yields: 3 quarts of ice cream

Banana Split Ice Cream

6	eggs
2	cups sugar
1	(14-ounce) can sweetened condensed milk
2	teaspoons vanilla extract
1	pint fresh strawberries, washed, drained, hulled and sliced*
2	ripe bananas, mashed
1	cup nuts, chopped
1	(8-ounce) container frozen whipped topping, thawed
	Approximately 1 cup milk
	Red food coloring (optional)

Beat eggs with mixer until frothy, gradually adding sugar and beating well until thick. Stir in the condensed milk and vanilla in the egg mixture. In a separate bowl combine the strawberries, bananas, nuts, and whipped topping. If you desire, you may add red food coloring to the mixture, stirring till you reach the color you desire. Add this mixture to the egg and milk mixture and stir. Pour into ice cream freezer and add enough milk to reach fill line of freezer. Freeze according to manufacturer's directions.

*If fresh strawberries are unavailable, you may use 1 (10-ounce) bag frozen strawberries, thawed.

Yields: 1 gallon ice cream

Vanilla Custard Ice Cream

6	eggs
1½	cups granulated sugar
2	cups whole milk
¼	teaspoon salt
3	tablespoons vanilla extract
4	cups half-and-half
4½	cups rock salt
2	(10-pound) bags crushed ice

Beat the eggs well until frothy. Add the sugar, milk and salt, mixing well. Pour ingredients in a large saucepan and cook over medium heat, stirring constantly until slightly thickened and mixture coats a metal spoon. Remove from the heat and add the 3 tablespoons of vanilla extract and the half and half. Cool the mixture and pour into the ice cream freezer and freeze according to manufacturer's directions.

Note: Try a variation by adding most any fruit which has been sweetened to taste, such as peaches, strawberries, and bananas.

The Deva's Chocolate Mousse

If you have any heavy whipping cream left over in the fridge, don't let it go to waste. This dessert is pure heaven. It takes a grand total of 15 minutes to make and 30 minutes in the fridge. If you have unexpected company, boy can you surprise them with this!

1	envelope unflavored gelatin
2	tablespoons cold water
3	tablespoons boiling water
¾	cup granulated sugar
⅔	cup dry cocoa
1½	cups heavy whipping cream
1	tablespoon vanilla extract

Sprinkle the gelatin over the cold water in a very small bowl. Stir. Let stand for 1 minute just to soften the gelatin. Add the boiling water to the gelatin, stirring until the gelatin is completely dissolved. The mixture will be clear. Set aside.

Using a cold medium-size mixing bowl, stir together the sugar and cocoa. Add the heavy whipping cream and vanilla extract, beating till stiff peaks. Now pour in the dissolved gelatin and beat until well blended.

Spoon this delicious delicacy into fancy serving dishes. Garnish with chocolate shavings or I simply break a Hershey's bar along the little squares and put a square of Hershey's chocolate in the mousse.

Yields: 4 servings

Chocolate Bread Pudding

4	slices white bread
4	eggs, beaten well
1	(13-ounce) can evaporated milk
¾	cup chocolate syrup
⅓	cup water
	Ice cream or sweetened whipping cream for topping, if desired

Preheat oven to 350-degrees and prepare an 8 x 8 x 2-inch baking dish by greasing. Place bread on the bottom of the baking dish. Mix together the eggs, milk, chocolate syrup and water, blending well. Pour this mixture over the bread, pushing bread down so as to soak up chocolate mixture. Cover and put in the fridge at least 1 hour. Bake at 350-degrees for 30 to 40 minutes until knife is inserted in the middle of custard and it comes out clean. Serve warm or cold.

Belle, the Chocolate Lab

Fudge Cake Pudding

A cake like dessert with pudding underneath. Very simple.

¾	cup all-purpose flour
1	cup sugar (divided use)
½	cup cocoa (divided use)
1	teaspoon baking powder
¾	teaspoon salt (divided use)
½	cup milk
2	tablespoons butter, melted
1	teaspoon vanilla
½	cup pecans, chopped
1⅔	cups boiling water

Mix the flour, ½-cup sugar, 3 tablespoons cocoa, baking powder, ½-teaspoon salt, milk, butter, vanilla and pecans in a small bowl until smooth. This will be the batter. Set this aside.

Grease a 10 x 6 x 2-inch baking dish and stir the remaining ingredients of cup of sugar, cocoa, and the salt. Add the boiling water with these ingredients. Now drop the batter by tablespoons into the sugar and cocoa liquid. Bake at 350-degrees for 40 to 45 minutes. Serve warm. This will be delicious with sweetened whipping cream.

Hint

For you chocolate lovers. Do you ever drip chocolate on your clothes? I sure do. Keep a bottle of hydrogen peroxide just for this. Dab the peroxide on the chocolate spot with a cotton ball or Q-tip and watch the chocolate disappear in front of your eyes.

Mama Gillis' Bread Pudding

When Mama Gillis asked me what I wanted for my Birthday several years ago, I told her I wanted her to make me a Bread Pudding. Little did I know that this would be the last dish I would eat of her cooking. She also gave me her handwritten recipe. I will believe to this day, she knew this would be the last dish that she would prepare for me. At any rate, I ate the whole pan and did not share with anyone. Mama Gillis' Bread pudding is so rich that you do not need a sauce to pour over it.

Grease with butter a 13 x 9 x 2-inch pan.

10   slices of bread
Approximately 1 stick of butter needed to butter the slices.

Butter and toast the slices of bread in the broiler. Toast until lightly brown. Lay the toasted bread slices side by side in the baking pan. Set aside while making the custard filling.

Custard Filling:
6   eggs, well beaten
2½   cups granulated sugar
5   cups half-and-half cream or you may use evaporated milk
    (You may use a mixture of both if you like.)
1 or 2 tablespoons vanilla extract *(You may use 1 tablespoon of coconut and 1 tablespoon of vanilla)*
3   cups flaked coconut (divided use)

In a large saucepan, combine the eggs, sugar and cream, stirring constantly until the milk starts to steam and just begins to boil. This mixture could scorch, so it's important to keep stirring. When you take the filling off of the heat, stir in the extract and 2 cups of the coconut. Be sure to stir the coconut in the milk real good for you want the coconut to soak in the custard. Now pour the custard carefully over the bread slices. Take your spoon and mash the slices of bread and also move the bread slices around so that the custard will soak into the bread. Sprinkle, using the last cup of coconut over the bread pudding. Bake in a 350-degree oven for 40 to 45 minutes or until a knife is inserted in the middle that shows clean. Watch the coconut while cooking, for you do not want the coconut to get too brown.

The Lord is my Shephard;
I shall not want.
He maketh me to lie
down in green pastures;
he leadeth me beside the
still waters,
He restoreth my soul;
he leadeth me in the paths
of righteousness for his
name's sake.
Yea, though I walk through
the valley of the shadow of
death, I will fear no evil:
for thou art with me; thy Rod
and thy staff they comfort
me.
Thou preparest a table before
me in the presents of mine
enemies; thou anointest my
Head with oil. My cup Runneth
over, surly goodness and mercy
shall follow me all the dayes of my Life
and I will dwell in the

*The 23rd Psalm,
handwritten by
Mama Gillis*

*Artwork by
Mama Gillis*

Pumpkin Custard

1	egg
¼	cup brown sugar, firmly packed
Pinch	ground allspice
Pinch	ground mace
Pinch	ground ginger
Pinch	ground nutmeg
¼	teaspoon ground cinnamon
1	teaspoon vanilla or maple extract
Pinch	salt
⅔	cup canned pumpkin or cooked pumpkin
½	cup evaporated milk

Beat the egg in a medium-size mixing bowl. Add all of the ingredients except for the pumpkin and milk, mixing well. Slowly stir in the pumpkin and milk. Pour into a 1-quart greased baking dish. Bake at 325-degrees for 20 to 25 minutes. Make topping while custard is cooking.

Topping:

2	tablespoons brown sugar
2	teaspoons all-purpose flour
1	teaspoon cinnamon
2	teaspoons cold butter
¼	cup pecans, chopped

While the custard is cooking, combine the brown sugar, flour, and cinnamon in a small bowl. Cut in the butter till it is very crumbly. Add the pecans. Sprinkle onto the custard and bake 15 to 20 minutes longer until knife inserted in center comes out clean.

Cakes, Frostings, Icings & Fillings

Created and decorated by the Divine Dixie Deva

We seemed to always have a cake around the house. Mama Gillis was a cake person. She always had homemade cakes at her house. I'm the same way. When I think of dessert, cake comes to mind. As you walked into Mama Gillis' kitchen you would see those ole timey pea-shelling pans (we also called them dish pans), in which she would convert to covers for her cakes. There was no way in the world that she could possibly own cake covers for all the cakes she baked at one time. I would just go down the row of her kitchen table and lift up the dish pan and choose what kind of cake I wanted. Of course, a whole lot of the times they were promised out and that meant hands off!

We Southerners always have a cake ready and willing to take to someone's home or church or just to have at the house for company drop-ins.

I don't want to leave my mother out on the cake issue. Mama is still keeping the tradition alive on cake baking. Just ask anyone in Albany, Georgia. You know, Mama Gillis didn't realize just how much influence she instilled in us while she was here on earth.

I will never forget one of the first cakes I made was a Tunnel of Fudge cake and it was a huge flop. When I dumped it out on the cake plate, I did just that. What I mean is that the fudge part just oozed out and my sister called it a "Mud Cake." That's what it looked like. Of course, at the time, I didn't think it was funny. She has never let me forget it, though.

I make my cakes from scratch, however, there are some recipes from box mixes that you can add several ingredients in them and get a good product. But, I figured by the time you do that, you might as well just make one from scratch. Your cake is as good as the ingredients you put in it; I don't care how you doll it up. I guess it's how you were raised. It's hard nowadays to go to a function and find a homemade cake. To me that is such a disappointment to see a store-bought cake. Anyone can pick up a cake from God knows where. It's the giving of yourself that means something to me. I never saw a box mix at Mama Gillis' house. Folks came from all over to eat her cakes.

I will have her 14-layer cake in the Grand Finale Section. Yes, that's what I said, a 14-layer cake! A lot of folks say that I'm just like her. Well, what a compliment!

I was raised to say Icing for that wonderful sweet condiment that you put on cakes or bar cookies. Now some cooks may have a "defined" definition for the word Frosting and Icing, but in this book, if Icing comes across in lieu of the word Frosting, that's what it is.

A lot of these recipes are what I call Specialty cakes. They would be great gifts at Christmas time or for a Birthday or just because.

Pineapple Pound Cake

⅓	cup Crisco
1	cup butter
2¾	cups granulated sugar
6	large eggs
3	cups all-purpose flour, sifted
1	teaspoon baking powder
¼	cup milk
¾	cup crushed pineapple and juice, undrained
1	teaspoon vanilla extract

In a large mixing bowl cream shortening, butter, and sugar well, beating until light and fluffy. Add eggs, one at a time, beating well after each addition. Sift together flour and baking powder, and add to the batter alternately with milk, beginning and ending with flour. Add vanilla. Stir in pineapple and juice. Blend well. Pour into a well-greased and floured 10-inch tube pan. Place in a cold oven. Bake at 325-degrees for 1½-hours. Very moist cake.

Icing:

¼	cup butter, melted
1½	cups powdered sugar
1	cup crushed pineapple, drained

Add melted butter and other ingredients in a large bowl, stirring until mixed well. If the icing is too runny, just add more powdered sugar, mixing until the desired consistency. Pour over warm cake.

Lemon Cheese Cake

This is an old-timey recipe. I would always make this for my mother for her birthday cake. It is one of her favorites. You used to find these cakes all the time in the bakeries down South, for they were a real popular cake. For those of you that don't know what this cake is about, it is a white layer cake and is iced with a lemon-like curd filling. It is a very delicate cake, yet rich.

There are different variations. You can add pineapple in the filling as an optional choice. I have also made this cake with the lemon filling between the layers and have iced the tops and sides of the cake with the Snow-Capped Icing recipe, which I will include below. You can also add a touch of coconut in the cake layers or to the Snow-Capped Icing to make it also different. Be creative in the kitchen.

Cake Batter:
- 2 cups sugar
- 1 cup Crisco or vegetable shortening
- 3 cups all-purpose flour
- 3 teaspoons baking powder
- 1 cup milk
- 6 egg whites, stiffly beaten

Cream the sugar and shortening together, beating until light and fluffy. Sift together flour and baking powder. Add flour mixture to the creamed batter, alternating with the milk, beginning and ending with the flour. Fold in the beaten egg whites. Bake in 3 greased and floured 9-inch layer cake pans. Bake in a 350-degree oven for 25 minutes or until toothpick test shows clean. Make sure cake is completely cool before you ice this cake with this filling.

Note: If you want to add coconut to this recipe, just add and stir in a ½-cup of flaked coconut before you add the egg whites.

Filling for Lemon Cheese Cake:
- 1½ cups granulated sugar
- ½ cup all-purpose flour
- 6 egg yolks
- ½ cup lemon juice
- Grated rind from two lemons
- 1 cup hot water
- ½ cup butter, melted

Mix sugar and flour and add beaten egg yolks, lemon juice, grated lemon rind, hot water and butter. Cook until smooth and thick over low heat. Spread between cake layers. Ice the sides and top with Snow-Capped Icing.

Optional choice: Drain 1 small can of crushed pineapple and add this in with the above ingredients and cook it till thick enough to spread. It's good with or without the pineapple.

Snow-Capped Icing

- 1 cup granulated sugar
- ⅓ cup water
- ¼ teaspoon cream of tartar
- 2 egg whites, room temperature
- 1 teaspoon vanilla extract

Combine the sugar, water and cream of tartar in a large saucepan, cooking over medium heat without stirring until the mixture reaches 232-degrees or spins a thread stage. While the mixture is cooking, beat egg whites till soft peaks. When sugar mixture reaches proper cooking temperature, slowly add to the egg whites, beating well. Add vanilla extract. This recipe yields enough to ice the tops and sides of the cake.

Heavenly Pecan Cake

If you want to be the "Belle of the Ball," I guarantee you will be with this recipe. Even if you haven't cooked for years, folks will think you have been if you make this cake. Check this one out. If you need a resource for pecans, look on my Resource Page. Remember I was born and raised in the pecan capital of the world. Believe it or not, this recipe is quite easy. Just turn that mixer on and go for it.

This cake is beautiful and wonderful for that dinner party. After icing the cake with the whipping cream, which is rich enough and a gorgeous sight, the Butter Pecan Sauce which is depicted below, adds that extra bang. The cake is most elegant without the Butter Pecan Sauce; the sauce is an optional choice.

Now, just to let you know in advance—did you notice the recipe calls for no shortening?

8	whole eggs
2	cups granulated sugar
1	tablespoon vanilla extract or butternut flavoring
1	cup all-purpose flour
1	teaspoon salt
4	teaspoons baking powder
5	cups pecans, chopped very fine

Grease and line with wax paper 3 (9-inch) pans. Preheat oven to 350-degrees. Beat eggs for 5 minutes at high speed. Yes, 5 minutes. Just think, if we didn't have mixers. Mama Gillis didn't have one for years. Add sugar, vanilla extract or butternut flavoring, flour, salt and baking powder. Beat another 5 minutes. Add 5 cups of pecans at low speed to moisten (1 minute). Pour into 3 greased and wax paper-lined 9-inch pans. Bake at 350-degrees for about 15 to 20 minutes. Remove immediately from pans to wire racks and cool completely. This cake will fall slightly, but this is okay.

Topping:
- 3 half-pints heavy cream, whipped
- 1 cup powdered sugar to taste
- 1 teaspoon vanilla extract
- ¼ cup pecans, chopped very fine, for topping the cake

Whip the heavy cream until stiff peaks, adding sugar gradually. Stir in the vanilla extract. You may need to add a little more powdered sugar, depending on your taste.

To assemble the cake:
Ice between the layers of the cake and the top of the cake with the sweetened whipping cream. If you choose to ice the sides of the cake, you will have plenty of whipping cream to do that, also. I like to put whipping cream on the tops and sides and sprinkle the top of the cake with chopped pecans. For a glamorous effect, I like to drizzle the cake with the Butter Pecan Sauce.

Butter Pecan Sauce:
If you really want to make this cake rich and dazzling, just drizzle along the sides and tops and then sprinkle the nuts on top. I have made this cake either way. Very easy to prepare and if you have any left over, use it on ice cream.

- ½ cup butter
- 1 cup pecans, chopped
- 1 cup light brown sugar, packed
- ⅓ cup heavy cream or a 1 small can evaporated milk
- ¼ cup light corn syrup or Karo

Melt butter in a saucepan, add the pecans. Heat the pecans till they are toasted and butter is lightly browned. Stir in brown sugar, cream and corn syrup. Cook on low heat till the sugar is dissolved. Stir often. This will make 2 cups of sauce.

Strawberry Delight Cake

This cake is nothing more than a 1-2-3-4 cake recipe with a custard sauce as a filling, topped with sweetened strawberries and sweetened whipped cream. This is a gorgeous cake when decorated with strawberries. You can tell I love custard.

1	cup butter, softened
2	cups granulated sugar
4	eggs, separated
3	cups all-purpose flour
1	tablespoon baking powder
½	teaspoon salt
1	cup milk
1	teaspoon almond flavoring
2	quarts strawberries-sliced in halves and sweetened to taste with
1	cup powdered sugar*
2	pints heavy cream whipped until stiff peaks and sweetened to taste
½	cup powdered sugar

Note: Some folks like to use granulated sugar to sweeten strawberries. Granulated sugar does not dissolve as well. Keep the strawberries in the refrigerator until ready to use. (Save out some of the prettiest whole strawberries for garnish.)

Cake Batter:
Cream butter; gradually add sugar, beating until fluffy. Add egg yolks, beating well after each addition. Combine flour with baking powder and salt. Add to creamed mixture alternately with milk—beginning and ending with flour. Beat egg whites until stiff, but not dry. Fold into batter. Pour batter into 3 (9-inch pans), which have been greased, floured and lined with wax paper. Bake at 350-degrees about 25 minutes. Do the toothpick test. When done, you must cool the cake layers completely before adding custard filling

Custard Filling:
½   cup sugar
3   tablespoons cornstarch
¼   teaspoon salt
3   egg yolks, slightly beaten
2   cups milk
1   teaspoon vanilla extract
1   tablespoon butter

Mix together sugar, cornstarch, and salt in a saucepan. Gradually add the egg yolks and milk to the sugar, cornstarch and salt mixture. Cook over medium heat until it thickens and boils for one minute. Then remove from heat and add the butter and vanilla extract. Cool completely.

To assemble the cake:
Spread custard filling between each cake layer. Top the custard with layer of sweetened strawberries, then top the strawberries with the whipping cream. (In sequence-custard, strawberries, and whipping cream) When you reach the very top layer of the cake, frost the top layer and sides with whipping cream and garnish the top with the whole strawberries. This cake will make the Grand Finale for a Dinner Party!

Gingerbread with Lemon Sauce

Who would remember what was served for dessert at their Brownie Fly-up service, but me. Gosh, that was "umpteen" years ago, at Avalon Methodist Church in Albany, Georgia. I was "flying up" to become a Girl Scout. I guess it impressed me so much for me to remember it that long ago. This is a comfort food.

¾	cup dark brown sugar
¾	cup dark molasses
¾	cup shortening, melted
2	eggs, lightly beaten
2½	cups all-purpose flour
½	teaspoon baking powder
½	teaspoon salt
2	teaspoons soda
2	teaspoons ginger
1½	teaspoons cinnamon
½	teaspoon cloves
½	teaspoon nutmeg
1	cup boiling water

Mix sugar, molasses, and shortening together. Add beaten eggs and mix well. Add sifted dry ingredients and beat till well blended. Then add boiling water and beat till smooth. The batter will be thin. Pour into a greased and floured 9 x 13-inch oblong pan. Bake at 350-degrees for 30 to 40 minutes. Serve warm with what else but, warm Lemon Sauce. Recipe is below.

Lemon Sauce:

¾	cup granulated sugar
2	tablespoons cornstarch
2	cups water
	Grated rind of 2 lemons
	Dash of salt
¼	cup butter
¼	cup lemon juice

Mix together sugar and cornstarch, add water gradually, cooking until thick and clear. Remove from heat and stir in remaining ingredients. Pour over Gingerbread. Sweetened Whipping Cream makes an excellent topping for Gingerbread also.

One Bowl Pineapple Cake

This is one of the easiest homemade cakes you can make. It takes no time at all. If you think a box mix is easy, think again. This is it. When volunteering to bring something sweet to an outing and at the last minute, I wonder how am I going to swing it; there are two recipes that I use. This is one of them. The other is the Fastest Real Chocolate Cake in Town. You will get raves and everyone can tell they're homemade cakes.

2	cups all-purpose flour
2	cups granulated sugar
¼	cup vegetable oil
	Pinch of salt
1	teaspoon soda
1	(20-ounce) can of crushed pineapple (Do not drain)
2	eggs

Mix all ingredients. Bake in a greased and floured 13 x 9 x 2-inch pan at 325-degrees for 30 to 45 minutes. While warm make icing and spread over cake.

Icing:
1	stick butter
1	cup granulated sugar
1	small can evaporated milk
½	cup coconut
1	cup pecans, chopped

Cook the butter, sugar and can of milk for 8 minutes and then add the coconut and pecans. Spread on the warm cake.

Sour Cream Pound Cake
My Wedding Cake Recipe

This is the recipe I used to make my wedding cake. I like to use almond flavoring, but you can use any flavoring you choose. In the South when you visit someone, so often there will be a Pound Cake under that cake top cover.

When I was a little girl, I remember going to a lady's house, and she was beating a Pound Cake in a huge bowl and guess what she was beating that cake with? Her hand. Yes, that's what I said, her hand. I won't ever forget that. She was the cutest thing. She was a little short lady and she was holding this huge bowl and giving the batter "the country." Years ago before mixers came into play, people mixed cake batter with their hands. That cake was the best Pound Cake I have ever had. I only wish I had her recipe. Isn't it funny, what sticks in your mind for years?

1	cup real butter (2 sticks)
3	cups sugar
6	eggs, separated
¼	teaspoon soda
3	cups all-purpose flour, sifted
1	(8-ounce) carton sour cream
1	teaspoon almond flavoring
1	tablespoon vanilla extract

Preheat oven 325-degrees. Cream butter until light and fluffy, adding sugar gradually, beating well. Add egg yolks one at a time, beating well after each addition. Combine the soda and flour, adding to the creamed mixture alternately with the sour cream, beginning and ending with the flour. Mix well. Stir in the flavorings. Whip egg whites (room temperature) till they are stiff peaks, but not dry. Fold the egg whites into the batter. Pour the batter into a prepared 10-inch tube pan that has been greased and floured. Bake for 1 hour and 15 minutes or until a spaghetti noodle or toothpick is inserted in the center and it shows clean. Ovens vary. It may need to cook another 5 to 10 minutes. When cooking a pound cake, do not open the oven door till at least 1 hour has passed while cooking.* Cool in the pan for 10 minutes and then remove from the pan. This is one delicious cake. You can ice the cake with any icing you prefer. My husband likes an icing on it.

Note: If you want to make another version of Strawberry Shortcake, prepare the recipe for the Sour Cream Pound Cake and pile the sweetened fruit on top of the cake and ice the tops and sides with sweetened whipping cream. This is decadent.

*When I was a little girl, if Mama Gillis or Mama would tell me not to slam the door when I was going outside, I knew she had a Pound Cake in the oven. She did not want a "sunken" Pound Cake. Now I never had a "sunken" Pound Cake she made, but I have made one, and if it happens to you don't throw it out. That's when you can bring out the fruit with the whipping cream and heck, not a soul knows that it is a "sunken" Pound Cake.

Cake created by the Divine Dixie Deva for her own wedding

The Fastest Chocolate Cake in Town

2	cups all-purpose flour
2	cups sugar
1	teaspoon baking soda
½	teaspoon salt
1	cup butter
1	cup water
⅓	cup unsweetened cocoa
2	eggs
½	cup buttermilk or sour milk
1½	teaspoons vanilla

Preheat oven to 350-degrees. Grease and lightly flour a 13 x 9 x 2-inch baking pan. Sift together flour, sugar, baking soda, and salt. Set aside. In a medium-size saucepan, combine butter, water and cocoa. Bring this mixture to a boil, stirring constantly. Remove from heat and add the cocoa mixture to the dry ingredients. Beat at low speed with electric mixer just until this mixture is combined. Add the eggs, buttermilk, and vanilla. Beat 1 minute. This batter will be very thin. Pour batter into prepared pan. Bake at 350-degrees for about 20 to 25 minutes. Now let's make the icing while the cake is baking. Make sure the children are here. They can lick the bowl.

Chocolate Icing:

½	cup butter
¼	cup cocoa
6	tablespoons evaporated milk
	(If the icing is too thick add a little more milk)
1	(1-pound) box powdered sugar, sifted
1	teaspoon vanilla
1	cup pecans, chopped (optional)

While cake is baking, combine in a saucepan butter, cocoa and evaporated milk. Bring to boiling point. Remove from the heat. Add the powdered sugar and vanilla and beat until smooth. Stir in the pecans. Pour this wonderful hot chocolate frosting over the warm cake. Spread the icing evenly. Cool the cake in the pan. You will be a hit with this cake, no joke about it. This would be a wonderful recipe to teach to your daughter for first time she bakes a cake. She will have a wonderful feeling of accomplishment with raves to "boot".

Milky Way Cake

8	Milky Way Candy Bars (15-ounces in total)
½	cup butter, melted
½	cup butter, softened (additional)
1½	cups granulated sugar
4	eggs
1	teaspoon vanilla extract
1¼	cups buttermilk
½	teaspoon soda
3	cups all-purpose flour
1	cup pecans, chopped

Preheat oven to 325-degrees. Grease and flour a 10-inch tube pan. Combine the candy bars and melted butter in a saucepan. Place over low heat until the candy melts, stirring frequently and set aside. Cream softened butter till fluffy, adding sugar gradually beating after each addition. Add eggs one at a time, beating well after each addition. Add vanilla extract, blending well. Combine the soda and buttermilk. Add the buttermilk gradually with the flour mixture to the creamed mixture, alternately, beginning and ending with the flour mixture. Beat well. Stir in the melted candy and nuts, stirring well. Pour the batter into the prepared pan and bake at 325-degrees for 1 hour and 20 minutes. Let cool in the pan 1 hour before removing from pan. Do not frost cake until cake is completely cool.

Frosting:

2	cups granulated sugar
1	cup evaporated milk
½	cup butter, melted
1	(6-ounce) bag semisweet chocolate chips
1	cup marshmallow crème
	Extra evaporated milk or cream

Combine the sugar, milk and butter in a heavy saucepan. Cook over medium heat, stirring frequently until the mixture reaches a soft ball stage or 234 to 240-degrees. Remove from the heat and stir in the chocolate chips and marshmallow crème. Stir until melted. You may need to add a little more milk for spreading consistency.

Peter Paul Mound Cake

This recipe brings this story to mind.

I want to share with you a trick Mama Gillis would play on Papa pertaining to the Almond Joy candy bars. Mama Gillis would have a stash of candy bars hidden away from her grandbabies in a huge closet in her bedroom. It had piles of quilts in there. Now under those quilts were candy bars such as Almond Joys, Mounds, Chocolate Covered Cherries, Milky Ways and a couple of boxes of Whitman's Samplers. Now remember, we didn't know anything about the candy stash. Yeah, right, I can smell chocolate ten miles away. Everyone that knows me knows I will float a loan for a piece of chocolate. Well anyway, on with the story.

Mama Gillis would slip in the closet and get the Almond Joys and ease the paper off of the candy bar and take the almonds off of the candy bar and glue the paper wrapper shut where it did not look like anyone had been in the candy bar. The Almond Joy bar instantly would become a Mounds bar.

I won't ever forget the time Papa went in the closet to get what he thought was an Almond Joy. Low and behold he opened it and a few choice words came out of this mouth along with "Ruthieee!" You could hear Papa grumbling something under his breath. Wonder what it was? Trust me. He knew that Mama Gillis had been in there.

When he would go into a Whitman's Sampler box of candy, someone would have pinched off all the candies to see what kind was in there. Now you know the Whitman's Sampler has a diagram on the box when you open it as to the different kinds of candy contained in the box. I remember hearing Mama Gillis saying, "Olen, I think a rat must have gotten in the box." Now Papa always said his grandbabies were devilish. Wonder where we got those mischievous ways?

Everyone likes Mounds candy bars. Even though this recipe doesn't require the Mounds candy bar in it, it tastes like it.

Cake Layers:
- 2 cups granulated sugar
- 1 cup shortening
- 5 eggs
- 1 cup self-rising flour
- 1 cup all-purpose flour
- 1 cup milk
- 2 teaspoons vanilla extract

Preheat oven to 350-degrees. Grease and flour 3 (9-inch) layer cake pans. Cream sugar and shortening, adding eggs one at a time. Beat well after each addition. Sift the two cups of flour and add alternately with the milk beginning and ending with the flour. Stir in the vanilla. Pour into 3 (9-inch) layer cake pans. Bake 25 to 30 minutes or until cakes test done. Ovens vary.

Filling:
- 1 cup granulated sugar
- 1 cup evaporated milk
- 1 pound frozen coconut or 1 (12-14-ounce) package coconut
- 12 large marshmallows
- 1 teaspoon vanilla extract

Make this filling while the cake is baking. Put sugar and milk in a large saucepan and bring to a boil. Add coconut and marshmallows to this mixture, stir and boil for 5 minutes. Add vanilla. Stack the cake while it is hot. Put this mixture between the cake layers (not over the top layer) while still hot. Now after making the filling; get ready to ice the cake with the wonderful chocolate frosting.

Frosting for the tops and sides of the cake:
- 2 pounds confectioners' sugar
- 1 cup butter
- 1 small can evaporated milk
- 6 tablespoons cocoa

Add all ingredients in a large mixing bowl. Beat until blended well. Then pour all ingredients into a large saucepan and bring to a boil, cooking 3 minutes. Stirring constantly. Beat until you reach spreading consistency. Ice top and sides of the cake.

Yellow Sheet Cake

This is a delicious yellow sheet cake that you can ice with any kind of frosting. This cake is very light. Just choose one of the icings in the Frosting Section.

2¼	cups cake flour, sifted
3	teaspoons baking powder
1	teaspoon salt
½	cup soft shortening or Crisco
1½	cups granulated sugar
2	eggs
1	cup whole milk
1½	teaspoons vanilla extract

Preheat oven to 350-degrees. Grease and flour the bottom of a 13 x 9 x 2-inch pan. Sift and measure flour, baking powder and salt. Set aside. Cream the shortening and sugar until fluffy. Add the eggs to the cream mixture and beat well on low speed. Alternately, add the dry ingredients with the milk, beginning and ending with the flour. Mix well. Stir in the extract. Pour batter in the pan and place on the center of the oven. Bake for 30 to 35 minutes.

Butter Cream Yellow Layer Cake

¾	teaspoon baking soda
¾	cup buttermilk
⅓	cup butter
⅓	cup Crisco or shortening
1	cup granulated sugar
3	eggs
2	tablespoons cornstarch
2	cups all-purpose flour
1	teaspoon baking powder
	Pinch of salt
1	teaspoon vanilla extract

Preheat oven to 350-degrees. Grease and flour 2 (9-inch) pans. Stir the baking soda in the buttermilk and set aside. Cream butter, shortening and sugar. Beat until fluffy. Add the eggs one at a time, beating well after each addition. Add the cornstarch and beat well. Sift together the flour, baking powder and salt. Add the flour mixture alternately to the creamed butter mixture with buttermilk mixture, beginning with the flour mixture and ending with the flour mixture. Lastly, add the vanilla extract. Pour the batter into 2 (9-inch) greased and flour pans. Bake at 350-degrees for 25 to 30 minutes until toothpick tests clean.

Butter Cream Cheese Frosting:

½	cup butter, softened
1	(3-ounce) package cream cheese, softened
2	cups powdered sugar, sifted
1	tablespoon cornstarch
1	tablespoon evaporated milk
1	teaspoon vanilla extract
½	teaspoon butter flavoring
½	cup pecans, chopped (optional)

Cream together the butter and cream cheese. Blend in the powdered sugar, cornstarch. Add milk, vanilla and butter flavorings. Fold in the pecans, mix well.

White Butter Cake

When I was a little girl, I always loved to go to the bakery and look at their decorated bakery cakes. I always dreamed of decorating cakes, which I do now. I love pink icing roses (pink is my favorite color) and the scrolls made with the bakery icing. The designs would fascinate me and still do. This cake has a very similar taste to a bakery cake, but tastes a whole lot better.

When I was expecting my son, my birthday was a few days before he was born. I was presented a bakery cake with pink roses. I ate the whole thing and I gained 7 pounds in 1 week. My OB doctor had a fit. I just plain couldn't help myself.

5	egg whites, room temperature* (divided use)
2½	cups cake flour, sifted
2½	teaspoons baking powder
¼	teaspoon salt
1	cup butter, softened at room temperature
1¼	cups granulated sugar
1	cup whole milk, at room temperature
1	teaspoon granulated sugar (additional)
1	teaspoon vanilla extract
½	teaspoon almond flavoring

Preheat the oven to 350-degrees. Prepare 2 (8-inch) cake pans by greasing and lining with wax paper. Grease the wax paper and lightly dust the pans with flour, shaking off the excess flour.

*When separating egg whites, put 2 egg whites in one small bowl and 3 egg whites in another bowl. Set aside for later use.

Sift the cake flour, baking powder, and salt three times and set aside. Place the butter in a mixing bowl and cream the butter until it is light and creamy. Add the sugar, gradually, beating until the batter is light and fluffy, about 5 minutes. Add the 2 egg whites into the creamed mixture, beating on medium speed until well blended. While still beating on medium speed; add the flour mixture gradually with the milk, beginning and ending with the flour. Stir in the flavorings. In a separate bowl, beat the 3 egg whites on low and gradually add the teaspoon of sugar till the mixture is foamy. Now increase the mixer to high and beat the egg white mixture till it has stiff peaks. Fold in the egg white mixture in the cake batter. Pour batter into the cake pans and bake for 30-35 minutes until toothpick tests clean. After cakes have baked, let them cool for 10 minutes in the pans and before turning out onto cake racks. Cool completely, before icing. Ice with desired Frosting.

Ann Gambrell's No Name Cake

1	box Butter Pecan cake mix
4	eggs
1	cup water
¾	cup cooking oil
1	can Butter Pecan Coconut Frosting
1	cup pecans, chopped (optional)

Preheat oven to 350-degrees. Prepare a tube pan spraying with baking spray. Mix all ingredients together, INCLUDING, the Butter Pecan Coconut Frosting. If using the nuts, stir in the nuts. Pour into the prepared tube pan and bake for 1 hour. Let cool in pan for 10 minutes before turning out onto a cake rack. Enjoy!

Deep South Peanut Butter Cake

½	cup butter, softened
½	cup peanut oil
1	cup crunchy peanut butter
2	cups granulated sugar
5	eggs, separated
2	cups all-purpose flour
1	teaspoon baking soda
1	cup buttermilk
1	teaspoon vanilla extract
1¼	cups coconut or 1 (4-ounce) can
5	egg whites, beaten until stiff peaks

Preheat oven to 350-degrees. Prepare 3 (9-inch) cake pans by greasing, flouring and lining with wax paper. Cream together the butter, peanut oil and peanut butter, beating well. Add the sugar gradually beating well until light and fluffy. Add the egg yolks, one at a time, beating well after each addition. Stir in the baking soda with the buttermilk, set aside. Gradually, add the flour to the batter, beating on medium speed, alternately with the buttermilk mixture, beginning and ending with the flour mixture. Stir in the vanilla extract and coconut, blending well. Lightly fold in the beaten egg whites into the batter. Pour batter in to the prepared pans. Bake for 25 minutes or until toothpick tests clean. Cool in pans 10 minutes before removing from pans. When completely cool, ice with Peanut Butter Frosting below.

Peanut Butter Frosting:

½	cup butter, softened
1	(8-ounce) package cream cheese, softened
½	cup crunchy peanut butter
2	(16-ounce) boxes confectioners' sugar, sifted
1	teaspoon vanilla extract
	Evaporated milk, a few tablespoons for spreading consistency
½	cup roasted peanuts, chopped, optional

Cream butter, cream cheese and peanut butter until fluffy. Gradually add the confectioners' sugar and vanilla extract, beating until smooth and creamy. If the icing is too thick add a few drops of evaporated milk and continue to beat until spreading consistency is reached. You will have enough icing to ice between the layers, top and sides. If using the roasted peanuts, sprinkle for garnishment on top of the cake.

Note: If I see that the amount of my icing is running slim, I always ice sparingly between the layers, so as to have enough for the sides and top.

Michigan Apple Cake with Caramel Glaze

I had to include a recipe using Michigan Apples. You can use your favorite kind of baking apples.

1	cup cooking oil
2	cups granulated sugar
2	eggs
2	teaspoons vanilla extract
3	cups all-purpose flour
½	teaspoon salt
1	teaspoon soda
1	teaspoon cinnamon
1	cup milk
3	cups apples, diced and peeled or (1-pound)
1	cup pecans or walnuts, chopped

Combine the oil and sugar and beat well. Beat in the eggs and vanilla extract. Sift together the flour, salt, soda and cinnamon. Add the dry ingredients to the oil and sugar mixture along with the milk. Now stir in the apples and nuts. Pour the batter into a greased and floured 13 x 9 x 2-inch pan. Bake at 325-degrees for 40 to 45 minutes.

Caramel Glaze:
1	cup light brown sugar
½	cup butter
¼	cup evaporated milk
1	teaspoon vanilla

Heat the butter and sugar together until melted. Add the evaporated milk and bring to a full boil. Cook 1 minute. Now add the vanilla. Spread over the cake. Cool, cut and enjoy!

Willie Kirk's Coconut Cake

This cake recipe was given to me by Mrs. Rachael Jones. The recipe was passed down by her mother, Mrs. Willie Kirk. "Mama made this cake every Christmas. It takes a while to make, but it is perfect for a Christmas cake," says Rachael.

Rachael is not only my best friend, but was my Matron of Honor. Her husband Floyd was my husband's best man. These are the dearest people in the world!

1	cup butter, softened
2	cups sugar
2⅔	cups all-purpose flour
1½	teaspoons baking powder
1	cup milk
1	teaspoon vanilla extract
7	egg whites

Beat butter with electric mixer until creamy. Slowly add 2 cups sugar, beating well. Combine flour, baking powder and add to butter mixture alternately with milk, beginning and ending with the flour mixture. Beat at low speed until well blended after each addition. Stir in the vanilla extract. Beat egg whites until soft peaks form and fold this into the batter. Pour into 3 (9-inch) greased and floured cake pans. Bake at 375-degrees for 25 to 35 minutes until toothpick comes clean. Cool in pans for 10 minutes, then remove from pans and cool completely.

Coconut Syrup:

1	fresh coconut, grated
	Coconut milk from 1 fresh coconut
2-3	tablespoons granulated sugar

Pierce one of the eyes of the coconut with an ice pick. Drain the milk before cracking the shell. Pour coconut milk through a mesh strainer into a 1 cup measuring container. Add enough water to make 1 cup of liquid. Set this aside. Crack coconut using a hammer. Pry the coconut off of the shell with a screwdriver. Remove the brown skin with a knife and shred coconut with a grater or food processor. Cook coconut liquid and the 3 tablespoons of sugar in a small pan over medium heat, stirring constantly, until the sugar dissolves. Set aside until ready to assemble cake.

Seven Minute Frosting:
- 4 egg whites
- 2 cups granulated sugar
- ½ cup water

Combine all ingredients in top of double boiler and beat at low speed until blended. Place over boiling water and beat at high speed for 7 minutes or until soft peaks form. Remove from heat and continue to beat until frosting is spreading consistency. Spread immediately onto cooled cake.

To assemble cake:
Place 1 layer of the cake on the cake plate and drizzle with the coconut syrup. Spread with the Seven Minute Frosting over the cake layer and sprinkle with ¼ of the grated coconut. Repeat this procedure with the second layer using 5 tablespoons of coconut syrup and 1 cup of Seven Minute Frosting. Top remaining layer with ¼-cup of the coconut syrup. Spread remaining frosting on the top and sides of the cake using the coconut that remains. Sprinkle and press the coconut on the sides of the cake. Cover and chill 24 hours before serving.

Red Velvet Ganache Cheesecake

Note: Cheesecake needs to be prepared the day before.

Oreo Crust
20   Oreo Cookies *(You may use any brand chocolate sandwich cookie)*
         Everyone knows how good Oreos are, though.*
¼   cup butter, melted

Prepare a 9-inch springform pan by spraying with baking spray. In a food processor or blender, crush Oreo cookies. Leave the crème filling in the cookie, while crushing. Mix the melted butter and Oreo cookie crumbs together. Press crumbs into a 9-inch springform pan. Place in the fridge while preparing the cheese cake.

3   (8-ounce) packages cream cheese, softened
1½   cups granulated sugar
4   eggs, beaten well
4   tablespoons unsweetened cocoa, sifted
1   cup sour cream
⅓   cup buttermilk
1   tablespoon vanilla extract
1   teaspoon white vinegar
2   (1-ounce) bottles red food coloring

Preheat oven to 325-degrees. Beat the 3 packages of cream cheese, adding the granulated sugar gradually and beat till light and fluffy. Add eggs, sifted cocoa*, sour cream, buttermilk, vanilla extract, white vinegar and the food color. While mixing, scrape mixing bowl often so that all ingredients are incorporated thoroughly. Pour into prepared Oreo crust.

*It is very important to sift the cocoa. Cocoa tends to be lumpy.

Bake at 325-degrees for only 10 minutes. After 10 minutes, reduce heat to 300-degrees and bake for 1 hour and 10 minutes until the center of the cheesecake will jiggle but the perimeter of the cake will be firm to the touch. Take a knife and very carefully run along the out edge of the cake. Now turn the oven off and let the cake sit in the oven with the door of the oven closed for 30 minutes. Take out of oven and cool while still in the pan for 30 minutes. Then cover with a single layer of wax paper on top of the cheesecake pan and place in the fridge. Chill for 8 hours. After cooling for 8 hours, prepare the Cream Cheese topping.

Cream Cheese Topping:
1   (8-ounce) cream cheese, softened
¼   cup butter, softened
3   cups confectioners' sugar
1   teaspoon vanilla extract
3   tablespoons evaporated milk

Beat 8-ounces of cream cheese with the softened butter till fluffy, add the confectioners' sugar gradually, beating until creamy. Blend in the vanilla extract and milk. Beat on high with mixer till light and fluffy.

Note: If the icing is too runny, add a little more confectioners' sugar. If the icing is too thick add a little more cream, till spreading consistency. While cake is still in the pan, frost the cake with the icing. You just want to ice the top of the cake. Now take the cake out of the springform pan, lifting off the sides of the cake pan, carefully. Place cake on a serving plate.

Ganache Topping:
1   (6-ounce) bag semisweet chocolate chips, melted
⅛-¼ cup half-and-half cream *(just to consistency of drizzling on top of cheesecake)*

For the Ganache topping, just melt the chocolate chips in a small saucepan on low heat, adding the cream. Stir. To obtain the consistency of drizzling on the cheesecake, you may have to add just a touch more cream. Now take a teaspoon and just drizzle the Ganache topping however you want to on the top of the Cheesecake. Another thing I like about cooking is the creativity involved.

Georgia Peach Shortcake

This is the ole timey version of shortcake. The ole timey version of shortcake is one that has one cake, somewhat like a big biscuit and you split it and load it up with your choice of fruit and sweetened whipping cream.

3	cups sifted all-purpose flour
3¼	teaspoons baking powder
½	cup granulated sugar
½	teaspoon salt
½	cup shortening
1	egg, well beaten
½	cup milk
1	big tablespoon butter, melted *(When I say big tablespoon that means it doesn't have to be exact)*

Preheat oven to 450-degrees. Sift together flour, baking powder, sugar and salt. Cut in the shortening until the mixture looks like coarse meal. Add the egg and milk. Mix with fork to form soft dough. On a floured surface, knead the dough about 20 times. Divide the dough in half and pat half of the dough into a greased 8-inch greased, floured and wax paper lined cake pan. Pour melted butter over the top. Now pat the remaining dough over the top. Bake for 30 minutes or until golden brown. Prepare your peaches or your favorite fruit while this shortcake is baking. Cool the shortcake 10 minutes and separate layers of the shortcake with the tines of a fork.

Filling:

4	cups of sliced and peeled fresh peaches *(You need to sprinkle ascorbic acid or Fruit Fresh to keep them from turning dark)*
1	cup powdered sugar, (divided use)
2	cups heavy whipping cream
1	teaspoon almond extract or vanilla extract

Sprinkle peaches with ½-cup of powdered sugar and refrigerate. Whip cream with the remaining ½-cup of powdered sugar until stiff peaks. Stir in almond extract. Now spread the bottom layer of shortcake with half of whipping cream. Top with the peaches. Now add the top layer and repeat procedure. To garnish-make a big dollop of whipping cream in the center of the shortcake, add a couple of peaches on the dollop and then a sprig of mint. This can be the finale of a wonderful summer time supper for your family. It's not hard and it's rewarding. Try mixing blueberries with your peaches. Of course, strawberries are the ole favorite.

Autumn Spice Cake

What better cake to start the season!

¾	cup butter, softened
1½	cups brown sugar, firmly packed
3	eggs
3	cups all-purpose flour
1	tablespoon baking powder
2	teaspoons baking soda
1½	teaspoons salt
½	teaspoon ground allspice
½	teaspoon ground cinnamon
½	teaspoon ground nutmeg
1	cup apple cider or apple juice
¾	cup milk

Preheat oven to 350-degrees. Cream butter, adding brown sugar gradually and beat until light and fluffy. Beat in the eggs one at a time, beating well. Set aside. Sift together the flour, baking powder, baking soda, salt and spices. Set aside. In a separate container or mixing cup, combine cider and milk. Blend the flour and spice mixture into the creamed mixture alternately with the cider and milk mixture, beginning and ending with the flour and spice mixture. Blend very well. Pour batter into 3 (8-inch) cake pans which have been greased, floured and wax-paper lined. Bake in oven for 25 to 30 minutes until toothpick tests clean. Cool completely before frosting this cake. Vanilla or either Caramel Icing would be delicious with this cake.

Vanilla Icing Recipe:

1	cup butter, melted
4	cups confectioners' sugar
½	cup dark corn syrup
2	teaspoons vanilla extract

Cream together the butter, sugar, corn syrup and vanilla extract, beating until smooth and creamy. Add more sugar until you have spreading consistency.

Coconut Pound Cake

2	sticks butter, softened
½	cups shortening or Crisco
2½	cups granulated sugar
5	eggs
3	cups all-purpose flour
1	teaspoon baking powder
½	teaspoon salt
1	teaspoon almond flavoring
1	teaspoon coconut flavoring
1	cup sweetened coconut
1	cup milk

Grease, flour and line a 10-inch tube pan with wax paper. Cream butter, Crisco and sugar, beating until light and fluffy. Add eggs one at a time and blend well after each addition. Sift dry ingredients together. Add flour mixture alternately with milk to the creamed mixture, beginning and ending with the flour. In a small bowl, mix flavorings with the coconut. Now stir in the coconut by hand in the batter. Pour batter into your prepared tube pan. Put cake in a cold oven at 325-degrees for one hour and 20 minutes. Some ovens vary. Use a spaghetti noodle and test in the center for doneness. As an optional choice try this recipe for Coconut Icing. This icing is basically more like a glaze to add that extra "pizzazz" to the cake.

Coconut Icing:

1	cup granulated sugar
1	cup evaporated milk
	Pinch of salt
2	teaspoons butter
¾	cup flaked coconut
3	tablespoons all-purpose flour
3	tablespoons evaporated milk (additional)
1	teaspoon vanilla extract or coconut flavoring

Combine the sugar, milk, salt, butter and coconut in a medium-sized saucepan. Bring the ingredients to a boil. In a small cup, combine the flour and the additional milk stirring to make a thickener. Add this to the coconut mixture along with the flavoring. Cook until the icing thickens. If you like the icing to be thinner, add a little more evaporated milk.

Upside-Down Apple Cake
An ole timey recipe

3	medium tart apples, peeled and sliced very thin
1	cup apple juice
1/3	cup butter
1	cup light brown sugar
1	box of your favorite brand Spice Cake Mix *(yes, I said cake mix)*
1/4	cup maraschino cherries, drain juice
1/2	cup walnuts or pecans, chopped
	Sweetened whipping cream or Vanilla Ice Cream

Preheat oven to 350-degrees. Grease a 13 x 9 x 2-inch baking pan and set aside. After peeling and slicing apples, simmer them in the apple juice until they are tender about 5 to 7 minutes. Drain juice from cooking apples, only to reserve it. Mix ¼-cup of the reserved apple juice, butter and light brown sugar in the 13 x 9 x 2-inch pan and place the pan in the oven just until the butter melts. Take out of oven and arrange the apple slices and maraschino cherry halves in the brown sugar mixture. Sprinkle the nuts on top of the apple and cherries. Prepare the Spice Cake mix recipe according to package directions, the apple juice for part of the liquid. Pour the cake batter on top of the fruit mixture. Bake for 40 to 45 minutes or till toothpick test shows done. Let stand 1 minute before turning the cake out of the pan. Serve warm with sweetened whipping cream or vanilla ice cream.

Cheesecake Deluxe with Raspberry Glaze

You may make this Cheesecake with or without the Raspberry Glaze. The Glaze is optional. But that is the beauty of this recipe. You may add your favorite fruit topping on it or just eat it plain.

Remember the show, "The Golden Girls?" Every time there was a crisis in their lives they sat down to eat Cheesecake. My waistline couldn't afford to do that.

Crust:
2	cups crushed graham crackers (*I like to use any kind of sweet cookies I have on hand*)
½	cup butter, melted
½	cup pecans, ground fine

Filling:
3	(8-ounce) packages of cream cheese, softened
1½	cups granulated sugar
5	eggs
3	tablespoons lemon juice
1	teaspoon vanilla extract

Topping:
1	(8-ounce) sour cream
½	cup granulated sugar
1	teaspoon vanilla extract

Preheat the oven to 350-degrees. Spray a 10-inch springform pan with baking spray. Combine all the crust ingredients and press them across the bottom and sides of the springform pan. Mix the filling ingredients by combining the cream cheese and sugar. Add the eggs one at a time, beating very well after each addition. Now beat in the lemon juice and extract. Pour the filling over the crust and bake for 45 minutes without opening the door of the oven. After cooking the cheesecake remove it from the oven and reduce the heat to 300-degrees. Mix all of the topping ingredients and spread this over the cheesecake. Return it to the oven and bake for 15 minutes more. Cool the cheesecake on cooling rack for several hours. Refrigerate overnight.

Raspberry Glaze (optional):
1   (12-ounce) bag frozen raspberries
¼   cup water
1   cup granulated sugar
2   tablespoons cornstarch

Place the raspberries in a saucepan with the water. Bring to a soft boil. In the meantime, mix the cornstarch and sugar and gently stir into the raspberries, gently stirring until the mixture is thick and clear. Cool in the fridge. After cooling in the fridge, spoon glaze over entire Cheesecake or you may just serve it over individual pieces.

Strawberry Cake

1   yellow cake mix
½   cup milk
4   eggs
1   cup vegetable oil
1   cup frozen strawberries, thawed
1   cup coconut
1   cup pecans, chopped

Preheat oven at 350-degrees. Grease, flour and line with wax paper 2 (9-inch) layer cake pans or a 9 x 13-inch pan. In a large mixing bowl, mix the cake mix, milk, eggs and oil. Beat until smooth and add the remaining ingredients. Bake for 30 to 35 minutes or until done. Let cool 10 minutes before removing from pan.

Frosting:
1   stick butter, softened
1½   (16-ounce) boxes powdered sugar*
1   cup coconut
1   cup pecans, chopped
1   cup frozen strawberries, thawed

Mix the butter and sugar together, beating until creamy. Add the rest of the ingredients and ice cake.

*If icing is too runny, you may need to add more powdered sugar.

My Hubby's Groom's Cake

German Chocolate Cake

This is the recipe that I made for my husband's Groom Cake. I had a beautiful garden wedding in Albany, Georgia. I topped the 3-tiered cake with a fruit basket arrangement while garnishing the cake with Dark Chocolate Buttercream icing.

After moving to the North, I found that most of the Northern weddings do not include a Groom's cake. On the same note, the average Southern wedding does not have a sit-down meal as the Northerns have at their weddings. Very interesting how different parts of the U.S. celebrate different events.

½	cup boiling water
1	(4-ounce) bar German Chocolate
2	sticks butter
2	cups granulated sugar
4	egg yolks, well beaten
1	teaspoon vanilla flavoring
2½	cups cake flour
½	teaspoon salt
1	teaspoon baking soda
1	cup buttermilk
4	egg whites, stiffly beaten

Melt the chocolate in the boiling water. Set aside to cool. Cream the butter and sugar together till the batter is very light and fluffy. Add the eggs yolks one at a time, beating well after each addition. Stir in the chocolate and add the vanilla flavoring. Mix well. Sift together the cake flour and salt. Stir the soda into the buttermilk. Add the flour alternately with the buttermilk, beginning and ending with the flour. Beat the egg whites until stiff peaks, but not dry. Fold egg whites into batter. Pour batter into 3 (8 or 9-inch) cake pans which have been greased and wax paper lined. Bake 35 to 40 minutes at 350-degrees.

Frost the top and in between the layers with icing. If you want to ice the sides, like I do, spread the icing a little thinner between the layers. I like a lot of icing on the tops and sides of a cake. You may want to double the recipe. You will have plenty of icing between the layers and you do not want to be stingy with it. You will have some leftover icing, also. The extra icing will keep in the fridge covered for a couple of weeks.

German Chocolate Icing
(Coconut Pecan Frosting):
1   (12-ounce) can evaporated milk
1½   sticks butter
4   egg yolks, slightly beaten
1   teaspoon vanilla extract
1½   cups sugar
1   (7-ounce) bag coconut
1½   cups pecans, chopped

Combine all of the ingredients, leaving the coconut and nuts to add later. Cook over medium heat, stirring constantly until mixture thickens, about 12 to 15 minutes. Take off heat and add the coconut and nuts. Cool icing before you ice the cake and enjoy.

Created and decorated by the Divine Dixie Deva

Luscious Lime Cake

This cake is light tasting and a compliment to any summer supper time meal. Very, very simple with one bowl needed for preparation. I bet I have your interest on this one.

1⅓	cups granulated sugar
2	cups all-purpose flour
½	teaspoon salt
1	teaspoon baking powder
½	teaspoon baking soda
1	(3-ounce) package lime Jell-O
5	eggs
1⅓	cups cooking oil
¾	cup orange juice
1	teaspoon lemon extract
1	teaspoon vanilla extract

Drizzle:

⅓	cup Key Lime juice
⅓	cup powdered sugar, sifted

Preheat oven to 350-degrees. In a large mixing bowl, add the sugar, flour, salt, baking powder, soda, and lime Jell-O. Add the eggs, cooking oil, orange juice, lemon and vanilla extract. Beat until well blended. Pour the batter into a 9 x 13-inch baking pan. Bake for 25 to 30 minutes. Remove cake from oven and let it cool for 10 minutes. While cooling the cake, mix the Key Lime juice and powered sugar; poke holes in the cake and pour over the cake. Cover the cake and put in fridge for approximately 8 hours. Cut in squares. Dollop squares with whipping cream. Garnish with lime slices. Serve with sweetened whipping cream.

*You can use cooled pie filling like lemon pie filling.

Lemon Coconut Sheet Cake

This is really a quick cake recipe to throw together and watch the compliments pour in!

1	cup butter
2	cups granulated sugar
5	eggs
2½	cups all-purpose flour
1	teaspoon baking powder
1	teaspoon baking soda
¼	teaspoon salt
1	cup buttermilk
1	cup coconut
1	teaspoon lemon extract
1	teaspoon coconut flavoring (optional)

Preheat oven to 350-degrees. Cream butter well and add sugar gradually and beat until the batter is light and fluffy. Add eggs one at a time, beating well after each addition. Add the flavorings, blending well. Combine the flour, baking powder, baking soda and salt. Add this mixture to the creamed mixture alternately with the buttermilk, beginning and ending with the flour mixture. Mix well. Stir in the coconut. Pour batter in a greased and floured 13 x 9 x 2-inch pan and bake for 35 to 40 minutes or until toothpick tests clean. Cool 10 minutes before taking cake out of pan. Cool cake completely before icing cake.

Lemon Butter Icing:

½	cup butter, softened
4	cups powdered sugar, sifted
	Evaporated milk
2	teaspoons lemon flavoring
1	teaspoon vanilla extract
1	teaspoon lemon rind, grated

Cream butter, adding powdered sugar gradually using enough evaporated milk for spreading consistency. Beat until smooth enough to spread. Add flavorings and lemon rind, mixing well. Ice cake and enjoy.

Cranberry Orange Tea Cake

2¼	cups all-purpose flour
1	cup sugar
1	teaspoon baking powder
1	teaspoon baking soda
¼	teaspoon salt
1	cup cranberries, chopped
1	cup pecans or walnuts, chopped
1	cup dates, chopped
2	tablespoons orange rind, grated
2	eggs, beaten
1	cup buttermilk
1	teaspoon orange flavoring
¾	cup vegetable oil

Preheat oven to 350-degrees. Prepare a 10-inch tube or Bundt pan by greasing and flouring. In a large mixing bowl, combine all of the dry ingredients; add the cranberries, nuts, dates and orange rind. Mix well. Set aside. In a separate bowl, mix the eggs, buttermilk, orange flavoring and oil. Add this mixture to the dry ingredients, stirring just until blended. Pour this batter in the cake pan and bake for 50-60 minutes or until toothpick tests clean. Cool in pan 10 minutes and then turn out on cake plate. Poke small holes in the cake with an ice pick or wooden pick. Pour the glaze on it. Garnish with orange slices and a few cranberries with mint sprigs.

Glaze:

½	cup orange juice
½	cup powdered sugar, sifted

Mix ingredients and pour onto cake. Some folks that I have served this to tell me they would rather have this than a Fruitcake.

The Divine Dixie Deva's Favorite Cake
Caramel Cake

1	cup butter, softened
2	cups granulated sugar
4	eggs, separated
3	cups all-purpose flour
1	tablespoon baking powder
½	teaspoon salt
1	cup milk
1	teaspoon vanilla extract or butternut flavoring

Cake Recipe:
Cream butter; gradually add sugar, beating until fluffy. Add egg yolks, beating well after each addition. Combine flour with baking powder and salt. Add to creamed mixture alternately with milk, beginning and ending with flour. Beat egg whites until stiff, but not dry. Fold into batter. Stir in the flavoring. Pour batter into 3 (8-inch) greased, floured and wax paper lined pans. Bake at 350-degrees about 25 minutes. Do the toothpick test. When done, you must cool the cake layers completely.

Ole Fashion Caramel Icing:

4	cups brown sugar, firmly packed
½	teaspoon salt
½	cup butter
1⅓	cups half and half
1	tablespoon vanilla extract
4	tablespoons (additional half and half)

In a heavy saucepan, combine the brown sugar, salt, butter and half and half. Stir until the mixture boils. Continue to boil until it reaches a soft ball stage of 234-degrees. Take off of the stove and cool to lukewarm or until you can touch the bottom of the pan. Do not stir during the cooling period. You may beat with a wooden spoon or beat with an electric mixer on high until the icing thickens or the icing begins to loose its gloss. Stir in the vanilla extract and additional cream. If the icing is too thin add a small amount of confectioners' sugar. If the icing is too thick, warm up a small amount of milk and stir in the icing. This recipe makes enough icing to ice a 3-layer cake or 13 x 9 x 2-inch cake. I make this recipe even if I make a 2-layer cake. You never know when you may have to cover up boo-boo's on the cake, if you know what I mean.

Japanese Fruit Cake

I grew up with this cake in our home during the Holidays. The Holiday season would not be the same without this cake. For those of you who do not know what this cake is all about, it is basically a layered fruit cake, either white or yellow cake layers along with spice layers. The layers are "chocked" full of a fruit filling. Delicious.

1	cup butter, softened
2	cups granulated sugar
4	eggs
3¼	cups all-purpose flour
½	teaspoon salt
1	teaspoon soda
1	cup buttermilk
1	teaspoon vanilla extract
1	teaspoon cinnamon
1	teaspoon allspice
1	teaspoon cloves
1	teaspoon nutmeg
1	cup raisins, chopped
1	cup pecans, chopped (optional)

Preheat oven to 350-degrees. Grease and flour and line with wax paper 4 (9-inch) cake pans. Cream butter and sugar together, beating till light and fluffy. Add the eggs one at a time, beating well after each addition. Sift flour, salt, and soda together. Add to creamed mixture alternately with the buttermilk, beginning and ending with the flour mixture. Stir in the vanilla extract. Pour half of the batter into 2 (9-inch) cake pans. To make the spice layers; add the cinnamon, allspice, cloves, nutmeg, raisins and pecans to the other half of the batter. Pour this in the other 2 (9-inch) cake pans. Bake at 350-degrees for 25 to 30 minutes or until toothpick tests clean. After cooking, cool in cake pans for 10 minutes before turning onto the cake racks. Cool thoroughly before icing the cake.

Japanese Fruit Cake Filling:
- 2 tablespoons butter
- 8 egg yolks, well beaten
- 1 cup golden raisins
- 3 cups granulated sugar
- ¼ cup lemon juice
- 2 teaspoons lemon rind
- 1½ cups flaked coconut
- 1 (8-ounce) can crushed pineapple, drained
- ½ cup pecans, coarsely chopped and toasted for garnish

Cook the butter, egg yolks, raisins, sugar, lemon juice, and lemon rind in the top of a double boiler. Cook over boiling water for about 20 minutes, stirring constantly until mixture thickens. If mixture does not thicken up enough, you may have to add a tablespoon of cornstarch, dissolved in a small amount of cold water. Add the coconut and pineapple and cook another 10 minutes until thickened again. Cool.

To assemble the cake:
Place 1 spice layer on bottom and spread with filling. Top with a yellow cake layer, spread with filling. Repeat with the other spice layer and spread with filling. Top with the last yellow cake layer and spread the filling. Spread the remaining filling around the sides of the cake. Top with the toasted pecans.

Mama Gillis' Christmas tree that she made out of chicken wire when I was little. I use it every year to decorate my home, along with Mama Gillis' homemade ornaments and what-nots.

Frostings or "Icings"

When Mama Gillis made cakes, she always had a lot of icing left over in the bowl and did not mind giving me a lot of it to eat. Mama Gillis just always seemed to understand the importance of me eating all of that good stuff. Now Mama was another story. When she was putting icing on the cake, especially the Caramel icing (my favorite), she never ever had any leftover icing. Every bit of that icing had to go onto that "blame" cake. I would always beg if I could lick the bowl, spoon or beaters. But one of my "precious" sisters would fight me for one or the other. Oh, how sometimes I wanted them to disappear. Temporarily, of course, you know.

Now most of my Icing recipes are following the cake recipes in the Cake section. But, I have included extra Icing recipes that you might like to have handy.

I am not a "skimper" when it comes to making icing. Have you ever had a cake that was all cake and just enough icing to make it look good? Well, I want to be able to smack my lips and say I had a decent piece of cake. So, do your child a favor and when you make an Icing for a cake, increase the icing recipe just a little or leave just enough to coat a big tablespoon for your child or "Big Child" (husband). They will love you for it.

Orange Drizzle

1	tablespoon butter
1	tablespoon lemon juice
1	tablespoon orange juice
	Grated rind of one orange
1¾	cups powdered sugar, sifted

Melt butter and add juices in a small saucepan. Add the grated orange rind and powdered sugar. Beat well. You may also grind up a little candied orange peel for that extra kick. This recipe would be wonderful to top sweet muffins, drizzle a pound cake, or even a coffee cake.

Sour Cream Coconut Frosting

Enough for 3 (9-inch) cake layers or 1 (13 x 9 x 2-inch) cake.

This is a real quick and easy yet delicious Coconut Frosting. If you do not want to make the Seven Minute Frosting for your cake, follow this recipe and you will get just as many raves.

1	(8-ounce) carton sour cream
2	cups granulated sugar
2	(6-ounce) packages frozen, grated coconut
1	(6-ounce) package frozen, grated coconut (additional)

In a large bowl, mix the sour cream, sugar and the 2 bags of coconut. Let sit for about 30-minutes at room temperature for the ingredients to soak together. After you frost the cake, add the additional (6-ounce) package of frozen coconut to the cake. Just sprinkle on top of the other.

Butter Cream Frosting

What can be better than the good ole faithful Butter Cream?

1	cup butter, softened
2	(16-ounce) boxes confectioners' sugar, sifted
	Pinch of salt
¼	cup evaporated milk
2	teaspoons vanilla extract*

Cream butter while adding sugar gradually. Beat well after each addition. Add salt. Add a little milk at time with the sugar until frosting consistency. Mix in the vanilla extract. You may double the recipe for larger cakes or to cover generously.

*I like to use almond flavoring for a richer taste.

Yields: icing for 2 (9-inch) layers

In my Cake Decorating classes, I have used the following recipes.

Decorating Icing

1	box powdered sugar, sifted
1	cup Crisco
1	egg white
3-4	tablespoons water
1	teaspoon vanilla extract *(I like to use almond extract)*

Combine the entire ingredients in a deep bowl. Beat the ingredients 10 minutes at slow speed. The consistency of the icing is very important. For flowers that are to be dried, reduce the water to only ½-tablespoon. You only want to tint the icing sparingly with the cake color.

Hint: To make dark red roses, I add a hint of COCOA to the red icing to make American Beauty Roses.

Royal Icing

2	egg whites
2	cups powdered sugar, sifted
1	teaspoon cream of tartar

Combine the ingredients in a bowl. Place the bowl in a pan of warm water. Beat with mixer until the icing stands in peaks. Cover the icing with a damp cloth to prevent crust from forming.

Decorating Cream Icing

1	cup Crisco
1½	cups powdered sugar, sifted
¼	cup evaporated milk
¼	teaspoon vanilla extract

Mix all ingredients in bowl at low speed. This icing does not harden. This icing is not to be used for flowers that you make in advance and to harden. This icing is great for borders, inscriptions, *etc.*

Note: For tracing inscriptions or designs, use a toothpick.

Butter Cream icing can be stored in an air tight container in the fridge for weeks or even months.

Lemon Cheese Filling

Why call it Lemon Cheese when there's no cheese in it? Beats me. This is an ole timey recipe, and that's what they call it!

2	cups sugar
4	whole eggs
1	(8.25-ounce) can crushed pineapple (drained)
1	rind lemon, grated
	Juice of 2 lemons
1	stick butter

Put all of the ingredients except butter in a double boiler. Cook until thick; add the stick of butter. Let cool before spreading between layers and sides and top of cake. Makes enough filling between the layers of a 3-layer cake or enough to ice between the layers, top and sides of a 2 (9-inch) layer cake.

Seven Minute Frosting

1	cup granulated sugar
⅓	cup light corn syrup or Karo
3	egg whites
¼	teaspoon cream of tartar
1	teaspoon vanilla extract

Place all ingredients in the top of a double boiler, except for the vanilla. Cook for 7 to 10 minutes beating with the electric mixer over the hot water until the frosting is spreading consistency. Remove from the heat and add vanilla extract and continue to beat a minute or two more. Makes enough icing for 3 (9-inch) cake layers.

Chocolate Seven Minute Frosting

Follow the above recipe for the Seven Minute Frosting, but add 1 (6-ounce) bag of semisweet chocolate chips into the Seven Minute Frosting recipe while it is still hot. Stir completely and spread onto cake.

Marbled Effect:
Just partially blend in 1 (6-ounce) bag of semisweet chocolate chips into the Seven Minute Frosting while it is still hot and spread onto cake. This would look great on a Deviled Food's Cake.

Ole Fashioned Cooked Chocolate Icing

3	cups granulated sugar
1	cup cocoa
1	cup evaporated milk
1	cup butter
1	teaspoon vanilla extract

Mix the sugar, cocoa, milk and butter in a heavy saucepan. Bring to boil and cook 2 to 3 minutes or until soft ball stage (234 to 240-degrees.) Stir in the vanilla extract. Remove from the heat and let cool without stirring until lukewarm. Bottom of pan will be touchable. Then beat until icing loses its gloss and is spreading consistency. If the icing gets too hard, add a little more evaporated milk. Enough icing for a 2 (8 or 9-inch) layer cake, or a 9 x 13-inch cake or a Pound Cake.

Hawaiian Cake Filling
Consists of Pineapple, Pecan, Coconut and Cherries

This will make enough filling or glaze to a 13 x 9 x 2-inch cake. Or if you like, you can make a yellow cake and use it as filling between the layers. Then top the sides and top of the cake with the Seven Minute Frosting. How does that sound. Makes your mouth water, doesn't it?

1	(20-ounce) can crushed pineapple (Do not drain)
3	tablespoons cornstarch
½	cup butter
1	cup granulated sugar
1	tablespoon butternut flavoring
1	cup flaked coconut
1	cup pecans, chopped
½	cup maraschino cherries cut in half

In a large heavy saucepan, combine the pineapple, cornstarch, butter, sugar and flavoring. Cook these ingredients until it is thick. Add the rest of the ingredients and heat thoroughly.

Remedy

Blackberry Cough Cordial

1	quart blackberry juice
1	pound granulated sugar
1	tablespoon each of the following: cloves, allspice, nutmeg and cinnamon
1	pint grain alcohol

Put all of the ingredients, except for the grain alcohol, in a large saucepan. Stir well and boil 15 minutes. Now add the pint of grain alcohol. Bottle this up and take 1 tablespoon at bed time when needed.

Cookies

My son, Jeff

Cookie Tips from The Divine Dixie Deva

I always cook my cookies on the middle rack in the oven. I always cool them on sheets of wax paper or parchment paper. Lining the cookie sheet with parchment paper in lieu of greasing the cookie sheet is a great option.

When making drop cookies and making one batch at a time, I like to cream my butter and sugar with a wooden spoon. Be sure to have your butter at room temperature. I find that when I cream by hand with the wooden spoon the dough is a little stiffer and my cookie is a lot better. When you are making several batches at a time, the mixer is the way to go. The dough will be stickier and will need to be put in the fridge for a little while. The mixer incorporates the ingredients a lot better than the wooden spoon and makes for softer dough.

When my children were little, I loved to have cookies for them to eat. But most of all, we had a wonderful time making them together.

Date Nut Balls

1	pound dates, chopped
½	stick butter
1	cup granulated sugar
2	eggs
1	teaspoon orange flavoring *(You may use your favorite spirits for flavoring)*
2	cups rice cereal
1	cup nuts, chopped
1	cup coconut

In a medium-sized saucepan, combine the dates, butter, granulated sugar, flavoring and eggs. Cook over low heat for 10 minutes, stirring constantly until thick. Remove from heat and add the rice cereal and nuts. Stir well to coat cereal and nuts. Line a cookie sheet with wax paper and roll into balls and then roll in the coconut. These may be stored in Christmas tins lined with wax paper.

Peanut Butter Brownies

In my Jams and Jellies section, you will find the story about my Peach-Picking Mama, Bernice—well, this is a recipe that she shared with me. It is a delicious and nutritious snack for the kids when they come home from school, and goes great with a big, tall glass of milk.

1	cup all-purpose flour, sifted
¾	teaspoon baking powder
¼	teaspoon baking soda
½	teaspoon salt
⅓	cup butter, softened
1⅓	cup brown sugar, firmly packed
½	cup chunky style peanut butter
3	eggs, beaten thick and lemon colored
1	teaspoon vanilla extract

Preheat oven to 350-degrees. Sift flour, baking powder, baking soda and salt and set aside. Cream butter and sugar until light and fluffy. Add peanut butter to the cream mixture and mix well also until light and fluffy. Add eggs and vanilla, mixing well. Fold in the dry ingredients, blending well. Grease a square oblong pan and pour mixture into the pan. Bake for 25 to 30 minutes.

Coconut Macaroons

2⅔	cups coconut
⅔	cup granulated sugar
¼	cup all-purpose flour
¼	teaspoon salt
4	egg whites
1	teaspoon almond flavoring
	Candied cherries (optional)

Combine the coconut, sugar, flour and salt in a mixing bowl. Stir in the egg whites and almond flavoring, mixing well. Drop mixture onto a lightly greased baking sheet. Garnish with candied cherry halves. Bake for 325-degrees for 20-25 minutes or until edges of macaroon is lightly brown. Remove from baking sheet immediately.

Yields: 2½ dozen

Snickerdoodles

1	cup shortening
1½	cups granulated sugar
2	eggs
2¾	cups all-purpose flour
2	teaspoons cream of tartar
1	teaspoon baking soda
½	teaspoon salt
1	teaspoon vanilla

Sugar and cinnamon topping:
2	teaspoons granulated sugar
2	teaspoons cinnamon

Cream the shortening and sugar, beating until light and fluffy. Add the eggs, mixing well. Sift together the dry ingredients, adding to cream mixture. Stir in the vanilla. Chill dough for 1 hour. Mix the sugar and cinnamon in a small bowl. After chilling the dough, shape into balls and roll into the sugar and cinnamon mixture. Bake at 400-degrees for 10 to 12 minutes. I love these cookies to dip in hot tea.

Butter Cookies

1¼	pounds butter, softened
1	pound box powdered sugar
1	tablespoon vanilla extract
2	eggs
6	cups all-purpose flour
	Granulated sugar to roll cookies in

Cream butter till fluffy, gradually adding sugar and vanilla. Add the eggs and beat well. Add flour, gradually mixing well after each addition. The dough will be very soft. Refrigerate for an hour or so. When ready to bake cookies, grease a cookie sheet and preheat oven to 400-degrees. Using your hands, make balls with the dough and roll into granulated sugar. Flatten with fork. Bake for 8 to 10 minutes or until light brown. For another variation, take the batter and make equal rolls, wrap in wax paper and freeze. Then simply slice into slices and bake the amount needed. These are wonderful for children coming over at the last minute or friends coming over for coffee.

Oatmeal Raisin Cookie (The ole favorite)

1	cup butter, softened
2	cups light brown sugar, firmly packed
2	eggs
2	teaspoons vanilla extract
3	cups oatmeal, quick cooking
1¾	cups all-purpose flour
1	teaspoon baking soda
1	teaspoon cinnamon
½	teaspoon salt
1½	cups raisins

Preheat oven to 375-degrees. Grease a cookie sheet. In a large bowl, cream the butter and sugar till fluffy. Now add the eggs and vanilla beating well. Stir in the oatmeal. Sift the dry ingredients together and add to the oatmeal mixture. Now fold in the raisins. Drop batter by teaspoonfuls about 2-inches apart. Bake for 8 to 10 minutes until edges are light brown.

Yields: 4 dozen

Peanut Butter Pecan Cookies

1⅓	cups shortening (Crisco)
1½	cups granulated sugar
2	beaten eggs
3	cups all-purpose flour
1½	teaspoon baking powder
¼	teaspoon salt
2	teaspoons vanilla extract
¼	cup milk
1	cup pecans, chopped
1	cup crunchy peanut butter

Cream shortening and sugar, add eggs and beat well. Sift flour with baking powder and salt. Add to creamed mixture alternately with milk. Add vanilla extract, pecans, and peanut butter and mix well. Drop by teaspoons on an ungreased cookie sheet one-inch apart. Bake 325-degrees until lightly brown. Let sit a few minutes after taking out of the oven and then remove and set on wax paper until cool.

Yields: 8 dozen

Sweet Molasses Cookies

When I use the spice cloves in this recipe, I think of Mama's Gillis' pocketbook. Mama Gillis always chewed Cloves chewing gum as well as Juicy Fruit. But she had several packages of Cloves in her pocket book and it reeked of Cloves chewing gum when you opened it. That comes to mind when I tear out the clove spice can and sniff it.

Note: Everyone says to throw out your spices if you haven't used them in a year. Well don't throw the cloves can out, just empty the can in a saucepan of water, steep it, and your house will smell wonderful.

I love to make these cookies in the Fall and Winter. Try them with a cup of hot tea or a big glass of sweet milk. Total comfort. Did I mention that "Southerners" call milk "sweet milk"? That is, regular homogenized milk. That means they don't want buttermilk.

¾	cup Crisco
1	cup brown sugar, packed
1	egg
¼	cup molasses
2¼	cups all-purpose flour
2	teaspoons soda
¼	teaspoon salt
½	teaspoon cloves
1	teaspoon ginger
1	teaspoon cinnamon
	Granulated sugar

Preheat oven to 375-degrees. Mix well shortening, sugar, egg and molasses. Combine dry ingredients and stir in the shortening mixture. Chill dough for about 2 to 4 hours. Roll into balls the size of walnuts. Dip the tops of the balls in granulated sugar. Place balls, sugared side up, 3-inches apart on a greased baking sheet. Bake for 10 to 12 minutes. Remove from baking sheet as soon as they come out of the oven.

Yields: 4 dozen

Greenville Tea Cakes

In my Soup section, I mention a real "Southern Lady" by the name of Mrs. Edna Lane Higgins. Well, this was her Tea Cake recipe. I just wish she knew that I have kept her recipe this long. It's been over 20 years since she gave it to me. I think she would have been pleased. As I am writing different recipes from friends and relatives that have long passed, I would have never realized what a true gift they shared. A gift that I can share with you as well.

1	cup granulated sugar
2	sticks margarine
1	cup oil
1	cup powdered sugar
2	eggs
2	teaspoons vanilla extract
4½	cups all-purpose flour
1	teaspoon soda
1	teaspoon baking powder
1	teaspoon cream of tartar

Mix the first 4 ingredients and cream well. Add eggs and vanilla and cream again. Next add dry ingredients. Put this mixture in a Tupperware container with an air tight lid. Put in refrigerator over night. Pinch dough off and roll into small balls and put on an ungreased cookie sheet. They spread out and make nice small cookies. Bake at 325-degrees for 15 minutes.

Kathryn's Sugar Cookie Recipe

My daddy is a "stickler" for good Sugar cookies. However, he calls them Tea Cakes. To me there is no difference. I would make and make them until I got one that he liked. Well, I got lucky on this one.

1	cup butter, softened
¾	cup granulated sugar
1	egg, beaten
1	teaspoon vanilla extract
2¼	cups all-purpose flour
½	teaspoon baking powder
¼	cup extra granulated sugar for rolling dough balls into and extra sprinkling for decoration. *If Christmas time, use the colored sugar to sprinkle.*

Preheat oven to 350-degrees. Grease a cookie sheet. Cream the butter, adding the sugar gradually, beating until light and fluffy. Add the egg and vanilla, beating well. Combine the flour and baking powder and beat in the cream mixture, mixing well. Have a little bowl of granulated sugar ready. Make 1-inch dough balls and roll the balls into the granulated sugar. Using the tines of a floured fork or the bottom of a glass, flatten the cookies on the greased cookie sheet. Bake 12 to 15 minutes or just until edges are a very light brown. Remove immediately to cool on wire racks or wax paper to cool.

If you want to add extra sugar, sprinkle more granulated sugar on them. I usually do not unless it's the Holidays, and then I use the colored sugar or sprinkles.

Yields: 3 dozen

Almond Crescent Cookies

When I was a little girl, my mother would make these delicious cookies at Christmas time and put them in a beautiful china dish. I have that dish now and every time I look at it, this recipe comes to mind.

2	sticks butter
5	tablespoons powdered sugar
3	cups all-purpose flour
1	teaspoon almond extract
1	teaspoon vanilla extract
1	cup pecans, chopped very fine
	Extra powdered sugar to roll cookies in

Melt butter and cool. Sift flour and sugar together. Add flour mixture to butter along with extract. Knead with hands until dough is well mixed. Add pecans. Pinch off small pieces and shape into crescents. Bake in a real slow oven at 300-degrees for about 20 to 25 minutes. DO NOT BROWN TOO MUCH. They should be a very light brown color. While warm, roll into the extra powdered sugar. I put a little powered sugar in a bowl and roll the cookies until the cookies are well coated with sugar. These will keep for a long time if you put them in an air tight container and taste better the day after you make them. The butter and the flavorings mellow in the cookie. Wonderful cookies for a wedding shower or wedding.

The Good Ole Faithful Blondie Bar Cookie

Back in the day in Albany, Georgia, there was an insurance agency called Walden & Kirkland Insurors, Inc. In my many careers, I was an insurance agent there, and Mrs. Marialis Hamlett, the boss's wife, gave me this recipe. These are some fine people, and I might add you could not have asked for a finer boss than was her husband, Mr. Hamlett.

Even though my real name is Kathryn, no one ever called me Kathryn; I was always referred to by Kathy, until I started to work for Mr. Hamlett. Ever since then, I go by Kathryn.

1	stick butter
1	cup brown sugar
1	cup white sugar
2	eggs
1½	teaspoons vanilla extract
1¾	cups all-purpose flour
½	teaspoon salt
1	cup nuts, chopped
1	package dates, chopped

Cream butter and all sugars. Add other ingredients in the order that are listed. Mix well after each addition. Spread in a greased 8 x 8-inch shallow pan. You might have to spread it with floured hands, because the dough is very stiff. Bake at 350-degrees for about 20 to 30 minutes or until it leaves the sides of the pan. If overcooked the edges will be dry. Cut into short strips or bars like brownies.

Fruitcake Cookies

2	pounds whole dates
½	pound candied cherries
½	pound candied pineapple
4	cups pecans or walnuts, coarsely chopped
3½	cups all-purpose flour
1	teaspoon soda
1	teaspoon salt
1	teaspoon cinnamon
1	cup butter
1½	cups sugar
2	eggs

Cut dates into chunks, cut cherries in quarters and slice pineapple in slivers.* Place fruit and chopped nuts in a large bowl. Combine flour, soda, salt and cinnamon and sift over fruit and nuts to coat. Cream butter and sugar until light and fluffy. Add eggs and beat well. Add to fruit mixture and mix well by hand. Drop batter by teaspoonfuls onto a lightly oiled cookie sheet. Bake at 325-degrees for 15 minutes. Do not over bake.

*When cutting dates and fruit lightly flour and cut with scissors. The flour keeps fruit from sticking to the scissors.

Yield: 12 dozen

War Jack

When I was a little girl this recipe was given to me by my next door neighbor, Mrs. Annette Lewis. Anne, her daughter and I made these cookies when we were little. This recipe is very similar to the Ole Faithful Blondie as mentioned earlier. I cared a lot for Mrs. Lewis and out of tribute, I wanted to include this in my cookbook. In my mind, I can still see the little cookie tin that held the wonderful little cookies.

A quick little story comes to mind. Our school bus was late picking us up quite often. Our school bus had to go down a road called Mud Creek Road which describes it quite well. Red clay surfaced the road and when it rained it was a horrible mess. The school bus would get stuck in the mud invariably every time it rained. If I had a big test in my first period class, I so prayed that it would rain, for I knew that I would miss the test.

Well, this particular morning, the school bus was late and I grew very excited. We did not want to stand out in the rain waiting on the bus, so Anne called her mother from her grandmother's house, where we caught the bus and told her the bus was late. I got on the phone and told Mrs. Lewis that I was taking a "rest day", since the bus was late and I would just walk to my house. She laughed and asked me what a "rest day" was and I told her it was a day that I would take from time to time to rest from school. Well, Mrs. Lewis called my mother and that ended my "rest days".

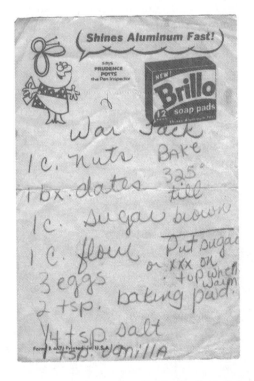

Even though Mrs. Lewis had a hand ending my "rest days", I had a lot of great memories spending time at her home.

1	cup nuts
1	box of dates, chopped or you may use the whole pitted dates and cut in half
1	cup granulated sugar
1	cup all-purpose flour
3	eggs
2	teaspoons baking powder
¼	teaspoon salt
1	teaspoon vanilla extract
½	cup powdered sugar to sprinkle on top of bars

Mix all ingredients together bake in a greased 8-inch square baking pan at 325-degrees till brown. Pour about a ½-cup of powdered sugar in the sifter and sift on top of the War Tack when they come out of the oven. Cut into bars. Store in tins. They are real chewy—wonder why she called them War Tack.

Brown Sugar Cut-Outs

1½	cups brown sugar, firmly packed
2½	sticks butter, softened
2	eggs
1	teaspoon maple flavoring
½	teaspoon vanilla extract
4	cups all-purpose flour, sifted
1	teaspoon baking powder
1	teaspoon salt
	Pinch of baking soda
	Granulated sugar for sprinkling cookies

Cream the butter and sugar together until fluffy. Add the flavorings and eggs, beating well. Now add the dry ingredients, beating well. Refrigerate the dough overnight. When you are ready to roll out the dough, use small amounts at a time and roll out ⅛-inch thick. Cut with lightly floured cookie cutters. Place on a greased cookie sheet. Sprinkle each cookie lightly with granulated sugar. Bake at 350-degrees for 8 to 10 minutes.

Coconut Washboard Cookies

½	cup butter
½	cup Crisco
2	cups brown sugar
2	eggs
¼	cup water
1	teaspoon vanilla extract
¼	teaspoon almond flavoring
4	cups sifted flour
1½	teaspoon baking powder
¼	teaspoon salt
½	teaspoon soda
1	cup coconut, shredded

Mix together the butter, Crisco, sugar and eggs. Stir in water, vanilla and almond flavoring. Stir in sifted flour, baking powder, soda and salt. Then mix in coconut. Chill dough for about 2 hours. Roll into balls the size of walnuts. Place 1½-inch apart on an ungreased baking sheet. With your fingers, flatten each ball into an oblong cookie. You can leave them round if you wish. Press each cookie with the tines of a floured fork making a washboard look. Bake 8-minutes in a 400-degree oven or until they are lightly browned. Makes about 5 dozen.

Hint

Making coconut cookies? Add toasted coconut to your cookies. Toast your coconut by placing it in the oven on 300-degrees for about 10 minutes, stirring occasionally. Crumble the coconut slightly before adding to the dough. Adds crunchiness and a whole lot of taste.

Jumbo P-nut Butter M & M Cookies

1	cup butter
1	cup peanut butter, crunchy or creamy
1	cup granulated sugar
1	cup light brown sugar, firmly packed
2	eggs
2	cups all-purpose flour
1	teaspoon baking soda
1	cup M & M candies, plain or peanut

Cream together butter, peanut butter, and all sugars until light and fluffy. Add eggs, beating well again. Mix baking soda and flour, adding this gradually to the creamed mixture, blending well. Stir in the candies. Drop ¼-cup dough onto greased cookie sheet 3-inches apart. Press 4 extra M & M candies onto the cookies. Bake at 350-degrees for 14 to 16 minutes or until edges are brown. Cool 3 minutes onto cookie sheet before removing on cooling rack or wax paper. Yields 2 dozen cookies.

Peanut Butter Fingers with Chocolate Icing

This is another recipe that we had for dessert at my Grammar School. No one ever traded any of their food for this, much to my dismay. Believe me I would keep a watch down the lunchroom table to see if anybody was leaving their Peanut Butter Fingers. I always lucked out, though. This recipe makes 4 dozen. Enough for the whole neighborhood.

1	cup butter
1	cup granulated sugar
1	cup brown sugar
2	eggs, beaten
⅔	cup peanut butter *(I like to use crunchy)*
2	cups all-purpose flour
1	teaspoon baking soda
½	teaspoon salt
2	cups oatmeal, old fashioned or quick cooking (I usually use the old fashion)
1	teaspoon vanilla extract

Cream the butter and sugars. Beat in the eggs and peanut butter. Sift together the flour, baking soda, and salt and add this mixture to the peanut butter mixture. Now mix in the oatmeal and vanilla extract. Bake in a greased 13 x 9 x 2-inch pan at 375-degrees for 25 minutes. While cooling, prepare the icing. Yummy!!!

Chocolate Icing:

1	cup butter, softened
2	cups powdered sugar*
1	cup dry cocoa*
½	cup evaporated milk
3	teaspoons vanilla extract
¼	teaspoon salt
½	cup peanut butter, creamy or chunky

Mix all icing ingredients together and spread onto bar cookies. If icing is too runny, add a little more powdered sugar.

Note: If your powdered sugar is lumpy, sift the powdered sugar and cocoa together.

The Redhead's Favorite Peanut Butter Cookies

1	cup shortening
1	cup granulated sugar
1	cup light brown sugar, firmly packed
2	eggs
1	teaspoon vanilla extract
1	cup crunchy peanut butter
2	cups all-purpose flour
½	teaspoon salt
2	teaspoons baking soda
1	cup oatmeal, uncooked (quick or old fashion)
	Extra granulated sugar
	Additional flour (¼ cup)

Preheat oven 350-degrees. Cream all of the sugars and shortening together. Beat until fluffy. Add the eggs and vanilla extract, beating well. Add the peanut butter and mix well. Sift together the flour, salt and soda and add to the creamed mixture. Stir in the oatmeal. Make about 1-inch balls and roll in the extra granulated sugar. Place on an ungreased cookie sheet about 1-inch apart. Using the tines of the fork, press down the cookies using a crisscross method. You will need to dip the fork in the flour to keep the dough from sticking. Bake for 12 to 15 minutes.

Yields: 5 to 6 dozen

Kathryn's Favorite Cereal Cookie Recipe

By looking at the ingredients at first glance, it favors another one of my recipes. However, the Rice Krispies make a difference. Notice how easy it is. The kids would love to make this one. Look at all of the onesy's in it. Easy to remember. If you have more than one child, line them up with a cup of one of the ingredients in their hand. Let them feel a part of this and make an adventure out of it, like Mama Gillis did to me.

1	cup shortening
1	cup oil
1	cup brown sugar
1	egg
1	cup coconut
1	cup pecan or walnuts, chopped
1	cup oatmeal, quick or old fashioned
3	cups all-purpose flour
1	teaspoon cream of tartar
1	teaspoon salt
1	teaspoon soda
2	teaspoons vanilla extract
1	cup rice cereal

Using a large size mixing bowl, cream the shortening, oil and brown sugar. Mix in the egg and then all other ingredients. Mix well. Drop by teaspoonfuls on an ungreased cookie sheet. Bake at 350-degrees for 12 to 15 minutes.

Gingerbread Bars with Lemon Glaze Icing

1¼	cups granulated sugar
1	cup butter, softened
1	egg
3	tablespoons molasses
3	cups all-purpose flour
1	teaspoon baking soda
2	teaspoons ground cinnamon
4	ounces crystallized ginger, coarsely chopped

Preheat oven to 350-degrees. In a large mixing bowl, combine all of the ingredients. Pour dough out onto an ungreased 15 x 10 x 1-inch jelly roll pan. With lightly floured hands, pat the dough down into the pan. Bake at 350-degrees for 15 to 20 minutes or just until the edges are lightly brown. Cool before glazing.

Frost with Lemon Glaze Icing:

1½	cups powdered sugar, sifted
2	tablespoons butter, softened
2	teaspoons lemon rind, grated
3	tablespoons lemon juice

Combine all of the ingredients and spread onto the Gingerbread Bars.

Elaine's Last Minute Drop Cookies

½	cup soft shortening
1	cup light brown sugar, firmly packed
1	egg
¼	cup buttermilk or sour milk*
1	teaspoon vanilla
2	cups all-purpose flour, sifted
½	teaspoon baking powder
½	teaspoon salt
½	teaspoon soda
¾	cup nuts, chopped. You may use coconut, currants or dates.

Cream together the shortening and brown sugar till light and fluffy. Add egg, beating well. Stir in the buttermilk and vanilla. Mix together the flour, baking powder, salt and soda. Stir in the flour mixture to the cream mixture. Fold in the nuts. Bake on a greased cookie sheet at 375-degrees for about 10 minutes or until lightly brown. I like to double this recipe.

* To make sour milk: 1 cup milk, adding 1 tablespoon vinegar, stirring to blend.

Freezing Bananas with a Story

How many times do you buy bananas and have them turn black before you use them, or you eat one or two and plan to cook something with them. Some people buy real ripe bananas at super cheap prices and freeze them. Let me tell you how to freeze them and then I will get on with the recipe.

Peel the bananas, mash them and in a small bowl, sprinkle just a teaspoon of lemon juice on the bananas. Stir the lemon juice into the mashed bananas. Then get a plastic zip-top freezing bag and freeze them. They will stay good at least 6 months in the freezer. You can use them to make Banana Cake or anything using mashed bananas. When you get ready to make the Banana Bars, take out the frozen bag of bananas and let them thaw.

Don't do like my daddy did! He heard that you could freeze bananas, so he put the whole bunch of bananas with the peeling on in the freezer. I guess he thought they would come out of the freezer looking like they went in there. Well, he was surprised!

Banana Bars

I usually double this recipe. If you want to add an icing on the bars, do so. That's what I like to do.

½	cup butter
1	cup light brown sugar, firmly packed
1	egg, beaten
1	teaspoon vanilla extract or banana flavoring
1	teaspoon baking powder
¼	teaspoon salt
1	cup mashed banana
1	(3½-ounce) can of flaked coconut or ¾-cup coconut
1¼	cups all-purpose flour
½	cup walnuts or pecans, chopped (optional)

Cream together the butter and light brown sugar. Add the beaten egg and flavoring. Now add the baking powder and salt, mixing well. Fold in the mashed bananas and the coconut and slowly add the flour, blending well. Stir in the nuts, if you use them. Pour batter into a greased 11 x 7 x 2-inch pan. This pan makes thin bars. Bake at 325-degrees for 40 to 45 minutes. Cut into bars. You can use a small square pan to make the bars a little thicker. It might take them a little longer to cook, though. The recipe below will make a quick and easy glaze to drool over the top. I like to make the icing while the Banana Bars are baking. Then I drool the icing over the warm bars and the icing seeps into the bars.

Icing:

½	cup butter, softened
1	teaspoon vanilla extract or banana
2	cups powdered sugar, sifted
2-4	tablespoons evaporated milk

If you want to add a little coconut, you may add ¼-cup coconut
I like to add ⅓-cup mashed banana. This is optional, though.

If you want more or a thicker icing, just double the icing recipe.

In a medium-sized bowl, cream together the butter and vanilla. Blend in the powdered sugar, one cup at a time. Add a little milk while beating. I usually don't use my mixer to beat this icing. With this small amount, I cream the butter with my wooden spoon. After you mix the ingredients, just spoon it over the bars.

Reese's Cup Chocolate Cookies

1	cup semisweet chocolate chips, melted
½	cup butter, softened
⅓	cup peanut butter, crunchy or smooth
¾	cup light brown sugar
1	egg, beaten
1	teaspoon vanilla extract
1¾	cups all-purpose flour
½	teaspoon baking soda
¼	teaspoon salt
8	(6-ounce) Reese's peanut butter candy cups, coarsely chopped

In a small saucepan, melt the chocolate chips, set aside. In a large bowl, cream the butter, peanut butter and brown sugar until fluffy. Add the egg and vanilla and beat well. Add the melted chocolate chips and mix well. Mix all dry ingredients together and then blend the dry ingredients into the creamed mixture. Mix well. Drop dough by tablespoons on a greased cookie sheet or one that has been lined with parchment paper. Space the dough 2-inches apart. Place several pieces of the candy on top of each cookie. Bake cookies for 18 to 20 minutes or until the cookies are set. The cookie centers will still be moist. Cool 5 minutes and then transfer the cookies on a cooling rack to cool.

Yields: 1½-dozen

Pies, Cobblers & Crunchers

Holiday Cranberry Raisin Pie

Sweet Potato Pie Story

Well, here is my Sweet Potato Pie recipe. I mention in the Canning Section that I had a Peach Pickin Mama called "Bernice". Well, here is another story.

I was expecting my second child and y'all know by now, I love to eat. Bernice birthed 12 children right by herself (that means she did not go to the hospital to have any of them). I was at Bernice's house, and I was huge with child. It's not like it is now where the girls are expecting and they are little petite things with a little bulge. I looked like a 5' 3" pot belly stove. Food was better when I was expecting than any other time in my life. Well-let's get on with the story.

Bernice was making Sweet Potato Pies and I was sitting lop-sided on her kitchen stool. She looked at me said "Honey, you sure are carrying that baby low". Well, I was 10 days late. I was never early having a child. "That baby is ready to come, I know it. I have birthed 12 children right by myself and I know. I want you to eat this whole Sweet Potato Pie and you will have this baby tomorrow." Well, she sure did not have to pry my arm in eating the pie. It was the best. I ate the whole thing, crust and all. Well, low and behold the next afternoon, my daughter was born. I always thought Bernice could have hung her M.D. shingle up. She hit the nail on the head. I really don't think it was a coincidence. Even though I was overdue, the baby could have been born 2 or 3 days after that.

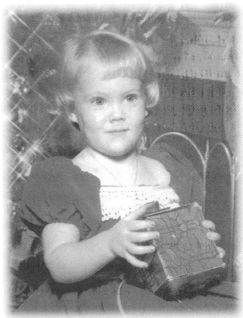

My daughter, Mandy. This is my "Sweet Potato Pie Baby"

Autumn Sweet Potato Pie

1   (10-inch) pie shell baked for 15 minutes at 400-degrees and cooled

Filling for pie:
Absolutely wonderful! I want to scoop and eat the filling right out of the pie.
- 3 egg yolks, beaten
- 2 cups cooked sweet mashed potatoes
- 1 cup granulated sugar* (You may want to add another ¼-cup)
- ½ cup evaporated milk
- 1 tablespoon cornstarch
- ¼ teaspoon nutmeg
- 2 teaspoon cinnamon
- 1 teaspoon orange flavoring
- 1 teaspoon vanilla extract
- 3 egg whites, beaten with ¼-cup granulated sugar

Beat egg yolks and add potatoes, sugar, milk, cornstarch, nutmeg and cinnamon in top of double boiler. Cook until it thickens about 12 to 15 minutes, stirring constantly. Taste the mixture. If the mixture is not sweet enough, this is the time to add a little more sugar to taste. Remove from the heat. Now add the orange and vanilla extract. Cool 10 minutes and then fold in the egg whites that have been beaten with ¼-cup sugar. Pour this mixture into the partially baked pie shell. Bake at 400-degrees until set for about 20 to 30 minutes. If you find the crust is browning excessive, cover with strips of aluminum foil around the edge of the pie shell.

Note: I like to use leftover pieces of dough and cut out leaves with a cookie cutter and place on top of the pie prior to cooking. At Christmas time, when I make the pie, I use my Christmas tree cookie cutter to garnish the pie.

Gerb's Peanut Butter Pie

This pie is better if prepared early in the morning or the night before serving.

Oreo or Chocolate Cookie Crust:
- 20   Oreo cream or any Chocolate cream Cookies-leave the cream in (this makes 2 cups crumbs)
- ½   cup granulated sugar
- ¼   cup butter, melted

Preheat oven to 375-degrees. Put whole cookies in the food processor and grind. Mix the sugar and butter together with the cookies. With the back of a spoon, press crumb mixture firmly on bottom and up the sides of a 10-inch pie plate. Bake 10 minutes. Cool completely by chilling at least 1 hour before adding this wonderful filling.

Filling:
- 2   (8-ounce) packages cream cheese, softened
- 2   cups creamy peanut butter
- 1½   cups granulated sugar
- 1½   cups heavy whipping cream

In a large mixing bowl, beat the cream cheese and peanut butter, adding the sugar gradually. Beat until this mixture is very light and fluffy. In a separate bowl that has been chilled, beat the whipping cream until soft peaks form, and then fold the whipping cream into the peanut butter mixture. Mix thoroughly. Pour the filling into the pie crust and chill at least 4 hours or overnight.

Topping for the pie:
- ½   cup heavy whipping cream
- 1   (6-ounce) bag of semisweet chocolate chips

In a saucepan, bring the cream to a light boil and remove from the heat. Stir in the chocolate chips until they are all melted and stir until smooth. Put the saucepan in the fridge for about 30 minutes to cool. Then pour this decadent topping over the pie. Chill the pie at least for another 30 minutes before serving, so that the topping will firm up.

Note: My husband can eat the whole pie. It seems like it takes a long time, but it doesn't. It is wonderful.

Elvis Pie

This recipe was given to me by Ms. Suzanne Anderson. She is from my hometown of Albany, Georgia. Suzanne is the 2004-2005 Ms. US Sophisticate. Her passion for crowns and gowns began when she was first awarded first runner-up in the Little Miss Albany Pageant in 1973. She's been chasing titles ever since.

As a true Southerner, Suzanne also loves college football, particularly the Auburn University Tigers. From September through December, you will find her at Auburn with her tailgate crew, the Blue Moon Krewe, hootin' and hollerin' for her beloved alma mater. She's a beauty and we go a long way back. We have had some good times! Thanks Suzanne.

½	ripe banana
1	(8-ounce) package cream cheese, softened
½	cup creamy peanut butter
½	cup sugar
2	teaspoons vanilla
½	cup Cool Whip
1	chocolate graham cracker crust
	Chocolate syrup (optional) *Now who would turn down the chocolate syrup!*

Mash banana. Set aside. Combine cream cheese and sugar. Beat at low speed until smooth. Add peanut butter, banana, vanilla and Cool Whip. Pour this mixture into pie crust. Refrigerate 3 hours before serving. If you like, add swirls of chocolate syrup on top of pie before refrigerating.

Banana Cream Pie

1	(10-inch) pie shell, baked and cooled*
⅔	cup sugar
2	tablespoons cornstarch
2	cups milk or half-and-half
2	egg yolks
1	tablespoon butter
2	teaspoons vanilla flavoring (divided use)
2	large ripe bananas, sliced
½	teaspoon lemon juice
1	cup heavy whipping cream
	Confectioners' sugar to taste

In a 2-quart saucepan stir together the sugar and cornstarch. Gradually stir in the milk, whisk to make smooth. Using the whisk again beat in the egg yolks until blended. Cook over medium heat, stirring constantly until mixture comes to a boil. Boil until mixture is thick about 2 minutes. Take off heat and stir in butter and 1 teaspoon of vanilla flavoring. Turn banana cream filling into a bowl and place plastic wrap on top to keep skin from forming. Refrigerate for one hour. Sprinkle lemon juice on banana slices to keep from discoloring. Place the banana slices in the pie shell. Pour the banana cream filling in the pie shell over the bananas. Now cover pie filling once again with plastic wrap and refrigerate overnight or at least six hours for pie to set.

At serving time, whip the whipping cream until stiff peaks. Gradually add enough confectioners' sugar to taste and then stir in the left over 1 teaspoon vanilla flavoring. Spread whipping cream topping over the entire pie and garnish with banana slices.

Yields: 8 slices

I like for my pies to have the high fluted edge, I always use a 10-inch pie shell.

Raspberry and Lemon Lush Pie

Crumb Crust:
- 1 cup graham cracker or cinnamon graham cracker crumbs
- ½ cup pecans or walnuts, toasted and chopped
- 3 tablespoons sugar
- ⅓ cups butter, melted

In a bowl combine the crumbs, nuts, sugar and butter. Press into a 9-inch pie pan. Bake at 375-degrees for 8 to 10 minutes.

Filling:
- ½ cup seedless red raspberry jam, melted slightly
- 1½ cups granulated sugar
- ½ cup cornstarch
- ½ teaspoon salt
- 1 cup water
- 2 egg yolks, slightly beaten
- 1 (8-ounce) package cream cheese, softened
- 2 tablespoons butter
- 2 teaspoons lemon peel, grated
- ½ cup fresh lemon juice

Spoon jam into the bottom of the cooled crust. Set aside. In a large saucepan, combine the sugar, cornstarch and salt. Stir in the water and egg yolks. Cook over medium heat until mixture thickens and boils. Boil and stir 1 to 2 minutes. Remove mixture from heat and add cream cheese and butter, stirring until melted. Stir in the lemon peel and lemon juice. Spoon lemon filling on top of the raspberry jam. Cover and chill for 1 to 2 hours.

Topping:
- 2 cups whipping cream
- ½ cup powdered sugar
- ½ teaspoon vanilla extract
- 1 (6-ounce) container fresh raspberries, rinsed and blotted with paper toweling
- Lemon zest and sprigs of mint

Whip cream on high speed with mixer until soft peaks, adding the sugar gradually. Stir in the vanilla. Spoon the whipping cream over the top of the pie or you may use a decorator tube with a large tip and make dollops of the whipping cream, if desired. Place raspberries over the top of the pie and decorate with the lemon zest and mint sprigs.

Yields: 10 to 12 servings

Holiday Cranberry Raisin Pie

2	(9-inch) double crust pie shells, commercial or homemade recipe
2	cups cranberries, fresh or frozen
2	cups raisins, dark or golden
1½	cups granulated sugar
⅓	cup all-purpose flour
¼	teaspoon salt
⅔	cup water
1½	tablespoons lemon juice
	Grated peel of one orange
½	teaspoon cinnamon
½	teaspoon almond extract
1	egg, slightly beaten
3	tablespoons butter, cut in slices
	Cookie cutters for crust*
	Additional granulated sugar to sprinkle

Preheat oven to 425-degrees. Using a 3-quart heavy saucepan, mix the cranberries, raisins, sugar, flour and salt. Add the water and stir frequently on medium heat until the cranberries pop open and the mixture is thickened. Cook about 5 minutes, still stirring to keep from sticking. Stir in the lemon juice, orange peel, cinnamon and almond extract. Cool slightly. Line a 9-inch pie plate with a bottom crust and pour the filling in. Dot with the pats of butter.

Note: Using my cookie cutters, I select one of the Holiday themes and cut several pieces of dough out of the top crust and place on top of the pie shell. I find this is much more attractive. In essence, the whole top crust is covered with dough in selected shapes. My favorite one is my tree cookie cutter for the Holidays. I use this on Mincemeat and all of my fruit pies I bake for the Holidays. At Valentines, when I make a cherry pie, I use my heart-shaped cookie cutters to cut hearts out of dough and place on top of the pie.

Place the dough on top of the filling, and brush the beaten egg on top of the dough. Sprinkle with additional granulated sugar. Bake at 425-degrees for 15 minutes and then reduce the heat to 375-degrees and continue to bake until the pie crust is nice and brown and bubbly. Cool before serving and top with sweetened whipping cream or ice cream.

Brown Paper Bag Apple Pie

When grocery shopping and at the check-out counter the grocery bagger always asks, paper or plastic? I always say paper.

Again, I want to emphasize that Michigan apples are absolutely the best. When I make this recipe, I never leave the kitchen without at least two pies. When I'm in the kitchen, I'm going to make my time count.

1	(10-inch) deep dish pie shell, uncooked
6	apples, cored, peeled, and diced
¾	cup granulated sugar
4	tablespoons all-purpose flour
3	tablespoons lemon juice
1	teaspoon cinnamon
½	teaspoon nutmeg
	Pinch of mace

In a large bowl, mix all of the ingredients together. Place the ingredients in the unbaked pie shell. Top the pie with the crumble topping.

Crumble topping:

1	stick butter, softened
½	cup all-purpose flour
½	cup brown sugar

Mix all of the ingredients together, using a pastry blender or by hand. Put the crumble topping in the fridge to firm up, so you have a more crumbly topping than soft product for the topping. Place the topping on the pie and put the pie into a large paper brown bag to bake. Secure the bag with a large metal clip. Bake at 375-degrees for 30 minutes and then reduce the heat to 350-degrees for 35 to 40 minutes. After removing the pie from the oven, tear the bag off of the pie. Serve with sweetened whipping cream or vanilla ice cream.

Note: The pie will get soggy if you do not remove the bag from the pie.

Pecan Pie

1	(9-inch) unbaked pie shell
1	cup pecan halves
3	eggs, beaten
1	tablespoon butter, melted
½	cup dark corn syrup (Karo)
½	cup light corn syrup (Karo)
1	teaspoon vanilla extract
1	cup granulated sugar
1	tablespoon flour

Preheat oven to 350-degrees. Place the pecan halves in the bottom of the pie shell and set aside. In a medium-sized mixing bowl, beat eggs until light and frothy, adding the butter, syrups and vanilla, blending well. Mix the sugar and flour and mix this with the egg mixture. Slowly pour the filling into the pie shell over the pecans. Before putting the pie in the oven, let the pie sit long enough for the pecans to rise to the top. This procedure will glaze the pecans nicely during the baking procedure. Bake for 45 to 50 minutes.

Buttermilk Pie

1	10-inch unbaked pie shell
½	cup butter, melted
2	cups sugar
4	tablespoons flour
3	eggs, beaten
1	cup buttermilk
1	teaspoon vanilla
	Dash of nutmeg

Note: I like to use butter flavoring in this recipe, also. You may use ½ teaspoon vanilla and ½-teaspoon butter flavoring.

Cream butter and sugar with mixer. Add flour, eggs and beat. Stir in buttermilk and flavorings. Pour filling into unbaked pie shell. Sprinkle with nutmeg. Bake at 350-degrees until pie is set approximately 40 minutes.

Cream Cheese Pudding Pie

Adorning this pie with Raspberry and Blueberry Topping makes a perfect dessert for the 4th of July or Memorial Day. Check the glaze section out for the topping recipes. For this whole recipe, you can use the food processor or blender. Simple and very easy. Once you start eating this pie, just be prepared to eat the whole thing.

Crust:
1	(9-inch) graham cracker crust, purchased or homemade
24	graham cracker squares
⅓	cup granulated sugar
⅓	cup butter, melted

Separate the crackers and put them in the food processor or blender, process until all crackers are crumbs.* Empty the crumbs in a bowl, add the sugar and butter, mixing well. Pour the crumb mixture into a 9-inch pie plate, pressing firmly against the bottom and sides. Bake at 350-degrees for 8 minutes until crust is lightly brown. Cool completely before adding the filling.

*If you do not have a food processor or blender, put all of the crackers in a 2-gallon zip-top bag. Close bag and crush them with a rolling pin or mashing the bag with your hands.

Pie Filling:
1	(8-ounce) package cream cheese, softened
2	cups whole milk
1	(5.5-ounce) package vanilla or lemon instant pudding mix
1	teaspoon vanilla extract

Place the cream cheese in the food processor or blender and process until soft and creamy. Add milk slowly to keep from splattering and mix thoroughly on high. Add pudding mix and vanilla extract, blending real well. Pour the filling into the cooled pie crust. Serve with sweetened whipping cream or with selected toppings.

Mocha Ice Cream Pie

I won 2nd prize in the Baker County Farm Bureau Dairy Contest for this recipe. I have always loved coffee ice cream and of course chocolate *(who doesn't)* and I came up with this recipe. If you do not want to go to the trouble of making homemade fudge topping, just substitute with the already prepared topping. You need to prepare this recipe at least the day before you serve it.

Coconut Pie Crust:
2   cups flaked coconut
3   tablespoons butter, melted

In a mixing bowl, combine coconut and melted butter. Spray the pie plate with baking spray. Spread the mixture evenly in a 9-inch pie plate. Press onto bottom and sides to form a firm crust. Bake 325-degree about 10 minutes or till crust is golden brown. Cool thoroughly. After cooling, refrigerate pie crust for filling. Refrigerate at least 4 hours.

Filling:
2   pints of coffee ice cream-softened (your favorite brand) Häagen-Dazs® – Wow!
1   cup fudge topping, commercial or my homemade kind *(see next column for recipe)*
½   cup salted peanuts, chopped
1   pint chocolate ice cream, softened
1   half-pint heavy cream, whipped with 4 tablespoons of confectioners' sugar

Spread 1 pint of the coffee ice cream over the crust. Spread half of the fudge topping over the ice cream; then sprinkle with half of the nuts. Freeze until firm. Then spread chocolate ice cream over the frozen mixture. Then add remaining chocolate topping and nuts. Freeze until firm. Spread remaining coffee ice cream over frozen mixture. Freeze several hours or overnight. Whip heavy cream until stiff peaks and pile on top of pie. Freeze until firm at least 1 hour. Garnish with chocolate curls and a few chopped peanuts. To serve pie, let stand 15 minutes. Cut into small wedges.

Fudge Topping:

¾	cup half-and-half (light cream)
1	cup sugar
¼	cup butter
½	cup cocoa
1	teaspoon vanilla flavoring
	Dash of salt

Heat milk and sugar, stirring constantly to rolling boil. Boil and stir 1 minute. Add cocoa and salt. Beat over heat with wire whisk until smooth. Take off heat, add butter and vanilla. Yields 1½-cups topping.

Fresh Blueberry Pie
By Mrs. Kalah Hardy

There was a couple in Leesburg, Georgia, who had a Blueberry and Apple Farm. I would go and pick blueberries every year from Mr. Hardy. Of course this was before Mama Gillis planted her blueberry bushes.

1	(10-inch) baked pie shell, which has been cooled
1	quart fresh blueberries
1	cup granulated sugar
1	cup water
3	tablespoons of cornstarch
⅛	teaspoon salt
1	tablespoon butter
	Few drops of lemon juice
1	carton fresh whipping cream, whipped and sweetened with
4	tablespoons powdered sugar
	Dash of vanilla extract

Wash and drain the blueberries thoroughly. Mix the sugar, salt and cornstarch in the saucepan. Gradually, add the water and then 1 cup of the blueberries. Cook over low heat, stirring constantly until the mixture is thick and clear and purple in color. Remove from the heat and add the butter and lemon juice. Cool slightly and stir in remaining berries. Pour into the baked pie shell. Refrigerate. When cold, cover with the sweetened whipping cream, which has a dash of vanilla extract in it. Refrigerate.

Ole Fashion Egg Custard Pie

This recipe was handwritten and given to me by my father's mother who we called "Grandma Pierce". She used to make this pie for my Daddy.

1	cup sugar
2½	tablespoons flour
	Pinch of nutmeg
3	eggs, well beaten
1	cup milk
2	tablespoons melted butter

Meringue:
2	egg whites
2	tablespoons sugar
1	(9-inch) unbaked pie shell

Combine the sugar, flour, and nutmeg. Beat eggs together and add to the dry ingredients. Beat well, add milk and stir in the melted butter. Pour into the crust and bake for 400-degrees for 10 minutes. Reduce heat to 325-degrees and bake for 30 minutes longer.

For meringue:
Beat egg whites and sugar until stiff peaks for the meringue. Spread onto custard and brown in oven, for 12 to 15 minutes at 325-degrees. Watch closely for it doesn't take long for meringue.

Lemon Chess Pie

1	(9-inch) unbaked pie shell
	(Use my Cream Cheese Pastry Crust Recipe)
2	cups sugar
1	tablespoon all-purpose flour
1	tablespoon cornmeal
¼	teaspoon salt
¼	cup melted butter
¼	cup lemon juice
	Grated rind of 2 lemons
¼	cup evaporated milk
4	eggs

Combine the sugar, flour, cornmeal, and salt. Add the melted butter, lemon juice, lemon rinds and milk, mixing well. Now add each egg, beating well after each addition. Pour in the pie shell and bake for 50 minutes at 350-degrees. Delicious.

Easy Apple Pie

I just bet you have had a couple of apples you just didn't know what to do with. Usually an apple pie recipe requires more than just two apples. But this one you use only a couple!

1	(9-inch) unbaked pie crust
1½	cups peeled, grated baking apples (2 large apples)
2	eggs
½	cup brown sugar, firmly packed
½	cup Karo or light corn syrup
½	stick butter, melted
1	teaspoon cinnamon
¼	teaspoon mace

Preheat oven to 350-degrees. Using your electric mixer, beat eggs, brown sugar, syrup, melted butter, and spices in a bowl. Stir in the grated apples and pour mixture into an unbaked pie shell. Placing your pie on a cookie sheet to prevent any spillover; cook for 50 minutes to 1 hour. Top each slice with a dollop of sweetened whipping cream.

Apple Cobbler

½	cup butter
1½	cups sifted self-rising flour
½	cup shortening (Crisco)
½	cup milk
2	cups finely chopped apples
1	teaspoon cinnamon
½	teaspoon mace
½	cup pecans or walnuts, chopped fine
2	cups sugar
2	cups water

Preheat oven to 350-degrees. Melt the butter in a 13 x 9 x 2-inch baking dish and set aside. Cut the shortening into the flour until it looks like small crumbs. Add milk and stir only until dough leaves the sides of the bowl. Turn dough out onto lightly floured board and knead just until smooth. Roll dough out into a large rectangle about ¼-inch thick. Mix cinnamon, mace and nuts over apples. Now sprinkle the apples over the dough. Roll the dough up like a jelly roll. Dampen the ends of the dough with a little bit of water to seal the dough. Slice dough into about 16 slices, ½-inch thick. Place in the baking dish with the melted butter. In a medium size saucepan, combine the sugar and water, stirring on medium heat until dissolved. Pour sugar water syrup over the roll. Do not worry if it looks too watery, the crust will soak it up. Bake for approximately one hour.

Peach Cobbler

	Pastry for a double pie crust
	(Your favorite homemade or commercial)
6	cups peaches, fresh or frozen and peeled
2	cups granulated sugar
½	cup all-purpose flour
2	teaspoons cinnamon
	Pinch of salt
1	cup water
½	cup butter, melted
1½	teaspoons almond flavoring
4	tablespoons, butter (Cut into slices)

Preheat oven to 375-degrees. Prepare a 3-quart baking dish by greasing with butter. In a large bowl, dredge the peaches in the sugar, flour, cinnamon and salt. Add the water, melted butter and almond flavoring. Set aside. Divide the pastry dough into 2 sections. Roll both pastry pieces of dough to ¼-inch thickness on a floured surface. Place the dough into the baking dish. Pour the peach mixture into the pastry dough. Place the slices of butter in the baking dish with the peach mixture. Now put the remaining pastry dough on top of the peach mixture. Cut several slits into the top of the pie crust to allow steam to escape. Sprinkle the top of the pie crust with granulated sugar. Bake for at least 1 hour until the juices start to bubble out of the slits in the pie crust and the top of the crust is brown. Serves about 8. Serve with sweetened whipping cream or vanilla ice cream.

Blackberry Cobbler

On Mama Gillis' farm, in the blistering hot sun we would go blackberry picking, and the one thing that we wouldn't forget to take with us was a big stick. Guess what that stick was for? Rattlesnakes. We would hit the blackberry bushes with that stick before we would stoop over and reach for the berries to see if a rattlesnake would shake his rattler. Lord, what we "Southern Women" will do for our Southern men! Papa loved his Blackberry Cobbler.

This is a 2-crust (top and bottom) cobbler.

Preheat oven to 425-degrees. Prepare a 12 x 6 x 2-inch baking dish or a 2-quart casserole dish by greasing well with butter.

Cobbler Dough:
- 2 cups all-purpose flour
- 1 teaspoon salt
- ¾ cup butter
- About 6 tablespoons ice cold water
- Extra flour

Cobbler Filling:
- 6 cups blackberries
- 1½ cups granulated sugar (reserve 2 tablespoons)
- 1 teaspoon cinnamon
- 4 tablespoons all-purpose flour
- ½ stick butter, cut into slices
- Sweetened whipping cream or vanilla ice cream

Sift flour and salt together. Using a pastry blender, cut in the butter with the flour till it resembles small peas. Sprinkle water, 1 tablespoon at a time, till the dough is able to rollup into a ball. Split the ball in halve and roll between 2 sheets of waxed paper. With floured hands press dough to fit the bottom of baking dish. Do the same with the other ball of dough and set aside for the top of the cobbler.

Filling:
Mix granulated sugar (all but 2 tablespoons), cinnamon, and all-purpose flour. Toss carefully with the blackberries. Fill the baking dish with the berry mixture. Dot the berry mixture with the slices of butter. Now top the cobbler with the other half of the dough and sprinkle with the reserved 2 tablespoons of sugar. Makes several slits in the pie crust. Bake for 15 minutes at 425-degrees and then reduce the heat to 350-degrees for 45 minutes or until the juice from the berries start to bubble out of the pie crust or until crust is brown. Top with sweetened whipping cream or vanilla ice cream.

Cranberry Cruncher

We had this for dessert when I was in grammar school around Thanksgiving time. You always have an extra can of cranberry sauce in your cupboard. Put it to good use!

1	cup uncooked old fashioned oats
½	cup flour
1	cup brown sugar
⅓	cup butter
1	(1-pound) can whole berry cranberry sauce

Mix oats, flour, and brown sugar. Cut in the butter until crumbly. Place half of this mixture in a greased 8 x 8-inch baking dish. Cover with the cranberry sauce. Top with the balance of the crumbly mixture. Bake 45 minutes at 350-degrees. Serve hot with sweetened whipped cream or vanilla ice cream.

Yields: 6 servings

Georgia Peach Dumplings

1	recipe double crust pastry
4	tablespoons brown sugar
¼	teaspoon cinnamon
⅛	teaspoon nutmeg
⅛	teaspoon mace
4	peaches, peeled, pitted, and halved
4	tablespoons butter
1	cup dark corn syrup or Karo dark corn syrup
3	tablespoons water
2	tablespoons butter, additional

Preheat oven to 425-degrees. Prepare a 13 x 9 x 2-inch pan by greasing. Roll out pastry on a lightly floured surface and cut (4) 7-inch squares. In a small bowl, combine the sugar, cinnamon, nutmeg and mace. Set aside. Place 4 prepared peach halves in the center of each dough square and then sprinkle 1 tablespoon of the brown sugar and 1 tablespoon of butter in the center of each peach half. Top the peach with the other half of the peach. Bring the edges of the dough over the peach to cover it, and moisten the dough with water to seal the peach. Place the peaches in the prepared pan and bake for 25 minutes until lightly brown.

While the peaches are cooking, mix together the dark corn syrup, water and butter in a 2-quart saucepan. Heat this mixture until the syrup boils and pour this over the dumplings. Cook 5 minutes more, basting the syrup over the dumplings. When serving, top the dumplings with ice cream or sweetened whipping cream and spoon the syrup on top of the ice cream or whipping cream.

*If you have a pastry wheel, using this to cut the dough would make it decorative.

Yields: 4 servings

Johnny Appleseed's Apple Dumpling

4	large baking apples, peeled and cored all the way through the apple
¼	cup brown sugar, firmly packed
1	teaspoon cinnamon
¼	teaspoon mace
4	tablespoons pecans or walnuts, finely chopped
¼	cup raisins, if desired
2	cups water or apple juice
1	cup granulated sugar
½	stick butter, melted

Preheat oven to 375-degrees. Combine the brown sugar, cinnamon, mace, raisins and nuts in a small bowl, mixing well. Fill the apple centers with the sugar and spice mixture. Set the apples aside while you prepare the pastry dough according to the recipe below.

2	cups all-purpose flour
1	teaspoon salt
⅔	cup butter
⅓	cup very cold ice water
	Extra all-purpose flour for rolling out dough

Combine the flour and salt. Cut in the butter until the mixture resembles little peas. Sprinkle in the water a tablespoon at a time, mixing lightly until the dough forms a ball. On a lightly floured surface, roll dough out to approximately a 14-inch square. Cut the dough into 4 (7-inch) squares. Place an apple on the center of each pie dough square. Wrap the apples with the dough and wet the edges of the dough to seal. Place the wrapped apples in the baking dish. Pour the water or apple juice, granulated sugar and butter around the apples. Bake for 40 minutes or until apples are tender. Delicious with sweetened whipping cream.

Yields: 4 servings

Apple Brown Betty

What do you do with the heels of your bread? Some folks just throw them out. Save them, and you can make a wonderful dessert. Delicious!
I always double this recipe.

6	slices of bread
⅓	cup brown sugar
¼	teaspoon nutmeg
½	teaspoon cinnamon
1	(21-ounce) can of apple pie filling
1	stick of butter, melted

Cut the bread into small cubes. Put bread into a bowl and soak the cubes of bread with the butter. Set aside. Mix the sugar, nutmeg, and cinnamon. Mix the apples with the sugar and spice mixture. Place the apple mixture in a greased baking dish. Now top with the bread cubes. Bake at 375-degrees for about 20 to 30 minutes.

Blueberry Buckle

½	cup butter
1	cup sugar (divided use)
½	teaspoon vanilla
½	teaspoon almond extract
1	egg, beaten well
1½	cups all-purpose flour (divided use)
1	teaspoon baking powder
¼	teaspoon salt
⅓	cup milk
2	cup blueberries
½	teaspoon cinnamon
¼	cup butter
	Sweetened whipping cream

Cream butter, ½-cup of the sugar, vanilla, and almond flavoring into a medium-sized bowl. Add beaten egg to this mixture. Sift together 1 cup of the flour, baking powder, and salt. Add the dry ingredients alternately with milk to the creamed mixture. Pour this mixture into a greased 10 x 5 x 2 baking dish. Cover with the blueberries. Combine the remaining ½-cup sugar, flour, cinnamon and butter, blending together to form a crumb topping. Sprinkle this mixture over the blueberries. Bake at 375-degrees for 40 to 45 minutes. Serve with sweetened whipping cream.

Pie Crusts

Choose any one of these crust recipes to put delicious fillings or to make delicious ice cream pies. Use your imagination!

Butter Pecan Coconut Crust
(Makes one 9-inch pie crust)

¼	cup light brown sugar, firmly packed
1	cup all-purpose flour, sifted
½	cup butter, softened
¼	cup pecans, finely chopped
¼	cup shredded coconut

Combine the brown sugar and flour. Cut in the butter with a fork until mixture resembles little tiny peas. Add the pecans and coconut, mixing well. With buttered fingers, press mixture into a 9-inch pie pan, evenly around the bottom and sides of the pan. Bake at 375-degrees for 12 to 15 minutes until lightly brown.

Chocolate Coconut Crust
(Makes one 9-inch pie crust)

2	squares unsweetened chocolate, melted
2	tablespoons butter, melted
2	tablespoons hot water
⅔	cup powdered sugar, sifted
1½	cups sweetened flaked coconut

Melt the chocolate and butter over very low heat, using a double boiler or a microwave. Stir in the hot water and the sifted powdered sugar. Now add the coconut, mixing well. Grease a 9-inch pie pan. Spread the coconut mixture on the bottom and sides of the pie pan. Chill until firm.

Coconut Crust
(Makes one 9-inch pie crust)

1⅓	cups flaked coconut
2	tablespoons butter, melted

Mix ingredients together and press into a 9-inch pie pan. Bake at 325-degrees for 12 to 15 minutes or until light brown. Cool before pouring filling in pie shell.

Walnut Graham Cracker Pie Shell
(Makes one 10-inch pie crust)

1	cup graham cracker crumbs, crushed fine
½	cup walnuts, chopped fine
¼	cup granulated sugar
¼	cup butter, melted

Mix all of the ingredients. Press into a 10-inch pie pan. Chill or bake in a 375-degrees oven for about 7 minutes. Delicious with Banana Cream Pie.

Cream Cheese Pastry Crust
(For one 9-inch pie crust)

1	stick butter, softened
1	(3-ounce) package cream cheese, softened
1	cup all-purpose flour

Soften the butter and cream cheese. Mix the butter and cream cheese until light and fluffy. Add the flour, blending well. Roll into a ball and wrap in wax paper and chill, for about 1 to 2 hours. Roll out onto a lightly floured surface. I also like to finger pat my pastry into the pie pan in lieu of rolling. Bake until 450-degrees until golden brown.

* I usually double this recipe for my regular use of pie crusts, especially if I want to make a top for my 9-inch pie crust. I love the rich taste that accompanies this crust. It is also wonderful to use for quiches, fried pies, etc.

Pecan Crust

(Makes one 9-inch pie crust)

Wonderful for all types of fillings, especially for Pumpkin Pie, Sweet Potato Pie.

1	cup pecans, chopped fine
2	tablespoons granulated sugar
1¼	cups all-purpose flour
¾	stick salted butter, cold (if you use unsalted, add ½-teaspoon of salt to the crust recipe)
3	tablespoons cold water

In a food processor, grind the pecans and sugar together. Place in a mixing bowl and set aside. Using the processor again, blend flour, butter and salt, (if using unsalted butter), until mixtures resembles corn meal. Add this to the pecan mixture. Add 3 tablespoons ice cold water and mix together until it holds shape. Press dough into the bottom and along the sides of a 9-inch deep dish pie pan, crimping the edges. Prick the crust with the tines of a fork and chill for 30 minutes.

This crust can be made in advance and also can be frozen. Wrap real well if you freeze it. When you are ready to bake the pie, line the inside of the pie crust with foil and fill the foil with rice or dried beans. Bake the crust in the middle of a preheated oven at 425-degrees for 7 minutes. Remove the foil along with the rice or dried beans and discard. Turn the heat down to 350-degrees and bake another 5 minutes more and let it cool.

Orange Vanilla Crust
(Makes one 8-inch pie crust)

1	cup vanilla wafer crumbs
3	tablespoons granulated sugar
2	teaspoon orange peel, grated
¼	cup butter, softened

Combine the sugar and vanilla wafer crumbs in a medium-sized bowl. Mix in the orange peel. Now add the softened butter, mixing well. Using buttered fingers, press the crumb mixture firmly on the bottom and sides of an 8-inch pie pan. Bake at 375-degrees for 8 to 10 minutes. Cool the pie crust before adding the filling of your choice.

Chocolate Cookie Dough Pie Crust
(Makes two 9-inch crusts*)

½	cup butter
1	cup granulated sugar
1	egg
1	teaspoon vanilla extract
1¼	cups all-purpose flour
½	cup cocoa
¾	teaspoon baking soda
¼	teaspoon salt

Cream together the butter and sugar. Add the egg and vanilla extract, beating well. In a separate small bowl, mix the flour, cocoa, baking soda, and salt. Add the flour mixture to the creamed mixture. Mix until a soft cookie dough is formed. Shape the dough into 2 (1½-inch) rolls. Wrap them in wax paper and chill in the fridge for several hours.

*Each roll makes 1 pie crust. When ready to make a pie crust, grease pie pan.
Take out cookie dough and slice into ⅛-inch slices. Arrange the slices of cookie dough with the edges touching on bottom and the sides of the pie pan. Bake at 375-degrees for 8 to 10 minutes. Cool completely before putting filling in the pie crust.

Boiling Water Pie Crust

(Makes two 9-inch pie crusts)

I received this recipe from a wonderful cook about 20 years ago. I have heard over and over that ice water makes the best crust. Well, this recipe is not made with ice water, but with boiling water. It makes the flakiest pie crust ever, but you know why? LARD. Look for lard near the meat counter. It will be in a box or plastic tub.

I know you have tasted pie crust that has tasted pasty. Try this one, it does not. This is a very pliable crust and is easy to roll; I can even talk on the phone and make it at same time, which is wonderful.

¾	cup lard
1	teaspoon salt
¼	cup boiling water
2	cups all-purpose flour, sifted
	Extra sifted flour

Place the lard and salt in a mixing bowl and pour the boiling water over it. Mix with a mixer or fork until creamy. Add the sifted flour, stirring quickly until the dough clings together. Form into a ball and chill in the fridge. Roll dough between 2 sheets of wax paper or on a lightly floured board. (This is where the extra flour comes in.)

If using a top crust, I like to use 1 slightly beaten egg and wash the top crust with the egg and sprinkle with granulated sugar.

If you prefer, you may just use a small amount of evaporated milk to lightly brush on the top crust and then sprinkle with granulated sugar. This procedure promotes even browning on the crust.

For pie shells that are to be filled later with a previously cooked filling; pre-cook the pie crust by pricking the pie crust with the tines of your fork before baking and bake for 15 to 18 minutes at 450-degrees.

Plain Pastry Dough

(Makes one 9-inch pastry shell)

1½	cups all-purpose flour, sifted
½	teaspoon salt
½	cup solid shortening
5	tablespoons ice cold water

Measure sifted flour into a large bowl. Add salt, stirring to blend. Cut in with a pastry blender ¼-cup of the shortening until the mixture looks like coarse meal. Now add the other ¼-cup of the shortening, cutting in this until the mixture looks like little peas. Add the ice cold water, one tablespoon at a time, mixing lightly with a fork. Shape the dough into a ball and roll out onto a lightly floured surface. I like to roll between sheets of wax paper, also lightly floured. Roll the dough at least 1-inch larger than the pie pan. You want enough dough to make fluted decorated edges. Fold the edges over and flute.

If the pie recipe calls for a baked pie shell, prick the shell with fork on the sides and bottom of the pie shell to prevent puffing and shrinking during baking. Bake 475-degrees for 10 minutes. Cool completely before filling with pie filling.

* I just double recipe to make 2 (8 or 9-inch) pie crusts.

Hint

Do you have pierced ears and own several pairs of big clunker earrings? When you place those big clunkers on your ears, do you have a feeling of insecurity that they will slip off or even worse rip your ear lobe? This is the main reason I had to get another piercing in my ear. A sure fire solution is a pencil eraser. Take the eraser off of that pencil. Put the eraser on the back of the earring, as you would the original prong. It will support the heaviest earring you have. Every pencil I own is missing the eraser. Personally, I would rather use the eraser than the backing that comes with the earring.

Something Sweet to Eat

Potholders hand-made by Mama Gillis

I was always asking Mama Gillis if she had something sweet to eat. The answer was not too far from me as I looked on her kitchen table. Here is a little story that comes to mind when I think of candy.

On Saturday mornings at Mama Gillis' house, we could not wait for the grocery bus to arrive. What was the grocery bus? It was a big red truck that had a lot of different items in it and would stop off in the rural areas to sell their wares. All of my tales are just aging me, that's for sure! Well, the grocery bus stopped off at the farm hands house, Jeff and Ira, who I just loved.

I remember that I was so little that I couldn't even reach up to the steps to tell the grocery man what I wanted or to even look inside of the grocery bus. I always wanted to see everything in there. I never got to look in there for it stopped coming to the farm, for whatever reason, before I grew a little taller or got older.

Mama Gillis always said the grocery bus had high prices. Well, to be honest, she said it would "rob you blind." It might have been that way, but we couldn't wait to run down to Jeff and Ira's house to catch it and buy some candy. We would get so upset if we went to Jeff and Ira's house and would find out the grocery bus had already gone. Remember "party lines"? We would try to call Jeff and Ira, but somebody was always on the party line and wouldn't get off. It seemed like an eternity for every Saturday to roll around for the grocery bus to return.

They had different candy that wasn't at the regular store, or that's what I thought. They had B-B-BATS. That was Molasses Peanut Butter Taffy on a stick. They also had Kits, which also was a taffy in different flavors like banana, chocolate, and strawberry. As I have grown up I know the grocery bus had candy that was indeed in the grocery stores, but just because it was the grocery bus, that made the candy different.

Part of Mama Gillis' front yard was a pecan orchard. We would pick up enough pecans for her to use in her cooking, and she would give us a little change to spend on the grocery bus. Sometimes, we would also get our extra money by selling Coca-Cola bottles.

Mama Gillis had a 1953 Blue Dodge Pickup truck and the bed of the truck was loaded up with Coca-Cola bottles. Now, when I say loaded up, I mean loaded up. She probably had $600.00 worth of Coca-Cola bottles in the back of that pick-up truck. Anytime we needed money we would just go get a few bottles and get our deposit at the grocery store and have money to spend. That was a whole lot easier than to pick up those "blame pecans" in the blistering hot sun while swatting gnats and flies.

Wouldn't it be nice to receive a nice tin box of wonderful homemade fudge, Georgia Pecan Pralines, Divinity, and Coconut Macaroons? Have you ever wanted to include your children in the wonderful spirit of giving at Christmas time or any of the Holidays? Valentine's would also be a perfect time of giving a homemade box of candies. Or one day just make a batch for someone, just because. Try anyone of these candy recipes. Go to your local cake/candy supply shop and you will find all kinds of those cute boxes, paper liners and bags that will represent any of the upcoming holidays.

Not only use your imagination and creativity, but also let your children use theirs. Sure it may mess up your kitchen, but what is all of that spray bottle cleaner that you have in the house for? Let the kids help you clean up the mess. They will use these memories to create memories for their children. Just think of all the time you spend shopping at the stores thinking of teacher's gifts, neighbor's gifts, your children's friends' gifts, etc. I have been there, I know.

Making your homemade candies is more economical and let's face it—everyone had better watch their pennies nowadays, but the main reason is the time you are going to spend with your children. This will create more memories worth anything you could purchase at the store.

Oh—I almost forgot to mention that Mama Gillis had a "sugar can," in which of course, she stored her sugar. Most kitchens today have all sorts of beautiful decorated canisters in them. She never had a real canister set that I know of. However, this particular "sugar can" was metal, bright red in color, with a mist of a little rust. I never saw her use anything else for a canister. It also had a white teacup in it to measure. In years that followed, Mama Gillis covered it with layers and layers of adhesive-backed shelf paper.

When that dreaded day came to clean up her estate, we went on a grand hunt for the "sugar can". I meant I had to have it and I still use it today. I have to be there with her in some way, some how.

Boy, do I have a weakness for candy and "glory be," this is also one of my favorite sections. I would float a loan for a piece of homemade fudge. The smell of chocolate fudge cooking in the kitchen is absolutely amazing. When you try some of the different choices I have for you, see which one you like. The following are some of my favorites, which I hope you enjoy.

Buttermilk Fudge

1	cup buttermilk
1	teaspoon soda
2	cups granulated sugar
2	tablespoons light syrup or Karo
1	stick butter
1	cup pecans or walnuts, chopped coarsely

Blend the soda and buttermilk, stirring well. Pour sugar into a large saucepan and add the buttermilk mixture, corn syrup and butter. Bring this mixture to a boil and cook to a soft ball stage or if using the candy thermometer, cook to 234 to 240-degrees. Remove from heat and beat well. Stir in the nuts. Drop by spoonfuls onto buttered wax paper.

Maple Pecan Buttermilk Candy

2	cups granulated sugar
1/4	teaspoon salt
1/2	teaspoon soda
1	cup buttermilk
2	tablespoons butter
1	teaspoon maple flavoring
2	cups pecans, chopped

Combine the sugar, salt, soda, and buttermilk in a large saucepan. Cook on medium heat, stirring often to keep the mixture from boiling over. Cook until the temperature reaches 234 to 240-degrees or a soft ball stage. Remove the pan from heat and add the butter, maple flavoring, and nuts. Have a cookie sheet ready, lined with wax paper. Drop candy by teaspoons. Cool.

Georgia Pecan Pralines

You don't have to go to Louisiana to enjoy Pecan Pralines. Years ago, I went to Savannah, Georgia, and visited the Riverfront Shops. All you could smell on Riverfront was the aroma of pecans, butter and sugar cooking, which adds up to the famous Pecan Pralines. You could go into most every shop and have samples of Pecan Pralines. Needless to say, I went in almost every shop.

I demonstrated Georgia Pecan Pralines on a TV spot before Christmas time, and I forgot to bring the brown sugar. Well, even though I had a finished product for the viewers to look at, I still had to go through the process of demonstrating how to make pralines. There was no time to run to the store and purchase brown sugar and the nearest thing that would look like brown sugar on TV that we found in the studio was coffee. I had a finished product, so no one was the wiser but us. It went off without a hitch. Thank goodness for the cameras in TV land.

1	(1-pound) box light brown sugar
	Pinch of salt
¾	cup evaporated milk
1	tablespoon butter
2	cups pecan halves

Mix sugar, salt, milk and butter in a medium size saucepan. Stir over low heat until sugar is dissolved. Add pecans and cook stirring over medium heat to soft ball stage (234 to 240-degrees). Remove the saucepan from the heat and let cool 5 minutes. Beat, using a wooden spoon, until mixture begins to thicken and it coats the nuts. Using a tablespoon, drop the candy into cup cake papers that are in muffin tins. You may also drop the candy onto a well buttered baking sheet. If the candy becomes stiff to drop into patties, just add a little hot water to the mixture. You can make miniature pralines, by using a teaspoon. Makes approximately 20 candies using the tablespoon and 40 patties using the teaspoon.

Note: Speaking of using coffee on the set in lieu of sugar, check this out using instant coffee for a wonderful flavor with this recipe.

Mocha Cream Pralines

To make a unique tasting confection—try this using the above Georgia Pecan Praline recipe and adding 1½-teaspoons of instant coffee to the sugar, milk, butter mixture and cook as above to make the Mocha Cream Pralines.

Old Time Chocolate Fudge

3	cups granulated sugar
½	cup cocoa
3	tablespoons white corn syrup or Karo
	Pinch of salt
⅔	cup evaporated milk
2	tablespoons butter
1½	teaspoons vanilla
1	cup pecans, chopped

Combine all ingredients, except for the butter, vanilla, and nuts in a medium size saucepan. Cook over medium heat, stirring frequently till mixture forms soft ball stage (234 to 240-degrees.) Remove from heat and add the butter without stirring. Now cool to lukewarm (bottom of pan will be touchable), without stirring. When cooled, add nuts, beating with a wooden spoon till mixture looses its gloss and thickens. Pour into a buttered 9-inch pan.

Note: I use an ole timey metal ice tray to pour my fudge up in, remember those. Grease it real well with butter. I take the dividers out while the candy is "setting up" When the candy has set or is almost firm, push the divider about ⅛-inch into the top of the candy and this will mark the squares of candy into equal portions and you can continue to cut equal portions. It makes a thick piece of candy.

Very Important Note: Do not forget to let your children lick the spoon and scrape the pan.

Kathryn's Blonde Fudge

3	cups granulated sugar
¾	cups evaporated milk
3	tablespoons light corn syrup or Karo
	Dash of salt
3	tablespoons butter
2	teaspoons vanilla extract
1	cup chopped pecans, coarsely chopped

Combine the sugar, milk, syrup, and salt in a heavy saucepan. Cook over medium heat, stirring until sugar dissolves. Reduce your heat to low and boil the ingredients until they reach a soft ball stage (234 to 240-degrees). Take off heat and add butter without stirring. Cool to lukewarm or until bottom of pan is where you can touch it. Now add the vanilla and beat the candy till it loses it gloss and starts to thicken. Stir in the nuts. Pour into a buttered pan.

Note: When I beat the candy, I sometimes fill a large bowl full of ice, put the saucepan on top of the ice bowl and beat with an electric mixer. This does speed up the process, but my preference is to beat the candy with a wooden spoon.

Peanut Butter Fudge

1	cup white sugar
1	cup light brown sugar
1	cup evaporated milk
	Dash of salt
1	cup marshmallows
½	cup creamy peanut butter
2	tablespoons butter
1	teaspoon vanilla

Cook sugars, milk and salt to soft ball stage or the temperature of 234 to 240-degrees. Add the marshmallows, peanut butter and butter, just before removing from the stove. Cool and add vanilla. Beat and pour into a buttered pan.

Top of the Stove Popcorn

I just bet most kids today cannot associate popping popcorn in anything but the microwave. Well, as I said earlier, I do not own a microwave. I just bet this would be a great rainy day fun thing, if you brought out your saucepan and popped the pop corn right on top of the stove. It is fun to see how long it will take to pop the last kernel of popcorn and the kids will like this.

We had a Chihuahua dog one time named "Cha-Cha". Well, I poured a lot of kernels in the boiler or saucepan and the top blew off along with mountains of popcorn floating out of it. Cha-Cha was the only house dog we ever had and boy, did she love popcorn. That day Cha-Cha had a ball tip-toeing all over the floor eating popcorn. There was popcorn rolling all over the stove as well as the counter tops. Now this "ole gal," can do some dillies.

Here is the recipe for the long time ago Traditional Popcorn:
Place a 3-quart aluminum or stainless steel saucepan on the stove. Using high heat, add 1½-tablespoon of vegetable shortening or 3 tablespoons of cooking oil. After the oil or shortening is hot, drop a drop of water in it. If it sizzles, it is ready. Add enough unpopped kernels of corn to cover the bottom of the saucepan. Stir the kernels of corn real fast with a wooden spoon until it starts to pop. Quit stirring. Take the spoon out and now cover the top of the saucepan. Slide the saucepan from side to side of the burner real fast to keep the corn from burning. You will hear lots and lots of popping. After the last kernel has popped, pour it in a large bowl and melt 1 stick of butter on the stove and pour all over the pop corn. Salt to taste. Now, isn't that more fun than popping popcorn in the microwave?

Popcorn Balls

Mama Gillis made these one time, and they were delicious. She made sure that she used real butter to shape them. I can still taste the syrup and butter. We had so much fun!

½	pound popcorn kernels
⅔	cup Karo syrup or light corn syrup
2	cups granulated sugar
⅔	cup boiling water
2	tablespoons vinegar
2	teaspoons cream of tartar
2	tablespoons butter
	Pinch of baking soda
2	teaspoons vanilla extract
	Extra butter

Pop the popcorn. Place the popped corn in a large pan or bowl. Combine the syrup, sugar, water and vinegar in a large, heavy saucepan, mixing well. Heat to boiling and add the cream of tartar. Blend well. Boil this mixture till it reaches to soft crack stage (275 to 290-degrees). If you are using the cold water test, cook the syrup until the threads separate into hard threads making sure they are not brittle. Remove the syrup from the heat and add the 2 tablespoons of butter, pinch of baking soda, and 2 teaspoons of vanilla extract. Mix well. Now the fun part begins! Pour this wonderful syrup over the popcorn. Taking the extra butter and smearing it all over your hands, mix the syrup over the popcorn. It will be warm, so don't burn yourself. Form the balls and lay them on wax paper.

Years ago, I would put food color in the syrup and make colored popcorn balls. You can do this and it is very pretty. The supermarkets now carry the colored plastic wrap. So wrap individual pop corn balls with the colored plastic or just plain clear plastic wrap and tie a pretty bow on it. Wouldn't this make a great gift for your child's friend for Christmas? Your child would love making these. You could even lightly press M & M's on top of the pop corn balls before the syrup sets up. Don't mash the M & M's though. Just lightly press them on top of the balls and then wrap them.

Easy-to-Make Marshmallow Popcorn Balls

½	cup butter
1	(16-ounce) bag marshmallows
3	quarts popped corn

In a heavy saucepan, on low heat, slowly heat the butter and marshmallows. Stir constantly until melted and smooth. Pour mixture over popcorn and mix until well coated. Using buttered hands, form into balls or shapes.

Southern Pecan Logs

This is a true Southern candy. This makes an excellent Christmas gift and its fun to make, too.

1	(7-ounce) jar marshmallow crème
1	(1-pound) box powdered sugar
2	teaspoons vanilla extract
1	bag Kraft caramels, unwrapped
2	tablespoons water
2	quarts pecans, chopped*

In a large bowl, mix the marshmallow crème, sugar and vanilla until all the sugar is worked into the crème. Divide this into three parts. Take each part and roll between your hands into long rolls. Lay this on wax paper and cut into pieces of about 2-inches long. Set aside. Meanwhile, melt the caramels in the top of a double boiler. Add the 2 tablespoons of water to the caramels. Stir. When the caramels are melted and smooth, pour over the rolls and drop the logs into a pan of chopped pecans. Coat each Pecan Log real good with the pecans.

*Place the pecans in a square pan in order to roll the Pecan Logs easily in the pecans.

Mints

By Elaine Ranew-Barrett

If there was ever a great cook, this gal is it. She came from a line of wonderful Southern cooks. She's a natural. We grew up together, and, not only is she a great cook, she's a wonderful mother, and most of all a treasured friend. She gave me this recipe for Mints years and years ago. I love her so much. Thanks, Laine (I have always called her Laine in lieu of Elaine. You know our Southern lingo). This is wonderful to make for weddings, showers, and parties. Just buy those candy molds and make these while you are watching TV. Laine and I made these together for a wedding one night while watching TV. (Who's wedding or which one?)

1   stick butter
1   egg white
1   box powdered sugar, sifted
    Dash of peppermint flavoring
    Food coloring of your choice, (optional)

Mix all ingredients by hand. Color with the food coloring of your choice. Mold in candy molds and let air dry. You can make these ahead of your party and freeze them.

Chocolate Peanut Clusters

2   pounds white chocolate
1   (12-ounce) package semisweet chocolate chips
1   (12-ounce) package milk chocolate chips
1   (24-ounce) jar, unsalted, dry roasted peanuts

Melt all chocolate in a double boiler over low heat, stirring until melted. You can use an electric skillet or microwave as well. Cool for five minutes, stirring the peanuts. Drop candy onto wax paper by tablespoons. Let the candy cool completely. After the candy has completely cooled, you may wrap individually and store in the fridge.

Truffles

Do you remember many years ago there was a candy bar by the name of 7-Up? Well it had seven different candies in one. It was absolutely delicious. Everyday after school, I would ride my bike to the Albany Drug Store and get this candy bar. The Truffle recipe brings this story to mind, for there are so many different variations you can try with it.

1	pound milk chocolate flavored coating, chopped
1	can sweetened condensed milk
½	teaspoon vanilla extract, or if you want different variations, try mint, orange flavoring
1	cup pecans, finely chopped
1⅓	cups flaked coconut

In a double boiler, melt the coating over hot water (130 to 140-degrees). Stir in sweetened condensed milk and flavoring. Add the pecans and coconut. Refrigerate for 30 minutes. After refrigerating, roll into balls.

Mocha Fudge

3	cups granulated sugar
2	tablespoons instant coffee granules
	Dash of salt
2	tablespoons of Karo or light corn syrup
½	cup half-and-half
1	cup evaporated milk
2	tablespoons butter
1	teaspoon vanilla extract

Combine the sugar, coffee granules, salt, corn syrup, half-and-half, and milk in a heavy 2½-quart saucepan. Bring to boil over medium heat stirring constantly. Cook to the soft ball stage of 234 to 240-degrees or until a soft ball is formed when a small amount of syrup is dropped in a cup of cold water. Turn off the stove. Add butter and vanilla. Cool to lukewarm to 110-degrees, without stirring. The bottom of the pan will be touchable. Beat the candy until the syrup becomes thick and its begins to lose it gloss. Pour this into a buttered 8 x 8 x 2-inch pan. Chill until firm. Cut into squares.

Two-Toned Georgia Crackers

1	(18-ounce) jar chunky peanut butter
1	(10-ounce) package of Ritz or Ritz like crackers
2	pounds of milk chocolate flavored coating or you may use the white chocolate coating

Spread peanut butter on 72 crackers and place these on wax paper lined cookie sheet. In a double boiler, melt your chocolate over hot (130 to 140-degrees) water. Keep adding more coating until all is melted. Dip your peanut butter covered cracker into the coating with the peanut butter side up. I use tongs and using them I can scoop the candy coating over the crackers. Lift out with the tongs and shake off the excess coating. Place on the wax paper lined cookie sheet. Refrigerate 15 minutes or until set. I like to make some of the milk chocolate and white chocolate. It's pretty in a tissue lined box for the Holiday giving. Makes 6 dozen.

Ambrosia Candy

2	boxes powdered sugar
1	can sweetened condensed milk
1	stick butter
3	cup nuts, chopped fine
1	can Angel flaked coconut

Mix the sugar, milk and butter. Add the nuts and coconut. Roll the candy into little balls and place onto a buttered cookie sheet and place in the fridge. Just another kind of candy to go into those Christmas tins.

Pecan Brittle

It's a toss up between Pecan and Peanut Brittle. Both are delicious. Being from Southwest Georgia, we could get both kinds of nuts without any problem.

2	cups pecans, chopped coarsely
1½	cups granulated sugar
½	cup water
½	cup Karo syrup or light corn syrup
1	tablespoon butter
½	teaspoon salt
1½	teaspoons soda
	Additional butter or cooking spray to grease candy surface

Have all of your ingredients measured and ready to use before starting this recipe. It is hurry up and wait procedure. Have 2 cookie sheets prepared by greasing generously with butter or cooking spray. Using a heavy saucepan, put sugar, water and syrup in the pan and bring to a rolling boil on medium-high heat. Prepare the surface in which you are going to pour your candy on with lots of butter or cooking spray. Keep testing the syrup mixture until the candy spins a thread. The thread will be about a foot long and will want to fly away from you. Add butter, stir and the pecans. Cook until foam is light brown in color. Continue to keep cooking until the foam rises. When the foam starts to rise, add the salt and soda and remove from the heat. Stir just enough to dissolve the soda. Stirring too much will make the candy too hard. Pour on greased cookie sheets. Using a large spoon, spread candy. Use a fork to lift from the sides and pull out and work towards the center to thin the candy out. Break in small pieces.

Peanut Brittle

As with the Pecan Brittle, you need to have all ingredients handy before you cook. Grease 2 cookie sheets generously with butter or cooking spray. Prepare your 2 cookies sheets by greasing real well with butter or spraying with baking spray. My preference is the butter, for the candy will have a slight buttery taste on the bottom.

2	cups granulated sugar
1	cup light corn syrup or Karo
½	cup water
1	cup butter
2	cups raw peanuts, chopped coarsely
1	teaspoon baking soda

Combine in a heavy 3-quart saucepan sugar, corn syrup, and water. Heat on medium-high heat stirring until all sugar dissolves. When the syrup starts to boil, blend in the butter. Stir often after the temperature reaches 230-degrees. Add the peanuts when the temperature reaches 280-degrees. Stir this mixture constantly until the temperature reaches 305-degrees, which is the hard-crack stage. Remove from the heat and quickly stir in the baking soda, mixing well. Pour the mixture onto the buttered cookie sheets. Loosen the candy from the cookie sheets when it is cool. Break into pieces.

Yields: 2½-pounds

Peter Pan's Cornflake Candy

1	cup granulated sugar
1	cup light corn syrup or Karo syrup
1	(12-ounce) jar creamy peanut butter
6	cups cornflakes

In a heavy boiler or saucepan, combine the sugar and corn syrup. Bring this to a boil and boil for 1 minute. Remove from the heat and stir in the jar of peanut butter. Beat until smooth. Add the corn flakes and stir until they are well coated. Roll into balls or drop by teaspoons on wax paper. This mixture will harden as it cools.

Divinity

My mother use to make the best Divinity. Let me rephrase that statement, before I get into big trouble. She still does make great Divinity, but since I have been up here in snow country, I haven't had any. My Daddy could eat his weight in it. Here is a recipe that I hope you enjoy. It's best to make this on a pretty day.

2	cups granulated sugar
½	cup light corn syrup or Karo
½	cup boiling water
2	egg whites, beaten stiff peaks with a pinch of salt
1	cup pecans, chopped

In a heavy saucepan, boil the sugar, corn syrup and water, mixing well. Cook over medium heat to 250-degrees or a hard ball. A hard ball is formed when a small amount of candy is dropped in cold water. Remove from the heat. Have your egg whites already beaten with the pinch of salt added, until they hold stiff peaks. Slowly, pour the hot syrup into the beaten egg whites. Beat until the candy stiffens. Fold in the nuts and drop on wax paper lined on a cookie sheet.

Butterscotch Haystacks

1	(6-ounce) package butterscotch morsels
2	teaspoons cooking oil
1	(3-ounce) can chow mein noodles
2	cups miniature marshmallows

Melt the butterscotch morsels in a double boiler. Stir in the cooking oil. In a large bowl mix the chow mein noodles and marshmallows. Pour the butterscotch mixture over the marshmallows and noodles. Mix with a fork. Using a teaspoon drop on wax paper. Chill at least 2 hours before serving.

Yields: 30 pieces

Rocky Road Candy

½	cup granulated sugar
½	cup evaporated milk
1	tablespoon light corn syrup or Karo
1	(12-ounce) package milk chocolate chips
1	cup miniature marshmallows
1	cup pecans, chopped coarsely

In a 2-quart saucepan, combine the sugar, milk, and light corn syrup. Bring to a boil over medium heat, stirring constantly. Boil for two minutes and remove from the heat. Add the chocolate chips, stirring until melted. Cool mixture until lukewarm (bottom of pan will be where you can touch). Stir in the marshmallows and nuts. You do not want the marshmallows to melt. Refrigerate uncovered for about 1 hour or until the mixture is firm. Drop the candy into small mounds onto wax paper. Let candy dry.

Yields: 35 pieces

Candied Apples

A recipe way older than me—not telling how old, though! Spend a little time preparing these and you will reap the awards!

10-12	tart red apples, washed, dried and blemished free
	Wooden sticks
2	cups granulated sugar
½	cup light corn syrup or Karo
¾	cup water
4	drops red food coloring or more
3	drops oil of cinnamon

(available at most cake supply stores or drug stores)

After washing and drying apples, remove the stem and insert a wooden stick. Set apples aside. Well grease a baking sheet with lots of butter. Combine the sugar, corn syrup, and water in the top of a double boiler. Place over low heat, stirring constantly until sugar is dissolved and the boiling starts. Stop stirring the syrup after it boils. Keep the sugar crystals from forming by wiping the sides of the saucepan with a fork that is wrapped with a thin cloth or with cheesecloth. Boil until the sugar syrup reaches 300-degrees. Remove immediately from the heat and plunge the pan into a bowl of ice cold water. I fill my sink with lots and lots of ice cubes and add water in the sink. Then you are ready for the big plunge. This stops the syrup from boiling. Then put the pan back over the hot water to keep it from hardening. Stir in the food coloring and oil of cinnamon. Blend thoroughly with wooden spoon. This recipe makes enough syrup for 10 to 12 apples. Start dipping apples immediately in the syrup. Twirl the apples slowly to coat evenly. Place the apples on the well-greased baking sheet, with the apple stick up.

Breakfast

Sketch by Ruthie Gillis

Even though this section indicates Breakfast Foods, most of these foods you could have at any meal. I don't know about you, but I love to have breakfast at night time.

I have always been a breakfast person. You either like to eat breakfast or you don't. Breakfast provides a huge kick-start in the day.

We always ate breakfast at Mama Gillis'. I'm sharing with you a couple of Grits stories later on in this chapter.

In addition to having Grits every morning, Mama Gillis would fix us cinnamon toast. Papa would always have his cornflakes or ham and red-eyed gravy with Hoecakes or biscuits. We would all drink Postum in the morning, which we loved. I still drink it sometimes. Papa would pour his Postum in a bowl to cool it and then drink it out of the bowl.

Postum is a hot beverage made with wheat and molasses and has a coffee taste. A whole lot of people have told me they have never heard of it. Well, just look on the counters at the grocery stores in the coffee section and you will find it. Delicious and nutritious. Great for kids when they want to be like adults and drink coffee.

Buttermilk Pancakes

1	egg
1¼	cups buttermilk
2	tablespoons oil
1¼	cup all-purpose flour
1	teaspoon sugar
1	teaspoon baking powder
½	teaspoon salt
½	teaspoon baking soda
¼	cup drained blueberries, optional
	Butter

Beat egg and add the buttermilk and oil. Sift together the dry ingredients and stir into the wet ingredients. Stir just until moistened. If you choose blueberry pancakes, fold them at this point in the batter. Heat your skillet or griddle. I use pats of butter. Do not let your butter burn or your pancakes will taste burnt. Heat your butter just until the butter starts to sizzle. Pour batter onto hot griddle at small amounts at a time. When bubbles appear around the edges, its time to flip the pancake. Cook the other side until golden brown. This recipe makes for 4 people. You may want to double this recipe.

Homemade Waffles

2¼	cups all-purpose flour
4½	teaspoons baking powder
¼	teaspoon salt
3	tablespoons sugar
3	eggs, separated
2½	cups milk
4	tablespoons butter, melted
4	tablespoons butter, melted (additional)

Preheat waffle iron while preparing waffle batter. In a large mixing bowl, combine flour, baking powder, salt, and sugar. Set aside. In a deep medium-sized bowl, beat the egg whites until stiff and set aside. Beat the egg yolks till frothy, adding milk and butter, blending well. Now add the flour mixture all at once and stir just enough to blend. Fold in the egg whites. Using the additional melted butter, brush onto waffle iron and cook waffles according to manufacturer's directions. Top waffles with confectioners' sugar or syrup. Check the Topping section for the Blueberry Topping and the Apple Dapple Topping.

Blueberry Waffles:
If you desire blueberry waffles, fold 1 cup of fresh blueberries into batter.

Ham and Cheese Quiche

For the Pie Crust:
- 1 (9-inch) pie crust or I like to make my own pie crust. I like to use the Cream Cheese pie crust especially with this recipe. Very rich.
- 1 stick butter, softened
- 1 (3-ounce) cream cheese, softened
- 1 cup all-purpose flour

Mix these 3 ingredients together. Chill for 1 hour. Using a little more flour to powder your hands; press the pie crust into the pie plate. Prick the sides and bottom of the crust with the tines of a fork. Now bake the crust in a 400-degree oven for 5 minutes. Set aside.

For the Ham and Cheese Quiche:
- 2 tablespoons all-purpose flour
- 1 cup sharp cheese, grated
  (Jalapeño Cheese would be excellent in this recipe.)
- 1 cup cooked ham, chopped
- ¼ cup onion, chopped
- ¼ cup green pepper, chopped (optional) or use ¼-cup red pepper, chopped (optional)
- 3 eggs, beaten
- 1 cup half-and-half cream
- Pinch of salt
- ½ teaspoon dry mustard
- Dash of cayenne pepper
- Dash of nutmeg

Combine the flour and cheese, sprinkling in the bottom of the pie shell. Now add the ham, onions, and peppers. Combine the eggs and half-and-half. Add the salt, mustard, cayenne pepper, and nutmeg to this mixture. Now pour gently in the pie shell. Bake at 350-degrees for 45 minutes or until the pie is set. To test, stick a knife in the middle of the pie. If it comes clean, it is done.

Rudolph's Breakfast Casserole

This is ideal to prepare the Night Before Christmas and pop in the stove Christmas morning while the kids are seeing what Santa brought them.

2	pounds your favorite sausage, mild or hot
½	cup onion, chopped
2	cups seasoned croutons
2	cups sharp cheese, shredded
1	(4-ounce) can mushroom pieces, drained (optional)
6	eggs
2½	cups whole milk (divided use)
½	teaspoon salt
½	teaspoon black pepper
	Pinch of cayenne pepper or dash of hot sauce
½	teaspoon dry mustard
1	can cream of mushroom soup
	(reserving soup to be used the next morning)
	Paprika to sprinkle

Grease a 9 x 13-inch baking dish. Brown the sausage with the onions. Drain grease. Set aside. Place the croutons in the baking dish. Sprinkle cheese and mushrooms on top of the croutons. Now spread the cooked sausage and onions over the cheese. Beat the eggs with 2 cups of milk, leaving the other ½-cup of milk for later use. Add seasonings to the milk, reserving the paprika. Pour the milk and egg mixture over the sausage. Cover and put in the fridge overnight.

The next morning preheat the oven to 325-degrees. Mix the remaining ½-cup milk and the cream of mushroom soup and pour over the top of the casserole. Sprinkle with paprika. Bake for 1 hour.

Baked French Toast

This also would be great to prepare The Night Before Christmas and pop in the oven Christmas morning.

If you are at the grocery store and see French bread on special—this is the time to pick up a couple of loaves. Sometimes you see them for as little as a buck a loaf. Use one loaf for this recipe and freeze the other loaf for future use.

Prepare this the night before serving. Easy as pie.

1	(1-pound) loaf of French bread, cut into 1-inch slices
8	eggs
2	cups whole milk
2	cups half-and-half or evaporated milk
½	teaspoon nutmeg
¼	teaspoon mace
1	teaspoon cinnamon
2	teaspoons vanilla extract or butternut flavoring
½	cup raisins, optional
1	cup butter, softened
1½	cups brown sugar, firmly packed
1½	cups pecans, chopped
3	tablespoons maple syrup or dark corn syrup

Grease a 9 x 13-inch baking pan. Arrange the bread slices in the baking dish. Using your blender, mix the eggs, milk, spices, and flavorings. If you do not have a blender, use your hand mixer. Blend the ingredients until smooth. Pour this mixture over the bread, mashing the bread down with a spoon or spatula to soak the bread real good. Sprinkle the raisins over the bread. Cover the baking dish and chill overnight.

The next morning, preheat your oven to 350-degrees. In a medium sized bowl, mix the butter, brown sugar, pecans and syrup. Mix well. Sprinkle this mixture on top of the bread and bake for 50 to 60 minutes.

Grits

When you go to a seafood restaurant in the South, you can just bet they will have Cheese Grits on the menu. If your child loves Mac 'N' Cheese, they will love Cheese Grits.

I like to serve this recipe with Beef Brisket as well as Fried Fish. But let's not forget this is for breakfast, too.

I have a story about the grits. We ate grits every morning at Mama Gillis' house. I ate my grits on a white platter. Mama Gillis would put a wad of butter in the center of the hot grits. I would take a spoon and go around the edge of my grits to eat them (because they were cooler around the edge) until I reached the middle of the grits. The wad of butter had melted somewhat, but the most of the center of the grits was oozing with that big slab of butter. That was the best part. To this day, I still eat my grits on that same platter.

Another grits story I want to share with you. My mother went to the hospital to have my baby sister. Well, my daddy cooked breakfast for us one of those mornings and naturally, it was grits, but they were grey in color.

I asked my sister why they looked gray and she told me they were scorched. Now this was the dramatic sister I told you about in an earlier story.

Well, with a lot of butter added, we still ate them. Bless his heart, at least he tried.

There is nothing better than a big, thick slab of Fried Ham, Grits and Red-Eyed gravy.

Look in the Sauces and Gravy section for the recipe of Red-Eyed Gravy and don't pour out that left-over coffee in the coffee pot. You will need it to make the Red-Eyed Gravy.

Cheese Grits

I made this recipe for Home Economics years ago during one of our demonstrations. Back then, I did not use the green chilies or even the Jalapeño cheese; I just used more hot sauce.

If you want to make this the day before, you may, and the flavors will blend together.

4	cups boiling water
½	teaspoon salt
1	cup grits, quick cooking type
2	cups sharp cheese, shredded
½	cup butter
½	cup evaporated milk
1	clove garlic, minced
	Dashes of Hot sauce to taste *or*
	Cayenne pepper to taste *(Personally, I like to use the Cayenne Pepper in lieu of the Hot Sauce, no vinegar taste)*
2	eggs, beaten
	Paprika to sprinkle

Preheat oven to 325-degrees. Grease a 2-quart casserole dish very well with butter. Bring the water and salt to a boil, add the grits gradually while stirring. It's very important to add the grits gradually into the boiling water; if you add them all at one time, you will have lumpy grits. Boil until thick according to package directions, about 5 minutes, stirring frequently. Add the cheese, butter, milk, garlic and hot sauce or cayenne pepper to taste. Stir until the cheese and butter are melted. Add the beaten eggs. Be sure to temper your eggs when you add them to this mixture. Tempering your eggs will prevent them from being scrambled in the process with the hot liquid. To temper the eggs, just stir in a small amount of hot grits mixture to the beaten eggs and then stir that mixture into the remaining grits. Pour into the greased baking dish, sprinkling with paprika, and bake 1 hour.

Breakfast Scramble

1	cup fully cooked ham, diced
3	green onions, sliced tops and all
2	tablespoons red bell pepper
¼	cup tomatoes, chopped
¼	cup zucchini, sliced
¼	cup butter, melted
8	eggs
¼	teaspoon salt
¼	teaspoon pepper
½	teaspoon dried dill
2	cups Swiss cheese or your favorite brand, shredded

In a non-stick skillet, sauté ham, green onions, red bell pepper, tomatoes, and zucchini in butter about 3 minutes or until the vegetables are just barely tender. Crack eggs into the skillet on top of the vegetables. Add the salt, pepper, and dried dill. Cook on low heat, without stirring, until the mixture just starts to set on the bottom and sides. Lift and fold the cooked eggs, so that the uncooked portion will flow to the bottom of the pan and it will cook. Try not to break open the yolks until almost completely cooked. Add the cheese and continue to cook 5 to 8 minutes or until the eggs are set but still moist. Remove from the heat and serve immediately. Do not cook too long for you do not want a dry product.

Hot Ham Brunch Casserole

Here is another recipe to use up the leftovers from that Easter Ham or use this for your Christmas morning Brunch.

2	cups ham, cooked and chopped
½	cup celery, chopped
½	cup green or red bell pepper, chopped
1	onion, chopped
¼	cup mayonnaise or salad dressing
	Salt and pepper to taste
4	slices bread
3	eggs, beaten
1	cup evaporated milk
1	cup beef or chicken stock
1	can cream of mushroom soup or cream of celery soup

Prepare this recipe the night before and refrigerate. Combine the first six ingredients and set aside the ham mixture. Grease an 8-inch square baking dish. Place the 4 slices of bread in the bottom of the baking dish. Pour the ham mixture over the bread. Combine the eggs, evaporated milk, and stock. Pour this mixture over the casserole. (Save the soup for the last step in the morning.) Cover and refrigerate overnight. The next morning, before baking, pour the soup on the top of the casserole. Bake at 400-degrees for one hour or until set.

Sausage and Hash Brown Casserole

2	pounds sausage, cooked and drained, hot or mild
1	(16-ounce) container sour cream
1	package dry onion mix
2	cups sharp or Cheddar cheese, shredded
1	can cream of chicken soup, undiluted*
1	cup onions, chopped
¼	cup red bell peppers, chopped
¼	cup green bell peppers, chopped
1	(30-ounce) bag hash brown potatoes, thawed
	Salt and pepper to taste
	Paprika to sprinkle

Cook and drain sausage. Set aside. In a small bowl, mix the sour cream and dry onion soup mixing together, setting aside to let the flavors blend. In a large bowl, mix the cheese, soup, sour cream mixture, onions, bell peppers, salt, and pepper together. Fold in the whole bag of the hash brown potatoes in this mixture. Layer this in a 9 x 13-inch baking dish starting with the hash brown mixture, then cooked sausage, hash brown mixture and finally the other half of the sausage. Sprinkle with paprika. Bake 1 hour at 350-degrees.

*You may use either Cream of Potato, Cream of Mushroom, or Cream of Celery soup

Hint

If you have a messy casserole dish that has baked on food and you need to get the crud off before you put it in the dishwasher, here's how. Just put liquid dishwashing detergent in the pan and sprinkle generously with baking soda. Fill the dish with water and let soak for about 15 minutes. The crud will come out with little or no scrubbing.

Meats, Main Dishes, Skillets & Casseroles

I am probably the only person in the world that doesn't own a microwave. I don't want one. But I will tell you the kitchen appliance that I could not do without, and that's an electric skillet. You can't get any better than a meal that cooks itself, and that meal is with a skillet. In this section you will find recipes that are perfect for a skillet.

Southern Baked Pork Loin
With
Sausage Stuffing and Mushroom Sauce

Pork Loin is another very economical way to serve your family great meals. It is a meat that you can dress up or dress down. It has absolutely no waste, for you can freeze the leftovers. When I see a Pork Loin in the store on sale, I never pass it up. You will find them wrapped two in a package, or packaged as one whole Pork Loin. If you can't use the entire Pork Loin, cut it in half and freeze the other half. Prepare a 1 (4-pound) Pork Loin, if you need a smaller amount.

2	(4-pound) boneless pork loins, center cut
1	teaspoon salt
1	teaspoon black pepper
4	cloves garlic, cut into slivers
	Heavy kitchen string (save for the stuffing)

In order to prepare the roasts for stuffing, you will need to butterfly them. This is a very simple method. Simply turn the roast fat-side down. Make a single lengthwise cut down the center of the loin, cutting within ½-inch of the other side. Spread the loin sides open. Pound both sides of the loin with a meat mallet to 1-inch thickness. Make tiny slits in both halves of the loin and insert the tiny slivers of garlic into them. Season with salt and pepper.

Yields: 12 servings

Sausage Stuffing:
This stuffing recipe is enough to stuff 2 (4-pound) pork loins.

8	fresh bread slices, wheat or white, whatever you have on hand
1	(1-pound) roll of your favorite brand of sausage
1	onion, finely chopped
2	celery stalks, finely chopped (Grind onion and celery together in food processor together)
1	cup chicken broth
1	cup apple juice (Save this for pouring in the bottom of the roasting pan)
1	cooking apple, diced (Do not peel)
1	chicken bouillon cube
1	teaspoon poultry seasoning
½	cup pecans, chopped
1	cup butter, melted

Cut bread into cubes, crust and all, and set aside. Cook the sausage in a skillet along with the celery and onions. Cook until there is no pink in color. Drain and discard the grease. Remove from the heat and stir in the bread, bouillon cube, broth, apple, poultry seasoning, pecans, and butter. Spoon 2 cups of the sausage stuffing on the bottom half of each pork loin and tie with a kitchen string at 4-inch intervals. Place the roasts in the roasting pan and sprinkle any leftover stuffing on top of the roasts. Pour apple juice in the bottom of the pan. Bake covered at 325-degrees for 2½ to 3 hours or until the internal temperature reaches at least 170-degrees. Ovens vary. The last 30 to 45 minutes of the cooking time, bake with the cover off of the roaster so that the roast will brown nicely. Take out of the oven and let the meat sit in the pan for 15 minutes to rest before slicing. This lets the juices seep back into the meat.

Mushroom Sauce:

1	stick butter
2	(8-ounce) packages fresh mushrooms, sliced
1	onion, finely chopped
2	cloves garlic, minced
½	teaspoon salt
1	cup white wine
½	cup Baked Pork Loin drippings

Melt the butter in a skillet on medium heat, adding the mushrooms, onions, and garlic. Sauté until tender, adding the salt, wine and pan drippings. Cook about 10 minutes and serve over the Southern Baked Pork Loin Roast.

Stuffed Pork Chops with Apple

Have you ever sat at your desk at work and wondered, "What can I fix for supper that would be a little different, yet tasty and quick?" Impress your husband during the week with this.

Most everyone has a couple of apples in their fruit bowl that they need to hurry up and use. This recipe serves both purposes.

8	(1-inch thick) pork chops*
4	tablespoons butter
1	cup apples, chopped (about 3 medium sized) you do not have to peel them.
2	tablespoons Worcestershire sauce
1	cup onions, chopped
1	cup celery, chopped real fine
¼	cup raisins, optional
	Salt and pepper to taste or you may use seasoning salt
1	egg, beaten
1	cup soft bread crumbs
½	cup apple jelly
	Salt and pepper to season

Stuffing part:
Melt butter in a large skillet or fry pan, adding the apples, Worcestershire sauce, onions, celery, and raisins. Season to taste with salt and pepper. Sauté these ingredients until the onions are tender. Remove from the heat and set aside while preparing the stuffing. In a small bowl, beat the egg and bread crumbs and mix together with the sautéed ingredients. Take each pork chop, season with salt and pepper, and cut a large incision, making a pocket in the side of each pork chop. Stuff 2 tablespoons of the sautéed mixture in each pocket. Place the pork chops in a greased baking dish. Cover with tin foil. Bake at 375-degrees for 1 hour. Melt the apple jelly in a small pan. After the pork chops finish cooking, brush the apple jelly over the pork chops. Put the pork chops back into the oven and bake without the tin foil on them for 15 to 20 minutes more.

*You could have the butcher make the incision or pocket in the chops for you.

This meal would be great with the traditional Green Bean Casserole.

Pork Chop Skillet Supreme

4	pork chops (½-inch) thick
2	tablespoons bacon grease or shortening
¼	teaspoon salt
¼	teaspoon pepper
¼	teaspoon paprika
¾	cup water
1	envelope dried onion soup mix
½	cup celery, chopped
1	(4-ounce) can mushrooms, chopped
¼	cup all-purpose flour
⅔	cup evaporated milk
¼	cup sour cream
3	cups cooked rice **or**
3	cups cooked egg noodles

Melt 2 tablespoons of bacon grease or shortening in a skillet on medium-high heat. This can be an electric skillet or cast iron skillet. While melting the grease or shortening, season the pork chops with the salt, pepper, and paprika. Brown the pork chops on both sides. Drain the grease, leaving about 2 tablespoons of the drippings behind in the skillet. Stir in the water, dried onion soup mix, and celery and cook over medium low heat for 30 minutes, until the pork chops are tender. Take the pork chops out of the skillet and set aside. Stir in the flour and evaporated milk into the liquid in the skillet. Add mushrooms and sour cream. Stir well. Now add the pork chops back into the skillet and simmer on low heat. Serve hot with cooked egg noodles or rice.

Pork, Cabbage and Apple Skillet

1	pound your favorite brand mild sausage
4	cups cabbage, shredded
¼	cup apple cider vinegar
¼	cup light brown sugar, firmly packed
1	teaspoon dried thyme
2	cooking apples, unpeeled and cut into wedges

Cook sausage in a large skillet until sausage is brown and there is no pink. Drain the drippings and discard. Add the cabbage to the skillet. Combine vinegar, brown sugar, and thyme and pour over the cabbage. Cover and cook for 5 to 8 minutes on medium heat. Add the apples and cover, cooking for an additional 5 minutes or until apples are tender.

Pork Chop and Spanish Rice Dish

6	shoulder pork chops
	Salt and pepper to season
2	medium bell peppers, seeded and cut into 6 (½-inch) rings with each pepper
	Garlic salt to taste, optional
1½	cups rice, uncooked
2	(8-ounce) cans tomato sauce
1	cup water
½	cup onion, chopped
1½	teaspoons salt (additional)
¼	teaspoon pepper (additional)

Sprinkle the pork chops with salt and pepper. Place the pork chops in a single layer in a 13 x 9 x 2-inch baking dish and then place the sliced bell pepper rings on top of the chops. Spoon the rice into, and all around, the bell pepper rings. Chop any other remaining pieces of the bell pepper and combine it with the tomato sauce, water, onion, 1½-teaspoons salt and ¼-teaspoon pepper. Pour this mixture over the pork chops and the rice. Cover tightly with foil and bake for 2 hours until the rice is tender. While cooking, baste a couple of times with the tomato sauce mixture.

Yields: 6 servings

Meat Balls with Dill Sour Cream Gravy

This recipe features pork as well as beef. The sauce, with a hint of dill, is delicious.

1	egg, beaten
1	pound ground pork
1	pound ground chuck or round
2	tablespoons grated onion
½	cup dry bread crumbs
2	teaspoons salt
¼	teaspoon pepper
2	teaspoons Worcestershire sauce
½	teaspoon marjoram
¼	cup water

Combine all of the ingredients in a large bowl, mixing well. Refrigerate several hours or overnight for the flavors to blend. Form into 1-inch meatballs, frying them in a heavy skillet in hot grease. Drain. Make Sour Cream Dill Gravy and pour over the meatballs.

Yields: 25 meatballs

Sour Cream Dill Gravy

You may use the same skillet in which you cooked the meatballs or use a medium-sized saucepan. If using the skillet, drain off the grease.

⅓	cup butter
⅓	cup all-purpose flour
1¼	cups water
2½	cups sour cream
¾	teaspoon dill seed or to taste

Melt the butter and blend in the flour. Add the rest of the ingredients, stirring constantly. Cook until gravy thickens and boils. Simmer for 5 minutes. Season to taste. Pour the hot gravy over the meatballs, or if you are using the skillet, just put the meatballs back into the skillet and reheat the meatballs back up with the gravy.

Yields: 1-quart

Beef Stew in a Skillet

⅓	cup all-purpose flour
½	teaspoon pepper
1	teaspoon salt
2	pounds boned chuck or bottom round, cut into 1½-inch cubes
¼	cup bacon grease or olive oil
½	cup onion, chopped
1	clove garlic, minced
	Additional 1 teaspoon salt
2	(10.5-ounce) cans beef broth*
1	package small carrots
5	medium potatoes, peeled and quartered
12	fresh mushroom caps
1	bay leaf
1	teaspoon dried parsley flakes
	Hot cooked rice or hot buttered noodles

Combine the flour, pepper, and 1 teaspoon of salt. Add meat cubes and toss them with flour until they are well coated. If there is any leftover flour, save it for later on in the recipe. Preheat skillet to 375-degrees. Melt grease or put olive oil in the skillet, and brown the meat on all sides. Turn the skillet down to 250-degrees. Stir in the chopped onion and garlic with the other teaspoon of salt and the reserved flour. Slowly stir in the broth. Bring to a boil and simmer with the vent closed for about 1 hour or until the beef cubes are tender. Add the vegetables and mushrooms and simmer another 45 minutes or until tender. Add the bay leaf and the dried parsley flakes. Add additional water, if necessary.

* If you do not have beef broth, substitute 4 bouillon cubes with 2½-cups of water. The bouillon cubes will dissolve in the hot skillet.

Serve with hot cooked rice or hot buttered noodles.

Beefy Noodle Supper Dish

1	pound ground chuck or ground round
½	cup onion, chopped
½	cup celery, chopped fine
1	can cream of mushroom soup
½	cup milk
½	teaspoon salt
	Dash of pepper
2	cups noodles, cooked and drained
2	cups sharp cheese, grated
	Bread crumbs

Preheat oven to 350-degrees. Brown meat and drain. Add onion and celery and cook until tender. Stir in soup, milk, and seasonings. Grease a 2½-quart casserole dish and start with a layer of noodles, meat mixture, and cheese. Repeat this sequence—noodles, meat mixture, and cheese. Top with the remaining cheese and bread crumbs. Bake for 20 to 30 minutes until cheese is melted.

Hamburger and Onion Pie

This is a quick after-school suppertime meal.

2	large Vidalia onions, sliced
1½	pounds ground chuck or ground round
1	tablespoon vegetable oil or bacon grease
1	teaspoon garlic, minced
1	teaspoon salt
¼	teaspoon pepper
1	(6-ounce) can tomato paste
2	cans vegetable beef soup, undiluted
2	cans refrigerated can biscuits

Brown the onion and ground beef in the bacon grease or oil. Add the garlic, salt and pepper in the skillet with the beef and onions. Drain the excess grease. Now add the tomato paste and the vegetable soup and mix well. Pour mixture into a baking dish and arrange the uncooked biscuits on top. Bake at 450-degrees for 15 minutes or until biscuits are done.

Beef Stroganoff

1	pound sirloin steak, ½-inch thick
¼	cup butter or bacon grease
½	cup onion, grated
¾	pound mushrooms, sliced
¼	cup all-purpose flour
1	teaspoon salt
¼	teaspoon pepper
¼	teaspoon dry mustard
½	teaspoon basil
1	tablespoon Worcestershire sauce
2	beef bouillon cubes
¼	cup burgundy wine
1	cup sour cream
½	teaspoon paprika
	Water
	Cooked noodles or rice

Pound the meat with a mallet until thin. Cut into 1-inch wide strips about 3-inches long. Melt grease or butter in a skillet and sauté the onions until clear and the mushrooms are tender. Remove the onions and mushrooms and set aside. Combine the flour with the salt, pepper, dry mustard, and basil. Toss the sirloin strips with the seasoned flour, and brown them in the pan that you used to cook the onions and mushrooms. Add enough water to make 1¼-cups of liquid. Add Worcestershire sauce, beef bouillon cubes, onions, and mushrooms to your liquid. Now add the burgundy wine. Stir mixture until well-mixed on medium heat. Cover and simmer until the meat is tender, about 30 to 45 minutes. Stir in the sour cream. Sprinkle with paprika. Do not boil. Serve with cooked noodles, hot cooked rice, or toast points.

Don's Grilled Eye Round Roast

Don was a great cook even though his last name was Cook. I had never known anyone to grill an Eye Round Roast until I met Don. It is tender enough to cut the finished roast into thin slices. If your husband likes to grill, this recipe will be for him. The flavor is awesome.

1	(2-3 pound) Eye Round Roast
1	small clove of garlic, cut into slivers

Make little slits in the roast and insert tiny slivers of garlic in the slits of the roast. Prepare the marinade ingredients the night before you plan to grill.

Marinade ingredients:
- ½ cup Worcestershire sauce
- ⅛ cup olive oil
- 1 teaspoon meat tenderizer (with No MSG)
- ½ teaspoon garlic powder
- 1 tablespoon parsley flakes
- 1 teaspoon black pepper
- 1 (1 or 2-gallon) zip-top bag (Now that they have come out with the 2-gallon size, I buy that size. I like to have plenty of room for my marinade ingredients as well as my meat.)
- 1 bag hickory chips
- Charcoal

Place all marinade ingredients in a zip-top bag. Place the roast in the bag along with the marinade and put in the fridge overnight. When ready to grill, have the meat at room temperature. Place charcoal on one side of grill, light the charcoal and let the coals ash over. While the coals are ashing over, place 3 cups of hickory chips in a large bowl with about 2 inches of water above the chips. Let the chips soak for about 30 minutes. After the coals have ashed over, place 1 cup of the soaked hickory chips on top of the coals. Using an aluminum foil 9 x 13-inch aluminum foil pan, lay the roast and cook over indirect heat. Do not cover the roast with tin foil. Midway through the cooking process, turn the roast so that it will be smoked on the bottom half. Also, baste with juices collected in the pan. After another hour of cooking, place another cup of soaked chips over the coals. Do this procedure one more time after an hour. Cook approximately a total of 4 hours. Cut into thin slices and enjoy.

Corned Beef and Cabbage Dinner

4-5	pounds corned beef brisket
1	tablespoon mixed pickling spice
1	medium onion, cut into half
1	medium cabbage, cut into wedges

Wipe the corned beef down with paper towels. Place in a large Dutch oven or pot and cover with cold water. Add all of the ingredients except for the cabbage. Bring to a boil and simmer about 10 minutes. Skim off the top. Cover and cook until tender, about 3 to 4 hours. Add the cabbage the last 20 minutes of cooking time. Remove the corned beef and cabbage and place on a serving platter. Slice the corned beef across the grain of the meat.

Note: With what's left of the corned beef, I make Reuben sandwiches!

Chuck Wagon Dinner

1	pound ground chuck or round
1	small onion, chopped
¼	cup celery, chopped fine
1	medium-sized green pepper, seeded and chopped
1	(16-ounce) can tomatoes*
1	(13-ounce) can French onion soup, undiluted
1	(10.75-ounce) can cream of mushroom soup, undiluted
1	cup long grain rice, uncooked
1	teaspoon chili powder
	Dash of hot sauce
1	cup Cheddar cheese, shredded

Brown ground chuck or round with onion, celery, and green pepper. Drain. Add the remaining ingredients, except for the cheese, mixing well. Pour into a lightly greased 13 x 9 x 2-inch baking dish. Cover with foil and bake for 1 hour at 350-degrees. Remove the foil and top with the cheese. Bake an additional 5-10 minutes or until cheese melts.

* 1 (16-ounce) can stewed tomatoes with celery and peppers can be substituted and is just as good.

Yields: 4 to 6 servings

Elegant Prime Rib Roast

1	(5-6-pound) prime rib roast
2	cloves garlic, cut into slivers
1	teaspoon salt
½	teaspoon pepper
1	tablespoon paprika
¾	cup all-purpose flour

Preheat oven to 325-degrees. Prepare roast by making several gashes in the roast to insert the garlic slivers. Combine the salt, pepper, paprika and flour. Rub the roast fat-side up with this mixture, place it (fat-side up) in the roasting pan uncovered, and bake. Roast till desired preference of doneness. Insert the meat thermometer into the thickest part of the meat.

Rare – 140-degrees on meat thermometer –
    Roast 1 hour and 20 minutes or 15 minutes per pound.
Medium – 160-degrees - 20 minutes per pound
Well done – 170-degrees - 25 minutes per pound

After cooking, allow the roast to stand 10-15 minutes before carving, so the juices can redistribute themselves. I like to serve Roasted Potatoes with this recipe. Look in the Side section for Roasted Potatoes.

The Divine Dixie Deva displays her Elegant Prime Rib Roast

Stuffed Cabbage Rolls

This recipe was demonstrated on a local television show called, "The Rozell Show," back in the 60s'. "Rozell" was a local TV celebrity that was featured in Columbus, Georgia, and she always had someone cooking on the set. I was just in awe. Maybe that's why I like to cook on TV. Wonder why the TV stations do not have kitchens on their sets now, like they used to? People still like to eat.

1½	pounds ground chuck or ground round (cooked and drained)
1	small onion, grated
2	teaspoons salt
½	teaspoon pepper
¾	cup cooked rice
2	(8-ounce) cans tomato sauce, divided use
12	large cabbage leaves
2	tablespoons oil
¼	cup brown sugar
¼	cup lemon juice
1	cup Cheddar cheese, grated (optional)*

Combine the first six ingredients with 1 can of tomato sauce. Set aside. Soak the cabbage leaves in boiling water for 4 minutes or until the leaves are flexible. Drain. Divide equal amounts of meat mixture on each leaf. Roll up and fold ends over and fasten with a toothpick or string. Brown in hot oil in a heavy skillet. Mix remaining tomato sauce, brown sugar, and lemon juice. Pour this over the rolls. Cover and simmer 1 to 1½ hours, basting occasionally with the sauce. During the last 15 minutes of cooking, sprinkle the cheese on top of the rolls, if desired.

Yields: 6 servings

Tonight's Meatloaf

If you have any meatloaf left, try meatloaf sandwiches. A neighbor of mine, Mrs. Annette Lewis, introduced them to me. I love them with salad dressing and catsup. The Lewis' were wonderful neighbors.

1½	pounds ground round or ground chuck
1	cup fresh bread crumbs
1	medium onion, chopped
¼	cup bell pepper, chopped very fine (optional)
¼	teaspoon pepper
1	teaspoon salt
1	teaspoon Accent
1	egg, beaten
½	can tomato sauce

Mix all the ingredients and form a loaf. Place in a loaf pan and bake at 350-degrees for 1½ hours. Baste with the topping sauce below. While the meatloaf is cooking, mix the topping ingredients and spread over the top of the meatloaf the last 30 minutes of cooking.

Topping:
½	can tomato sauce
2	tablespoons prepared mustard
3	tablespoons vinegar
3	tablespoons brown sugar
1	tablespoon Worcestershire sauce

Round Steak Supper Dish

2	pounds beef round steak (Have your butcher tenderize twice)*
4	tablespoons butter
¼	cup onion, chopped
½	cup celery, chopped
2	cups fresh bread crumbs
½	teaspoon salt
½	teaspoon powdered sage
	Pinch of pepper
1	tablespoon water
	Flour
3	tablespoons fat or bacon grease
1	(10.5-ounce) can cream of mushroom soup
2	teaspoons Worcestershire sauce
1	clove of garlic, minced
½	cup water

*If you do not have your butcher tenderize your steak, you will need to pound the steak with a mallet. Then cut it into 4 pieces.

Melt the butter in the skillet and sauté the onion and celery until tender. Add bread crumbs, salt, sage, pepper, and water to the meat pieces. Roll up and fasten the meat with toothpicks. Dip the meat in flour and cut each piece of meat in half. Melt the fat in the skillet, and brown on all sides. Combine the soup, Worcestershire sauce, garlic, and water. Pour over the meat. Cover and simmer about 1 hour and 30 minutes. Serve gravy over the meat.

Note: I watch the sales paper, and when I see round steak on sale, I stock up. Ask the butcher to tenderize the round steak twice. If you didn't know, look at the difference in the price of cube steak and round steak, it is the same thing. Round steak just hasn't been cubed or tenderized.

Down Home Country Fried Steak

Have you ever eaten at a Boarding House or Truck Stop? I ate at a truck stop once when traveling on I-75 in South Georgia, and everyone was sitting at the table with a Lazy Susan in the middle of the table laden with vegetables and anything you could possibly want to eat. Naturally, Country Fried Steak was on the menu.

2	pounds boneless top round steak, ½-inch thick
2	eggs, beaten
2	tablespoon evaporated milk
2	cups cracker crumbs, ground fine
¼	cup vegetable oil
	Salt and pepper to taste

Trim the fat from the steak. Using a wooden meat mallet, pound the "daylights" out of it. Cut the steak into serving pieces. Beat the eggs, blending the milk together with the egg. Dip the pieces of the meat into the egg mixture and then dredge them in the cracker crumbs. Brown the steak slowly on low heat for 45 to 50 minutes. Watch carefully, for it will burn easily due to the cracker crumbs. Sprinkle with the salt and pepper and serve.

All Beef Meatball Recipe

Look in the Gravy section and simmer these meatballs in the Stroganoff Gravy.

2	pounds ground round or chuck
½	cup onion, chopped
1	egg, beaten
½	cup fine bread crumbs
2	teaspoons sugar
¼	teaspoon allspice
1½	teaspoons seasoned salt
	Pinch of pepper
	Bacon grease or oil (Just enough to cover a 12-inch skillet.)

Preheat the skillet hot enough that you can sprinkle a drop of water in it and the water sizzles. Mix all of the ingredients together, forming into 1-inch balls. Brown the meatballs and add them to your favorite spaghetti sauce recipe or use them with a Sour Cream Gravy on top of rice and or noodles.

Cube Steak Dinner

½	cup butter
6	pieces cube steak
	All-purpose flour, enough to dredge the steaks in
2	onions, sliced
1	(4-ounce) can mushrooms, sliced or pieces, undrained
1	(10.5-ounce) can cream of mushroom soup
1	cup buttermilk
1	teaspoon salt
¼	teaspoon pepper
1	teaspoon paprika
5	medium potatoes, sliced *(You may leave the peeling on them, scrub real well. Lots of vitamins in the peel)*
3	medium carrots, sliced

Melt the butter in a large skillet. While the butter is melting, dredge steaks in the flour and brown steaks slowly in the butter on medium heat. Remove the steaks from the skillet and add onions and sauté till they are clear and tender. Add mushrooms with liquid along with the drippings from the steak, soup, buttermilk, salt, pepper, and paprika. Keep this on the eye of the stove on low heat until you are ready to put it into the casserole. Preheat oven to 350-degrees. In a 2½-quart baking dish, layer the potatoes, carrots, along with the steak and onion mixture. Bake uncovered for 1 hour and 20 minutes until the potatoes and carrots are tender.

Hint

When you are in a pinch and expecting company to come and you look once over the house and see, whoops—the silver is all tarnished—grab the tube of toothpaste quick! Take the toothpaste and a moist cloth and squirt some toothpaste on the silver dish, then take the cloth and rub. The sparkle of silver will appear before your very eyes. Rinse it in the sink with hot water and magic appears. Dry it with a dry cloth. I usually keep a tube of the white toothpaste handy.

Swiss Steak Dinner

2-4	pounds round steak (1-inch thick)
½	cup all-purpose flour
4	tablespoons bacon grease or shortening, (divided use)
3	onions, peeled and sliced
2	teaspoons salt
¼	teaspoon pepper
1	clove of garlic, minced
1	stalk celery, chopped
1	(14-ounce) can tomatoes
1	teaspoon Worcestershire sauce
½	cup green pepper, sliced into ¼-inch slices
1	cup tomato or V-8 juice

Have the butcher tenderize the round steak or you can do it yourself. To tenderize the meat yourself, lay the meat on a board and sprinkle the meat with flour. Pound with a meat mallet until the flour has absorbed into the meat. Preheat your skillet or fry pan to at least 350-degrees.* Using only 2 tablespoons of the fat, melt the grease and add the onions. Sauté onions until transparent. Remove the onions from the fat and add the remaining 2 tablespoons of grease, browning steak well on both sides. Season the steak with the salt and pepper. Add the onions back to the skillet along with the garlic, celery, tomatoes, Worcestershire sauce, and green pepper. Cover and simmer on low, if using the fry pan. If you are using an electric skillet, lower the heat to 250-degrees. During the simmer process, add the tomato or V-8 juice. Simmer for 1½-hours until fork-tender.

* If you are not using an electric skillet and you need to test to see if the fry pan is hot enough, I usually just drop some droplets of water into the skillet and if they "hiss," the grease is ready.

Super Easy Taco Filling

1	pound ground round or chuck
1	medium onion, chopped
1	can cream of tomato soup, undiluted
1	can chili beef soup, undiluted
1	(14-ounce) can chili and beans
½	teaspoon chili powder (Suit to taste)
	Dash of sugar
1	box of Taco shells
	Lettuce, Chopped
4	red ripe tomatoes, diced
2	cups Sharp cheese, shredded
1	(8-ounce) carton sour cream

Brown ground round or chuck with onion. Drain if any grease. Stir in the soups and chili beans. Add chili powder and sugar. Stir while heating on medium heat. Prepare taco shells according to package directions. Fill the tacos with lettuce, tomatoes, cheese, and sour cream.

Humongous Hamburgers

Now, listen to this. Mama Gillis made the biggest Hamburgers anyone has ever seen. The meat was literally coming out of the light bread. Now, light bread is regular sandwich bread in a loaf. We never had Hamburger Buns. So, you get a piece of bread and look at it and picture a Hamburger that was about ½-inch out of the bread on all sides.

Now, Papa could barely eat two of them. Of course, we did have the peas and butterbeans on the side, and anything else she cooked that we wanted.

This recipe is depending on how thick you want them and how big. If you have five people, mostly men, this amount of meat I would start with first.

Here is what she put in her Hamburgers.

3	pounds ground chuck or ground round
2	teaspoons Seasoning Salt
2	slices light bread, crumbled up
2	eggs, beaten
	A little evaporated milk just to moisten the mixture along with the eggs, but not much.
	Minced Onion (optional)

Mix together and fry in a skillet on medium high. Flip often. Pat with paper towels. You may need to add salt and pepper to taste. I have never been one to add a great deal of salt in anything. Just enough to enhance the taste, not to overpower it.

The Divine Dixie Deva's Hamburgers

Follow Mama Gillis' recipe, except leave out the seasoning salt and add 1 packet of dry onion mix in the hamburger meat.

Proceed with the rest of the recipe.

Kathryn's Stuffed Cheese Burgers with Salsa

2	pounds ground chuck or round
1	(16-ounce) package dry ranch mix or ½ package of dry onion mix
1	teaspoon black pepper
2	tablespoons Worcestershire sauce
	Cheese slices (You will need 1 cheese slice for every hamburger)

Mix the hamburger meat with all of the ingredients except for the cheese. Shape into thin patties. Take two hamburger patties and put a slice of cheese between the two. Seal the patties real well by pressing the edges together. You may fry or bake the hamburgers. Sometimes it's quicker to bake the burgers in a 350-degree oven until they are no longer pink if you have a lot of them to cook. However, I usually fry them on the stove for that fry taste, if I am just cooking enough for a few folks.

Here's my Homemade Salsa Recipe that I like to put on top of my Hamburgers

3	large tomatoes, chopped
½	red onion, chopped
1	clove garlic, minced
	Dash of sugar
½	green pepper, seeded, cored and chopped
1	jalapeño pepper, seeded, chopped
2	tablespoons olive oil
1	tablespoon Dry Italian Seasoning*

Combine the above ingredients and let sit in the fridge for several hours so that the flavors will blend.

*If you do not have the dry Italian Seasoning, substitute by omitting the olive oil and add 3 tablespoons of prepared Italian dressing.

Weenies N' Crescents

8	hot dog Weenies, partially split
4	slices of cheese cut into 8 strips
1	(8-ounce) can refrigerated crescent rolls

Fill each weenie with a cheese strip. Separate the crescent dough into eight triangles. Place the weenies on the wide end of each triangle and roll up. Place on a greased cookie sheet, cheese side up. Bake 375-degrees for 15 minutes. Great for a Friday night to graze on while the kids are watching a movie.

Yields: 8 Weenies

Beefaroni

This meal is great to prepare during Summer vacation for the kids. It's quick and easy. Double the recipe and freeze a batch. You know there is a lot you can do with a pound of hamburger!

½	cup onions, chopped
¼	cup butter
1	pound ground chuck or round
1	(16-ounce) can diced tomatoes
2	teaspoons salt
	Pinch of sugar
1	tablespoon Worcestershire sauce
	Couple of dashes of hot sauce
1	cup macaroni, uncooked
1	cup Cheddar cheese or sharp cheese, grated.

Sauté onions in butter till tender. Add the ground chuck and brown. Drain any grease. Add the tomatoes, salt, sugar, Worcestershire sauce, and hot sauce. Bring to boil and add uncooked macaroni. Stir and cut down the heat. Cover and simmer until the macaroni is tender. Uncover the pan and sprinkle the cheese last in the skillet. The cheese will melt just enough and you are ready to serve it up.

Yields: 6 servings

Beef Brisket

1	(4-5 pound) boneless beef brisket (Brisket has such a great flavor)
1	envelope dry onion soup mix
¼	cup Worcestershire sauce
1	(14-ounce) can beef bouillon
1	large cooking bag
1	clove garlic, peeled
1	tablespoon black pepper

Preheat oven to 300-degrees. Make tiny slits in the brisket and insert the garlic in the slits. Rub both sides of the brisket with the pepper. In a 9 x 13-inch baking dish, put the brisket in the large cooking bag. Empty the contents of the dry onion mix, Worcestershire sauce and can of beef bouillon in the cooking bag. Make several slits in the cooking bag. Bake the brisket for approximately 4 hours or until temperature reaches at least 170-degrees for well-done. Let the meat rest about 15 minutes to let the juices redistribute before cutting. When cutting, cut diagonally across the grain of the meat.

Chicken Herb Dinner with Sweet Taters and White Taters

1	(4½-pound) chicken, washed and patted dry
2	teaspoons dried rosemary
1½	teaspoons sage
1½	teaspoons thyme
½	stick butter
	Salt to taste
	Pepper to taste
1	bay leaf
⅓	cup olive oil
	Paprika to sprinkle
2	large sweet potatoes, peeled and sliced
7-8	new potatoes, scrubbed and sliced lengthwise

Preheat oven to 450-degrees. Combine the rosemary, sage, and thyme with the olive oil. Rub half of the olive oil mixture on the inside of the chicken. Place the bay leaf on the inside of the chicken along with the half-stick of butter. Brush the additional olive oil mixture over the outside of the chicken. Place in a large baking dish and surround the chicken with both kinds of the potatoes. Sprinkle the chicken with paprika. Cover with foil and bake for 30 minutes at 450-degrees. Now reduce the heat to 350-degrees and take the cover or foil off of the chicken and continue cooking approximately 45 more minutes until potatoes are done and the chicken reads at a temperature of 190-degrees.

A great fall suppertime meal.

Mama Gillis' Fried Chicken

I was telling the truth when I said we had Fried Chicken every day. In the recipe below, every ingredient was what Mama Gillis used to fry her chicken. I could just about bet my red hair on this. I wonder if she ever knew that I was taking in all of her secrets.

She always bought whole chickens and cut them up herself, instead of buying the chicken already cut up. I would not take a "purty" for her teaching me how to cut up a chicken, for I cut up my own chickens today. It's more economical to cut up your own, and besides, my favorite pieces are the pulley bone (wishbone) and the drumsticks. You can find already cut-up chicken in the grocery stores, but the butcher typically does not cut the chicken where you can actually have the pulley bone. If you want the chicken to have a pulley bone, just buy a whole chicken and ask the butcher to cut it in a country-fry style.

When I would call Mama Gillis and tell her I was coming to see her, she would always ask me what I wanted her to fix me to eat. I always said Fried Chicken. Sometimes, she would tell me that she didn't have one thawed up. Magically, when I got there after a couple of hours, there was a platter of Mama Gillis's Fresh Fried Chicken ready and waiting for her "grandbaby." And just for the record, it wasn't a "bucket of chicken," if you know what I mean. Talk about giving of one's self and giving her love, which was what it was. I know for sure that she sometimes just plain didn't feel like cooking, especially when she got older.

If you are lucky enough to own a heavy black cast-iron skillet, that's the trick. I use Mama Gillis' cast-iron skillet. If you don't have one, just use a regular skillet.

If you want Fried Chicken for the next day for lunch or supper, soak your chicken the night before in the buttermilk mixture. You don't have to, but it sure makes it better.

1	(2-3 pound) fryer chicken, cut-up
1-2	cups buttermilk
4	tablespoons Worcestershire sauce
1	teaspoon garlic powder
¼	teaspoon onion powder
1	teaspoon salt
¼	teaspoon black pepper
	Paprika to sprinkle
1½	cups all-purpose flour
1½-2	cups Crisco oil
	Additional Salt in shaker
	Additional Pepper in shaker

Wash chicken pieces real well and set aside. In a large bowl, combine buttermilk, Worcestershire sauce, garlic powder, onion powder, salt, pepper, and paprika. Mix together. Place the chicken pieces in the bowl with the buttermilk mixture. Toss the chicken real well, coating each and every piece of chicken with this mixture. Let the chicken sit in this mixture at least 30 minutes or more. I prefer to let the chicken marinate overnight. Pour grease in the fry pan or skillet and heat until the grease is 350-degrees on medium high heat. Place flour in a zip-top bag. Remove chicken from the buttermilk mixture, sprinkle each piece with the additional salt and pepper, and dredge in the flour mixture. Place the meatier pieces in the fry pan first, and then add the bonier ones. Fry in the hot grease, turning each piece often until golden brown. Put the lid on the fry pan for about 10 minutes and then take the cover back off, turning pieces again. The whole process usually takes about 35 to 40 minutes depending on the size of your chicken. Drain chicken on paper towels. Check the Chicken Gravy recipe out.

Chicken Gravy

If there is a lot of "crispy" left from frying chicken in the fry pan, be sure to make gravy from that. Chicken gravy has a distinct taste and is light brown in color, and the "crispy" adds that much more flavor.

¼	cup drippings along with the "crispy"
¼	cup all-purpose flour
2	cups evaporated milk
½	cup water
	1 or 2 chicken bouillons cubes*
	Salt to taste
	Pepper to taste

Be sure to add the bouillon cube, before you add the salt to taste, because bouillon has salt already in it. You may have to add additional salt to taste.

First of all, drain all of the drippings or fat from the skillet, but ¼-cup of the drippings. Using a wooden spoon, scrape the skillet lightly, until you get up all of the "crispy" residue. Keeping the skillet hot, add the ¼-cup flour and then add at least 2 cups of milk, stirring constantly, now add the water. If you like, you may add one or two chicken bouillon cubes to add that much more flavor. Keep stirring until the gravy thickens and comes to a good boil. Add a little more water or milk, just enough for desired thickness in the gravy. Boil 2 or 3 minutes. Salt and pepper to taste. Put the top of the skillet on and simmer gravy on very low heat for 2 minutes. That's it. It's easy you just have to practice.

Quick Supper of Oven Fried Chicken with Dressing

- 1 (3-4 pound) chicken, cut up
- 1 cup all-purpose flour
- 1 teaspoon salt
- ¼ teaspoon pepper
- Cooking oil

Dressing:
- ½ cup butter
- ¾ cup celery, diced
- ¾ cup onions, diced
- 1 (14-ounce) can chicken broth
- ⅓ cup milk
- 1 (10.5-ounce) can cream of chicken or cream of mushroom soup
- 1 (14-ounce) bag herb seasoned stuffing
- Black pepper to taste
- Paprika

Preheat oven to 350-degrees. Grease a 13 x 9 x 2-inch baking dish. Mix the flour with salt and pepper in a large zip-top bag. Coat the chicken with the seasoned flour mixture by placing the chicken in the bag and shaking. In a heavy skillet, pour ¼-inch cooking oil and heat until sizzling hot. You need to just brown the chicken in the hot grease, do not completely cook it. Set aside. In a separate skillet, sauté onions and celery with butter until transparent, stir in the broth, and heat until it boils. Cut the heat down and add milk and soup, stirring until smooth. Add the stuffing mix and mix well with the ingredients.

Place the stuffing or dressing mix in the center of baking dish and arrange chicken pieces around the dressing. Sprinkle chicken and dressing with black pepper and paprika. Bake for 50 to 60 minutes until chicken is completely done.

Chicken and Dumplings

Chicken and Dumplings were just a side dish at Mama Gillis' house; remember we had Fried Chicken everyday. Hope you enjoy it!

I wish I could show you how Mama Gillis would make her Dumplings. As I am writing this recipe to you, I can just see her draping the dough over her little fingers and putting the dumplings in the hot, boiling chicken stock.

1	large chicken, boiled
2	quarts chicken stock
1	can cream of chicken soup *(You could use cream of celery if you prefer)*
6	Tablespoons butter
	Salt and Pepper to taste
4	chicken bouillon cubes

Boil the chicken until tender. Remove the chicken from the bones and cut into small pieces. Set the chicken aside while preparing the dumplings. Save the liquid for the stock. If there is not enough stock to make 2-quarts, add enough water to do so. *(This is where I add my chicken bouillon cubes with the water.)* Even if I have enough broth, I still add the bouillon cubes for flavor. Add soup, butter, salt and pepper. Keep hot while making the dumplings.

Dumplings:

$1/3$	cup shortening or lard
$2/3$	cup milk
$1\frac{1}{2}$-2	cups all-purpose flour
	Dose of black pepper*
2	quarts chicken stock *(See note)*

Place flour in a large bowl. Cut in shortening, adding milk, and stir until moistened. Add more flour if needed to make soft dough. Take small amounts of dough and roll them to ¼-inch flat. You do not want your dumplings thick. It will take longer to cook and they will be gummy. Ugh! Cut into strips. Drop the dumpling strips into the hot boiling chicken stock. Cut the burner to medium heat, boiling gently. Boil 2 to 3 minutes, stirring gently. Always dip the spoon into the boiling stock and gently move the dumplings away from each other—this eliminates the dumplings from sticking together. Fold in your chicken and simmer for 20 to 30 minutes. Add a dose of black pepper. This is a wonderful recipe. **Note:** a dose is a little more than a dash.

Note: At any given time while boiling the dumplings, the stock reduces significantly, just add more water, or if you have another can of chicken broth, feel free to add.

Yields: 6 to 8 servings

Chicken on a Shoe String Budget

I would make this recipe when I found chicken drumsticks on sale. Raising children on a single income is hard, but you can do it and have good meals. They will like helping you prepare this. Put this meal together in no time, and throw it in the oven while you are helping the kids with their homework or bath.

	Juice of one lemon
¼	cup butter, melted
1½	cups cracker crumbs
½	teaspoon garlic salt
½	teaspoon paprika
¼	teaspoon black pepper
2	pounds chicken drumsticks (10 to 12 pieces)

Combine the lemon juice and melted butter in a shallow dish. In another dish or zip-top bag, combine the crumbs, garlic salt, paprika, and black pepper. Dip the chicken first in the lemon juice and butter mixture. Then coat the drumsticks in the cracker crumb mixture. Arrange the drumsticks in a shallow baking dish and cover with foil. Bake for 45 minutes at 400-degrees. Remove the foil and turn the chicken. Bake another 15 to 20 minutes more. This will serve four people.

Chicken Pie

1	(2½-3 pound) fryer
1	teaspoon salt
½	teaspoon pepper
5	medium potatoes, peeled and cut into chunks
3	large carrots, scraped and cut into ½-inch slices
2	stalks celery, cut into ½-inch slices
1	(17-ounce) can English peas, drained
½	cup butter
1	cup all-purpose flour
1	cup milk
1	can cream of chicken soup or cream of celery soup
2	chicken bouillon cubes
	Salt and pepper to taste
1	cup sharp Cheddar cheese, shredded
	Pastry dough for a double crust 9-inch-pie

Grease a 13 x 9 x 2-inch casserole dish. Place chicken in a large pot and cover with water, adding 1 teaspoon salt and ½ teaspoon pepper. Bring to a boil, cover, and simmer until tender, about 1 hour. After chicken has cooked, place pot and all in the fridge to rush chilling. When chilled, take the chicken off of the bones and cut into chunk-like pieces. Reserve broth to cook vegetables. Using the same pot in which you cooked the chicken, place potatoes, carrots, and celery and cook with reserved broth until vegetables are tender. Take the vegetables out of broth and place potatoes, carrots, celery, English peas, and chicken in the casserole dish. Reserve the remaining broth for the sauce. Melt butter in a saucepan, stirring in the flour. Gradually add milk, reserved broth, cream soup, and bouillon cubes. Add salt and pepper to taste. Cook, stirring constantly until sauce is thickened. Pour sauce over the vegetables. Sprinkle cheese over the sauce and vegetables. Prepare pastry dough by rolling to fit the casserole dish. Make slits in the pastry dough to let the steam escape when pie is cooking. Bake at 400-degrees for 45 to 50 minutes until crust is golden brown.

Chicken Supreme

This recipe would indeed be excellent for a Sunday night gathering or dinner party. It is enough for 12 servings. If you wanted to trim it in half, you could make it as the recipe calls for and freeze the rest for later. You need to prepare this recipe the day before you serve it.

12	chicken breasts
2	cups sour cream
¼	lemon juice
4	tablespoons Worcestershire sauce
4	teaspoons celery salt
4	teaspoon paprika
4	teaspoons garlic salt
½	teaspoon pepper
2	cups dry bread crumbs*
1	cup butter, melted
	Extra paprika for sprinkling on top

In a large bowl combine sour cream, lemon juice, Worcestershire sauce, celery salt, paprika, garlic salt, and pepper. Add chicken breasts to the sour cream mixture, coating each piece well. Let stand covered in the refrigerator overnight. The next day, preheat oven to 350-degrees. Remove the chicken from the sour cream mixture and roll into bread crumbs, coating evenly. Arrange the chicken breasts in a single layer in a 13 x 9 x 2-inch greased baking dish. Melt butter and shortening in a small pan. Spoon half of the melted butter over chicken. Bake the chicken uncovered for 45 minutes and spoon the rest of the melted butter mixture over the chicken. Sprinkle with paprika and bake for 15 minutes more or until chicken is nicely browned.

Hint: *Speaking of the dry bread crumbs, pick up the bags of those herb-seasoned bread cubes that you use for stuffing. Swirl them in the blender and you have dry bread crumbs. The extra seasoning would make this recipe that much better. Try it.

Chicken or Turkey À La King

½	cup butter, melted
⅓	cups all-purpose flour
1	cup milk
2	cups chicken broth
½	teaspoon black pepper
	Pinch of cayenne pepper
1	teaspoon paprika
	Salt to taste
1	egg yolk, slightly beaten
1	(4-ounce) jar pimentos, chopped and drained
1	(4-ounce) can sliced mushrooms, drained
2	cups chicken or turkey, cooked and chopped

Note: You may serve over cooked rice, noodles, cornbread squares, or toast points.

Melt butter over low heat. Take off of the heat and stir in the flour and mix until smooth, gradually stirring in the milk. Put back on the stove and add the chicken broth, black pepper, cayenne pepper, paprika, and salt. Cook over low to medium heat, stirring constantly until the sauce is slightly thickened. Gradually add the egg yolk and continue to cook, stirring for 1 minute or more. Add the pimentos, mushrooms, and chicken or turkey. Simmer until all ingredients are heated throughout. Spoon the mixture over rice, noodles, cornbread squares, or toast points.

Cornish Hens with Wild Rice

6	Cornish Hens (1 per person)
1	teaspoon salt
1	teaspoon paprika
1	teaspoon garlic powder
1	teaspoon black pepper
1	box Uncle Ben's Long Grain Wild Rice
1	bunch spring onions, chopped
½	cup celery, chopped fine
1	(8-ounce) can mushroom, sliced or pieces or ½ pound fresh mushrooms, sliced
1	stick butter
2½	cups chicken broth
1	teaspoon marjoram
2	dashes nutmeg
	Large roaster pan with cover and rack

Preheat roaster to 450-degrees. Wash the hens well and pat dry. Season with salt, paprika, garlic powder, and black pepper. Place the rack in the roaster and place 3 hens on each side. Set aside while preparing the rice mixture. In a large skillet, sauté rice, onions, celery, and mushrooms in the butter. Combine the chicken broth and the rest of the spices, blending well. Add the rice mixture in the center of the hens in the roaster; cover and cook for 30 minutes on 450-degrees. After 30 minutes, reduce heat to 350-degrees for approximately 1 hour and 30 minutes.

Yields: 6 servings

Kathryn's Manicotti Meal

8-10	Manicotti shells
1	pound ground chuck or round
½	pound ground Italian sausage
1	clove garlic, minced
1	medium onion, chopped fine
1	cup cottage cheese, large or small curd
1	cup Mozzarella cheese, shredded
½	teaspoon salt
¼	cup mayonnaise
1	(15.5-ounce) jar of your favorite spaghetti sauce
½	teaspoon oregano
1	teaspoon sugar
½	cup Parmesan cheese, grated

Preheat oven to 350-degrees. Prepare a 13 x 9 x 2-inch pan by greasing with baking spray. Cook Manicotti shells according to package directions. Drain and rinse in cold water and set aside. In a skillet, sauté ground chuck or round and Italian sausage, garlic, and onion until meat is no longer pink. Drain off the drippings and discard. Add the cottage cheese, Mozzarella cheese, salt and mayonnaise to the skillet, stirring real well. Now it's time to stuff the shells with the meat mixture. Stuff the shells with about 1 to 2 heaping tablespoons of meat mixture into the shells. You have more than enough meat mixture. Arrange the shells in the baking dish and the leftover meat mixture. Simply place it in the baking dish along the sides of the stuffed shells. Mix the spaghetti sauce, oregano and sugar together and pour over the shells. Sprinkle the shells with the Parmesan cheese. Bake, covered with tin foil over the baking dish at 350-degrees for 20 minutes. At the end of 20 minutes, take the cover off and bake 10 additional minutes.

Saturday Night Lasagna

1	(16-ounce) box lasagna noodles
2	tablespoons cooking oil
1½	pounds ground chuck or ground round
½	cup onion, chopped
2	(26-ounce) jars spaghetti sauce
1	(16-ounce) carton cottage cheese, small curd
4	cups (1-pound) Mozzarella cheese, shredded
2	eggs, lightly beaten
1	cup Parmesan cheese, grated
	Salt & pepper to taste
	Dash of sugar
	Dash of nutmeg
1	cup water

Preheat oven to 350-degrees. Grease a 13 x 9 x 2-inch baking dish. Cook lasagna noodles according to package directions. Drain and rinse in cold water and stir in the cooking oil. Set aside until ready to use. Brown ground chuck or round until it is crumbly and no longer pink. Add onion and cook until transparent. Drain off any grease. Add the 2 jars of spaghetti sauce to the ground chuck or round, blending well. In a bowl, combine the cottage cheese, Mozzarella cheese, eggs, Parmesan cheese, salt, pepper, sugar and nutmeg. Set aside. Spread about ⅓ of the spaghetti meat sauce in the 13 x 9 x 2-inch baking dish. Layer a third of noodles, cheese mixture, and then spaghetti meat sauce again and so on. Repeat this procedure ending with the cheese mixture on top. Now pour in the water around the sides of the pan, carefully. Cover the lasagna tightly with tin foil. Bake for 40 minutes. Remove the foil and bake for 10 to 15 minutes longer. Let stand for 10 minutes before serving. Be sure to save the leftovers, for it tastes even better the next day.

Note: If you want to add ground Italian sausage, do so. In lieu of 1½-pounds of ground chuck or round, use 1 pound of ground chuck or round and add ½ pound of Italian sausage to the ground chuck or round.

Vegetarian Pie

1	(10-inch) deep dish pie shell, unbaked (homemade or commercial)
1	(1-pound) eggplant, peeled and cubed
1	medium-size onion, chopped
1	clove garlic, minced
1	stick butter
1	teaspoon salt
	Pinch of cayenne pepper
½	teaspoon oregano
½	teaspoon basil
1	small zucchini, sliced into thin slices
⅔	cup evaporated milk
1	egg
3	cups Mozzarella cheese
	Paprika to sprinkle

Preheat oven to 375-degrees. In a skillet, sauté the eggplant, onion, and garlic in butter until the ingredients are tender. Add the salt, cayenne pepper, oregano and basil, mixing well. Line the bottom of the pie shell with the zucchini slices. Pour cooked mixture over the zucchini. In a separate bowl, mix the milk, egg and Mozzarella cheese. Place the pie shell on a cookie sheet to prevent spillovers when baking. Slowly pour this mixture over the vegetables. Sprinkle with paprika. Bake at 375-degrees for 30 to 35 minutes.

Casseroles

Being a working wife and mom, I have always had a great respect for casseroles. On the weekends I would always make an extra casserole and freeze it, which helped me out tremendously. A lot of the casserole dishes I have included in this book are perfect for a main dish. Just add a congealed salad, fruit salad, or your favorite green salad to finish out for a balanced meal.

Italian Sausage and Black-Eyed Pea Casserole

1	pound Italian sausage
½	cup onion, chopped
½	teaspoon garlic powder
¼	teaspoon black pepper
2	(15-ounce) can black-eyed peas, undrained
4	tablespoons cornstarch
¼	cup water
	Dash of hot sauce, if desired
	Cooked rice, if desired

Cook sausage in a skillet until no longer pink, draining off grease. Add onion, garlic powder, and pepper and cook until onions are transparent. Add black-eyed peas to the sausage mixture. After filling one of the empty cans with water, add to the peas and sausage. Bring this mixture to a boil, reduce heat on the stove, and simmer for 25 minutes, stirring often. Mix the cornstarch with the water and add this to the pea mixture, stirring until thickened. This is delicious when served over rice.

Yields: 6 servings

Sausage Rice Casserole

This recipe was given to me several years ago by my mother, Catherine Pierce.

1	(1-pound) sausage roll, mild or hot
2	onions, chopped
1	box long grain and wild rice mix
1	(10.75-ounce) can cream of mushroom soup
2	(10.75-ounce) cans of cream of chicken soup
1	cup water
1	(4-ounce) can mushrooms, undrained
1	(2.5-ounce) package almonds, toasted

Cook the long grain and wild rice mix according to package directions and set aside. Fry sausage and onions. Drain sausage grease and discard. Add all the other ingredients mix together. Pour into a greased 9 x 13-inch baking dish. Bake at 350-degrees for 30 to 40 minutes. If you use (2) 8 x 8 or 9 x 9-inch pans, you can freeze one and bake one.

Hominy Hot Pot

1	(30-ounce) can white hominy or 2 (15.5-ounce cans)*
1	tablespoon butter or oil
¼	cup onion, chopped
¼	cup green pepper, chopped
1	pound ground chuck or ground round
1	teaspoon salt
¼	teaspoon pepper
¼	teaspoon chili powder
¼	teaspoon sugar
1	(16-ounce) can tomatoes

Drain hominy and set aside. Sauté onion and green pepper in oil. Add ground chuck or round and cook until lightly brown. Drain excess fat. Add salt, pepper, chili powder, sugar, and tomatoes. Stir, and allow to simmer 10 minutes. Add hominy and simmer for 30 minutes.

*It is hard to find 30-ounce cans, sometimes.

Any Meat Casserole

Now if you have any kind of meat left over in the refrigerator, use it for this recipe. This recipe will make a nutritious meal in minutes and save you the cost of one of those pizzas.

1	cup macaroni, cooked
¼	cup butter, melted
¼	cup onion, finely chopped or 3 tablespoons of dry onion flakes
¼	cup all-purpose flour
1	teaspoon salt
¼	teaspoon pepper
2	cups milk
1½	cup chopped, cooked meat whether it be ham, chicken, beef or cooked ground beef.
1	cup of cheese, grated, any kind that you like

Mix all of these ingredients together or you may save the cheese for the topping. Pour into a greased baking dish. Bake in a 350-degree oven until bubbly and serve. Now, tell me how quick was that? And very nutritious.

Taco Bake

2	pounds ground chuck or ground round
2	onions, chopped
1	package taco seasoning mix
1	cup water
	12-14-ounces nacho chips, broken
1	(15-ounce) can chili with beans
1	(8-ounce) can tomato sauce
2	cups sharp cheese, grated
1	(8-ounce) sour cream
	Chopped lettuce
1-2	cup tomatoes, chopped
	Picante sauce, Salsa sauce or taco sauce
	Extra sour cream

Brown ground chuck or ground round with onions. Drain off grease. Stir in taco mix and 1 cup of water. Simmer for 5 minutes and set aside. Place crushed chips in an ungreased 9 x 13-inch casserole dish. Layer with meat and onion mixture over the crushed chips. Mix the chili beans with the tomato sauce and place on top of the meat mixture. Top with cheese. Bake at 350-degrees for 30 minutes. After baking, top with the 8-ounces of sour cream. Bake 10 minutes longer. Before serving, top with chopped lettuce, chopped tomatoes, picante or taco sauce, and extra sour cream.

Yields: 10 to 12 servings

Turkey and Wild Rice Casserole

1½	cup cooked wild rice (white rice may be substituted)
4	tablespoons butter
1	cup celery, chopped
1	cup onion, chopped
3	cups turkey, coarsely chopped
1	(10.5-ounce) cream of mushroom soup
1	(10.5-ounce) cream of chicken soup
1	can water chestnuts, drained
1	(3-ounce) can mushroom stems and pieces
3	tablespoons soy sauce
¼	teaspoon pepper
2	tablespoons butter, melted (additional)
½	cup dry bread crumbs

Preheat oven to 350-degrees and grease a 3-quart baking dish. Cook rice according to the package directions. Sauté the celery and onion with the 4 tablespoons butter. In a large bowl, combine all of the ingredients together except for the additional butter and crumbs. Place the mixture in the baking dish and top with the 2 tablespoons of butter and bread crumbs. Bake for 30 to 45 minutes until hot and bubbly.

Yields 6-8 servings

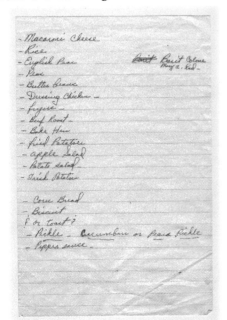

One of Mama Gillis' menus

Hot Turkey Casserole

2	cups potato chips, crushed
1	cup sharp cheese, grated
1	tablespoon butter
½	cup pecans, chopped fine
½	cup celery, chopped fine
½	cup onions, chopped fine
3	cups cooked turkey, chopped coarsely
¼	cup salt
¼	cup black pepper
	Dash of cayenne pepper
⅓	cup mayonnaise
2	tablespoons lemon juice
	Paprika to sprinkle

Combine the crushed potato chips and cheese. In a lightly greased 8-inch square baking dish, press half of this mixture on the bottom. Set the remaining potato-chip mixture aside. Melt the butter in a small skillet and sauté the pecans, onions, and celery. In a bowl, combine the turkey, celery, and onion mixture along with the rest of the ingredients, except for the reserved potato-chip mixture. Spoon over the potato-chip mixture in the baking dish and top it off with the reserved potato-chip mixture. Sprinkle with paprika. Bake at 400-degrees for 15 minutes.

Macaroni and Cheese Ham Casserole

This is another quick and easy meal to prepare for supper, using those cheap boxes of macaroni 'n' cheese mixes. Adding a vegetable and/or Jell-O salad with this dish would be a nice supper for any family.

1	(7.25-ounce) box macaroni and cheese mix
4	tablespoons evaporated milk
6	eggs (divided use)
1	cup Swiss cheese, grated
2	tablespoons all-purpose flour
1	can cream of mushroom soup
1	cup ham, chopped
1	(4-ounce) can mushrooms, sliced or pieces, drained
¼	cup onion, chopped fine

Grease a 2-quart baking dish and set aside. Prepare the box of macaroni and cheese according to package directions, using 4 tablespoons of milk and adding only 2 of the 6 eggs. Mix well. Spread this mixture over the bottom of the baking dish. In a separate bowl toss the cheese with the flour, and add the remaining 4 eggs, soup, ham, mushrooms, and onion. Pour this mixture over the macaroni. Bake at 350-degrees for 20 minutes. Cover with aluminum foil and bake for 20 minutes more or until set. Let stand at least 10 minutes before serving.

Hint

Do you have a bag of marshmallows that are hard? Never throw them out. Here is a way to soften them.

Take a quart jar and put a stalk of celery into the jar. Yes, I said celery. Then put as many marshmallows in the jar as you can fit into it. Close the lid tightly and let them stand for a day or so and the marshmallows will become soft again. If the marshmallows are extremely hard, let them stay in the jar a little while longer.

I never throw out marshmallows. If all else fails, always top them on a Baked Sweet Potato or a Sweet Potato Casserole.

All Kinds of Salads

These salads are great to fix in the morning before leaving for work. Then when you come home, you have something already prepared to add to your main dish. Some of these could be used for a light dessert. Take your pick at any of these. I guarantee you will find one that you like.

Note: Scoop out melons and tomatoes to make an excellent presentation in serving salads. As you know, a scooped out watermelon is the ticket for a large container in which to serve a fruit salad. In addition, a scooped out watermelon that has been dried out with paper toweling makes for a pretty presentation of macaroni, chicken, or even turkey salad.

Sweet congealed salads are one of my favorites, and you will find a good mix of all different salads in this section.

Holiday Fruit Salad

This is indeed a gorgeous gelatin salad that you will make every year. It will become a traditional recipe for years to come.

- 2 (3-ounce) packages black cherry gelatin
- 1½ teaspoons unflavored gelatin
- 2 cups boiling water
- 1 cup red wine
- 1 cup fresh cranberries, ground
- 1 teaspoon grated orange rind
- 1 cup mandarin oranges, drained (Save the juice)
- 1 (8.25-ounce) can crushed pineapple, undrained
- 1 cup pecans, chopped

Mix black cherry gelatin and unflavored gelatin together. Add boiling water and stir to dissolve. Add enough water to the reserved mandarin juice to make 1 cup. Stir in the gelatin mixture, and add the red wine. Chill the mixture until it begins to thicken, then fold in the cranberries, orange rind, mandarin oranges, pineapple, and pecans. Chill in greased 7-cup mold or 2-quart baking dish. Serve this on lettuce leaves and decorate with extra mandarin orange sections and orange twists.

Orange Mandarin Salad

This is one of my favorite salads. It is real showy. I use a ring mold with this recipe. I put my topping in the center and garnish it with a few mandarin orange slices in the middle along with a sprig of mint. You can also put this salad in an oblong dish and spread the topping on top of the chilled salad.

1	large package orange gelatin
2	cups boiling water
1	(6-ounce) can concentrated orange juice
2	(11-ounce) cans mandarin oranges, drained
1	(16-ounce) can crushed pineapple, drained
½	pint whipping cream, whipped
1	(3.5-ounce) package lemon instant pudding
1	cup milk

Dissolve the gelatin in 2 cups of boiling water. Add the frozen orange juice and stir until dissolved. Let cool in the refrigerator until slightly thickened and then stir in the mandarin oranges and pineapple. Place in a ring mold or an oblong dish. Chill until firm. Unmold your salad and now you're ready for the topping.

Topping for Salad:
Blend the pudding and milk, then fold in the whipping cream. Place in the center of the ring and garnish it with a few mandarin orange slices along with a sprig of mint, or spread over the top of the salad.

Yields: 8 servings

Mandarin Orange Delight

This is a very old recipe.

2	(3-ounce) packages orange Jell-O
2	cups boiling water
1	pint vanilla ice cream
2	(11-ounce) cans mandarin oranges, drained

Dissolve the gelatin in boiling water. Add the ice cream gradually, stirring until dissolved. Chill until partially set. After chilling until partially set, beat the mixture until fluffy. Fold into the mandarin oranges. Spread into a greased 8 x 8 x 2-inch square pan. Chill until set and cut into squares at serving time.

Yields: 8 servings

Fruit and Nut Salad

Many years ago, I will not say how long ago it was, I was in the organization of Future Homemakers of America. We had a luncheon, and one girl's mother fixed this salad. I never asked for the recipe, however, by memory I just put all of the ingredients together that I could remember. I had never had a fruit salad with sour cream in it until then. It is the quickest salad there is to make. Promise!

1	(20-ounce) can chunk pineapple, drain juice
1	(11-ounce) can mandarin oranges, drain juice
1	jar maraschino cherries, red or green (or both!) with juice
1	cup coconut
1	cup small marshmallows
1	(8-ounce) carton sour cream
2	tablespoons powdered sugar
1	cup nuts, chopped
1½	cups green or red seedless grapes

Mix all of the above ingredients and refrigerate overnight. Serve the next day. Put in a beautiful crystal bowl and garnish with a big dollop of sweetened whip cream and top with a maraschino cherry that has a stem.

Yields: 10 to 12 servings

Tutti-Fruity Salad

1	(16-ounce) can sliced peaches, drained
1	(8.25-ounce) can pear halves, drained
1	(3-ounce) package strawberry gelatin
1	cup boiling water
1	(6-ounce) can frozen concentrated lemonade
3	cups Cool Whip, thawed

Chop fruits and set aside. Dissolve gelatin in boiling water. Add the frozen lemonade and stir until melted. Chill this mixture until slightly thickened. Fold in the Cool Whip and then the fruit. Spray a 9 x 5-inch loaf pan with baking spray and pour the mixture into the pan. Freeze until firm, preferably overnight. Remove from mold and slice.

Yields: 8 to 10 servings

Orange Cheese Salad

Check this one out. Quick and easy, yet wonderful for a buffet dinner.

1	(3-ounce) package orange gelatin
1	(12-ounce) carton small curd cottage cheese
1	(11-ounce) can mandarin oranges, drained
1	(8-ounce) can crushed pineapple, drained
1	(9-ounce) package Cool Whip topping

Sprinkle cottage cheese with DRY orange gelatin. Set the mixture aside until the jello becomes moist. Mix. Add drained mandarin oranges and pineapple. Fold in the Cool Whip, which has been partially thawed. Toss this together until thoroughly mixed. Chill in the refrigerator and serve.

Note: You may substitute a small can of drained fruit cocktail in lieu of the mandarin oranges and pineapple.

Yields: 8 to 10 servings

Asa's Blueberry Salad

This recipe is well over 30 years old. Asa was a dear elderly man that gave me this recipe. Believe it or not, he made his suits and all of his wife's clothing. They don't make men like that now, do they?

1	(8.25-ounce) can crushed pineapple, drained and save juice
2	(3-ounce) boxes blackberry gelatin
3	cups boiling water
1	(15-ounce) can blueberries, drained
1	(8-ounce) cream cheese, softened
1	(8-ounce) sour cream
½	cup powdered sugar
¼	cup chopped nuts

Dissolve gelatin in boiling water and stir in pineapple juice. Chill until consistency of egg whites. Stir in pineapple and blueberries. Pour into a 10 x 6 x 1¾-inch pan. Chill until firm. Combine sour cream, cream cheese and sugar. Beat until smooth and well blended. Spread over salad. Top with nuts.

Yields: 8 servings

Cranberry Congealed Salad

1	(3-ounce) box raspberry gelatin
1	can congealed cranberry sauce
1	envelope unflavored gelatin
1	cup cold water
1	(8-ounce) or small can crushed pineapple, drained
½	cup celery, minced
1	cup pecans or walnuts, chopped
	Sweetened whipping cream, optional

Dissolve the raspberry gelatin in 1 cup boiling water. Add cranberry sauce and stir until almost dissolved. Add unflavored gelatin to 1 cup cold water to soften and pour into raspberry mixture. Add the other ingredients and pour into an oiled ring mold. This will make a pretty Christmas or Thanksgiving mold. You may put mayonnaise in the center of the ring or lightly sweetened whipping cream that has been whipped in the center of the ring.

Yields: 6 servings

Bing Cherry Salad

2	small packages black cherry gelatin
2	(6.5-ounce) bottles of Coke
1	(16-ounce) can Bing cherries, drained
1	(20-ounce) can crushed pineapple, drained and reserve juice

Add enough water to the reserved pineapple juice to equal 2 cups of liquid. Pour the liquid into a saucepan and bring to a boil. Stir in the gelatin until it dissolves. Add Coke. Chill mixture until it thickens and then fold in the fruits. Pour into a greased mold and chill until firm.

Yields: 8 to 10 servings

Mama's Christmas Fruit Salad

We have had this salad at Christmas and Thanksgiving time for as long as I can remember. My oldest sister slips leftovers to take home with her before anyone else can get to it.

2	small packages raspberry gelatin
2	cups boiling water
1	(20-ounce) can crushed pineapple, undrained
1½	cups cottage cheese
1	cup pecans, chopped

Boil water and add to gelatin until dissolved. Add the crushed pineapple, cottage cheese, and pecans. Pour mixture into a 7 x 12-inch oblong dish.

Yields: 8 to 10 servings

Orange Sherbet Gelatin Salad

2	(3-ounce) packages orange gelatin
1	cup boiling water
1	pint orange sherbet
1	(11-ounce) can mandarin oranges, drained *(Save a few for garnish)*
1	cup heavy whipping cream, whipped
	Additional sweetened whipping cream, optional
	Mint Sprigs and reserved mandarin oranges

Dissolve the gelatin in boiling water. Add the sherbet and mix well. Put in the fridge, and when partially set, fold in the mandarin oranges along with the whipped cream. Oil a 1½-quart ring mold and pour the mixture into the mold. Chill until set. This salad sets up quickly.

Yields: 6 to 8 servings

Kathryn's Citrus Salad

This salad is full of fruit. It's good, pretty, and colorful.

3	large packages lemon or orange Jell-O
4	cups boiling water
5	cups cold water
2	cups carrots, shredded
1	navel orange, peeled and sectioned
1	grapefruit, peeled and sectioned
	Sprig of mint

In a large bowl, dissolve the gelatin in boiling water. Then stir in cold water. Chill until gelatin mixture just begins to thicken. Fold the carrots in the gelatin mixture. Cut your orange and grapefruit sections in half and fold into the gelatin mixture. This makes a large salad, yielding 10 to 12 servings. Pour the mixture into 2 (6-cup) greased molds or 1 (3-quart) bowl.

Dressing:

1½	cups of mayonnaise or salad dressing
¼	cup orange juice
2	tablespoons orange rind, grated

Mix these ingredients together. Chill. Serve with the salad.

Note: I save a couple of orange and grapefruit sections. Unmold the salad on a nice plate of lettuce. Garnish with the orange and grapefruit sections along with the sprig of mint.

Yields: 10 to 12 servings

Pickled Peach Salad

I love Pickled Peaches. This is a Southern dish, and very few folks in the North have heard of it. Girls, the men love them. Save your syrup from these delicious peaches to make this recipe. You'll find My Mother's Pickled Peach recipe right here in this book. So, you have absolutely no excuse for not making this salad.

1	cup pickled peach juice
1	small box peach or lemon jello
1	cup ginger ale
1	cup pickled peaches, chopped
½	cup pecans, chopped

Boil pickled peach juice and pour over the jello. Add ginger ale and chill until slightly thickened. Then add your chopped pickled peaches and pecans. Pour into a greased 1-quart mold. Chill. Unmold onto lettuce.

Yields: 4 to 6 servings

Simply Southern Pear Salad

As you see the recipe, you will see why I'm calling this "Simply." Great addition for a quick meal.

1   large can pear halves, drain juice from pears *(do not throw it out-save it, freeze it, and drink it)*
     Salad dressing or mayonnaise
     Sharp cheese, grated
     Maraschino cherries

Simply put a dollop of salad dressing or mayonnaise on the little indention of the pear halves. Sprinkle grated sharp cheese on the dressing, then finish it off with a cherry. If one can of pears isn't enough for your family, get two. Simple enough!

For another variation:
Fill the cavity of the canned pear with a mound of the following:
1   (3-ounce) package cream cheese, softened
     Small amount of evaporated milk mixed with the cream cheese
     Pecans or walnuts, finely chopped for topping

Layered Fresh Fruit Nut Salad

If you are in the mood for a salad, this recipe will make the most delicious summer meal you have ever had. I make this salad sometimes for supper. You can add any kind of fruit. Try using different varieties of fruit, like cantaloupe, peaches, apple chunks, etc. This will make enough for 2 good-size servings. Of course, I could eat the whole recipe.

1	pint fresh strawberries, washed, stemmed and sliced (Save a few for garnish)
½	cup fresh blueberries
1	cup fresh or canned pineapple chunks
2	bananas, sliced
½	teaspoon lemon juice
1	cup green or red seedless grapes
1	(16-ounce) carton cottage cheese, large or small curd
½	cup cashew nuts (whole or pieces) You may add more
½	cup maraschino cherries, drained and blotted with paper towel

Greens to line the serving plate. Start layering the fruit on the greens or you may mix up the fruit; follow with cottage cheese and then top with the cashew nuts. Add Poppy Seed dressing on top of that.

Poppy Seed Dressing:
You may use a commercial dressing or try this recipe for Poppy Seed Dressing!

½	cup orange juice
¼	cup honey
2	tablespoons apple cider vinegar
1	teaspoon salt
2	tablespoons Dijon mustard
1	teaspoon orange rind, grated
1	tablespoon onion, minced
1	cup vegetable oil
1½	tablespoons poppy seeds

Pour all ingredients in a glass jar, except for the poppy seeds. Put the lid on top of the jar and shake. Add the poppy seeds and give it another good shake. Pour this dressing over this wonderful fruit salad. Store in the fridge if any remaining dressing. You may want to double the recipe.

Yields: 1 cup

Apple Salad

This recipe would make a delightful addition to chicken, tuna, or turkey salad with deviled eggs, making a nutritious cold plate on a hot summer day.

In the South, there are plenty of those days. A wonderful, nutritious salad.

1	red delicious apple, unpeeled
1	yellow or green delicious apple, unpeeled
1	tart apple, unpeeled
½	cup miniature marshmallows
½	cup pecans or walnuts, coarsely chopped
½	cup raisins or ½-cup chopped dates
1	small banana
	Juice of 1 lemon
¼	cup of maraschino cherries, drained well by blotting with paper towel
1	cup coconut
	Salad dressing or mayonnaise

Chop apples. Remember to leave on the peel. Pour lemon juice over the apples and bananas and mix well. Mix the rest of the ingredients and add enough mayonnaise or salad dressing as desired. Serve on a bed of lettuce. Lemon juice keeps the apples and bananas from turning dark.

Yields: 4 to 6 servings

Southwest Georgia Grape Salad
By Stan and Ann Gambrel

Stan Gambrel is the Creator of The Big Pig Jig, a Memphis in May Sanctioned Contest held in Vienna, Georgia.

2	pounds green seedless grapes
2	pounds red seedless grapes
1	(8-ounce) cream cheese, softened
1	(8-ounce) sour cream
½	cup granulated sugar
1	teaspoon vanilla extract

Wash grapes and dry thoroughly, using paper toweling. Spread grapes on paper towels and blot dry. Place grapes in a serving bowl. In a small bowl, mix cream cheese, sugar, and vanilla extract. Pour this over the grapes, mixing well.

Topping:

¾	cup light brown sugar, firmly packed
1	cup pecans, chopped

Mix the brown sugar and pecans together. Sprinkle on top of grape salad.

Yields: 10 to 12 servings

Marinated Tomato Salad

	Dash of garlic salt
	Dash of black pepper
	Dash of sugar
¼	teaspoon basil
1	tablespoon dried, minced onion
1	tablespoon wine vinegar
2	tablespoons olive oil
3	medium fresh tomatoes, sliced ¼-inch
	Lettuce leaves to line serving platter

Mix all ingredients, except for the tomatoes and lettuce, whisking to blend well. Very carefully, place the sliced tomatoes in the bowl with the marinade. Cover and put in the fridge for at least 1 hour for flavors to blend. Line the serving platter with lettuce leaves. Arrange the tomato slices on the platter. Spoon the marinade on the tomato slices.

Sweet Potato Salad

A different twist for sweet potatoes. This is perfect for a luncheon or picnic.

1	pound sweet potatoes, peeled, cooked and cubed (about 2 cups)
1	cup ham, cooked and cubed
2	cups miniature marshmallows
1	(8-ounce) can pineapple chunks or tidbits, drained (reserve juice)
½	cup celery, chopped fine, optional
½	cup flaked coconut, optional (Coconut is almost a must)
½	cup walnuts or pecans, chopped

Dressing:

½	cup mayonnaise or salad dressing
½	cup sour cream
¼	cup orange juice
1	teaspoon orange rind, grated

Combine sweet potatoes, ham, marshmallows, pineapple chunks, celery, coconut, and nuts in a large bowl. For the dressing, combine in a smaller bowl the salad dressing or mayonnaise, pineapple juice, sour cream, orange juice, and orange rind. Mix this well. Pour over the sweet potato mixture. Toss this mixture until well blended. Chill in the fridge to blend all flavors.

Yields: 10 to 12 servings

Luncheon Shrimp Salad With French Dressing

2½	pounds raw shrimp*
1½	tablespoons salt
	Shrimp and Crab boil
3	cups celery, minced
8	green onions, chopped
3	hard-boiled boiled eggs, minced
	Lettuce
	Tomato slices
	Additional 2 hard cooked boiled eggs, sliced in wedges

*Cook shrimp in salted boiling water until they turn pink, about 5 minutes. Clean under cold water. Combine the shrimp, celery, onions, minced eggs, and French dressing (recipe below). Place in a covered container and refrigerate overnight. Serve this salad on a bed of lettuce and garnish with tomato wedges and additional boiled egg wedges.

*I like to use crab boil to cook my shrimp, for it adds additional flavoring to the shrimp. However, a lot of the time I have the fish market clean and cook my shrimp for me. It usually costs extra to do that procedure, but is well worth the additional dollars.

French dressing:

1	can tomato soup
½	cup white vinegar
½	cup salad oil
¼	cup sugar
2	tablespoons Worcestershire sauce
1	tablespoon prepared mustard
1	teaspoon celery salt *(You may use regular table salt- I prefer celery salt)*
1	teaspoon paprika
½	teaspoon pepper
1	clove garlic, minced

Combine these ingredients and chill overnight to blend flavors.

Yields: 10 to 12 servings

Mixed Bean and Bacon Salad

I have never particularly cared for the ole version of the Three Bean Salad. In that recipe, the beans were cold, and I particularly think beans taste better warm. However, I changed the recipe somewhat by adding a little bacon and black gold and heating the beans. Remember when I say black gold, I'm referring to bacon grease. I also have added more than 3 beans to this recipe. So, that is why I call this Mixed Bean and Bacon Salad. You can pick any three or use all five beans in this recipe.

1	(16-ounce) package bacon cooked and drained *(reserve the bacon grease)*
½	cup sugar
2	tablespoons cornstarch
1	teaspoon salt
¼	teaspoon pepper
1	cup apple cider vinegar
¼	cup water
1	(15-ounce) can each kidney beans, green beans, lima beans or butter beans, wax beans, and pinto beans (Drain beans)

First, I cook my bacon on a cookie sheet at 350-degrees for 20 to 25 minutes. Drain on paper towels real good and pour up the grease. Crumble up bacon and set aside. Blend sugar, cornstarch, salt, and pepper. Stir in the bacon grease. Then add vinegar and water. Stir this real good. Add the beans to the pan and stir real good. Cover and simmer about 15 minutes. Add the crumbled bacon, saving some for garnish.

Note: If your bacon is real lean, which is a good thing, you may not have the required amount of bacon grease. It will be close, so don't worry about it.

Yields: 6 to 8 servings

Supreme Egg Salad

I love egg salad by itself or in a sandwich. Hollowed-out green or red peppers or firm red tomatoes that have been cut into quarters make an excellent presentation to fill up with the egg salad. Great for a picnic, too.

8	hard-boiled eggs
4	tablespoons mayonnaise or Miracle Whip salad dressing
1	teaspoon sugar
1	teaspoon honey mustard
½	cup sharp cheese, grated (A little more for garnish)
4	tomatoes, unpeeled and insides scooped out
	Several slices of bacon, which have been cooked, drained and crumbled. Save some extra bacon for garnish
	Black pepper to taste
	Paprika to sprinkle on top of tomatoes

To boil eggs, place them in enough cold water to cover completely. On medium high heat, bring them to a boil with the lid on. When they come to a boil, reduce heat to medium for 12 minutes. After that, quickly pour cold water on them. This keeps the yolk bright yellow instead of that green color. Remove the shells and then chop the eggs.

To make the salad, add the mayonnaise or salad dressing, sugar, mustard, and cheese. Leave a little cheese for garnish. Add black pepper to taste. Then stir in the crumbled bacon leaving a little of the bacon to garnish the tomatoes. Fill the tomatoes with the salad. Top with a little grated cheese, a few crumbles of bacon, and a sprinkle of paprika.

Yields: 4 servings

Judy's Bean Salad

From the kitchen of my dear friend
Sharon Dillard, Albany, Georgia

¼	cup vinegar
½	cup sugar
¾	cup Wesson oil
1	teaspoon salt
	Dash of crushed red pepper flakes
2	(14.5-ounce) cans French cut beans, drained
1	(15-ounce) can carrots, Julienne style, drained
1	large Vidalia onion, thinly sliced
1	(15-ounce) can Leseur peas, drained
½	bell pepper, finely chopped
4	stalks celery, finely chopped
1	cup of good quality mayonnaise
	Sprinkle with paprika for color

Mix vinegar, sugar, oil, salt, and red pepper. Stir in the green beans and carrots. Place in glass or earthen bowl, and cover with thin slices of onion. Weigh down the onions with a plate and leave **out** of refrigerator overnight. The next morning, remove the onions and discard. The flavor of the onions has permeated into the green beans and carrots while setting overnight. Combine the can of drained peas, chopped bell pepper, and celery with the marinated ingredients. After mixing well, pour into a colander, draining excess liquid. Be sure to place a bowl under the colander while the salad is in the fridge getting cold. While in the fridge, there will be more liquid draining off.

Remove from the fridge and place in a serving bowl, adding 1 cup of mayonnaise just before serving. Sprinkle with paprika for color.

Yields: 12 servings

Southern Snowflake Ambrosia

True Southerners spend hours in the kitchen preparing their holiday meals. Ambrosia is a traditional dish that graces our tables. Here is my version of Ambrosia. Mama Gillis put apples and bananas in her Ambrosia along with the oranges. I like my Ambrosia in a beautiful crystal bowl.

Do you know how I peel my oranges? With a spoon. Many years ago a friend of mine taught me this. Once you learn the technique, you will put your paring knife down.

12	oranges, peeled, seeded and sectioned
2	(20-ounce cans of crushed pineapple), undrained
1	cup miniature marshmallows
1½	cups sweetened coconut, divided
1	(10-ounce) jar of maraschino cherries, undrained
1	tablespoon almond extract
½	cup powdered sugar

Mix all ingredients in a big bowl and use only 1 cup of the coconut. Stir. Pour ingredients into your glass bowl. You can make this the night before. It's better this way, as all the ingredients have time to mellow. Add ½-cup of the coconut on top of the Ambrosia before serving.

Note: After adding the ½-cup of coconut on top of the Ambrosia, top it off with a couple of maraschino cherries with the stem for garnish.

Yields: 10 to 12 servings

Hint

Do you hesitate to buy oranges to make Ambrosia or other recipes, because you hate to peel them? Put the knife back in the drawer. Get a spoon instead. Cut into the peel of the orange, using the spoon. Do not cut into the membrane with the spoon. Slide the spoon and move the spoon to the inside of the orange peel. This will loosen the peel. Continue to move the spoon all around the inside of the orange peel to fit the curve of the orange itself. You will not break the membrane of the orange with this procedure. The peel slips right off of the orange. You also will not need a knife, except to slice the orange. Now go out and buy that bag of oranges for the holidays to make that Ambrosia.

Lamb Salad with Vinaigrette Salad Dressing

Let your taste buds roll.

4	cups mixed lettuce greens (mesclun), rinsed and dried
	Salt and pepper to taste
¼	cup purple onion, chopped fine
½	pound fresh mushrooms, sliced
½	cup mandarin oranges, drained
1	pound of lamb, cooked and thinly sliced

Mix greens and all salad ingredients except lamb. Divide salad mixture among four plates. Place the lamb slices in the center of each salad. Drizzle with the Vinaigrette Salad Dressing.

Vinaigrette Salad Dressing:

2	cloves of garlic, minced
½	teaspoon salt
2	teaspoons Dijon mustard
	Juice of 1 fresh lemon juice
1	cup olive oil
¾	teaspoon sugar
	Salt to taste
	Fresh ground pepper to taste

In a small bowl, combine the garlic, salt, mustard, and lemon juice, mixing well. Slowly add the olive oil, whisking until thick, and lastly add the sugar, salt and pepper. Makes 1 cup salad dressing.

Note: This recipe would be ideal for that leftover lamb you may have at Easter.

Yields: 4 servings

Sour Cream Potato Salad

4	medium potatoes, cooked, peeled and cubed
½	cup celery, chopped fine*
¼	cup onion, chopped fine
1½	teaspoons salt
¼	teaspoon pepper
1	teaspoon celery seed
1	(8-ounce) carton sour cream
½	cup mayonnaise or salad dressing*
1	tablespoon mustard
2	pinches sugar
1	tablespoon vinegar (apple cider or white)
4	boiled eggs, minced
	Paprika to sprinkle

In a large bowl, combine the potatoes, celery, onion, salt, pepper, and celery seed. Toss ingredients. In a separate small bowl, mix the sour cream, salad dressing, mustard, sugar, and vinegar. Add the sour cream mixture to the potato mixture and toss well. Now fold in the eggs lightly. Chill for 3 to 4 hours to blend flavors.

*These ingredients you can add more or less of depending on your taste.

Yields: 6 to 8 servings

Slaw

A BBQ Sandwich Favorite

3	pounds cabbage, shredded
1	green pepper, chopped fine
1	red pepper, chopped fine
1	carrot, grated
2	medium onions, chopped fine
2	cups sugar
1¼	cups vinegar (apple cider or white)
1	tablespoon salt
2	teaspoons celery seed
1	teaspoon mustard seed

In a large mixing bowl, mix the cabbage, peppers, carrot, and onions. Cover and put in the fridge for at least 2 to 3 hours. Combine the sugar, vinegar, salt, celery, and mustard seed in a pan on the stove; heat on high until the salt is dissolved and boiling. Pour the hot vinegar mixture over the cabbage, peppers, carrots, and onions. Cover once again, and chill for at least 2 to 3 hours or overnight. You can pack this in freezer containers and freeze for later use.

* This is delicious with BBQ sandwiches or fried fish.

Yields: 8 to 10 servings

Creamy Bacon, Lettuce, Tomato Salad

Put this salad in a beautiful glass bowl to display.

Dressing:
1	(.7-ounce) envelope Italian dressing mix
¼	cup sour cream
¼	cup mayonnaise
¼	cup milk

Salad makings:
1	large head Romaine lettuce, washed, blotted with paper towels and torn into bite size pieces
1	pint cherry tomatoes
½	pound bacon, cooked, crumbled
2	cups sharp Cheddar cheese, shredded

Combine the dressing mix, sour cream, mayonnaise and milk, mixing well to blend. If you have a blender, that would be ideal. Put in the fridge. Combine the lettuce, cherry tomatoes, bacon, and cheese. Adding the dressing last, toss it to combine all of the ingredients. Refrigerate until serving time.

Yields: 6 to 8 servings

Tomato Soup Mold Salad

2	cans tomato soup
1	soup can boiling water
1½	packages unflavored gelatin
½	cup cold water
1	cup nuts, chopped fine
1	(3-ounce) package cream cheese
½	cup celery, chopped
3	tablespoons chili sauce
3	tablespoons mayonnaise

Mix the tomato soup and water. Dissolve the gelatin in the cold water and add to the soup mixture. Add all of the other ingredients, pour into a well-greased mold, and put in the fridge. Unmold and serve on lettuce leaves and top with mayonnaise and a thin tomato wedge.

Yields: 4 to 6 servings

Fruit Bowl Salad with Fruit Dressing

2	cups fresh blueberries
2	cups fresh strawberries, hulled and sliced
2	cups green grapes, seedless
2	cups cantaloupe cubes
2	cups honeydew melon cubes
2	cups watermelon cubes

Combine all fruit in a large fruit bowl and mix well. Put in the fridge to chill.

Note: Makes a large quantity. This recipe is easy to break down in a smaller quantity.

Fruit Dressing:
2	cups raspberry sherbet
1	(8-ounce) of your favorite fruit yogurt or vanilla

Mix the sherbet and yogurt together. Serve the dressing with the Fruit Bowl Salad or any Fruit Salad.

Note: You may want to double the Fruit dressing recipe, depending on amount used.

Taco Salad

1	(8-ounce) cream cheese, softened
1	(16-ounce) container sour cream
1	(15-ounce) can Hormel chili with or without beans
1	onion, chopped
1	medium size jar salsa
8	ounces Sharp cheese, shredded
	Paprika to sprinkle
	Nacho chips

In a separate bowl, mix cream cheese and sour cream. Using a large oblong or square glass dish, layer the salad on the serving dish in order, starting with the mixture of cream cheese and sour cream. Sprinkle paprika on top of shredded cheese for color. Serve with nacho chips.

Yields: 6 to 8 servings

Hint

Perpetual Vanilla Extract? Have you looked at the prices for vanilla extract lately? The prices are incredibly outrageous. Many years ago, I quit buying vanilla extract. I make my own. Just go to the liquor store and purchase any brand (cheapest) 750 ml bottle of vodka or rum. Purchase a bottle of the whole vanilla bean pods found in the spice section. Very carefully, split open the vanilla bean pods (this method will release the little beans); slip the whole bean pod with the little beans in the bottle of vodka or rum. Place the top back on the bottle of spirits and shake the bottle every day for at least a month or so. Keep an extra bottle of spirits in your cupboard so that when your vanilla gets low, fill it back up with the spirits. You will have vanilla flavoring for a very long time. I have several bottles in my cupboard, so that I have a fresh one and an aged, ready-to-go bottle. I keep adding the beans to the bottle, as they weaken. I have never taken the beans out of the bottle.

Every year after the holidays, you will find the spices at a cut-rate price. This is the time to buy another bottle of vanilla bean pods and another bottle of spirits. In addition to using this wonderful homemade vanilla extract in your many dishes you prepare, don't forget to use this vanilla extract in making your homemade vanilla ice cream, it will taste like a very expensive popular brand. Just think of the dough that you save. Lord knows how much money I've saved using this method.

Soups, Sandwiches, Spreads & Relishes

Soups

Lunch time at my grammar school in Albany, Georgia, was the best—except when they had Split Pea soup. Everyone at the table would finish their milk off first and then pour the Split Pea soup in the milk cartons. That was probably the only time we drank all of our milk. It didn't take long before the teacher got wise. In those days, we were supposed to try everything on our plate. If you are wondering where my recipe for Split Pea soup is in this section, keep wondering. I lost my appetite for it.

Personally, I would rather have soup any ole day of the week instead of a salad at the beginning of a meal. It's filling and comforting.

Cream of Mushroom Soup

5	tablespoons butter, divided use
½	pound fresh mushrooms, sliced (Save a few caps for garnish)
3½-4	cups water
½	onion, sliced
	Dash of cayenne pepper
1	teaspoon paprika
4	tablespoons flour
1	cup half-and-half
½-1	cup whole milk
2	beef bouillon cubes

Heat 1 tablespoon butter in a skillet and sauté the mushroom slices until softened. Bring the water and bouillon cubes to a boil in a large saucepan, reducing heat to medium high and simmer the onions until tender, about 30 minutes. Set aside. Melt remaining butter in a saucepan that will hold up to 4-quarts. Add the mushroom mixture and whisk the flour and half-and-half to make a thick sauce. Stir in the milk, a dash of cayenne pepper, and paprika and heat all the way through. Slowly stir the onion mixture and stir until the soup is smooth and heated all the way through. Divide the soup between 6 soup bowls and garnish with mushroom caps. Sprinkle with additional paprika. This is an excellent soup.

Zucchini Soup

Years ago, I lived and worked on one of the largest plantations in southwest Georgia. I had the distinct pleasure of meeting a very fine "Southern Lady" by the name of Mrs. Edna Lane Higgins. I loved her so much. I could just sit and talk with her for hours. She was the first "Southern Lady" that I had ever met that had married a "Yankee." She always made the remark that he was a wonderful husband. I only wish that she had been around to know that I, too, eventually married a "Yankee", and am pretty proud of it.

She gave me this wonderful recipe of Zucchini Soup. She was a fine cook.

6	zucchini (5-6 inches long), peeled and diced
3	bunches of spring onions, using the tops, chopped; or 2 cups chopped white onions
	Reserve 1 bunch of spring onions for garnishment for bowls of soup
1	stick butter, melted
2	(14.5-ounce) cans chicken broth*
¼	teaspoon curry powder
	Salt and pepper to taste

Cook the zucchini and onions in the butter until tender. Now put all the ingredients, about 2 cups at a time, including the zucchini, in the blender and purée until creamy. Cook depending on how thick you want your soup. (Figure 1 cup of puree with 1 cup chicken broth.) Pour up and garnish with a few sprigs of spring onions. You may serve this soup hot or cold.

*I like to use equal amounts of homemade chicken broth. Some of the broth will cook down as you cook the soup. You may want to have an extra can of broth handy to thin the soup when you heat it.

Cheddar Cheese Soup

2	cups potatoes, peeled and diced
1	cups carrots, sliced
½	cup celery, chopped fine
⅓	cup onion, chopped fine
2	cups water
½	teaspoon salt
1	pinch black pepper
2	tablespoons butter
2	tablespoons all-purpose flour
2	cups half-and-half cream (You may use regular milk)*
1	cup (4-ounces) Cheddar cheese, grated
1	cup (4-ounces) American cheese, grated
1	cup cooked ham, cubed
	Dash of cayenne pepper
	Paprika

*For soups with that extra richness, I like to use half-and-half in lieu of milk. Just remember that is my own preference. Whole milk will make a wonderful product.

In a large saucepan, combine the potatoes, carrots, celery, onion, water, salt, and black pepper. Bring the ingredients to a boil on medium heat, stirring occasionally, and cook for about 15 minutes. Now reduce the heat to low and cook until the vegetables are tender. This will be about 15 minutes more. You do not want the vegetables to be mushy. DO NOT DRAIN. Now in another saucepan, melt the butter and stir in the flour. Cook, stirring constantly on medium until the mixture or roux is smooth. Now add the milk gradually, stirring often until mixture thickens and boils (about 10 minutes). Boil one minute longer and remove from the heat. Now stir in the good part—the cheeses. Stir until the cheese is melted. Stir cheese sauce into undrained, cooked vegetables and ham. Cook this mixture on medium heat until the soup is heated throughout, stirring often. Now add the cayenne pepper. You want a little kick, so add this to taste. Pour into 6 small soup bowls and sprinkle with paprika.

Creamy Broccoli Soup

This recipe was given to me by Betty, my Mary Kay buddy. A great friend in Albany, Georgia. Thanks Betty. If you want to use a crock pot in this recipe, combine all of the ingredients first, then transfer to the crock pot.

2	tablespoons onion, minced
3	tablespoons butter
3	tablespoons flour
1¼	teaspoon salt
1¼	teaspoon pepper
3	cups whole milk
3	cups chicken broth
2	cups fresh broccoli, chopped
2	cups carrots, thinly sliced
3	potatoes, peeled and diced
1	can minced clams (optional)

Sauté onions in butter. Stir in flour and salt and pepper. Gradually add milk, stirring constantly. Bring to a boil. Add broth, vegetables, and clams. Heat over low heat about 25 minutes, being careful not to boil.

Taco Soup

2	pounds lean ground chuck, ground round, or ground turkey
1	large onion, chopped (approximately 2 cups)
4	(14.25-ounce) cans whole tomatoes cut up
1	(15.25-ounce) can whole kernel corn, drained
1	(16-ounce) can kidney beans, (Do not drain)
1	(16-ounce) can pinto beans (Do not drain)
1	(4-ounce) can chili peppers, diced
1	package taco seasoning mix
1	package Hidden Valley Ranch Salad Dressing mix
1	teaspoon sugar
	Grated sharp cheese, enough for your own preference
	Sour cream
	Tortilla chips
	Paprika to sprinkle

While browning the meat, sauté the onion until transparent. Add all the other ingredients and simmer for 2 hours, stirring frequently. Pour into soup bowls. Serve with dollops of sour cream, top with grated sharp cheese and tortilla chips on the side. Sprinkle cheese with paprika to bring out the color. Delicious.

Onion Soup

⅓	cup butter
4	large onions, sliced very thin *(depending on how much onion you like in soup)*
1	(46-ounce) can beef bouillon
¾	cup water
1	cup Parmesan cheese, grated
	Croutons (optional)

Sauté the onions in the butter. Add the bouillon. Dilute the mixture with ¾-cup of water and simmer. Pour soup in oven-proof soup bowls. Put a few croutons on top of the soup and then the Parmesan cheese. Slip the soup in the oven to melt the cheese, just for a second, though. It's delicious.

Note: You know what would be good on this, if you did not have croutons? If you have Rye bread or even some rye cocktail square bread, toast the bread and place a slice of Swiss cheese on the toast and let it melt in the oven. Then place it on top of the soup and let it float on the soup. If using the regular size rye bread, just cut out circles with the top of a jar or cookie cutters and then put the cheese on top of that and toast.

Yields: 6 good-size servings

Turkey Soup
A meal in itself

1	large onion, chopped
1	cup celery, chopped fine
6	tablespoons butter
6	tablespoons all-purpose flour
½	teaspoon pepper
1¼	teaspoons garlic salt
½	teaspoon dried thyme
½	teaspoon parsley flakes
1½	cups milk or half-and-half cream
4	cups cooked turkey, cubed
4	carrots cut into ¼-inch pieces
2	medium sized potatoes, peeled and diced
2	cups turkey or chicken broth*
1	(10-ounce) package green peas (Frozen)

In a large boiler, sauté onions and celery in butter until tender. Stir in the flour and all of the seasonings while gradually adding the milk. Stir constantly until thickened. Add the turkey, carrots, and potatoes. Now add enough broth until soup is the desired consistency. Cover and simmer for about 15 minutes. Now add the frozen green peas. Cover and simmer until peas are tender, for about 15 minutes.

*When you initially cook your turkey, be sure to save the broth. Freeze it until you get ready to make your soup.

Yields: 6 servings

Creamy Corn Chowder

6	slices of bacon that has been fried, just until crispy. *Be careful not to burn. Save the grease for the recipe.*
½	cup onions, chopped
½	cup celery, chopped
1	cup potatoes, diced
1	teaspoon salt
	Pinch of black pepper
½	cup water
3	tablespoons flour
2	cups milk *(I like to use 1 cup of can milk or half-and-half and 1 cup of whole milk)* This makes the soup rich.
1	(15.25-ounce) can creamed corn
1	(4-ounce) jar pimentos, chopped
	Dash of cayenne pepper
1	cup sharp cheese, grated

If you use a large fry pan, this will eliminate you using an extra pan for making the Chowder. After frying the bacon, crumble it leaving out 2 slices. Add onions, celery, and the potatoes and brown them slightly in the bacon grease. Add the salt and pepper. Add ½-cup of water to this mixture, cover and cook until almost fork-tender. Blend the flour into the milk along with the can of creamed corn and pimentos. Now add this mixture to the vegetables. Stir constantly until this mixture boils. Add cayenne pepper to taste. Spoon into 4 bowls, topping with the grated cheese. Using the 2 reserved slices of the bacon, cut into halves and put on top of each bowl of soup.

Egg Drop Soup

This is a delicious soup. I like to make it when I don't feel good or I say when I feel "puny." It gives you a boost.

4	cups chicken stock or broth
2	tablespoons soy sauce
1½	cups fresh mushrooms, sliced or 2 (6-ounce) cans mushrooms, drained
1	(4-ounce) can bamboo shoots, drained
½	cup carrots, shredded
½	cup frozen peas
½	teaspoon white pepper *(If you don't have white pepper, just use the black pepper)*
⅓	cup rice vinegar (You may use distilled vinegar)
2	tablespoons cornstarch
½	cup cold water
3	eggs, slightly beaten
	Green onions, to garnish

In a large pot, combine the stock or broth, soy sauce, mushrooms, bamboo shoots, carrots, and peas. Bring to boil over high heat. Reduce the heat to a simmer and continue cooking with the pot covered for about 5 minutes. Stir in the pepper and vinegar. In a separate bowl, combine the cornstarch, cold water and stir this in the soup mixture. Keep cooking until the soup begins to thicken. Now slowly stir in the eggs. Serve immediately and garnish with the green onions.

Yields: 6 (½-cup) servings

Cream of Bacon and Potato Soup

Do you have leftover mashed potatoes? Try out this soup. Your family will love it.

1	cup celery, chopped
½	cup onion, chopped
½	cup water
4 or 5	slices bacon *(If you want to cook a few more slices to garnish or add more to the soup, your preference)*
2-3	tablespoons bacon grease
2	tablespoons all-purpose flour
1	cup leftover mashed potatoes
2	tablespoons butter
3	cups milk *(I like to use half evaporated milk and half whole milk. This makes it richer and yes, more fattening. But what can I say?)*
	Salt and pepper to taste
	Dash of cayenne pepper
2	cups sharp cheese, grated *(Try using the Jalapeño cheese, but omit the cayenne pepper—unless you are brave. Save 1 cup for topping)*

Combine the onions, celery, and water in a medium-sized saucepan. Boil until tender and set aside. In a large skillet, brown the bacon. Take the bacon out of the skillet and set aside leaving the bacon grease. Keep the heat on medium high and combine the bacon grease, butter, and flour in the skillet. Blend well. Gradually add the milk with the flour mixture, stirring and blending well. Now fold in the mashed potatoes, stirring well. Do not leave the stove! With all of this starch, it will scorch. Heat just to boiling. Now add the celery, onions, and bacon (crumbled). Fold in the 1 cup of cheese. Season to taste and top each bowl with grated cheese. If you have any more leftover bacon, break a slice of cooked bacon in half and garnish on top of the cheese.

Homemade Chicken Soup

1	(46-ounce) can chicken broth
1	can cream of chicken or celery soup, undiluted
1	soup can water
½-1	pound boneless uncooked chicken, skinless and cut into bite-size pieces*
1½	cups medium egg noodles, uncooked
½	cup carrots, sliced thin, uncooked
1	cup potatoes, peeled and sliced thin
⅓	cup onion, chopped
⅓	cup celery, chopped
¼	teaspoon black pepper
½	teaspoon salt or salt to taste
1	teaspoon dill weed

In a large saucepan, combine all of the ingredients, bringing to a good rolling boil on medium heat. Lower the heat to simmer and cook until the chicken is no longer pink and the vegetables and noodles are tender. Stir frequently to keep from sticking.

Note: If soup is too thick, add a little milk or water to your liking.

*If you like a meatier soup, use 1 pound of chicken.

Yields: 6 servings

Sandwiches & Spreads

Attention ladies! I know the men in your life know what an "intake manifold" is on your car. Well, listen to this—a quick, hot and tasty sandwich spread heated right from the "intake manifold" itself. Yes, siree—bobtail! This is how to do it.

Place an unopened can of Underwood Deviled Ham or Roast Beef sandwich spread on the "intake manifold" of your car. When you reach your destination, try smearing it on a slice of bread. It's hot and delicious.

I did this on numerous occasions when traveling back and forth to the glorious Gulf of Mexico in a 1971 Chevrolet pickup truck. While I was 75-100 miles from getting to the beach or that far from home, this is what I would do to stop the hunger pains.

Try the same with baking potatoes, either sweet or regular. Wrap in tin foil and place on the "intake manifold." See, there are ways that you don't have to stop at a restaurant.

I don't know if the newer vehicles have a flat "intake manifold." I'm not much on what's inside of a vehicle.

Here are some very simple sandwiches—great on a summer day.

Sometimes we had these on Saturday nights when we got back from buying groceries at the Piggly Wiggly. That was usually the only time we ate sandwiches. They were a treat, for we did not have them often.

Lord, y'all, Mama Gillis made the best sandwiches in the world. It could have been because it was Mama Gillis who made them. But she would make a plain bologna sandwich or pineapple sandwich taste as good as a steak.

Mama Gillis never believed in slapping cold meat like bologna on a piece of bread without boiling it first. Now you may think why in the world would she boil it? Well, this is what she told me, and as I think about it, I believe Mama Gillis might have had a crystal ball.

Mama Gillis always told me that there were far too many preservatives in cold cuts. Only, she never used the word preservatives. She just said you never knew what was in there, just like hot dogs. She boiled the "devil" out of the hot dogs. Why, when she got through boiling those hot dogs, they were peeled wide open.

But to get back to Bologna sandwiches. Naturally, if we had a Bologna sandwich, the bologna had to be boiled first. We would just put the Bologna with mayonnaise and sliced tomatoes on the light bread, sprinkle with salt and pepper, and that was it.

Whenever I would give a Wedding Shower or Tea, I would always include a plate of little finger sandwiches. You can also cut the sandwiches with those decorative cookie cutters. A lot of these recipes could also be put on crackers and be used for great appetizers.

To give it that finished look. I make little cream cheese flowers on the sandwiches.

1	(8-ounce) package cream cheese, softened
	Food coloring
	Decorating tubes

Mix the cream cheese. Add the coloring and mix well. Fill decorating tubes, and pipe little flowers on top of the sandwiches. Don't forget to make the leaves—you will get raves. Let your kids help you. They will have a ball.

Note: I always use the thin sliced bread for appetizers.

Pineapple Spread

1	(3-ounce) package cream cheese
2	tablespoons pineapple juice
3	tablespoons walnuts or pecans, chopped

Combine cheese, pineapple juice, and nuts. Blend well. Spread on bread or crackers.

Hot and Spicy Apricot Spread

1   (18-ounce) jar apricot preserves
8   ounces of cream cheese
3-4   tablespoons or horseradish to taste (If you want a kick)

Mix well and spread onto sandwiches.

This is another way to use this recipe and is just as tasty. Using the same ingredients, mix the apricot preserves with the horseradish. Place an 8-ounce block of cream cheese on the serving platter. Pour the Apricot Preserves mixed with the horseradish over the entire block of cream cheese. Serve with assorted crackers.

Pineapple Cheesy Nut Spread

1   (8-ounce) cream cheese, softened
1   cup of Swiss cheese, grated
2   tablespoons half and half cream or evaporated milk
       Dash of curry powder
       Dash of ginger
1   (8-ounce) can crushed pineapple, well drained
½   cup pecans, finely chopped

Combine cream cheese, Swiss cheese, cream, curry and ginger, mixing well. Stir in pineapple and nuts. Chill. Wonderful!

Chilly Cheese Spread

1   (3-ounce) package cream cheese, softened
1   tablespoon good quality mayonnaise or salad dressing
1   tablespoon chili sauce
1   tablespoon sweet pickle relish
1   teaspoon onion, grated
1   hard-boiled egg, chopped (optional)

Soften the cream cheese and add the other ingredients, blending thoroughly. Spread onto sandwiches. Makes ¾-cup spread.

Georgia Peach Spread

1	rib of celery, finely chopped in food processor
1	fresh peach, peeled and cut up
1	(3-ounce) package of cream cheese, softened
1	tablespoon mayonnaise or Miracle Whip salad dressing
1	dash almond extract

After chopping celery in a food processor, add the peach, and puree. Add cream cheese, mayonnaise, and extract. Mix well. You may have to add a little more mayonnaise or salad dressing, just a dab for spreading consistency.

Ham Salad Spread

We often forget what we can do with leftover ham. Put this to good use. Don't pay the deli when you can prepare it for pennies.

3	cups fully cooked ham, ground
½	cup Miracle Whip or mayonnaise (You will see that I am a Miracle Whip buff-it has a sweeter taste.)
¼	cup sweet pickle relish, drained
1-2	tablespoons prepared mustard
	Dash of celery salt
1	boiled egg, diced (optional)

Some folks like to omit the dry mustard and put a tad of prepared mustard-just a tad.

When grinding the ham, knife chop and then pulse chop the ham in the food processor. You do not want the ham to come out of the processor mushy, the product will not be as tasty. Add the rest of the ingredients. Mix well and store covered in the refrigerator. Serve with sandwiches or assorted crackers. Makes about 3 cups. To make an excellent appetizer, shorten the lengths of celery stalks and stuff them with this tasty spread. Pretty, too!

Different variations to mix into the Spread:
Add a handful of minced raisins
Add ¼-cup of chutney

Creamy Ham N Cheese Sandwich Spread

2	cups cooked ham, shredded
1	(4-ounce) cream cheese, softened
	Dijon mustard to taste or you may use
	Hot Chutney to taste
	Cocktail Square Bread *(This bread is in loaves and you may find these at any Deli. It comes in several varieties, including Rye Squares, Pumpernickel, Sour Dough, etc.)*

Mix all of the ingredients. Spread on any of the breads described above.

Bologna and Cheese Sandwich Spread

½	pound bologna
1	small onion
4	medium sweet pickles
1	teaspoon celery seed
½	pound (2 cups) American cheese, grated
½	teaspoon salt
½	teaspoon pepper
¾	cup good quality mayonnaise or salad dressing

In your food processor, grind together the bologna, onion, and sweet pickles. Pour the mixture in a medium-sized bowl and add the other ingredients, blending thoroughly. Spread onto sandwiches.

Yields: 3 cups

Deviled Egg Spread

We often forget to use our most convenient items we have on hand. Check your cupboards before you run to the grocery store. If you like Egg Salad, you will love this.

1	dozen hard-boiled eggs, finely chopped
1	tablespoon prepared mustard
¼	cup sweet pickle relish*
¼	cup finely chopped celery* (optional)
½	teaspoon salt
1	(12-ounce) package of bacon, cooked, drained and crumbled (optional)
⅓	cup Miracle Whip or mayonnaise
	Dash of hot sauce to taste
	Paprika to sprinkle

*You may use either one or both of the ingredients. I like using one or the other, not both.

Blend together all ingredients except eggs. Lastly, add the boiled eggs. Sprinkle with paprika. Makes about 3 cups spread. Wonderful.

Note: When I use the tomatoes for this recipe, as in putting the Deviled Egg Spread in them for the container, I do not finely chop the boiled egg, I chop them but leave the pieces bigger. You want a little more substance. Great for a Cold Plate in the summer when the weather is warm and a great luncheon idea! Hollow out the inside of about 4 or 5 unpeeled, firm tomatoes. Line a plate with lettuce. Pile the spread inside each tomato. Don't forget to sprinkle paprika on the finished product. Put a tiny sprig of parsley or a sliver of cooked bacon on top. Adds great color and is pretty tasty.

Tuna Sandwich in a Hot Dog Bun

I know everyone has leftover hot dog buns. Sometimes we forget that hot dog buns can be utilized in other ways. If your child likes tuna fish, pack this nutritious sandwich in his lunch box. Try Ham Salad with this, too.

1	(7-ounce) can tuna, drained
½	cup sweet pickle relish, drained
¼	cup celery, chopped fine, optional
2	tablespoons onion, minced
1	hard-boiled egg, chopped fine
1	tablespoon lemon juice
¼	teaspoon salt
	Dash of pepper
½	cup good quality salad dressing or mayonnaise
4	hot dog buns, lightly buttered

Combine all of the ingredients, except for the hot dog buns. Mix well. Fill the hot dog buns and put in the fridge until you are ready to pack your lunch.

Egg Salad Sandwich in a Hot Dog Bun

4	hard-boiled eggs, chopped fine
2	tablespoons good quality salad dressing or mayonnaise
	Pinch of salt
	Pinch of pepper
2-3	tablespoons sweet pickle relish, drained
4	hot dog buns, lightly buttered

Combine all of the ingredients, except for the hot dog buns. Fill the hot dog buns with the salad and keep in the fridge until you are ready to pack a lunch.

Pizza Dogs

Another great way to use up hot dog buns. This is great also to take fishing.

1	pound ground round or chuck, browned and drained
¾	teaspoon garlic salt
⅔	cup tomato sauce
1	cup Muenster cheese or whatever string cheese is on sale
¼	teaspoon oregano
	Pinch of sugar

Combine all the ingredients, cook, and let cool. Fill the hot dog buns with this mixture. Wrap in foil and bake at 350-degrees for 15 to 20 minutes. Cook this while you are getting everything ready to go fishing in the morning. After baking, just place them, still individually wrapped just like they came out of the oven, in an aluminum pie tin. Wrap a sheet of foil over this. This will keep them nice and toasty and you can store the pie tin under your fishing boat seat.

Cranberry Cheese Sandwich Spread

1	(8-ounce) block cream cheese, softened
¼	cup pecans, chopped
¼	cup cranberries, dried
⅛	cup orange juice concentrated, undiluted
	Cinnamon to taste

With an electric mixer, beat the cream cheese until soft and creamy. Pour into a medium-sized bowl and add the other ingredients, stirring to combine well. Cover the bowl and put in the fridge to let flavors mellow. Spread onto assorted breads or crackers.

Pineapple Sandwiches

The Pineapple Sandwiches were absolutely wonderful. The best part of eating them was letting the pineapple juice drool down your arms. You may wrinkle your brow on that, but in Southwest Georgia on a summer day, that feels good. Anything cold feels good.

Some folks have never thought about eating Pineapple Sandwiches. Try it, you will like it!

Anyway, here's how Mama Gillis made the Pineapple Sandwiches.

1	(20-ounce) can of cold crushed pineapple, drained*
	Mayonnaise or Miracle Whip
2	slices of light bread

We were not stingy with the mayonnaise or Miracle Whip. The middle part of the sandwich where the pineapple and mayonnaise went together was the best part, after you ate all of the crust of the bread.

Note: If Mama Gillis did not have crushed pineapple, we made Pineapple Sandwiches with the sliced pineapple. We just had straight mayonnaise in the hole of the pineapple, though.

Now, I believe I may have told you that light bread in the South was just plain white bread. We ate Sunbeam bread. Do you remember that advertisement of Sunbeam bread, where the little girl with gorgeous blonde curls and blue eyes tore the bread in half and it always tore in half every time, perfectly?

Potato Chip Sandwich

	Potato chips
2	slices of light bread
	Mayonnaise or Miracle Whip

One handful of potato chips, and don't crush them either. The fun in eating the Potato Chip sandwich, other than the taste of it, is the crushing of the chips between your teeth.

Orange Pineapple Spread

1	(3-ounce) package cream cheese, softened
1	tablespoon orange juice
1	teaspoon orange rind, grated
4	tablespoons crushed pineapple, drain juice

Double or triple this recipe when making large quantities.

Beat the cream cheese until creamy, adding the rest of the ingredients. Spread on assorted sandwiches or crackers.

Note: This spread would make very attractive and tasty sandwiches for a bridal or baby shower. Remember how I mentioned to decorate the sandwiches with cream cheese flowers.

Pumpkin Butter

Use with buttered toast, biscuits or tea breads.

3	cups fresh cooked pumpkin, mashed
1	cup granulated sugar
2	tablespoons butter
½	teaspoon ground cinnamon
¼	teaspoon ground ginger
¼	teaspoon ground nutmeg
½	teaspoon white vinegar

Combine all ingredients in a heavy saucepan, mixing well. Cook over low heat for 1 hour, stirring often.

Yields: 2½-cups

Good Ole Southern Pimento Cheese Spread

This is my favorite sandwich spread in the whole world. I'm drawn to the refrigerator when I have a bowl of this in there.

1	(8-ounce) block of sharp cheese, grated
1	(4-ounce) small jar of pimentos, diced
	Miracle Whip or Mayonnaise*
	Black Pepper to taste

Enough Miracle Whip salad dressing to make it easy to spread-not too much though. You do not want the salad dressing to overpower the cheese and pimentos. A little dash of red pepper, if desired. That's it.

*You may use mayonnaise in lieu of Miracle Whip. Miracle Whip makes the pimento cheese sweeter.

Bacon Spread

1	cup of sharp cheese, grated
½	small onion, grated
1	(12-ounce) package of bacon cooked, drained and crumbled
½	cup Miracle Whip salad dressing (you may need a little more, just enough to make it easy to spread)

Also, a big slab of a tomato would be good on this sandwich spread.

Mix well and spread on sandwiches.

Italian Sandwich Spread

1	(8-ounce) package cream cheese, softened
2	cups of Sharp cheese, grated
1	(.7-ounce) envelope of Good Seasons Italian Salad Dressing mix
¼	cup Miracle Whip salad dressing
	Dash of garlic powder

Mix the ingredients and spread on sandwiches or crackers.

Deviled Ham Spread

1   (4.25-ounce) can deviled ham
½   cup sour cream
2   teaspoons pickle relish*

*You could add a little chutney in the place of pickle relish if you like.

Mix together. Spread on sandwiches.

Honey Raisin Spread

When you need a boost, try this on a sandwich or crackers. This would be a healthy choice for mid-morning snack.

½   cup peanut butter
¼   cup honey
⅓   cup chopped raisins

Combine ingredients, mixing well. Spread on crackers, toasted bread, or wheat thins. A great and healthy treat—core an apple, and put a spoonful in the core of the apple.

Strawberry Cream Cheese Spread

1   (8-ounce) package of cream cheese, softened
½   cup fresh strawberries, sliced

Mix the ingredients and serve with ginger snaps.

When I would go to Panama City Beach, Florida, on a whim for the day, I would pack this and a fruit salad. How refreshing under that blazing sun. With me living here in Michigan, I miss those last-minute sporadic trips to the beach.

Cranberry Relish

1	(16-ounce) package fresh cranberries
2	oranges
2	cups granulated sugar
1	(3-ounce) package lemon-flavored gelatin
1½	cups boiling water
½	chopped celery
½	cup chopped pecans or walnuts

Sort and wash cranberries. Drain. Quarter and seed the oranges. Grind the oranges, cranberries, and celery in your food processor or blender. Combine the cranberry mixture and sugar and stir well. Let stand until the sugar melts. Dissolve the gelatin in boiling water and cool. Add the gelatin and pecans to the cranberry mixture. Stir well and chill.

Jar up a couple half-pints and give these to the neighbors for a quick gift for their Thanksgiving or Christmas Dinner and it's one less thing they have to prepare. They will appreciate this. If you jar this up, keep it in the refrigerator.

Yields: 2-quarts

Hint

Do you have a leftover bag of potato chips with just the remaining crumbs in there. Don't throw it out. To ½-cup of potato chip crumbs, add ½-cup of your favorite grated cheese. Sprinkle over the top of any casserole, such as Macaroni and Cheese or any favorite Tuna Casserole, or Baked Casserole, etc. Bake as usual.

Sides & Vegetables

sketch by Ruthie Lee Gillis

Cooked Apple Wedges

This is delicious to eat as a side dish for dinner or for breakfast.

4	tablespoons butter
1	tablespoon lemon juice
5	cups apples, peeled and cut into wedges
⅓	cup light brown sugar, firmly packed
	Cinnamon to taste

Melt butter in a large skillet over medium heat. Mix the apples and lemon juice and pour into fry pan. Sprinkle with brown sugar. Brown apples lightly on both sides, turning once. If the apples are not tender, cover the pan and cook over low heat until they are tender. Sprinkle in the cinnamon to taste.

Yields: 4 to 6 servings

Apples, Onions & Beer

I have never acquired the taste for beer. The closest I have been to beer is to use it as a setting lotion for my hair. That's the truth. But this recipe is great and would be fitting to pair up with pork.

1	pound small onions, peeled and cut into quarters
½	cup butter
1	cup beer
½	cup maple syrup or maple flavored syrup
4	small apples, peeled, cored and sliced into thick slices
1	tablespoon spicy brown mustard
1	tablespoon white vinegar
½	teaspoon poultry seasoning

In a large skillet, melt butter and sauté the onions under tender. Add the beer and syrup and heat until boiling. Cook uncovered about 15 minutes, stirring often until the liquid is almost evaporated. Now stir in the remaining ingredients. Cook over medium heat, stirring often until apples are tender. Serve warm.

Yields: 6 servings

Apples Stuffed With Sweet Potatoes

Picture this side dish at your next holiday meal. Red and green apples stuffed with creamy sweet potatoes surrounding a scrumptious Baked Pork Loin. Great way to use up leftover sweet potatoes from a meal. This would be also be perfect to jazz up a weekday suppertime meal and serve it with Fried Pork Chops.

6	medium size baking apples, washed and cored
2	cups sweet potatoes, cooked and mashed*
¾	cup brown sugar, firmly packed
½	teaspoon salt
½	teaspoon cinnamon
4	tablespoons butter, melted
¼	cup maple syrup
1	cup pecans, chopped
	Cinnamon sugar to sprinkle
4	tablespoons butter, melted (extra)
	Aluminum foil

Wash and core the apples, but do not core them all the way through. When removing the pulp, make the opening at least 1¼-inch wide. Using aluminum foil, cut 6 squares of foil approximately 7-inches square to fit around the bottom and sides of each apple. Set aside. Mix together the sweet potatoes, brown sugar, salt, cinnamon, melted butter, and maple syrup. Fill the cavity of each apple generously with the sweet potato mixture, piling the potato mixture on top of each apple. Sprinkle the tops of the apples with the 1 cup pecans. Top the pecans by sprinkling cinnamon sugar on each apple. Place the apples in a greased baking dish.* Drizzle the extra 4 tablespoons of butter over the apples. If you have any leftover sweet potato mixture, just mound it around the apples in the baking dish. Bake at 350-degrees for 30 to 40 minutes.

*Again, you may use leftover mashed sweet potatoes from a previous meal to prepare this dish or simply open up a can of sweet potatoes and prepare them according to the recipe.

Yields: 6 servings

Asparagus and Pea Casserole

A great Easter dish!

2	cups English Peas, drained
1	(10.5-ounce) can asparagus, drained*
1	teaspoon salt
¼	teaspoon black pepper
1	(4-ounce) jar pimentos, chopped (you do not have to drain)
2	hard-boiled eggs, chopped (optional)
1½	cups Ritz crackers or Ritz-like crackers, crushed
1	cup evaporated milk
1½	cups sharp cheese, shredded (Cheddar is fine)
	Dash of Paprika
1	stick butter, melted

*You may use fresh Asparagus. Cook, drain, and cut the asparagus into 2-inch pieces.

Preheat oven to 350-degrees. Grease a 2-quart casserole dish. Mix all ingredients except for the melted butter and paprika, and place in the casserole dish. Pour melted butter over the top. Sprinkle with paprika, and bake for 30 minutes at 350-degrees.

Yields: 6 servings

Sour Cream and Green Bean Casserole

2	tablespoons butter
2	tablespoons all-purpose flour
½	teaspoon salt
	Pinch of pepper
¾	cup milk
½	cup sour cream
1	(17-ounce) can French-style green beans, drained
½	cup Swiss cheese, shredded
2	cups Funyuns onion flavored rings, crumbled

Melt butter in a saucepan over low heat. Blend in the flour, salt, and pepper. Cooking over low heat, stir the roux until smooth. Remove from the heat and add the milk. Return the saucepan back to the stove and heat until thick. Now remove from the heat one more time and add the sour cream, stirring until blended. Grease a 1½-quart baking dish and pour the green beans in the dish. Add the sour cream mixture, blending well into the beans. Top with the Swiss cheese and top the cheese with the crumbled onion-flavored rings. Bake 20 to 25 minutes at 325-degrees. To garnish for serving, place whole onion flavored rings on the casserole dish. (This is a little different twist to the traditional Holiday Green Bean Casserole.)

Yields: 4 servings

Pole Beans and New Potatoes

2	pounds new potatoes
1	teaspoon salt
1	pound fresh pole beans or fresh Blue Lake snap beans
1	ham hock or small piece smoked ham (side meat) to season*
1	teaspoon sugar
½	teaspoon black pepper
1	cup evaporated milk or half-and-half
½	cup whole milk
1	stick butter
	Salt and pepper to taste

Wash potatoes well and peel off narrow strip in the center of each potato. Cook the potatoes in boiling water, adding one teaspoon of salt in the water. Cook until just barely tender, about 15 to 20 minutes, depending on the size of the potatoes. Drain the potatoes and set aside. In a large saucepan, boil the ham hock or piece of side meat in water for about 10 to 15 minutes. Sprinkle in ½ teaspoon black pepper with the side meat. Add the beans to the ham hock, adding the 1 teaspoon of sugar, and boil until tender-about 15 minutes. Do not drain the water. (I usually do not add extra salt to the beans while cooking as the smoked ham hocks have salt in them.) Now combine the potatoes with the beans, seasoning* meat, half-and-half, milk, butter, and salt and pepper to taste. Heat throughout without boiling. Just barely stir the potatoes.

* "Season" is a Southern term for "flavor".

Yields: 6 to 8 servings

The Old Favorite of Broccoli Rice and Cheese Dish

2	(10-ounce) packages chopped broccoli, cooked and drained
¾	cup onion, chopped
¾	cup celery, chopped
4	tablespoons butter
3	cups rice, cooked (divided use)
1	(10.75-ounce) can cream of mushroom soup
1	(10.75-ounce) can cream of chicken soup
1	(8-ounce) jar Cheez Whiz
	Paprika to sprinkle

Cook broccoli as directed on package, drain, and set aside. Sauté onion and celery in butter until tender. Add broccoli, both kinds of soups, Cheez Whiz and one cup of rice to the sauté mixture. Mix well and set aside. Grease a large baking dish. Line the baking dish with the remaining 2 cups of cooked rice. Now add the broccoli mixture. Sprinkle with paprika and bake 30 minutes at 350-degrees.

Yields: 6 to 8 servings

Hilda's Broccoli Casserole

3	eggs, beaten
3	(10-ounce) boxes broccoli spears
1	can cream of mushroom or cream of chicken soup
1	cup mayonnaise
2	cups Cheddar cheese or Colby cheese, grated
	Salt and Pepper to suit taste
	Sprinkle with paprika

Steam broccoli just until tender. Drain well and cut up in pieces. Add the other ingredients in a large bowl. Mix well. Pour ingredients into a greased casserole dish and sprinkle paprika on top. Bake at 375-degrees for 30 to 45 minutes or until firm to touch.

Yields: 8 servings

Broccoli and Cauliflower Casserole

1	(10-ounce) package frozen broccoli, chopped
1	(10-ounce) package frozen cauliflower, chopped
1	(10.75-ounce) can cream of mushroom soup
1	(10.75-ounce) can Cheddar cheese soup
½	cup evaporated milk
1	tablespoon Worcestershire sauce
1	can French Fried onion rings*

Mix 1 cup of water with broccoli and cauliflower and cook about 10 minutes. Remove from heat and drain well. Mix the soups, milk, and Worcestershire sauce. Pour over broccoli and cauliflower and mix thoroughly. Pour into casserole dish and bake for 20 to 25 minutes at 400-degrees. The last five minutes, top the casserole dish with the French fried onion rings.

*Instead of purchasing a small can of fried onion rings, I buy the bag of onion rings found in the potato chip aisle. In my opinion, they are better, and if it is around the holidays you have some left for that Green Been Casserole. There's enough left for your kids or that Big Kid.

Yields: 6 to 8 servings

Orange Glazed Carrots

When I was a teenager, I grew a garden and planted carrots. The green stalks were growing like crazy, but I couldn't understand where the carrots were. When Mama Gillis came by, I asked her about it, and she went and pulled one up. I had no idea that carrots grew in the ground!

4	cups carrots, sliced
½	cup butter, melted
2	tablespoons light brown sugar
1	teaspoon cornstarch
¼	teaspoon salt
	Dash cloves
	Dash ginger
¼	cup orange juice
	Fresh parsley for garnish or dried parsley flakes

Cook carrots in boiling, salted water until fork tender—about 10 minutes. Drain well. Melt butter in a saucepan, add the rest of the ingredients, except for the parsley, and stir until thickened. Pour over the hot carrots. Sprinkle with fresh parsley or parsley flakes.

Yields: 6 servings

Fried Okra

2	pints fresh okra
	Cornmeal and all-purpose flour (Mix half cornmeal and half flour)
	Salt and pepper to taste
	Dash cayenne pepper
	Oil or better yet bacon drippings

Heat oil to 375-degrees. While preheating the skillet, wash okra and pat dry with paper towels. Slice into ¼-inch slices. Put the cornmeal and flour in a paper sack and shake, mixing well. Now add the okra, a few pieces, at a time until well-coated. Fry the okra until golden brown. Drain on paper towels and season with salt and pepper.

Yields: 4 to 6 servings

Scalloped Corn Casserole

½	pound bacon, cooked and drained
1	(17-ounce) can creamed corn
3	eggs, beaten
½	cup half-and-half
½	cup onion, chopped
2	tablespoons butter, melted
½	cup herb-seasoned stuffing mix
	Salt and pepper to taste
	Paprika

Preheat oven 350-degrees. Break the cooked bacon into small pieces. Combine all ingredients in a mixing bowl and mix well. Pour this mixture in a greased casserole dish. Sprinkle with paprika. Bake for about 45 minutes until center of the mixture is firm.

Yields: 6 servings

Creamy Cauliflower Dish

1	medium-sized cauliflower
	Salt and pepper to taste
1	(8-ounce) container sour cream
1	cup Cheddar or sharp cheese, shredded
1	cup cracker crumbs
1	stick butter, melted
	Paprika to sprinkle

Preheat oven to 350-degrees. Prepare a 2-quart casserole dish by greasing with butter. Rinse the cauliflower and separate the flowerets. Using a 2-quart saucepan, boil the cauliflower in salty water for 10 minutes. Drain. Season with salt and pepper. Place half of the cauliflower in the casserole and spread half of the sour cream and half of the cheese over the cauliflower. Place the other half of cauliflower with the other half of the sour cream and half of the cheese. Top with cracker crumbs and pour the butter over the cauliflower and then sprinkle with paprika. Bake 20 to 25 minutes until bubbly.

Yields: 4 to 6 servings

Fresh Country Cream Corn

Mama Gillis always called this "Roast Nears." We ate more corn fixed like this than on the cob. I could eat it cold. If you have a cast-iron skillet, this is the best way to fix it. Don't forget, you need to have a big slab of real butter floating on the top.

12	ears of fresh corn, scraped off of the cob
1	stick of butter, melted
2	tablespoons of bacon grease
	Water
½	cup evaporated milk

Scrape the corn off of the cob into the skillet. Add the butter and bacon grease and just enough water to make the mixture creamy. Remember, corn has a lot of starch in it. Cook on the top of the stove over low heat for about 20 minutes, stirring often. This will scorch if you don't keep it stirred. Now add the can of evaporated milk in the skillet and bake for 30 minutes longer in a 350-degree oven. You will need a skillet that has a handle that is heat-resistant or wrap the handle with several layers of aluminum foil, or you may simply grease a baking dish and pour the corn mixture into the baking dish and cook as recipe specifies. As far as I'm concerned, this is the best way to eat corn.

Yields: 4 servings

Corn and Okra Side Dish

6	ears fresh corn on the cob, scrape the corn off of the cob
1	beef bouillon cube
½	cup boiling water
¼	cup butter
1	medium onion, cut into strips
1	(10-ounce) package frozen cut okra, thawed
½	teaspoon salt
¼	teaspoon pepper
	Dash of sugar

After scraping the corn off of the cob, dissolve the bouillon cube in the boiling water. Set aside. Melt the butter in a large skillet. Sauté the onion until crispy. Add the corn and okra, bouillon mixture, salt and pepper. Mix well. Bring to a boil. Add the dash of sugar. Reduce heat, cover, and simmer until tender— about 20 to 30 minutes, stirring often. You do not want this to scorch.

Yields: 6 servings

Fried Eggplant with Parmesan Cheese

This recipe tells how to fry eggplant. Adding Parmesan Cheese is totally optional. It adds that something extra.

1	large eggplant, peeled and cut into ¼-inch slices
1	cup milk *(I use can milk or evaporated milk)*
1	egg, beaten
1	cup all-purpose flour
1	teaspoon baking powder
1	teaspoon salt
	Pinch of black pepper
	Parmesan cheese
	Crisco oil for frying

In a large skillet, heat oil to 375-degrees. Combine milk and egg, mixing well. Mix the flour, salt and black pepper. Dip the eggplant into the milk and egg batter. Then dip into the flour mixture. Fry until golden brown. Drain on paper towels. Now sprinkle with Parmesan cheese.

Out-of-Season Cream Corn

Here in Michigan, when it is snowing and blowing, I think of the summer meals down South. Well, here is a recipe that tastes the nearest to the Fresh Country Cream Corn when fresh corn is not available. I had a food critic at my home for supper, and he couldn't tell the difference. I did not let on either.

2	(16-ounce) bags whole kernel corn, frozen
1	stick butter, softened*
1	large can evaporated milk
	Salt and Pepper to taste
	Blender

*If you have bacon grease in the fridge like I do, cut down on the butter and use the bacon grease. It's better anyway.

Preheat oven to 350-degrees. Butter a 2-quart baking dish. Pour one bag of whole kernel corn in the blender. You may need to do one bag at a time, depending on the quantity your blender holds. Take a half stick of butter and throw it in there with half of the can of evaporated milk. Pulse until most of the kernels are no longer kernels. You want a few kernels left in there. If there are a lot of kernels, folks will know what you did. Pour that batch in the baking dish. Now, do the other bag of corn just like you did the first batch. Just pour it on top of the other one in the baking dish. Season the corn with 1 teaspoon salt and ¼ teaspoon pepper for both bags. You may want to add a little more salt to taste. This will make enough for 6 people for supper. It is quick and great. If you need to cut down on the quantity, just do one bag of corn. Bake for about 25-30 minutes until bubbly. Check while baking in oven; you may need to stir occasionally.

Note: At the super markets in Georgia, they have the fresh creamed corn in roll packets year round. I wish here in Michigan they would have these, but buddy, can I improvise! I was taught if there was a will, there is a way, thanks to my depression-era relatives. I hope parents today are teaching their children to be conservative. Kids need to be taught to "make something out of nothing," whether it be in the kitchen or otherwise.

Okra, Corn, and Tomatoes Side

Eat this with a big ole slab of buttered cornbread!

6	strips bacon, which has been cooked and crumbled (reserve the bacon grease)
5	good-sized fresh tomatoes, peeled and chopped
2	cups okra, washed and cut into 1-inch slices
1	can whole kernel corn, drained
1	onion, chopped fine
¼	cup celery, chopped fine
½	teaspoon salt
½	teaspoon black pepper
1	teaspoon sugar

After cooking bacon, leave the bacon grease in the skillet, and add all other ingredients in the skillet, including the bacon. Put the lid on the skillet and reduce heat to simmer, stirring often. Cook until okra is tender.

Yields: 5 to 6 servings

Hint

Keep your old panty hose. Why? Store your Vidalia onions in them. How do you do this? Put an onion in the hose, tie a knot, put another onion in there, and tie a knot and so on. Keep going till you reach the panty part. Cut the panty part off and toss. Hang the onions up on a nail. Your onions will get air and will keep longer. When you need an onion, just cut the part off where the onion is and you will not bother the other onions. Keep them out of sight in the carport or barn.

My Secret Little Side Dish

Girls, if there is one dish that I can share with you, this is it! I call this "My Secret Little Side Dish."

Keep this in mind if you have been home ALL day and your spouse or significant other is due home ANY minute and you have been busy goofing off and/or enjoying your freedom—the clock is ticking and you see that, OH MY GOSH—It's almost time for them to get home and you haven't cooked anything for supper. What do you do in the nick of time? Let me tell you! I have had a world of practice, trust me!

Slice up some of those good ole' onions, Vidalia if you can find them (they come from Georgia). Put them in a skillet, one that you can put into the oven—preferably a cast iron one. Put those onions in that pan with a stick of butter and you can add fresh mushrooms if you like. You want to have this IN the stove. Sight unseen. You get my drift.

The point I'm making is the aroma of your kitchen when he walks in. It's wonderful! Why he will come in there and think! Oh, my baby, you have been cooking all day. He will not have a clue that all you have in the oven is a bunch of sliced onions, mushrooms, and butter. Now this will give you some time to catch up on supper while he is laid out horizontally in his easy chair. He will even take a snooze while he smells that aroma in the oven. And guess what girls? This will make a wonderful side dish to add to any meal. Be sure to season it with salt and pepper and maybe a little paprika. You can also serve this dish over pork chops, steak, and hamburgers.

Remember this is OUR LITTLE SECRET!

Sauted Onions

Same dish as Secret little side dish, except cooked on top of the stove.

4	onions, sliced ¼-inch thick
4	tablespoons butter
½	pound fresh mushrooms

Heat skillet on medium heat and melt butter. Add the onions and mushrooms and stir often until golden brown in color. Season with seasoning salt and pepper.

Cheese Onions with a Hint of Sherry

This would be wonderful to serve with fried fish or ham. Delicious.

25	small onions, about the size of a golf ball
2	teaspoons seasoned salt
4	tablespoons butter
4	tablespoons all-purpose flour
1¾	cups milk*
1	cup sharp cheese, grated *(You can use any kind of cheese if you prefer)*
2	tablespoons dry sherry wine

Peel the onions and place them in a large boiler. Barely cover with water and add salt. Bring to boil. Cook on medium heat about 15 minutes or until tender. Drain the onions real well and place the onions in a greased baking dish. Now you are ready to make the roux or the sauce to put on the onions. Melt the butter in a saucepan on medium heat. I use the same saucepan that I cooked the onions in. I just throw the water out and start the sauce. No need to have every pan out in the kitchen. Now that you have the melted butter, add the flour, stirring until smooth, still on medium. Cook 1 minute, stirring constantly until smooth. Gradually add the milk, still stirring constantly, until thickened and smooth. Now add the cheese, stirring until the cheese melts and it is smooth. Stir in the sherry and pour the sauce over the onions. Bake for 350-degrees for 20 to 30 minutes.

*When using the milk, I like to use part evaporated milk and part whole milk. This makes the sauce richer.

Yields: 6 to 8 servings

Stuffed Vidalia Onions

When this South Georgia onion crop comes in, always look for a Shriner, whether it is in Southwest Georgia or Michigan. I was quite surprised to find this wonderful product here in Michigan.

6	medium Vidalia onions
1	(16-ounce) roll sausage, mild or hot, cooked and drained
1	(4-ounce) can mushrooms, stems and pieces chopped, drained
1	tablespoon pecans, finely chopped
3	tablespoons butter
	Salt and Pepper to taste
1	tablespoon rosemary garlic seasoning *(optional-but I love this)*
1	cup beef bouillon or consommé
	Grated Parmesan cheese
	Paprika

Peel and core onions, leaving the shells about ½-inch thick. Reserve the pulp and chop the core part of the onion. This will be for the filling. Cook the onion shells in boiling water until just tender. Drain and cool. Melt the butter and sauté the mushrooms and the chopped onions. Add the pecans in the butter and cook for about 10 minutes. Add the cooked sausage and season to taste with salt, pepper, and rosemary seasonings. Arrange the onions in a greased baking dish. Pour the beef consommé around them. Bake at 300-degrees for 30 minutes. Sprinkle with Parmesan cheese and paprika. Continue to bake for 30 minutes longer. This recipe can be prepared the day ahead and refrigerated with a cover on it until time to bake.

Yields: 6 servings

Baked Pears and Pineapple

1	(20-ounce) can pineapple chunks or tidbits, drained Reserve the 1 cup of the pineapple juice
1½	tablespoons cornstarch
½	cup granulated sugar
8	medium-sized pears, peeled and sliced
6	tablespoons butter, melted
6	tablespoons light or dark brown sugar
1	cup coarse bread crumbs
½	cup sharp cheese, grated (optional)*

Combine the pineapple juice and cornstarch. Add the granulated sugar and cook over medium heat until thickened. Set aside. Place the pears in a greased 8-inch square baking dish. Pour the pineapple chunks or tidbits over the pears. Combine the butter and brown sugar, adding the bread crumbs, and stir. Pour the juice over the pears and pineapple and sprinkle with the bread crumbs. Bake for 30 minutes at 350-degrees.

*If you want to try the cheese, which it is wonderful, sprinkle the cheese before adding the bread crumbs.

Yields: 6 to 8 servings

Cooked Pear Wedges

Mama Gillis had two huge pear trees, and I would wait anxiously for the fall to get here to use these pears to make this recipe.

I believe the species was the 'Conference' and 'Bosc' pear. They were big speckled pears. I made all kinds of things with them, as did she.

Using the same recipe and technique as for the Cooked Apple Wedges, substitute pears for the apples. You will have to cook them a little while longer, though, because the meat of the pear is thicker than the apple. Add a little more sugar and cinnamon to taste. I like to use the spice mace along with the sugar and cinnamon. But just a dash of mace; remember mace is very pungent. Pears also make great cobblers.

Mama Gillis always had English Peas with Cream Sauce on her table. English Peas is the Southern term for green peas. These were the first vegetables that came out of her garden. She would fix her English Peas in a lot of different ways, such as English Peas with Dumplings or English Peas with New Irish Potatoes and Cream Sauce. These are real treats, and I hope you like them too!

English Peas with Cream Sauce

	Smoked side meat or ham hock*
2	tablespoons all-purpose flour
2	tablespoons butter
½	teaspoon salt
¼	teaspoon black pepper
1	cup evaporated milk *(You may use regular whole milk)*
	Pinch of sugar
2	cups fresh English peas or
	1 (10-ounce) bag frozen green peas, unthawed
1	cup water

*In a separate saucepan, boil your smoked side meat or ham hocks with just enough water to cover the meat, until the meat is tender. Set aside.

In a large-sized saucepan, melt your butter on medium heat, stirring in flour, salt, and black pepper, and gradually stirring in the milk. Add the pinch of sugar, green peas, and side meat along with the stock of the side meat. This will give the peas a wonderful flavor. Bring to a boil, stirring often. Cook on medium heat for about 20 minutes until peas are done and sauce has slightly thickened. This recipe makes a light sauce. If you want a thicker sauce, just add more flour. If by any chance the sauce is thicker than you like, just add a little water. I always add an extra dose of black pepper. Mama Gillis would always have very visible black pepper in this dish.

Note: I like to double the recipe, however, I never add extra side meat. The side meat for one single recipe is adequate.

Yields: 4 to 5 servings

English Peas and New Irish Potatoes with Cream Sauce

1½	pounds small new potatoes, scraped*
1	teaspoon salt
1½	cups fresh or 1 (10-ounce) bag frozen peas, unthawed
2	tablespoons all-purpose flour
	Dash of sugar
2	tablespoons butter
½	teaspoon salt (additional)
¼	teaspoon pepper
1	cup evaporated milk

*There are several ways you can present the potatoes in this dish. You can scrape them, peel a narrow strip of peel around the center of each potato in lieu of scraping, or if you prefer, and some of your potatoes are a little larger than you like, just quarter or half them.

In a large saucepan, cover potatoes with water and add 1 teaspoon salt to the water. Boil for about 10 minutes. Now add the peas and let the water come back to a boil and cover and boil for 15 to 20 minutes or until the potatoes are fork tender. Taste your peas and make sure they are done and add the dash of sugar. Do not drain your water; this will be part of your liquid. Meanwhile, melt butter in a small saucepan, stir in flour, salt and pepper. Gradually add the evaporated milk until a thick cream or sauce is formed, stirring constantly. Gradually stir this mixture in the potato and English Pea mixture. Stir and season to suit taste. I like to add an extra dose of black pepper.

Yields: 6 servings

Years ago, I worked as an agent for a local insurance company and I was sitting there at my desk one day and looked up and saw a very tall, stately, black-headed young lady getting out of a Red Mercedes convertible. This gal was as close to looking like "Wonder Woman" as you could get. She came waltzing in the insurance company, and from that day on Sharon became the most wonderful friend, as well as "running buddy," you could get.

She introduced me to the officials at the Memphis in May sanctioned contests, which I have been judging ever since. For you readers who do not know what the Memphis in May contest is, it is the World Championship BBQ Contest. On one occasion, after judging this contest, we were so stuffed after eating BBQ that we had to lay down in the car just to breathe.

She so graciously gave me the following recipe, which would be great as a side dish with BBQ. It is out of this world.

Marinated Black-Eyed Peas

By Sharon Dillard-Albany, Georgia

4	(15-ounce) cans of black-eyed peas, drained and washed
¾	cup vegetable oil
¾	cup red wine vinegar
1	cup onions, chopped very fine
1	cup green pepper, chopped very fine
4	ribs of celery, chopped very fine
1	clove of garlic, minced
1	teaspoon salt
1	teaspoon hot sauce or to taste
1	teaspoon black pepper
1	can of Rotel diced tomatoes and green chiles, drained
	Several dashes of crushed red pepper

Mix all ingredients, except for the can of tomatoes and green chiles. Marinate this mixture for at least three days. Just before serving, add the diced tomatoes and green chiles. It will put hair on your chest!

Yields: 6 servings

English Peas and Dumplings

2	(10-ounce) bags frozen green peas
	Salt to taste

Dumplings:
⅓	cup shortening
1½-2	cups all-purpose flour
⅔	cup milk
	Dose of black pepper*
4	(14.5-ounce) cans chicken broth

Place shortening and flour in a large bowl. Cut in the shortening until it resembles little peas. Add the milk and stir until moistened. Add more flour if needed to make soft dough. Take small amounts of dough and roll them to ¼-inch flat on a lightly floured covered surface; you do not want your dumplings to be thick. It will take longer to cook and they will be gummy. Ugh! Cut into strips.

In a large heavy saucepan, empty chicken broth into the pan and let it come to a rolling boil. Drop the dumpling strips into the boiling stock. Continue to dip your spoon in the hot boiling broth as you place the dumplings in the broth. This will prevent the dumplings from sticking together. You do not want to stir, for this will tear your dumplings. Keep the broth at a rolling boil. As the dumplings are beginning to be completely cooked and not gummy, add the 2 bags of frozen green peas. You may have to add a little more water, or if you like, you can add evaporated milk. Cook the peas until done, by tasting. You may have to add salt to taste. Add the dose of black pepper. This is a wonderful recipe.

A dose is a little more than a dash.*

Yields: 8 servings

Pineapple Casserole

Back in the '90s this recipe became a big hit. It's a wonderful potluck dish as well as different side that a lot of folks have not tried yet. If you need one more dish for that family gathering, this is it.

2	(20-ounce) cans pineapple, drained
6	tablespoons pineapple juice
6	tablespoons flour
1	cup sugar
2	cups sharp cheese, grated
1	stick butter, melted
3	cups cornflakes*

Mix flour, sugar, and pineapple juice. Add pineapple and cheese. Pour into a greased 2-quart baking dish. Crumble the corn flakes to cover the top of the mixture. Then pour melted butter over the corn flakes. Bake for 350-degrees for 30 to 45 minutes. When it starts bubbling and turns a golden brown, it's done.

*You may substitute Ritz or Ritz-like crackers in this recipe in lieu of the corn flakes. Just use one stack of crackers and crush. Place on top of the casserole as you would the corn flakes and pour the melted butter on top.

Yields: 6 to 8 servings

Mashed Potato Meringues

3	pounds or 9 medium potatoes, peeled and split lengthwise
¼	cup butter, melted
1	small onion, chopped very fine
½	cup evaporated milk
1	egg, beaten well
1-1½	teaspoon of salt
	Pinch of pepper

Cover the potatoes in water, adding 1 teaspoon salt in the water. Boil covered for 35 to 40 minutes or until fork-tender. Drain potatoes and place the potatoes over low heat 1 or 2 minutes to dry them out. Mash potatoes thoroughly until no lumps remain. Set aside. In a small skillet, melt the butter and add the chopped onion, sauté until tender, but not brown. Remove this mixture from the heat and add the evaporated milk, beaten egg, salt and pinch of pepper. Beat the potatoes with the electric mixer and gradually add the egg and onion mixture. Drop the mixture by heaping tablespoon onto a greased cookie sheet, using the spoon to make rounded mounds. Bake at 350-degrees for 20 to 25 minutes until the meringues are set.

Yields: 6 to 8 servings

Potato Balls

This is a very old recipe, and if you like potatoes, you will love these. For a nice presentation, the Potato Balls would look great displayed around the edge of a roast. They are easy to make, and you only need a few ingredients.

6	medium-size potatoes, peeled and cubed
1/8	cup evaporated milk* *(see note below)*
	Salt and pepper to taste
1	egg, beaten
1½	cups cornflakes, crushed

Cook potatoes in boiling water until fork tender. Drain well. With your electric beater while the potatoes are still hot, beat in milk and salt and pepper to taste. Add the egg and beat in well. Crush cornflakes and set aside in a bowl. Dip your hands in cold water to make the potato balls; this will make the potatoes less likely to stick when rolling into balls. Roll the potato balls in the crushed cornflakes and place them in a baking pan that has been sprayed with cooking spray. Bake at 250-degrees for 30 minutes or until serving time. The oven is at a low temperature and the potatoes will be fine to stay in the oven for a little longer if need be while getting supper ready. To serve them with Pot Roast, you can just spoon the gravy over them at serving time or even have some melted butter in lieu of the gravy.

Note: You want the potatoes to be thicker than usual, because you will be shaping them into balls.

Cheese Potato Souffle

If you want to do a little something different with mashed potatoes, this will be a family pleaser. Especially for those men folks. Your children will like this, also.

3	cups mashed potatoes *(Approximately 6 medium)*
½	cup evaporated milk
1	cup sharp cheese, grated
2	eggs, separate the whites from the yolks. Beat the yolks until light.
	Salt and pepper to season
	Cayenne pepper—just a "smidgen" or dash to taste
	Paprika to sprinkle

Peel, boil, and drain potatoes. Mash potatoes and set aside. Heat milk in a double boiler and add cheese. Beat this mixture until smooth. Add the cheese and milk mixture to the mashed potatoes. Season the mashed potato mixture with the salt, pepper, and cayenne pepper. Add the beaten egg yolks. Beat the egg whites until stiff. Fold in the egg whites into the mixture and pour into a greased baking dish. Sprinkle with paprika. Bake in a 350-degree oven until lightly brown.

Yields: 6 to 8 servings

Roasted Potatoes

This is as easy as it gets.

	Potatoes (Peel as many as you think your family can eat) Leave whole.
2	sticks butter, divided use
	Paprika
	Salt and Pepper to taste.

Peel the potatoes, leaving whole and par-boil 15 to 20 minutes, just until tender. Drain the potatoes well. Preheat oven to 350-degrees. While you are preheating the stove, place one stick of butter in the baking dish to melt. You are greasing your baking dish and melting the butter at the same time. Place the potatoes in the baking dish and turn potatoes over and over in the butter to coat well. Then sprinkle paprika on them. Bake approximately 30 to 45 minutes. Every now and then, turn the potatoes over in the butter. Melt the other stick of butter and brush additional butter on them. Season with salt and pepper to taste.

Swedish Green Potato Casserole

There is a secret ingredient in this recipe. If you like spinach and if you like potatoes, you will like this recipe. Now, I have given the secret ingredient away.

6-8	large potatoes (3 pounds), which have been peeled, cubed and boiled
¾	cup half-and-half or evaporated milk
1	teaspoon sugar
½	cup butter, melted
2	teaspoons salt
¼	teaspoon pepper
2	tablespoons chives, chopped
2½	tablespoons fresh dill, chopped or 1½-teaspoons dried dill
1	(10-ounce) package frozen spinach, drained

Heat the milk (do not boil) in a small saucepan and set aside. After boiling the potatoes, drain them well. Mash with the potato masher and then beat the potatoes on high, whipping them real good. Add the heated milk, sugar, butter, salt and pepper. Beat until light and fluffy. Now add the chives and dill. Meanwhile, prepare the spinach according to the package directions, draining well. Squeeze with paper toweling to get out excessive water. Add the spinach to the potato mixture and beat until well blended. Pour into a well greased 2-quart baking dish. Bake at 400-degrees for 20 to 30 minutes.

Yields: 6 to 8 servings

Mama Gillis' Fried Sweet Potatoes

At almost every meal at Mama Gillis' house there was a stack of Fried Sweet Potatoes. I know you're probably wondering where on our plate we could put them. Well, we found room on the plate, as well as our stomachs. Very easy to prepare.

6	sweet potatoes, medium size peeled, sliced and cut about ⅜-inch thick slices
	Crisco Oil for frying
	Granulated sugar to sprinkle

Heat ¼-inch of oil in your skillet till hot. I always sprinkle a tiny drop of water in the grease; if it sizzles it's time to fry. Fry the sliced potatoes until the potato is soft when poked with a fork and golden brown. Drain on paper towels. Sprinkle with granulated sugar. You could also mix granulated sugar and cinnamon to sprinkle if you like. Mama Gillis just used the granulated sugar.

Yields: 6 servings

Sweet Potato Bread

Only this is not bread. Years ago in the old South, Sweet Potato Bread was called "bread," if it wasn't in a pie crust.

2	cups cooked and mashed sweet potatoes (3 medium)
½	cup granulated sugar
1	stick butter, melted
2	eggs
½	cups self-rising flour
1	(14-ounce) can sweetened condensed milk
1	teaspoon vanilla flavoring
1	teaspoon cinnamon
1	cup raisins
½	cup coconut (optional)
1	cup walnuts or pecans, chopped

Preheat oven to 300-degrees. Cream the sweet potatoes, butter, and sugar in a large bowl. Beat until fluffy. Add the eggs, self-rising flour, condensed milk, vanilla, and cinnamon. Mix well and fold in the nuts, raisins, and coconut. Pour this mixture into a greased 14 x 11-inch pan. Bake for 45 to 60 minutes until done.

Yields: 6 servings

Sweet Potato Crunch

I hope you do not tire of Sweet Potatoes, for I love them and I have several recipes. Enjoy!

3	cups sweet potatoes, cooked and mashed
1	cup granulated sugar
½	teaspoon salt
2	eggs, slightly beaten
½	cup evaporated milk
¼	cup butter, melted
1	teaspoon vanilla extract*

*Try using lemon or orange flavoring in your sweet potato recipes. You will find this is delicious. Mix all ingredients together and pour into a greased baking dish. Top this dish off with the topping below.

Crunch Topping:

¼	cup butter
1	cup brown sugar, firmly packed
⅓	cup flour
1	cup chopped pecans or walnuts

Melt butter and add brown sugar, flour, and chopped pecans or walnuts. Mix together well and place on top of sweet potatoes. Bake at 350-degrees for 35 minutes.

Yields: 6 to 8 servings

Brown Rice

1	stick butter, melted
2	cups long grain rice, uncooked
2	(14.5-ounce) cans beef consommé
2	(10.75-ounce) cans French onion soup
1	package dry onion soup mix
1	(8-ounce) can mushrooms, sliced or chopped, drained
1	can water chestnuts, optional

Melt butter in 3-quart greased baking dish. Add rice and other ingredients. Cover with aluminum foil and bake at 350-degrees for 1 hour.

Spanish Rice

2	(8-ounce) cans tomato sauce
1/2	cup water
1/3	cup onion, chopped
1/3	cup green pepper, chopped
1/4	cup butter
1	teaspoon sugar
1/2	cup prepared mustard
1/4	teaspoon salt
1/4	teaspoon black pepper
6	cups cooked rice

Combine all of the above ingredients, except for the rice, in a large saucepan. Stir and bring to a boil and cover for 15 minutes. Stir in the cooked rice and remove from the heat. Cover and let stand at least 5 minutes before serving.

This would be delicious with Meatloaf and a Fruit salad.

Yields: 8 servings

Butternut Squash Casserole

This is a sweet side dish; it can be used as a dessert.

2	cups butternut squash, peeled, cooked and mashed
1	stick butter, melted
1	cup evaporated milk
3	eggs, slightly beaten
1	cup granulated sugar
½	teaspoon ginger
½	cup coconut, optional
1	teaspoon vanilla extract or
1	teaspoon coconut flavoring

Preheat oven to 350-degrees. Combine all of the ingredients in a mixing bowl and mix well. Pour ingredients in a well-greased casserole dish. Place baking dish in a pan of water to cook. Bake for 45 minutes or until a knife is inserted in the middle of the pudding and comes out clean.

Yields: 6 servings

Ole Favorite Squash Casserole

2	cups yellow squash, cooked and mashed
1	can cream of chicken soup
1	cup sour cream
1	carrot, grated
1	medium onion, grated
1	cup sharp cheese, grated
	Salt and pepper to taste
	Dash of cayenne pepper
	Paprika to sprinkle on top
¼	cup butter, melted
	Breadcrumbs or cracker crumbs

Combine in a large bowl the cooked squash, soup, sour cream, carrot, onion, and cheese. Now season with salt, pepper, and a dash of cayenne pepper. Pour this mixture in a greased baking dish. Sprinkle bread or cracker crumbs and pour the melted butter on top. Bake at 350-degrees for 30 minutes.

Note: Using a dash of cayenne pepper in cheese dishes brings out that punch, especially in squash dishes to help out the flavor.

Yields: 6 servings

Summer Squash Patties

I just love this recipe. I so look forward for summer to get here and for squash to come in so I can prepare this.

2	cups uncooked summer squash, grated
2	teaspoons onion, grated
2	teaspoons sugar
½	teaspoon salt
	Pinch of black pepper
	Few grains of red pepper
½	cup all-purpose flour
2	eggs, well beaten
4	tablespoons butter, melted

In a medium-sized bowl, mix the squash, onion, sugar, and seasonings. Let stand for 30 minutes. Drain off any liquid that may have set up during the 30 minutes. Now, add the flour and eggs to the mixture. Melt butter in a large non-stick skillet. Drop batter by tablespoons on the hot skillet. Cook on both sides until light brown. Serve immediately. If the mixture tends to be too runny, just add a little more flour to the mixture.

Yields: 6 servings

Baked Stuffed Tomatoes

4	medium-sized red tomatoes
4	tablespoons butter
2	tablespoons onion, minced
¼	cup green pepper, chopped fine
1½	cup seasoned croutons
¼	cup mayonnaise
¼	cup sour cream
1	tablespoon prepared mustard
¼	garlic salt
	Dash of pepper
1	cup Parmesan cheese, grated

Preheat oven to 350-degrees. Scoop out centers of tomatoes with a spoon, using the tomatoes as a shell. Reserve the meat of the tomatoes. Melt butter, and sauté the onion and green pepper until tender. Stir in the croutons, the meat of the tomato, mayonnaise, sour cream, mustard, garlic salt, dash of pepper, cooking for 2 minutes on low, stirring constantly. Stuff the tomato shells with crouton mixture. Top with Parmesan cheese. Place in a shallow baking dish. Bake at 350-degrees for 15 to 20 minutes.

Yields: 4 servings

Fried Red Tomatoes

- ½ cup all-purpose flour
- ½ teaspoon baking powder
- ¼ teaspoon salt
- Salt and pepper to taste
- 1 egg, beaten
- ⅓ cup evaporated milk
- 6 firm ripe tomatoes, sliced and not peeled
- Canola or vegetable oil

While preparing the tomatoes, heat your skillet with canola or vegetable oil. Combine the flour, baking powder, and salt in a medium-sized mixing bowl. Add the beaten egg to the milk and stir. Add this mixture to the dry ingredients and mix well. Salt and pepper the tomato slices and dip in the batter. Fry until brown on both sides. Serve hot.

Yields: 6 servings

Vegetable Trio Bake

This recipe is a medley of vegetables which makes for a delightful addition to any meal.

- 1 small can English peas
- 1 (15.25-ounce) can shoe peg corn
- 1 (14.25-ounce) can French-style green beans
- ⅓ cup onion, chopped
- ⅓ cup celery, chopped
- ⅓ cup green or red pepper, chopped
- 1 (8-ounce) carton sour cream
- 1 cup sharp cheese, grated
- ½ stick butter
- 1 stack Cheese Ritz or Cheese Ritz-like crackers, crumbled

Drain all vegetables and combine them in a greased baking dish. Top with the sharp cheese and then top the cheese with sour cream. Dot with slices of butter and then finish the dish off with the cracker crumbs. Bake at 350-degrees until nice and bubbly.

Yields: 6 servings

Fresh Tomato Garden Pie

1	(10-inch) pie shell, unbaked
3	large tomatoes, peeled and sliced
1	teaspoon of salt, divided use
6	bacon slices, which have been cooked, drained. *(reserve the bacon grease)
3	medium sized sweet onions, peeled, halved and sliced
1	cup of sharp cheese, grated
1	cup of mayonnaise
¼	teaspoon black pepper
⅓	cup grated Parmesan cheese
¼	cup dry bread crumbs

Place tomato slices on a paper towel and sprinkle ½-teaspoon of salt on the tomatoes. Let them stand at least 30 minutes. This will absorb the liquid in the tomatoes and will not make the pie crust soggy. Bake the pie crust at 425-degrees until lightly brown for only 10 minutes. Cool while preparing the rest of the recipe. Cook bacon and save the grease to use later in the recipe. Crumble the bacon and set aside. Sauté the onions in the reserved bacon grease till they are tender, and scoop them up and place in the cooled pie shell. Now place the tomatoes on top of the onions. Stir together the mayonnaise and sharp cheese with the remaining ½-teaspoon salt and the ¼-teaspoon pepper. Spread this mixture over the top of the tomatoes. Combine the Parmesan cheese with the breadcrumbs. Sprinkle over the top. Bake at 350–degrees for 30 minutes till golden brown. Lastly, top with the crumbled bacon. Garnish with a couple of slices of Roma tomatoes.

*If you like, when you cook the bacon, cook it partially and then crumble the bacon on top of the pie before you cook it. I have made it both ways. I have completely cooked the bacon and put the bacon on after the pie has baked for 30 minutes. Personally, I like to partially cook the bacon, because all of the juices from the bacon seeps into the pie while it is cooking.

Yields: 8 servings

Fried Green Tomatoes

Whether you like the green or red tomatoes or both, here is the recipe for the green ones, in hopes for you to use up all of those leftover green ones on the vines.

1	egg, slightly beaten
½	cup evaporated milk
½	cup cornmeal
¼	cup all-purpose flour
1	teaspoon salt
½	teaspoon pepper
3	green tomatoes, medium sized and sliced
	Vegetable oil

Combine the egg and milk and mix well. In a separate bowl, stir together the cornmeal, flour, salt and pepper. Dip tomato slices in the egg mixture and dredge in the cornmeal and flour mixture. Fry tomato slices in hot oil just until brown, turning only one time. Drain on paper towels. Serve hot.

Yields: 4 to 6 servings

Tomato Casserole

2	(28-ounce) cans whole tomatoes
2	cups your favorite cheese, grated (divided use)
3	cups unseasoned croutons
3	medium onions, sliced
1½	teaspoons garlic salt
½	teaspoon oregano
1½	teaspoons sugar
2	teaspoons butter
6	slices bacon, fried and drained

Layer the tomatoes, 1½-cups cheese, croutons, and onions in a greased baking dish. Combine the seasonings and sprinkle over the tomato mixture. Crumble the bacon on top of this. Sprinkle with ½-cup of the remaining cheese and dot with butter. Bake uncovered at 350-degrees for 30 minutes.

Yields: 6 servings

Cranberry Apple Pineapple Casserole

This recipe is very pretty to serve for the holidays. I love it. This is one of the quickest recipes to prepare when you need another side dish.

So easy to prepare. It could be used as a dessert as well as a side dish.

3	cups red **unpeeled** apples, sliced very thin
2	cups cranberries
1	cup crushed pineapple, drained *(reserve the juice for the topping)*
1	tablespoon lemon juice
1¼	cups granulated sugar
½	teaspoon salt

Place apples, cranberries, and pineapple in a greased 9 x 13-inch baking dish. Sprinkle with the lemon juice. Combine the sugar and salt, mixing with the fruit. Prepare the topping below.

Topping:
½	cup brown sugar
⅓	cup all-purpose flour
1½	cups old-fashioned oatmeal
½	cup pecans or walnuts, chopped
½	cup butter, melted
1	egg yolk, beaten
1	teaspoon orange extract

Combine the brown sugar, flour, oatmeal, and nuts, stir in the melted butter, egg yolk, and orange extract. If you need a little more moisture in this, add about ¼-cup of the reserved pineapple juice. Spread topping on top of the fruit. Bake at 350-degrees until bubbly for 30 to 45 minutes.

This would be an excellent dish for the little one in your family to help you with. It is very showy and a big dish; they would feel a great accomplishment to help with this recipe.

Yields: 6 to 8 servings

Mexican Macaroni

This is an excellent picnic side dish. It is a whole new twist for macaroni and cheese. Can be served hot or cold. Makes two, 1½ quart baking dishes.

1	(10-ounce) package small elbow macaroni
1	(10-ounce) can tomatoes with green chiles
2	cloves garlic, chopped
½	cup olive oil
1	cup longhorn cheese or hot pepper jack cheese, grated
1	(32-ounce) can tomato juice
1	(10-ounce) jar salad olives with pimentos, drained and chopped (optional)
2	(4-ounce) jars pimento, chopped
	Salt and pepper to taste

Cook macaroni according to package directions. Drain. Run cold water through the hot macaroni, blanching it. In a small skillet, cook the garlic in the olive oil slowly, but do not brown. In a large bowl, mix the macaroni, tomatoes with the green chiles, garlic, and cheese, ¾ of the can of tomato juice, olives, and pimentos. Reserve the remainder of the tomato juice for reheating. Grease the two baking dishes and pour the macaroni mixture in the two dishes. Bake at 350-degrees for 40 minutes. To reheat, pour the remaining tomato juice in the dishes. The salad keeps in the fridge for 4 or 5 days.

Yields: 4 to 6 servings

Mama Gillis' Baked Macaroni N' Cheese

This is very easy. You do not have to make the white sauce separately. Just sit back and listen to how Mama Gillis told me to make this many years ago. I can just hear her now explaining this to me.

Just to warn you-she loved butter, cream and cheese.

2	cups elbow macaroni, uncooked
1	stick butter
1	(12-ounce) can evaporated milk
2	cups sharp cheese, grated
	Black pepper to taste
	Paprika

Boil macaroni according to directions on package. **DO NOT DRAIN WATER.** Do you want to know why? I asked her. She said that the water you boiled the macaroni in was full of starch. Why throw it out? The starch water is the thickening. Put a stick of butter in it. The hot water will melt the butter. Then pour this mixture into a 2-quart greased baking dish. Some of the water in which you boiled the macaroni boiled away in the process. Pour enough of the can of milk in this baking dish to just about cover the macaroni. Then add about 1½-cups of the grated cheese and stir until melted leaving ½-cup for the topping. Stir in just enough black pepper to taste. Then add the remaining grated cheese and sprinkle a little black pepper and paprika on top of the casserole. Bake at 350-degrees for about 30 to 35 minutes.

Yields: 6 to 8 servings

Good Ole Southern Cornbread Dressing With Giblet Gravy

Save your old biscuits and freeze them till you're ready to make the dressing.

4	cups cornbread crumbs (Cornbread recipe below)
5	biscuits (crumbled) or 2 cups day-old bread, crumbled
3	cups hot chicken or turkey broth
1	cup celery, finely chopped
1	large onion, chopped
4	tablespoons butter
2	cups hard-boiled eggs, optional
½	cup butter, melted (additional)
1	teaspoon salt
1	teaspoon pepper
2	teaspoons poultry seasoning
¼	teaspoon cayenne pepper to taste
3	eggs, beaten slightly
1	can cream of chicken or cream or celery soup, undiluted
3	cups of hot chicken or turkey broth (extra)*
	Paprika to sprinkle

Crumble bread into a mixing bowl. Add boiling broth. Cover and let sit 5 minutes. Melt the 4 tablespoons of butter and sauté the onions and celery, just until tender. Set aside. In a large bowl, add all of the other ingredients in the order given, except for the extra chicken broth. Add soaked bread, celery, onions, and the remaining ingredients, thoroughly mixing. (You now have all of the ingredients, except for the extra broth.) Add just enough of the extra broth so that the dressing will be moist like a thick batter, but not dry. You may not need to use all of the broth; save the rest of the broth and freeze it. Pour into a 9 x 13-inch baking dish which has been sprayed with baking spray or greased well with butter. Sprinkle with paprika. I always check the dressing while cooking, and, if after 30 minutes of cooking the dressing looks a little drier than I would like, I add a small amount of the reserved broth to the dressing. Just pour easily into the pan to dampen it; there is no need to stir it. Continue baking. Bake for approximately 1 hour at 400-degrees or until nice and light brown. Serve with chicken or giblet gravy.

Yields: 10 to 12 servings

Giblet Gravy:

¼	cup butter
¼	cup flour
½	teaspoon salt
1½	cups chicken broth
½	cup evaporated milk
¼	cup cooked turkey parts, chopped real fine (gizzard and liver). *Now, if you don't want to use the gizzard and liver, that's fine. Just use the neck.**
1	hard-boiled egg, chopped
	Pepper to taste

Melt the butter and add the flour and salt, blending well. Add the chicken broth, milk, and turkey. Cook on medium high until thick, stirring constantly. Now add the chopped boiled egg, stirring well. Add pepper to taste.

*I bake the turkey neck while baking the turkey, and I pull the pieces off of the turkey neck and use this for the meat in the giblet gravy.

Cornbread Recipe for the Dressing:
You may use any of your favorite cornbread recipes. It's best to make your cornbread a few days before and freeze it to have on hand.

4	tablespoons bacon grease
2	cups buttermilk
2	eggs
½	teaspoon salt
½	teaspoon soda
1	cup cornmeal
½	cup self-rising flour

Preheat oven to 400-degrees. Place your cast iron skillet in the oven with the bacon grease while the oven is preheating. Just keep an eye on it. You don't want the grease to overheat. Then mix all ingredients together by hand. **Do not beat**. Mix ingredients just enough to moisten them. Then pour this mixture in the skillet on top of the hot bacon grease and cook for about 30 minutes until done. This will make enough for your Dressing recipe.

Hint: To dress up your Thanksgiving Plate, open a can of jellied, strained cranberry sauce. Cut a half-inch slice from the cranberry mold. Using a star-shaped cookie cutter, cut a star out of the cranberry slice. This will be very attractive to place on your plate, in lieu of the round jellied slice.

Snappy Spinach Casserole

If you are tired of the Traditional Green Bean Casserole for the holidays, and you like spinach, try this. This is a little different twist.

2	(10-ounce) packages frozen spinach, cooked according to package directions
4	tablespoons butter
4	tablespoons onions, chopped
4	tablespoons flour
½	cup buttermilk
½	teaspoon salt
½	teaspoon pepper
¾	teaspoon garlic powder
2-3	drops of hot sauce
1	(6-ounce) roll of jalapeño cheese, cut up in small pieces

After cooking the spinach, drain it well, reserving ½-cup liquid. I use paper towel to squeeze out the excess moisture. Melt the butter, and sauté onions, cooking until tender. Add flour, stirring well, and add the buttermilk along with the reserved spinach liquid. Add the seasonings and cheese, stirring until cheese has melted. Lastly, add the spinach and mix well. Pour into a greased baking dish. Now you're ready to make the topping.

Topping:
1	stick butter, melted
1½	cups herb stuffing mix

After melting the butter, pour butter over herb stuffing mix and then sprinkle the topping on your spinach casserole before heating. Bake at 350-degrees until heated throughout, about 30 to 35 minutes.

Yields: 6 to 8 servings

Syrups, Sauces, Toppings, Glazes & Gravies

Enjoy the sweet sauces for that Banana Split party or Sops for biscuits and pancakes. I've included ole' timey recipes from Red-Eye Gravy to Hog Sauce which will make your mouth water.

Blueberry Sauce

This is excellent to put on waffles, pancakes, pound cake, or ice cream.

¾	cup granulated sugar
½	cup water
	Pinch of salt
1	tablespoon cornstarch
2	cups blueberries, fresh or frozen
1	tablespoon lemon juice
	Pinch of cinnamon

Combine sugar, water, salt and cornstarch. Cook, stirring often, until mixture boils and thickens. Add berries and heat to boiling. Simmer for 5 minutes. Stir in lemon juice and the cinnamon. Let sauce cool slightly.

Peach Blueberry Sauce

Use the above recipe and add ½-cup fresh sliced and peeled peaches. You may want to sprinkle a little Fruit-Fresh on them before adding to the sauce to keep that beautiful color.

Sweet Strawberry Sauce

2	pints fresh strawberries, sliced
½	cup powdered sugar, sifted
3	tablespoons kirsch

Stir all ingredients together and chill overnight for the flavors to blend. Serve over vanilla ice cream. Makes about 2½-cups of the best sauce.

Raspberry Sauce

1	carton frozen raspberries
½	cup sugar

Drain the juice from the raspberries. Set the raspberries aside. Add the sugar to the juice, and boil the liquid. Pour this syrup over the raspberries. Chill.

Apple Dapple Topping

1	tablespoon cornstarch
¾	cup granulated sugar
½	cup water or apple juice
1	tablespoon lemon juice
½	teaspoon cinnamon
2	cups apples, chopped (peeled or unpeeled, whatever your preference)

Combine the cornstarch, sugar, water or apple juice, lemon juice, cinnamon and apples. Mix well. Cook stirring often on medium heat until mixture thickens and boils until well-heated. Take off heat and cool slightly. Enjoy on pancakes, waffles, biscuits, or even ice cream.

Cinnamon Apple Topping

Try this on pancakes or waffles.

1	(21-ounce) can prepared apple pie filling
2	tablespoons butter
	Pinch of cinnamon
	Pinch of mace

In a small pan, combine the above ingredients and stir on low heat until all ingredients are nice and warm. Enjoy!

Rum Sauce

Wouldn't this be good drizzled on a piece of Sour Cream Pound Cake, ice cream, or pie? A cake with spirits brings the holidays to mind!

2	tablespoons butter
¾	cups granulated sugar
½	cup light brown sugar, firmly packed
1	tablespoon cornstarch
2	tablespoons cold water
2	cups boiling water
1	teaspoon vanilla flavoring
1	tablespoon rum to start with and then to taste
1	teaspoon lemon juice

Melt butter in a medium-sized saucepan and stir in both kinds of sugar. Meanwhile in a small saucepan, boil the 2 cups of water, mix the cornstarch with the cold water, and add the cornstarch paste to the boiling water. Let water return to boiling and then add the boiling water mixture to the butter and sugar mixture. Boil hard for 5 minutes. Take off the heat and add the vanilla flavoring, rum, and lemon juice. What's left after serving, store covered in the fridge. This will keep for several weeks.

Gooey Caramel Pecan Sauce

Honey, you can eat this stuff just by itself! But ice cream or cake would put this to the ultimate.

⅓	cup butter
½	cup granulated sugar
1	cup Karo syrup or light corn syrup
1	egg
1	tablespoon vanilla extract
1	cup pecans, chopped and toasted

Combine all ingredients except the pecans in a 1-quart saucepan. Cook over medium heat, stirring constantly, until mixture comes to a boil. Now stir in the pecans.

Yields: 2 cups

Hot Fudge Topping

½	cup granulated sugar
¼	cup butter
⅓	cup water
2	tablespoons Karo syrup or light corn syrup
1	(6-ounce) package of semisweet chocolate chips
1	teaspoon vanilla

In a 1-quart saucepan combine sugar, butter, water, and corn syrup. Cook over medium heat, stirring constantly, until mixture comes to a full boil. Boil for 3 minutes. Remove from heat and add the chocolate chips and vanilla. Stir with a wire whisk until smooth.

Yields: 1½-cups

Chocolate Sauce

½	cup Karo or light corn syrup
1	cup granulated sugar
1	cup water
3	squares unsweetened chocolate
1	teaspoon vanilla extract
1	cup evaporated milk

Combine the light corn syrup, sugar, and water. Blend well. Cook until a soft ball stage which is 234 to 240-degrees. A soft ball is reached when a small drop of syrup is dropped into a cup with ice cold water and it forms a soft ball which flattens upon removing from the ice water. Remove from heat and add the chocolate squares and stir until the chocolate is melted. Add the vanilla extract and slowly add the evaporated milk. Cool. This recipe will make a little over 3 cups of sauce. Store covered in the refrigerator, and it will keep a long time. You can serve it warm or cold.

Brown Sugar Hard Sauce

You can tell that I like any recipe that resembles Caramel, Butterscotch, or Pralines. This Hard Sauce is just like it says; it's thicker than the other sauces. Try a dollop on Apple Pie.

2	tablespoons butter, softened
½	cup light brown sugar, packed
½	cup powdered sugar, sifted
	Pinch of salt
1	teaspoon vanilla extract

Cream the butter until fluffy, adding the sugars gradually, beating well after each addition. Stir in the vanilla extract. Put in the fridge to chill.

Creamy Butterscotch Sauce

Serve Hot!

⅓	cup butter
1	cup light brown sugar, firmly packed
⅓	cup heavy cream

In a small saucepan, melt butter on low heat, stir in brown sugar and cream. Bring to a boil and simmer for 3 to 5 minutes, without stirring. Remove from heat, stir well, and serve warm.

Brown Sugar Butter Sauce

1	cup water
1	tablespoon cornstarch
1	cup light brown sugar, packed
3	tablespoons butter
½	teaspoon vanilla

Dissolve the cornstarch in water. Pour into a medium-sized saucepan. Add brown sugar and butter. Bring to a boil, stirring constantly. Cook until thickened. Stir in vanilla.

Georgia Praline Sauce

1	cup brown sugar, packed
½	cup evaporated milk or you may use half-and-half
¼	cup light corn syrup or Karo syrup
3	tablespoons butter
1	teaspoon vanilla
1	cup pecans, broken in half (you may use chopped pecans)
	Pinch of salt

Combine all of the above ingredients, stirring constantly over medium heat for about 10 minutes until the mixture is smooth and creamy. If there are any leftovers, store in a covered container. In order to reheat, add a little more cream in a saucepan and stir.

Yields: 2 cups

Pineapple Sauce

This pineapple sauce can be used for an ice cream topping or you could use it for a beautiful and tasty sauce for your Thanksgiving ham. This is a sweeter sauce.

2	tablespoons cornstarch
2	tablespoons water
1	(15.5-ounce) can pineapple, crushed or tidbits, juice packed
¾	cup granulated sugar
½	cup water
1	tablespoon lemon juice

Mix together cornstarch and water until smooth. In a small boiler or saucepan, mix the cornstarch and water mixture along with the rest of the ingredients. Bring to a boil and reduce heat and simmer, stirring for about 8 to 10 minutes or until thickened.

Marshmallow Sauce for Sundaes, Cakes

¾	cup granulated sugar
¼	cup water
12	large marshmallows
	Pinch of salt
1	egg white

Note: To cut the marshmallows, dip scissors in cold water and cut each marshmallow in quarters.

Combine the sugar and water in a medium-sized saucepan. Simmer for 5 minutes, stirring constantly. Add the marshmallows to the sugar syrup and stir until the mixture is nice and smooth. In a separate bowl, beat the egg white until stiff, adding the salt. Slowly fold in the marshmallow mixture. Delicious!

Zippy Pineapple Sauce

Try this sauce over Baked Ham and Baked Pork Loin.

½	cup pineapple preserves
2	tablespoons prepared mustard
1	tablespoon horseradish

Combine the above ingredients in a small saucepan and stir over low heat.

Yields: ¾-cups

Pineapple Raisin Sauce

If you are wondering what to do with that leftover ham and you have just enough to skim a few slices off, this would be a welcome change. Compliments galore!

¾	cup unsweetened pineapple juice
	Dash of Worcestershire sauce
½	cup raisins
1	tablespoon vinegar
	Pinch of cloves
2	teaspoons cornstarch
2	tablespoons water

Combine all ingredients except for the cornstarch and water. Bring to a boil and cook until the raisins are good and plump. Dissolve the cornstarch with water and gradually add to the raisin mixture. Cook until mixture is clear, stirring constantly.

Raisin Sauce

Another great Raisin Sauce that is a little bit sweeter. Try this on a Roasted Pork Loin.

1	cup raisins
1	cup water
¾	cup pineapple juice
1	tablespoon cornstarch
	Pinch of salt
	Pinch of pepper
1	teaspoon dry mustard
⅓	cup light brown sugar
2	tablespoons drippings from the ham

Boil the raisins in the water for at least 10 minutes. Combine the cornstarch, salt, pepper, mustard, and brown sugar in your pineapple juice and add to the raisin and water mixture. Bring to a boil. Now add the ham drippings. Mix together and cook until thickened, approximately 5 minutes, stirring constantly.

Pineapple Glaze for Ham

¼	cup light brown sugar
1½	tablespoons cornstarch
1	teaspoon dry mustard
½	teaspoon cloves
1	(20-ounce) can crushed pineapple with juice

In a medium-sized saucepan, combine all of the ingredients, except for the pineapple. Mix well and stir in the pineapple and juice. Cook over medium heat until slightly thickened. Spoon and brush the ham with glaze during the last 30 to 45 minutes of cooking.

Apricot Honey Glaze

1	cup honey
1	(8-ounce) frozen orange juice concentrate, thawed
⅓	cup apricot preserves or jam
¼	cup soy sauce
½	teaspoon nutmeg
¼	teaspoon cloves

Mix all ingredients together in a medium-sized bowl. Spread as a glaze on a Roasted Pork Loin or Ham the last 30 minutes of cooking.

Plantation Hard Sauce

1	stick butter, softened
1	half pint heavy whipping cream
¼	cup powdered sugar (You might need to add a little more depending on your taste)
1	teaspoon vanilla

Cream butter and add the whipping cream. Beat with your mixer on high until its starts to peak, adding sugar a little at a time. Then fold in the vanilla. This sauce can also be put on cakes or pies at serving time. Oh, by the way, it's without calories! (Don't believe everything you read.)

Brandy Sauce

Delicious with any Pound Cake recipe for a wonderful treat for the holidays.

¾	cup granulated sugar
1	tablespoon cornstarch
1	cup water
1	tablespoons brandy
3	eggs, lightly beaten

Combine the sugar and cornstarch in a small saucepan. Gradually stir in the water and boil until the mixture is thickened. Beat the eggs in a small bowl and set aside. Add a small amount of the hot liquid into the egg mixture. Not too much; you do not want to cook the yolks. Then stir in the eggs into the saucepan. Remove the sauce from the heat and add the brandy. Cool.

Cranberry Sauce

This is a beautiful sauce for the holidays to use for your ham or turkey.

3	cups fresh cranberries
1½	cups brown sugar, firmly packed
½	teaspoon ground cloves
½	cup water

Wash the cranberries. Mix the cranberries, sugar, cloves and water in a medium-sized saucepan. Boil mixture until sugar melts and cranberries are tender. You may pour this sauce over your ham or serve the sauce separately.

Cheesy Cheese Sauce

This is a basic but good Cheese Sauce to make. It would be a delicious sauce to top broccoli or asparagus.

- 2 tablespoons butter
- 2 tablespoons all-purpose flour
- 1 teaspoon salt
- 2 cups milk
- ½-1 cup sharp cheese, grated
- Dash of cayenne pepper
- Dash of paprika

Melt butter, adding flour and salt and mix well. Now add the milk and cheese. Cook over low heat until thick, stirring constantly. Now add a dash of cayenne pepper to taste. Add a dash of paprika for color.

Zippy Meatloaf Topping

You might want to double the recipe to use as a condiment for your meatloaf.

- ¼ cup catsup
- Pinch of sugar
- 2 tablespoons vinegar
- 1 teaspoon Worcestershire sauce
- ½ teaspoon chili powder
- 1 tablespoon onion, chopped

Combine and mix all of the ingredients in the order as they are given in the recipe. Blend the ingredients very well. Now spread this topping on the top of your meatloaf prior to cooking.

Hop Sopping Syrup

1	cup Karo (light corn syrup) or cane syrup
¼	cup butter
	half-and-half or evaporated milk, just enough to thin the syrup out with.

Place the butter and syrup in a saucepan. Heat the syrup just until it boils. Stir in just enough half-and-half or milk to thin the syrup. Pour on pancakes or your biscuits.

Flavored Nut Butter

½	cup pecans or walnuts, chopped
½	cup butter, softened
3	tablespoons dark corn syrup
1	teaspoon maple flavoring
2	pinches nutmeg

Cream all of the ingredients together, blending well. Use on pancakes, waffles, or you favorite flavored breads.

Yields: ¾-cup flavored butter

Maple Syrup Cream

1	cup heavy whipping cream, whipped
½	cup maple syrup

Whip the heavy whipping cream till it mounds. Heat the maple syrup in a small saucepan till hot. Slowly fold the maple syrup into the whipping cream. Spread onto pancakes or French Toast. Delicious!

Honeybee Syrup

1	cup honey
½	stick butter

Using a double boiler, melt the butter and honey, stirring until well blended. Serve hot over pancakes, biscuits, or waffles.

Yields: 1½-cups

Honey Butter

½	butter, room temperature
1	cup honey, room temperature

After both ingredients have reached room temperature, blend both ingredients, beating until fluffy. Store in a covered container in the fridge.

Sour Cream Gravy

2	tablespoons all-purpose flour
2	tablespoons meat drippings or butter
⅓	cup water, can broth, or juices from meat
1	cup sour cream
	Salt and pepper to taste

Combine the flour and drippings. Blend in the water, broth or whatever liquid you are using along with the sour cream. Stir over low heat until thickened. Add salt and pepper to taste.

Onion Gravy

4	tablespoons meat drippings or meat fat
4	tablespoons all-purpose flour
2	cups onions, sliced into rings or 1 cup onion, diced
2	cups beef consommé or beef stock
2	teaspoons Worcestershire sauce
¼	cup mushrooms, sliced or chopped (optional)
½	cup sour cream or ½-cup evaporated milk *(This added makes for a creamier gravy)*
	Salt and pepper to taste

Sauté the onions in the meat fat or drippings. Add the flour, whisking until a smooth paste. Add the stock or consommé and Worcestershire sauce. Slowly whisk in the sour cream or evaporated milk. Now add the mushrooms and seasonings, while simmering with the cover on until the sauce is thickened.

Stroganoff Gravy

If you have some leftover steak from the night before, cut the steak into thin strips and toss the steak strips into this gravy and heat until piping hot.

You can also make your favorite meatball recipe and simmer them with this delicious gravy. Serve the meatballs with this gravy.

1	(4-ounce) can sliced mushrooms, drained
2	tablespoons butter
1	can cream of mushroom soup, undiluted
½	package onion soup mix
1	(8-ounce) carton sour cream
1	teaspoon instant coffee
½	cup cooking sherry
1	teaspoon paprika

Melt butter in skillet and sauté mushrooms. Add the remaining ingredients to the mushrooms and mix well. Heat until bubbly. Add meat and serve over noodles or rice. If the gravy is thicker than you like, just add a little evaporated milk or water to the gravy and stir well while heating.

Mama Gillis' Red-Eye Gravy

This is as near to Mama Gillis' Red-Eye Gravy as I can remember. Please enjoy!

1	(1 to 2-inch) thick slice cured ham
¼	cup butter, lard or shortening
1	teaspoon sugar
	Pinch of salt
½	cup hot water
⅓	cup hot coffee
	Additional salt and pepper to taste

Fry the ham in the shortening, butter or lard. (I use my black cast-iron skillet.) Remove the ham and set aside. Drain the fat or drippings and reserve for later use. Add the sugar and salt to the skillet and brown well. Pour in the hot water and coffee and add the reserved fat or drippings and heat. You may add the ham back to the skillet to flavor the gravy that much more. Serve with grits or "sop" with biscuits. Season with salt and pepper.

Mama Gillis' Sawmill Gravy

½	pound your favorite pork sausage, cooked and drained
¼	cup butter
⅓	cup all-purpose flour
3	cups whole milk
½	teaspoon salt
½	teaspoon black pepper
	Pinch cayenne pepper
	Paprika

Cook and drain sausage, set aside. In a large skillet, melt butter over low heat, stirring in flour until smooth. Cook on medium heat and gradually add milk, continue to stir to eliminate lumps. Stir until the mixture is creamy and thickened. Stir in the salt, and peppers. Sprinkle with paprika.

Cocktail Sauce

2	tablespoons fresh lemon juice
1	cup chili sauce
½	cup catsup
1½	tablespoons prepared horseradish to taste
½	teaspoon Worcestershire sauce
½	teaspoon celery salt
	Dash of hot sauce to taste
	Dash of red pepper to taste

Blend ingredients. Chill and enjoy over oysters, crab, or shrimp.

Homemade Tartar Sauce

When you cook fish, you most certainly can purchase commercially prepared tartar sauce. Most of the time you never use it up and it just sits there in the fridge.

Try this recipe. I promise you, that you will never, ever buy anymore commercially prepared tartar sauce. The sauce is as good as the fish itself. It is very simple to make. You will see.

1	cup mayonnaise
⅓	cup pickle relish, minced *(I like to use the Sweet Pickle Relish, however, if you like a more sour taste use the dill pickle relish).*
1	tablespoon chives, minced
1	teaspoon parsley, minced
⅓	cup onion, minced
1	teaspoon fresh lemon juice
1	tablespoon pimento, minced

Combine all of the ingredients in a blender. Mix and chill.

Basic Recipe for White Sauce

Thin Sauce:
- 1 tablespoon all-purpose flour
- 1 tablespoon butter
- 1 cup half-and-half or evaporated milk
- ¼ teaspoon salt
- Dash of pepper

Medium Sauce:
- 2 tablespoons all-purpose flour
- 2 tablespoons butter
- 1 cup half-and-half or evaporated milk
- ¼ teaspoon salt
- Dash of pepper

Thick Sauce:
- 4 tablespoons all-purpose flour
- 4 tablespoons butter
- 1 cup half-and-half or evaporated milk
- ½ teaspoon salt
- Dash of pepper

Melt the butter in a double boiler. Add the flour and seasonings. Mix to form a smooth paste or roux. Add the milk gradually, stirring to keep a smooth consistency. Simmer for 15 minutes, stirring well.

Variations:
Cheese sauce: Add 1 cup grated cheese to the hot sauce, stirring until melted.

Celery Sauce: Sauté 1 cup thinly, sliced celery in a small amount of butter. Add to the basic sauce. Substitute celery salt in lieu of the regular salt in the basic recipe. Stir well.

Different areas of the United States prefer different kinds of sauces. Texas prefers more of a catsup-based BBQ sauce, while the Carolinas prefer a more mustard-based BBQ sauce. As you probably have guessed, the Divine Dixie Deva likes it all. Mama Gillis made a more mustard-based sauce. Here are a couple of different sauces.

BBQ Slather and Sop Sauce
Mustard and vinegar base

¾	cup prepared mustard
¾	cup red wine vinegar
¼	cup granulated sugar
2	teaspoons Worcestershire sauce
1½	teaspoons black pepper
½	teaspoon salt
	Few dashes of hot pepper sauce
2	tablespoons butter

Mix all ingredients in a medium-sized saucepan. Cook and stir on medium high heat until boiling. Reduce the heat and simmer for about 30 minutes. Serve with your favorite BBQ sandwiches.

Hog Sauce
Catsup base

I like this on pulled pork or chopped pork sandwiches.

1	cup catsup
1	cup light brown sugar, firmly packed
½	cup real lemon juice
¼	cup butter
¼	cup onions, minced
1½	teaspoons Worcestershire sauce

Mix all ingredients in a medium-sized saucepan. Bring them to a boil on medium heat. Reduce to simmer and heat for 30 minutes more.

Samples of BBQ sauces for judging at the "Memphis in May" World Championship BBQ Contest

Jams, Jellies, Preserves & Pickles

I always had such a warm comfortable and secure feeling to walk in Mama Gillis' kitchen to see her, elbows deep in the preserving kettle. Mama Gillis never wasted a watermelon, or cantaloupe rind or anything. She never ceased to amaze me as to how many containers she owned to put pickles, watermelon or cantaloupe preserves to brine in.

Well, guess what? Her granddaughter, the Divine Dixie Deva, is the same way. I have more pots, pans and containers-mostly from Mama Gillis' kitchen-that I still use. It gives me a warm comfortable feeling. If there is a special utensil that a loved one uses to cook with, and you have a desire for it, please let them know you would like it someday when they pass on. Have them write your name on it. Just be sure you get it.

As I have mentioned, I have Mama Gillis' wood cook stove that she used to can with. Well, when I was a little girl, the wood cook stove was housed in a little wooden house where we would can green beans and tomatoes.

Thank goodness, I had enough forethought to ask her for it before she passed on. When that day came, I was encouraged to sell it for I was told that the stove was so heavy that it may cave my kitchen floor in.

Well, it has been on two different kitchen floors, one in the South and one in the North, and I still have a floor to walk on. Not only is the wood cook stove in pristine shape, the floor is too. It also made the trip quite nicely 979 miles from Albany, Georgia to Michigan.

Thank God, I did not listen to everyone's comments, and I went on my gut feeling.

Bernice and Me in the Peach Orchard

Many years ago, when canning and preserving time rolled around, I would look forward to peach picking time in the peach orchards of Desoto, Georgia. They have acres and acres of the most gorgeous peaches.

I had the most wonderful friend who I loved dearly, Bernice. She was my canning buddy, and I asked her if she wanted to go to the peach orchard with me. She was so excited, so we took off to the orchard. As the afternoon rolled on, we became so engrossed in picking the peaches that we barely realized that we were all alone. I showed some concern that two women had no business being in the middle of those acres of peaches without a soul knowing where they were. No sooner than I said this, she ripped out a pistol and told me not to worry about a thing-that she would take care of us. From that day on, Bernice was my Peach-Picking Mama. We were inseparable. I have a couple of recipes of hers that I would like to share. She has long passed now.

I'm sure you read what she told me about eating a whole sweet potato pie! Look for that story in the Pie section.

Note: There was only one thing that I did teach Mama Gillis about cooking, even though she did not listen to this hint. She always peeled peaches and tomatoes with a little paring knife. Several foot tubs of peaches and tomatoes lined the front and back porch. I taught her to dip the peaches and tomatoes in boiling water for 30 seconds to 1 minute or until the skins started to split. Then dip them in cold water and the skins would slip right off. I was grown before I learned that trick, and by that time, Mama Gillis did not want to change her old habits of peeling them with her paring knife.

Bernice's Peach Preserves

1½	quarts fresh peaches, peeled and diced
1	orange, diced
	Grated orange rind from 1 orange
	Juice of two lemons
1	cup maraschino cherries, including juice, chopped
6	cups granulated sugar
	Fruit Fresh-Sprinkle on peaches to keep color

Mix ingredients and cook until desired consistency. I liked my preserves to be real thick. Keep this stirred constantly. Pour into hot jars, adjust lids, and process in your water bath canner for 5 minutes at 212-degrees.

Yields: 3½-pints

Bernice's Cherry Pear Preserves

10	cups ripe pears, peeled and grated
5	pounds granulated sugar
3	cups **more** granulated sugar
3	(10-ounce) jars maraschino cherries, chopped, with juice
2	(20-ounce) cans crushed pineapple, with juice

Combine all ingredients in a large pot or kettle. Cook until a little syrupy. Cook until the juice drops a sheet off a spoon as in jelly test.* Then jar up in your hot jars. Adjust lids. Process in boiling water bath canner for 15 minutes at 212-degrees.

Y'all this is great on ice cream and even pound cake.

*Jelly Test – Boil the jelly on medium high to high heat, boiling briskly. Watch the mixture closely. Dip a spoon, not a wooden spoon, in the syrup and lift the syrup spoon up so that the syrup will run off of the sides of the spoon. Just before it becomes to the jelly point, the jelly will drop from the sides of the spoon in two drops. In just a second or two, after dipping the spoon in the hot syrup, you will have reached the jelly point when the mixture runs together and slides off of the spoon in one sheet. A candy thermometer can be used and the temperature will be between 220 to 222-degrees.

Peach Peeling-Peach Seed Jelly

This recipe came in handy with all of those peaches that Bernice and I would pick. We would only pay $4 a bushel for the finest peaches you could ever find. Mama Gillis taught me not to waste anything. So, we didn't waste any peaches with this recipe. The jelly was delicious, too. A lot of my girl friends wanted this recipe

There is a lot of pulp in the peeling and on the seeds, so save peelings and seeds when canning or freezing peaches. Place peach peelings and seeds (minimum 4 quarts) in a heavy pan. **Barely** cover with water. Bring to a boil and let simmer for 30 minutes. **Cover and let stand overnight**. Strain juice through several layers of cheese cloth. Measure 3 cups of juice into pan. Add 1 package of powdered pectin. Bring to a vigorous boil, adding 3 cups sugar. Boil juice rapidly until drops sheet off a spoon as in the jelly test. Skim off foam. Pour into sterilized jars to within ½-inch of top. Put on the cap and screw the band firmly tight. Process in boiling water bath canner for 5 minutes at 212-degrees.

Your kitchen smells so good during canning time. The spices reek in the kitchen and it is such a comforting feeling to one's self.

Cinnamon Apple Sticks

This recipe for Cinnamon Apple Sticks, I made this recipe well over 25 years ago. Mama Gillis helped me with this. I always called her several times a day. She never cared that I was turning her loose from a chore. She always had a sweet word to say to me. These are wonderful and colorful to give for Christmas gifts.

18	tart apples, peeled and cored
6	cups sugar
3	cups water
1	(9-ounce) package red cinnamon hearts
3	drops red food coloring

Cut each apple into eighths using corer or apple wedger. Combine sugar, water, cinnamon hearts and food coloring. Bring to a boil and boil for 3 minutes. Add apples to syrup and cook till transparent. Pack into hot jars. Cover with syrup. Adjust lids. Process in hot water bath canner for 25 minutes at 212-degrees.

Mayhaw Jelly

Stop. If you live anywhere other than Southwest Georgia, don't expect to find this berry. However, read the story for some amusement and if you are game to try the jelly. Look on my Resource page and you will find out where you can get the:

"Cadillac of All Jellies"

A tip from The Divine Dixie Deva—It has been known that a jar or two of this wonderful Jelly has kept a certain person from several speeding tickets. Whoops, did I indicate a bribe?

If you have never eaten Mayhaw Jelly, you are missing something. Again, the Cadillac of all Jellies. Mayhaws are found in the bogs of Southwest Georgia. They resemble a cross of a crab apple and plum.

If the Southern folks would have turned their swamp land into crops of Mayhaws like the Northerners did cranberries, Yeah, buddy—we surely would have had something there. As you have probably guessed, this is my favorite jelly.

Just to let you know how much I like it, listen to this story...

You have to adorn yourself in hip boots to wade in the water, wear long-sleeve shirts for the "skeeters" and of course, wear a hat for the blistering sun. If you are lucky and have a boat, that's the ticket to get out into the marshland. Last, but not least, you have to bring a couple of bed sheets to lay in the water, so when you shake the trees the berries will fall on them. Oh! Did I tell you to watch out for the water moccasins and alligators?

Every year in May, I would go to these lengths to get these wonderful berries. After getting the berries and extracting the juice, I would freeze the juice in several gallon jugs. Later during the year, particularly at Christmas, I would make my jelly. Folks in Southwest Georgia would almost float a loan for this jelly.

This is how I would make my spending money for my kids' Christmas presents, by making Mayhaw jelly. I had a list of folks that would call me every year for gifts of jelly. Even the college kids wanted jars of jelly with them at college. I made quite a little "stash."

Well, if you are lucky enough to live near Southwest Georgia or know someone to get these berries for you (it will cost you, though)—here's the recipe. You can use this recipe for crabapples, also.

In Southwest Georgia just about everything in your garden comes in at the same time and you have to get it while you can, because of the heat. You cannot afford to let something like Mayhaws go to waste.

Again, look on the Resource page and you can order Mayhaw jelly without having to worry about the water moccasins and alligators.

Mayhaw Jelly Recipe

Wash the berries off real well-lots of dirt, believe me. Put the berries in a large pot. Cover the berries with water. Let them come to a rolling boil. You do not want to let them boil too long, for you do not want the berries to burst open on the first boil. You would be losing some of the berry juice, since you are going to pour this water out. Skim the crud off along with the foam from the berries. Then let this cool so you won't burn yourself pouring off the water.

Cover the berries with water one more time. Let this come to a boil again. Skim the crud and foam off again. Do not pour this water out. Now, let the berries cook till the berries burst open. They will be boiling real good. Your kitchen smells wonderful by this time with this berry aroma. Can't forget it. It brings back so many memories.

After the berries have burst wide open, let them cool until you can strain them up. Let me tell you how I did this in detail. I took a piece of cheesecloth and a strainer with a large bowl under this. I laid my cheesecloth in the strainer and poured the juice from the pot along with the berries in the cheesecloth. I let the juices flow through and then I took the cheesecloth and squeezed real hard. I was not about to let any of the juice go to waste, as hard as it is to fetch it. Then I had nothing left in the cheesecloth but scrub, and I discarded that.

I made sure that the berry juice was good and clear. If it wasn't, I would strain it again with another clean piece of cheese cloth. Now here is the method of actually preparing the jelly.

(Recipe continues on following page)

Now you see why I froze my juice for later use. I was "tuckered out" by this time.

4	cups prepared juice (If you are short on juice – *e.g.* 3¾-cup juice to make 4 cups of juice – just add ¼-cup of water. I never added more than ¼-cup, though.)
1	box pectin
5½	cups granulated sugar

Have your jelly glasses ready. When I say ready, I mean sterilized. I did not have a dishwasher then so I used my large wedding cake pans and put water in the bottom of them turned my jelly jars upside down and cut on the eye of the stove. When they boiled for about 10 minutes, they were hot and ready to use. In a large kettle or Dutch oven, I mixed my pectin with my juice and brought the juice quickly to a boil, stirring occasionally. Then I added all of my sugar. When this came to a rolling boil, I cooked it, stirred it for 1 minute, and skimmed it again with a metal spoon. Now the juice was ready to pour in the jars. I kept this procedure up till all my juice was gone. This one recipe only made about 4 pints of jelly. I always process my jellies in a hot water bath canner for 5 minutes at 212-degrees.

The jelly has a beautiful reddish-peach color and is wonderful. If you ever want to find any of these berries, Colquitt, Georgia is the Mayhaw Capital of the World.

Pear Honey

8	cups pears, peeled and cored
5	cups sugar
1	(20-ounce) can of crushed pineapple, undrained
2	boxes of powdered pectin

Peel and core pears and put them through a processor and blend. Mix all ingredients and boil until thick and clear, somewhere between 30 to 45 minutes. Put in jars and seal. Also, process this in your hot water bath canner for 5 minutes at 212-degrees.

The pears that we have in Southwest Georgia are very firm. In other areas where you do not have these nice, big, firm pears to choose from, select the firmest ones at the produce stand.

Strawberry Rhubarb Jam

I never made anything with Rhubarb until I married my "Yankee" husband and moved to Michigan. He loves it.

3	cups sliced rhubarb
2	cups sliced fresh ripened strawberries
2	tablespoons grated orange peel
⅓	cup orange juice
1	box powdered fruit pectin
5½	cups sugar

Combine the fruits in a large saucepan. Add the orange peel and juice. Mix in the fruit pectin. Stir over high heat until mixture comes to a rolling boil. Immediately stir in the sugar, bring to a rolling boil, and continue to stir. Boil one minute and set aside. Stir the mixture for about 5 minutes and ladle the jam into hot sterilized jars. Seal immediately. Process 5 minutes in a hot water bath canner at 212-degrees.

Strawberry Fig Preserves

3	cups figs, mashed
2	(3-ounce) packages strawberry Jell-O
3	cups granulated sugar

Mash figs and combine with the other ingredients in a big kettle or Dutch oven. Bring to boil over medium heat, stirring occasionally. Boil for at least 3 minutes. Skim off the top of the jelly and then pour into sterilized jars and process for 10 minutes with hot water bath canner.

Blueberry Peach Jam

4	cup (4-pounds) peaches, peeled and chopped
4	cups (1-quart) blueberries
2	tablespoons lemon juice
½	cup water
1	stick cinnamon
½	teaspoon whole cloves
¼	teaspoon whole allspice
5½	cups granulated sugar
5-6	half-pint jars, hot and sterilized

Combine the peaches, blueberries, lemon juice, and water in a large kettle or Dutch oven. Bring to a boil, cover and reduce the heat to low, and simmer for 10 minutes. Make a cheesecloth bag and place the spices in the bag, tying securely. Add the spices and sugar to the fruit mixture, bring to a boil, stirring constantly. Boil on high for 20 to 30 minutes until the mixture thickens and the temperature reads on a candy thermometer at 220-degrees. Stir this mixture constantly. Remove from the heat and skim the foam off of the top of the mixture with a metal spoon. Toss the spice bag. Ladle the hot jam into the sterilized jars, leaving a headspace of ¼-inch. Cover at once with the metal lids and screw on jar bands. Process in a hot water bath for 10 minutes.

Vidalia Onion Relish

1½	gallons ground Vidalia onions (approximately 16 medium onions)
½	cup salt
1	quart apple cider vinegar
1	teaspoon turmeric
1	teaspoon mixed pickling spice
1	teaspoon pimento, chopped
4½	cups sugar

Grind up enough Vidalia onions to make 1½-gallons and then add ½-cup salt. Let stand 30 minutes. Squeeze the juice from the onion and salt mixture. Throw out the juice. Add vinegar, sugar, spices, and pimento to the onions. Bring to a boil and cook for 30 minutes, stirring often. (By this time your sinuses will say a big thank you.) Fill hot, sterilized jars with the cooked relish. Leave ½-inch headspace in jars. Cover with lids and process in a hot water bath canner for 10 minutes.

Yields: 8 pints

Winter Cranberry Chutney

1	(1-pound, 14-ounce) can fruit cocktail
½	cup orange juice
½	cup sugar
¼	cup brown sugar
¼	cup apple cider vinegar
½	teaspoon ground cloves
¼	teaspoon mace (my favorite spice in the whole world)
¼	teaspoon red pepper
½	teaspoon salt
2	cups cranberries
1	cup chopped, unpeeled apples
1	tablespoon candied ginger, finely chopped
1	small clove of garlic, minced
¾	cups of seedless raisins

Drain fruit cocktail and measure 1¼-cups of fruit cocktail syrup. Reserve the fruit. If there is not enough syrup to make 1¼-cups, add enough water to make it. Combine the syrup and the next 8 ingredients in a large boiler or kettle, with the exception of the fruit cocktail. Bring to a full boil, stirring often. Add the cranberries and the remaining ingredients. Cook until the cranberries pop open about 5 minutes. Now stir in the fruit cocktail. Simmer and continue to stir often until mixture thickens slightly. This will take about 15 minutes. Pour into hot, sterilized jars and process in hot water bath canner for 10 minutes. You may also store this in the refrigerator. This thickens as it cools.

Note: This makes wonderful a Christmas gift. Make extra. It is a great addition to your holiday meal. Try it.

Yields: 2½ pints

Georgia Peach Chutney

4	quarts peeled peaches, finely chopped
1	cup seedless raisins
1	hot red pepper, seeded and chopped
5	cups vinegar (apple or white vinegar)
2½	cups light brown sugar (You may want to add another ½-cup, if not sweet enough after tasting.)
¼	cup mustard seed
2	tablespoons ground ginger
2	teaspoons salt
1	clove of garlic, minced (this is optional)

Combine all of the ingredients in a large kettle or Dutch oven and cook slowly until thick. This will take about 40 minutes. Stir often to prevent sticking. After combining all ingredients, taste, and you may want to add another ½-cup of brown sugar. Pour boiling chutney into jars, leaving ½-inch headspace. Process 10 minutes in a hot water bath canner.

Note: You may substitute pears with this recipe. You may substitute 1 cup chopped onions in lieu of the 1 cup raisins in either version. I like to add chutney on my hams.

Canned Peach Chutney

This is a quick and easy Peach Chutney recipe using canned peaches. This will make 2 cups, just enough for a supper time meal. For the holidays, this would be ideal to accent a pork loin or a baked ham.

1	(1-pound) can peach slices, natural juice, drained
¾	cup apple cider vinegar
½	cup brown sugar
½	small onion, chopped fine
1	apple, peeled, cored and coarsely chopped
1	teaspoon mixed pickling spices
	Lemon juice from 1 lemon

Chop the peaches, leaving large chunks. Combine the rest of the ingredients in a large saucepan. Cook on medium for about 20 minutes, stirring occasionally until slightly thickened. Let cool and serve either cold or at room temperature. This is just enough for a couple of meals. Canning and processing this recipe is not an option.

Pear Chutney

4	quarts pears, peeled and finely chopped
1	cup seedless raisins
1	hot red pepper, seeded and chopped
5	cups apple cider vinegar
3	cups light brown sugar
¼	cup mustard seed
2	tablespoons ground ginger
2	teaspoons salt
7	pint jars, hot and sterilized

Combine all of the ingredients and cook slowly in a large kettle or Dutch oven. Cook until thick about 40 to 50 minutes, stirring often to keep from sticking. Pour the boiling mixture into the hot jars and leave a ½-inch headspace. Cap the jars and process in a hot water bath for 10 minutes.

Delicious with any kind of meat, particularly Pork Loin Roast.

Mama's Pickled Peaches

Remember that Pickled Peach Salad? Well, here is the recipe for the Pickled Peaches. Just use the leftover juice left in the jars after the peaches are gone for the recipe of Pickled Peach Salad. Believe me, it will not take long before they are gone!

Make a syrup as needed for the peaches:

24	firm ripe peaches (about 6 pounds), peeled
4	cups granulated sugar
2	cups water
1 ½	cups apple cider vinegar (you may use white vinegar)
	Mama uses the white vinegar. I like the apple cider vinegar.
4	tablespoons mixed pickling spices

Combine the sugar, water, and apple cider vinegar in an 8 to 10-quart Dutch oven. Stir constantly until sugar has dissolved. Tie 4 tablespoons of mixed pickling spices in a little bag and let simmer in syrup. Peel peaches and drop in this boiling syrup. After the peaches come to a boil, cut the heat down to a simmer for about 5 minutes, carefully turning them over in the syrup while cooking. Remove peaches and pack into hot, sterilized pint jars. Let stand a few minutes. Peaches will shrink and you will be able to put another peach or two in the jar. Pour hot syrup on top of the peaches. Seal and process in hot water boiling bath for 20 minutes.

***Note:** To make a spice bag—just cut a 6-inch square of doubled cheesecloth, put spices in it, gather it up and tie it with a string. The string needs to be long enough to pick up out of the pot.

Yields: 5 pints

Pepper Sauce

As far as I can remember, my Daddy has always eaten Pepper Sauce with his Butter Beans, Peas, Greens, etc. This is a common practice for most Southern men to douse enough Pepper Sauce on their food until they break out in a sweat. This must be a "He Man thing." I still haven't figured this one out.

Hot Pepper Sauce

Small hot peppers (Jalapeno, Banana or Hungarian)
Apple Cider Vinegar
Sterilized jars

Wash and drain the peppers, making slits in each of the peppers. Pack the jars tightly with the peppers, leaving a ½-inch headspace. Boil enough vinegar to fill the jars within ½-inch headspace. Adjust the lids and seal the jars. Boil in a hot water bath for 5 minutes.

I did not specify how many of any ingredients in this recipe. This is just one of those recipes that you need to make enough in proportion to your peppers.

Sweet Red Pepper Sauce Syrup Recipe

This is a Sweet Red Pepper Sauce recipe. It is not really hot but a sweet and tangy condiment. Again this is another recipe that you will need to make enough syrup in proportion to your sweet red peppers.

1 cup sugar
2 cups apple cider vinegar

Mix together in a large saucepan. Heat until boiling to dissolve sugar, stirring occasionally. Wash the outside of the peppers, remove the seeds, and cut into thin strips. Put the strips into ice water to crisp the strips. Have your jars ready for the peppers. Make enough syrup to fill the jars. Fill the jars with the peppers, and then fill with boiling hot syrup and seal.

Kathryn and Bernice's Vegetable Soup Base

This recipe is wonderful to "put up" your garden's bounty.

- 2 quarts tomatoes, peeled, chopped
- 1½ quarts potatoes, peeled and cubed
- 1 quart fresh lima beans
- 1 quart fresh corn, cut from the cob
- 1½ quart carrots, sliced
- 2 cups celery, sliced
- 2 cups onion, chopped
- 1½ quarts water
- Salt (½ teaspoon to each jar)
- 7 quart jars, sterilized and hot

Combine the vegetables and water in a large kettle. Bring to a boil over medium heat, stirring frequently to prevent scorching and sticking. Boil 5 minutes. Spoon into hot sterilized jars, leaving 1-inch headspace, adding ½-teaspoon salt to each jar. Cover at once with lids and seal tight. Process in pressure canner at 10 pounds of pressure (240-degrees) for 1 hour and 25 minutes.

Yields: 7 quarts

Bounty Fresh Vegetable Beef Soup for Supper

In the winter, when you have a desire for Fresh Vegetable Beef soup, purchase 1½ pounds of lean stew beef in 1-inch cubes. In a heavy saucepan, season the stew beef with salt, pepper, and garlic salt. Cover with water and boil. Cut the heat down to simmering for about 1 hour until tender. Now, add a quart of your Vegetable Soup Base, and a few splashes of Worcestershire sauce. You may have to add more liquid, depending on how thick you want your soup. I always like to add 1 (46-ounce) can of tomato juice or V-8 juice to my soup for some of the liquid. Add a pinch of sugar. Bring to a boil and simmer until vegetables are heated throughout. Make a pan of cornbread, and there you go. Something to stick to your ribs.

Note: You may also use 1½-pounds of ground chuck or round in lieu of the stew beef in this recipe. Just brown the ground chuck and drain off any grease, season as per the directions above.

Mama Gillis' 9-Day Pickle
(The Ultimate)

Try the 9-day pickle recipe. This recipe she gave to me and wrote in her own handwriting.

If you are looking for a very crisp, sweet pickle recipe, this is it.
Well, I have tasted and made pickles all of my life and this pickle is far better than any pickle recipe I have tasted. Now you may have a better one, but I haven't found it.

Lord, at pickle making time, Mama Gillis had every container within reach full of these things brining away. For every container she used, she had a plate to weight them down, in order to keep the pickles in the brine.

I am writing this recipe just as Mama Gillis' hand wrote it. The "Notes" are my addition.

Note: A measure of cucumber pickles is not mentioned, purposely. This is another recipe that you will make enough brine solution and syrup according to the quantity of your cucumbers.

Use fresh cucumbers 3 to 5-inches in length. Wash and drain the cucumbers and slice. You are to make enough brine to cover your pickles, regardless of how many pickles you have. Continue making brine to cover the amount of pickles and lay a plate on the pickles to keep your pickles under the brine solution. After the third day in the salt solution, you will see that some of the pickles have shrunk in size.

1-3 days...1 cup canning salt to 1 gallon fresh cool water. Each day for these 3 days, change in fresh water with 1 cup canning salt to one gallon fresh cool water.

Note: Dissolve the salt and water well before you pour over the pickles.

4-6 days...1 tablespoon alum to 1 gallon cool fresh water each day for 3 days then.* Everyday, you are to rinse the pickles off just like you did for the salt and start with new alum water.

6-9 days...Mix up the vinegar and sugar and let come to a boil. Stir your sugar good to dissolve in the vinegar, so it will not burn the boiler (saucepan).

Now...the way you do this–

1 cup vinegar (*I like apple cider vinegar and Mama Gillis used this, too.*)

2 cups granulated sugar

In your big kettle continue to make enough of this solution until you have enough fixed up for your pickles, and this will be enough to cover your pickles.

Each day, take the pickles out of this vinegar solution, boil again, and then pour the same vinegar back over the pickles while the solution is boiling hot. DO NOT RINSE THE PICKLES OFF WITH WATER LIKE YOU DID IN THE PREVIOUS STEPS.

Note: I always made a pickling spice bag out of a clean, thin cotton material. You can use several layers of cheesecloth or I take an old clean T-shirt and cut two 6-inch squares. In each square I pour about 2 tablespoons of mixed pickling spice, tie them up with dental floss or fishing line and let them stay in the vinegar and sugar solution. I also boil the bags when I bring the vinegar and sugar solution to a boil.

On the 9th day, lift the pickles out by hand and put them loosely in your clean, sterilized jars. Let the vinegar solution come to a rolling boil again. Pour while good and hot over the pickles in the jars and seal. Toss the spice bag on this day; you will not have a need for it any more.

Be sure you let your vinegar go around your pickles in your jars, so it will cover your pickles good before sealing. After sealing according to manufacturer's directions, process in a hot water boiling bath for 5 minutes.

Note: If you run slim on vinegar and sugar solution in the stages of filling up the jars with pickles and pouring the vinegar solution over them, just make up some more with the same recipe as above and let it come to a rolling boil and pour over the pickles.

Pickle Tips from the Deva: Never use iodized salt in making pickles, for it will discolor the pickles. I always get the canning salt. However, you may use the non-iodized salt, but canning salt is the better choice.

Always make sure that you do not use an aluminum container. Use a big plastic bowl, glass, or even some sort of crockery product.

(Recipe continues on following page)

Again, be sure you weight the pickles down in the brining solution by laying a plate on top of the pickles, for the pickles will rise to the top. You need to keep the cucumbers below the brine.

You will notice that the pickles will start to shrink during the pickle making process.

You may use apple cider vinegar or white vinegar, but choose one of good quality. Personally, I like to use apple cider vinegar. I usually purchase my cucumbers from a farmer or farmer's market, for if you buy them from the store, usually they have that wax finish on them, which you will have to "scrub the daylights," out of them in order for the brine to penetrate through.

This is a personal note Mama Gillis wrote to me:

Kathy, if you have any trouble understanding this, please feel free to call me every day before you make your changes.

I had to have help to begin my first and I do not mind helping you any way I can.

I hope you can read this-I am in a big hurry to go see about what is in my garden this morning before Mary C. comes (Mary C. is my mother).

Love, Mama Gillis.

Note: If I ever need sweet pickle relish to make deviled eggs, potato salad, or macaroni salad, *etc.*, I chopped some of these up very fine. They are very crisp and fresh tasting.

Quick and Easy Sweet Pickles

30	small cucumbers
2	cups lime
2	gallons water
2	quarts apple cider vinegar
8	cups granulated sugar
3	teaspoons whole cloves
1	teaspoon salt

Wash and slice the cucumbers ¼-inch thick.* Using a large plastic or glass bowl, dissolve the lime in the water and place the cucumbers in this solution. Place a plate on top of the cucumbers, weighting them down in the solution. If you do not weigh them down, the cucumbers will rise to the top. Cover the cucumber slices with plastic wrap or a lid to fit the bowl. Let them stand in the solution for 24 hours. After 24 hours, rinse the solution off of the cucumbers in clean, cool water. Make sure you rinse the cucumbers well. Now cover the cucumbers with water and let them stand in this water for 3 hours. Drain the water off after the 3 hours. Mix the vinegar, sugar, cloves, and salt together, dissolving well, and pour over the cucumbers. Let them stand in the solution overnight, weighting them down again with a plate. The next morning, bring the vinegar solution and cucumbers to a rolling boil, boiling 35 to 40 minutes. Skim any foam off of the top. Fill the jars within a ½-inch of the top of the jar. Cap the jars and process in a hot water bath for 10 minutes.

*Do not use an aluminum container.

Note: Mama Gillis taught me how to make pickles and the procedure behind it. Every summer of my life that Mama Gillis lived, I have watched her make pickles.

Yields: 11 pint jars

Red Pepper Relish

2	dozen red bell peppers, seeded
7	medium onions
2	tablespoons mustard seed
2	tablespoons salt
3	cup apple cider vinegar
3	cups sugar

In your food processor, grind the red peppers and onions. Save the liquid. In a large kettle, combine all of the ingredients with the reserved juice. Boil 30 minutes, stirring frequently. Pack this mixture into sterilized pint jars. Fill within ½-inch of the top of jars. Process the filled jars in a hot water bath for 5 minutes.

Fresh Tomato Salsa

7	quarts ripe tomatoes, peeled, cored, and chopped
4	cups long green chili peppers, seeded and chopped
½	cup jalapeno peppers, seeded and finely chopped
5	cups onions, chopped
5	cloves of garlic, minced
2	cups bottled lemon juice
2	tablespoons salt
2	tablespoons sugar
1	tablespoon pepper
1	tablespoon ground cumin
3	tablespoons oregano

Combine all ingredients in a large pot except for the cumin and oregano. Bring to a boil, stirring often to keep from sticking. Reduce the heat to a simmer. Simmer for 10 minutes and continue to stir. Add the cumin and oregano and simmer 20 minutes more. Ladle into prepared pint jars, leaving ½-inch headspace. Wipe the rims of the jars. Seal and process for 15 minutes in a hot water boiling bath.

Yields: 13 pints

Ole Fashion Apple Butter

2	gallons apple sweet cider
1	gallon apples, washed, stemmed, peeled, cored and quartered
4	cups light brown sugar, firmly packed
1½	tablespoons cinnamon
½	tablespoon allspice
¼	teaspoon mace

Place the cider in the kettle. Boil the cider down rapidly on high heat, uncovered, until the cider is reduced to 1 gallon of liquid. After preparing the apples, add them to the cider. Reduce the heat to medium and boil the apples with the cider for approximately 2 hours. Stir frequently with a wooden spoon to keep from burning or sticking. Add the sugar and spices and stir until they are dissolved. Continue to boil until the apples begin to settle down and become more like an applesauce, pulp mixture. Simmer and stir gently. Meanwhile prepare your canning jars by sterilizing. Pour apple butter into the hot sterilized jar, leaving ½-inch headspace. Be sure to wipe the rims of the jars. Seal and process in a hot water bath canner for 20 minutes.

What more thoughtful gift could you give to someone? A jar of Apple Butter with a loaf of homemade bread?

Note: I always smell the apples, and if they have a good fragrance, they are usually the most flavorful.

*Michigan has some dynamite apple orchards. That is a highlight of mine in the fall to go to their orchards, eat their homemade doughnuts, and drink the best apple cider in the world.

Yields: 10 half-pints

Squash Pickles

12	cups squash, sliced
2	cups onions, sliced
1	tablespoon pickling salt
1	cup green pepper, seeded and diced
2	cups vinegar (5% acidity)
3½	cups granulated sugar
1	teaspoon celery seed
1	teaspoon mustard seed

Combine the squash, onions, and salt in an 8 to 10 quart Dutch oven. Let stand for 1 hour. Combine all of the other ingredients, bring them to a boil. Pack squash and onions into hot, sterilized pint jars, adding the vinegar mixture and leaving a ¼-inch headspace for the jars. Cover and seal at once, processing in the hot water boiling bath for 15 minutes.

Yields: 4 pints

Wild Cooking, Fishing & BBQ

I'm not all just the domestic type of woman—there's another side of me—

I love to fish and hunt, but nothing is better than catching a "mess of fish" and cooking it right on the spot. If you have done it, you know you can't beat the taste. What fun! One of my favorite spots is Econfina, Florida. It's a real neat hunting and fishing camp.

Watch out for the wild hogs! During my first visit there about 15 years ago one of them tried to get in the tent with me; scared me to death, but that was the "rush" and made it that much more fun. Now girls, if you go there, this is a fishing camp for men, or at least it started out that way. Don't take your curling irons, it's rustic.

The camp has an inlet of fresh water that leads out to the Gulf of Mexico. After you leave the inlet you are out into that vast beautiful Gulf and it looks like the biggest diamonds you have ever seen shining in the sunlight. There is nothing like it. If you ever have the chance to visit Econfina—do so. The last time I went to Econfina was 7 years ago. From what I have been told it hasn't changed that much. That's the charm in it.

The fishing is incredible—Salt Water Cat, Reds, Speckled Trout, and Cobia. Just a hint for you folks that may want to go fishing out there—use the "Salty Dog" fishing tackle for the Speckled Trout and Cut-Bait Mullet to catch the Trout and Catfish. I've never caught Cobia, so who knows what to use for bait on that.

Don't forget to visit "Rock Island"—It's an island 10 miles from the mouth of Econfina in the Gulf—don't do like we did and wait too long to leave Rock Island. I was exploring it and the tide went out and we couldn't leave. We had to spend the night on that deserted island, and I mean deserted, except for the raccoons that kept us up all night. They stole every bit of food we had.

During my exploring on the island, I noticed a little hut with a mattress and a shelf that had potatoes (the potatoes had no eyes in them). Fresh potatoes. What did that tell me? Someone was coming back to eat them and the potatoes hadn't been there too long. No joke, Mullet fishermen spend the night there sometimes. I've been told that pirates have visited the island.

You know, I think that I should not have been too worried about the raccoons.

Pack your frying pan—you will need it!

Enough of the stories—Let's get on with the recipes!

Quick hint: Fishing with chicken livers? Save your panty hose for bait. Why? Cut tiny squares of panty hose and put chicken livers in there. The panty hose will stay on the hook better than just plain chicken livers.

Papa's Oyster Stew

As far back as I can remember, Mama Gillis and Papa had Oyster Stew on Friday nights. We would make a trip to the Piggly Wiggly store for her fresh oysters. She would always make sure she purchased a gallon of fresh "sweet milk" for Papa's Oyster Stew. What is "sweet milk"? It is a Southern phrase for whole homogenized milk, not buttermilk.

1	pint oysters, fresh or frozen, reserving the liquor
¼	cup butter
1	quart whole milk
1½	teaspoons salt
	Pinch of black pepper
	Pinch of paprika
	Saltines

Thaw oysters, if frozen. Drain the oysters, saving the liquor. Check each oyster for any remaining shell fragments. Melt butter in a medium-size saucepan, adding the liquor and the oysters. On medium heat, cook the oysters about 3 to 5 minutes or until the oysters edges start to curl. Gradually, add the milk, salt, and pepper, stirring frequently. Heat this mixture until it is heated through. Do not boil. Bowl up the stew, sprinkle with paprika and serve with saltines, serving immediately.

Note: If you want a heartier stew, you can also add the following:

½	cup chopped onion, sautéed
½	cup chopped celery
1	cup cooked, diced potatoes
1	(8-ounce) can whole kernel corn, undrained for variation

Important note: When preparing recipes with fresh oysters, take a few minutes and pick up the oysters one by one to look for any bits of shell left on them.

Yields: 6 servings

Fried Oysters

½	cup butter
½	cup cooking oil
1	pint oysters, fresh or frozen and drained
2	eggs
2	tablespoons cold evaporated milk
¼	teaspoon salt
¼	teaspoon black pepper
½	cup all-purpose flour
2	cups saltine crackers, crushed fine

You will need to have 3 bowls at your finger tips. One bowl for the egg mixture, another bowl for the flour, the third bowl for the crushed crackers. While preparing the oysters, heat the butter and oil in the skillet or fry pan until the grease is 375-degrees.* If you have no thermometer, heat the grease until a 1-inch cube of bread browns in the grease in 1 minute. In one bowl, beat the eggs, milk, salt, and pepper together. Dip the oysters into the egg mixture and then the flour bowl. Dip the oysters back again into the egg mixture and then roll the oysters into the cracker bowl. Let the oyster rest 5 minutes before frying, so that the cracker crumbs will adhere to the oysters. Fry them at least 3 to 5 minutes or until the oysters are lightly brown. Drain on paper towels. Serve with quartered lemons and cocktail sauce.

***Note:** Fry a few oysters at a time. If you put too many oysters in the frying pan all at one time it will lower the temperature of the oil and you will not get a good product.

Yields: 6 servings

Fried Shrimp

1½	pounds raw shrimp, peeled and deveined
1	egg, beaten
2	tablespoons evaporated milk
1	teaspoon salt
2	cups fine cracker crumbs or cracker meal
	Fat or shortening for deep frying.

Thaw the shrimp if they are frozen and dry them with paper towels. Beat together the egg, milk and salt. Dip the shrimp in egg mixture and roll the shrimp in the cracker crumbs or meal. Fry shrimp in the deep fat until golden brown about 3 minutes. Drain on paper towels.

Yields: 4 to 6 servings

Scalloped Oysters

1	pint oysters, drained and picked clean of any shell fragments, reserve juice
2	cups crushed Ritz or Ritz-like crackers
½	cup butter, melted
½	teaspoon salt
½	teaspoon pepper
¾	cup half-and-half cream
¼	cup oyster juice
¼	teaspoon Worcestershire sauce
	Paprika to sprinkle

Preheat oven to 425-degrees. Grease a shallow baking dish generously with butter. Combine the cracker crumbs, melted butter, salt and pepper. Spread half of the cracker crumb mixture on the bottom of the casserole dish. Cover with half of the oysters. Add the other half of the cracker crumb mixture and the rest of the oysters. Combine the oyster juice, half-and-half, and Worcestershire sauce and pour over the oysters. Sprinkle with paprika Cook for 30 minutes.

Yields: 4 to 6 servings

Scalloped Oysters with Corn

½	cup Ritz cracker or Ritz-like crackers, crushed into crumbs
½	cup fine dry bread crumbs
1	teaspoon salt
½	teaspoon pepper
1	stick butter, melted
	Pinch of mace
	Pinch of thyme
2	dozen large oysters, reserve juice *(Check oysters for any shell fragments)*
1	(15.25-ounce) can whole kernel corn, drained
1	cup Parmesan Cheese, grated
¾	cup half-and-half or heavy whipping cream

Note: In this recipe you will have two layers, so judge the quantity of the oysters and corn when layering.

Preheat oven to 375-degrees. Melt butter in a large skillet. Combine the cracker crumbs, bread crumbs, salt, pepper, mace, and thyme; blending well. Grease a flat, medium-sized baking dish generously with butter. Place a ¼-inch layer of crumb mixture on the bottom of the baking dish. Follow with a layer of the drained oysters. Then make a layer of corn on top of the oysters. Follow with a layer of crumbs. Repeat the procedure with the remaining oysters and corn. Finish off with the crumbs for the topping. Sprinkle with Parmesan cheese. Using the reserved juice from the oysters, add enough milk to make a cup of liquid. Pour this mixture carefully all over the dish. Bake for 40 minutes.

Yields: 6 to 8 servings

Fried Florida Scallops

1	pound bay scallops
2	eggs, beaten
2	tablespoons evaporated milk
	Pinch of black pepper
½	cup all-purpose flour
1¼	cups dry bread crumbs
4	tablespoons butter

Rinse the scallops real well to get any shell fragments off and drain on paper towels. Beat the eggs, milk, and pepper in a medium-size bowl. Place the flour and bread crumbs in separate containers. Roll the scallops in the flour. Dip in the egg mixture and roll in the bread crumbs. Melt the butter in a skillet on medium high heat. Pan fry the scallops until nice and brown on both sides about 3 minutes.

Yields: 4 to 6 servings

Pan-Fried Walleye

1	egg, beaten
2	teaspoons honey
2	cups Ritz or Ritz-like crackers (about 50), crushed
½	teaspoon salt
6	Walleye Fillets (about 2 pounds of fish)
½	cup cooking oil
	Lemon wedges

In a small bowl, beat egg and add the honey. In a plastic zip-top bag, combine the crushed crackers and salt. Dip the fish in the egg and honey mixture and then shake in the bag until the fish is well coated with the crumb coating. In a skillet, cook fish in the oil 3 to 5 minutes or until golden brown and the fish flakes easily with a fork. Serve with lemon wedges.

Yields: 4 to 6 servings

Fried Frog Legs

I only wish I knew someone who goes frog gigging up here in Michigan, for I haven't had any Fried Frog Legs since I left Georgia.

Seafood buffets in the South usually have Fried Frog Legs included on their menu. One night, I went to a Seafood buffet in my hometown, and a gentleman was constantly watching me at the buffet line. He became obsessed with the quantity of Frog Legs that I had on my plate. It became almost a race to see who could eat the most Frog Legs. The Seafood Buffet was more like a Frog Leg Buffet.

To give you a heads up, if those legs are fresh, they may jump a little in the fry pan while you are frying.

- 6-9 pair of frog legs
- Salt and pepper to taste
- 1 tablespoon lemon juice
- 2 cups bread crumbs, crumbled fine
- 1 egg, beaten
- 1 stick butter

Wash the frog legs and remove the skin by turning it down and pulling it off like you would a glove. Wash the legs and dry them with paper towels. Season with salt, pepper, and sprinkle with lemon juice. Put bread crumbs in a zip-top bag. Place butter in the fry pan and melt butter on medium high heat. Dip the legs in the beaten egg and dredge in the bread crumbs. Pan fry the frogs legs about 10 to 12 minutes until they reach a golden brown.

Yields: 4 to 6 servings

Pan-Fried Fish

Pan-Fried Fish is the art of cooking smaller fish, whether it is Trout, Bream or Blue Gill, in a pan. What we call Bream fish in the South are called Blue Gill in the North.

2	pounds fish fillets
1	teaspoon salt
1	teaspoon pepper
¼	teaspoon cayenne pepper, if desired
1	egg, slightly beaten
1	tablespoon milk
1	cup yellow cornmeal
1	cup all-purpose flour
½	teaspoon paprika
	Oil (Enough to cover the bottom of the skillet) (⅛-inch of oil or butter)

If fish is frozen, thaw. Rinse the fish and dry with paper towels. Cut into serving size pieces, sprinkling with salt and pepper. Mix egg and milk in a flat dish. In a zip-top bag, mix the cornmeal, flour, and paprika. Dip the fillets in the egg and milk mixture and then in the cornmeal and flour mixture. Heat the oil or butter in a heavy skillet or fry pan until hot. Ease the fish in the skillet, barely moving them with tongs. Pan-fry the fish on medium heat, for 4 to 5 minutes until brown on one side, turn and brown on the other side. The whole process takes around 8 to 10 minutes. Drain on paper towels.

I can brag a lot about the Gulf of Mexico and its fishing, but nothing holds a candle to the Great Lakes and its fishing opportunities. God spent a lot of extra energy when he created the beautiful State of Michigan. I'm very proud to live here amongst the gorgeous Great Lakes.

Yields: 4 to 6 servings

Baked Fish

I love fish for breakfast. If you want to kick-start your day in addition to getting your protein, here's the ticket. If you get a chance, just try baking fish one time for breakfast for your main course in lieu of bacon or sausage, and you will see that I'm right as rain.

You can serve Baked Fish in so many ways. You can compliment the Baked Fish by stuffing it with so many different variations as well as topping the Baked Fish with Sautéed Mushrooms and a Wine sauce. Let your imagination roll.

Here is a basic recipe for Baked Fish.

2	pounds fish fillets
2	tablespoons butter, melted or you may use olive oil
	Juice of 1 fresh lemon
	Minced onion, (optional)
	Fresh Bread crumbs, 2 or 3 slices of fresh bread, crumbled
	Paprika to sprinkle for color
	Salt and pepper
½	cup all-purpose flour (to dredge the fish in)

Preheat oven 350-degrees. Grease a baking dish with butter or olive oil. Lightly coat your fish in the flour. Place your fish in the dish and squeeze fresh lemon juice over the fish. Add minced onion and drizzle a little melted butter on the fish. Sprinkle with the bread crumbs and paprika. Bake at 350-degrees until the flesh of the fish will flake easily with a fork. Season with salt and pepper. Approximate cooking time is 12-minutes per pound.

Yields: 4 servings

Deep Fried Fish

Deep Frying Fish is different than Pan frying. You usually Deep Fry when you have large amounts of fish and large fillets of fish. Deep Frying is just what it says, 3-4-inches of hot oil cooking your fish with the temperature at 375-degrees. Blot the fish with paper towels to remove excess moisture. This will prevent splattering. Season with salt and pepper, dip in beaten egg, then in a cornmeal and flour mixture or cracker crumbs mixture. Ease the fish down into the hot grease and the fish will rise to the top when done and will be lightly brown in color.

Note: Do not use the grease for chicken or other foods for it will retain the flavor of fish.

Please note that there are so many different coatings you can buy in the supermarkets or you may make your own. I like to use a combination of cornmeal and flour mixture.

When I fry oysters, I like a crisper taste, so I use the cracker crumb coating. It is your own preference.

Note: Go to the Sauce section of my book and you will find the most delicious Tartar Sauce recipe.

Baked Bluefish

I have prepared this fish on two occasions, one for a hearty breakfast and the other for a delicious supper time meal.

I caught the Bluefish at Port St. Joe, Florida at the "Wall". If any of you have ever gone fishing at Port St. Joe, you have probably heard about the great fishing at the "Wall."

Believe it or not, I had just been released from their hospital after a two-week stint due to a Sting-Ray bite that almost ended me. It started into a wonderful vacation, but ended in disaster. The day I was released from the hospital, I had to go fishing or get something out of the deal. I went to the "Wall," and low and behold, I caught a huge Bluefish. There was a sweet little Cuban lady that helped me get the fish in for it was a big one. She then explained to me that I needed to "clean it," right there on the spot or the meat would not be good. Thanks to her and the Bluefish, my disaster vacation seemed a little brighter.

This is how I cooked the Bluefish.

- 2   (16-ounce) fillets
- 2   cups fresh bread crumbs, crumbled coarsely
- 2   cloves garlic, minced
- 1   teaspoon salt
- 1   teaspoon pepper
- 1   stick butter, melted
     Juice of one fresh lemon
     Paprika to sprinkle

Preheat oven to 350-degrees. Prepare a shallow, flat baking dish by greasing it well. Place the fillets in the dish. Mix the bread crumbs with the garlic, salt and pepper. Add the melted butter to the crumb mixture. Spread the crumb mixture on top of the fish and then squeeze the lemon juice on top of the mixture. Sprinkle with paprika. Bake for about 30 to 45 minutes until fork easily flakes the meat of the fish.

Yields: 4 servings

Broiling Fish

Broiling fish is obtained by placing the fish fillets on a pan several inches below the direct heat source. To prevent the fish from drying out, you can baste the fish while broiling with olive oil, melted butter or I like to use an Italian dressing. Typically, the fish does not take more then 5 to 6 minutes to cook on each side, depending on how thick the fillets are. You usually do not have to turn the fillet more than one time. You can determine the doneness when the fish is pierced with a fork and flakes easily.

Basic Recipe for Broiling Fish

The ingredients are basically the same for Baking Fish.

- 2   pounds fish fillets
- 2   tablespoons olive oil or melted butter
    Juice of 1 fresh lemon
    Salt to sprinkle
    Pepper to sprinkle
    Paprika to sprinkle

Place the fish fillets, skin side up, on a well-greased broiler pan. Salt and pepper the fillets; squeeze on the lemon juice and finally, brush with melted butter or oil. Sprinkle with paprika. Broil for no more than 5 to 6 minutes, turn the fillet over and repeat the ingredients. Broil on this side until fork easily flakes the fish.

Yields: 4 servings

The Divine Dixie Deva's Big Catch

...and Bigger Catch. Panama City, Florida

Game Bird Orange Sauce
"For that Wild Thang"

Whether Dove, Duck, or Goose try this sauce.

1	cup orange marmalade
¼	cup white wine
2	oranges, rind and juice
2	tablespoons lemon juice

Combine all ingredients in a medium size saucepan, mixing well. Cook on low at a simmer until all the sauce thickens.

Roasted Goose Glazed with Currant Sauce

1	(9 to 10 pound) whole goose
1	whole onion
1	whole apple, unpeeled
2	cloves garlic, peeled
2	celery stalks
	Salt and Pepper to taste
	Rosemary seasoning (optional)
	I purchase this at a local restaurant supply house
1	stick butter
1	cup apple juice
¼	cup olive oil
	Paprika to sprinkle
4-5	Bacon Strips (uncooked)

Preheat oven to 450-degrees.* Wash goose real well inside and out and pat with paper towels. Using a sharp fork, prick the lower part of the breast skin of the goose. This will loosen up the fat in the goose. Be careful not to prick the actual meat. Season the goose by sprinkling with salt, pepper, and rosemary seasoning inside and out of the goose. Fill the cavity of the goose with the onion, apple, and cloves of garlic, celery stalks, and the stick of butter. Pour apple juice in the bottom of the pan. Pour olive oil over the top of the goose and then sprinkle with paprika. Cover the breast of the goose with the bacon strips. The bacon adds that extra kick of flavor. Place goose on roaster rack breast side up. Cook the goose with the roaster cover on, and place in the oven at 450-degrees for 30 minutes **only** and then lower the oven to 350-degrees. *(This is what I call the "jump-start method")*. Continue to cook with the cover on until the Goose registers 190-degrees in temperature.

You may glaze the last 30 minutes with the Currant Sauce. The Goose will cook approximately 2½-hours.

Currant Glaze:

1	(12-ounce) jar favorite brand of currant jelly
½	cup light corn syrup or Karo
2	dashes red pepper

Empty the whole jar of currant jelly in a small saucepan. Mix the corn syrup and currant jelly well, heating until the mixture is smooth enough to brush on as a glaze. Add dashes of red pepper for that extra kick flavor.

Continue to brush the glaze on the goose until you reach the glaze you desire, even after the goose has cooked you can continue to brush on the glaze. Make extra, for this glaze is also great for a dipping sauce for the goose.

Currant Orange Glaze and Dipping Sauce:
For a tangy taste sauce: Add the juice and rind from 2 whole fresh oranges. Combine this with the previous ingredients, stirring on low heat to combine the flavors.

Note: If you choose to add spirits, add Sherry to taste to the contents of the currant jelly, blending well.

Plantation Smothered Quail Rice n' Gravy

When I worked on a Southern Plantation many years ago, my taste buds turned to dishes with quail and dove. I might add, this was quite an interesting job.

Since moving to the North, quail is hard to find, so I order mine from a supplier. Try this dish—your husband or significant other will love you for it.

8-10	quail *(This recipe works better if quail has been butterflied)**
	Seasoned salt
	Pepper
6	tablespoons bacon grease or olive oil
1	medium-size onion, sliced
2	(4-ounce) cans mushroom slices or pieces, undrained **or** 1 pound fresh mushrooms, sliced
1	cup all-purpose flour
2	cups long grain rice, uncooked
1	(10.75-ounce) can cream of mushroom soup
1	soup can water
	Paprika

Preheat oven to 350-degrees. Grease a 13 x 9 x 2-inch baking dish. In a large skillet, sauté the onion and mushrooms with the bacon grease, butter or olive oil. Do not brown too much. Scoop the onions and mushrooms out and set aside. You will be using the same grease to brown the quail. Salt and pepper the quail. Put the one cup of flour in a paper bag, and add the quail. Shake the bag until the quail is coated with flour. Brown the quail in the bacon grease that you previously used. Place the browned quail in the baking dish. Mound the rice in the center of the dish. Dilute the mushroom soup with 1 can of water. Sprinkle the onions and mushrooms on top of the rice. Pour the cream of mushroom mixture over the quail and rice. Add the can of mushrooms with the liquid. Sprinkle with paprika. Cover tightly with foil. Bake in the oven for about 1 hour. After 45 minutes check the rice and make sure that it is completely done. If it looks like it needs a little water, add about ¼-cup, then close foil and cook for about 15 minutes longer.

Note: This is a wonderful dish for a Dinner Party. Folks will rave. Especially if those folks are hunters. Most men eat at least 2 quail each; women usually eat just 1, except for me. So figure on this.

*Butterflied is simply splitting the quail along the breastbone with a knife to completely flatten. This may already be done to quail bought locally.

Fried Quail

I love to eat quail for breakfast with grits or cheese grits. Try it. That way I will not eat lunch, you know I'm trying to watch my calorie intake. Yeah-right! For the Cheese Grits, go to my Breakfast section.

The night before I cook my quail, I marinate them in a bowl or extra large zip-top bag.

Marinade ingredients:
- Enough buttermilk to cover the quail
- Several splashes of Worcestershire sauce.

12	quail
	Salt and pepper
2	eggs, beaten well
¼	cup buttermilk or evaporated milk
2	cups all-purpose flour (Put in a zip-top bag)
1	quart shortening

Drain off marinade and discard. Have your shortening heating up while you do the following to prepare the quail. Cut the quail in halves and season with salt and pepper. Mix the eggs and buttermilk and dip the quail in the mixture. Now shake the quail in the flour, coating well. Fry until golden brown.

Yields: 6 servings (2 quail each)

Mama Gillis' Fried Squirrel

The first time I had fried squirrel, I fell in love with it. Papa was a "cracker jack" shot and from time to time would give Mama Gillis some squirrel to cook. I remember to this day sitting down and eating fried squirrel.

1	squirrel, cut into pieces
½	teaspoon salt
¼	teaspoon pepper
	Dash of cayenne pepper
½	cup all-purpose flour
¼	cup shortening

Combine the salt, peppers, and flour in a paper bag. Shake the pieces of the squirrel in the flour mixture. Melt the shortening in a large skillet. Brown the squirrel. Lower the temperature on the stove, covering the skillet. Cook on simmer for about 45 minutes to 1 hour until the squirrel is tender. Remove the cover of the skillet the last 10 minutes to crisp the outer surface of the meat.

Yields: 1 to 2 servings

Papa Gillis' Catch

Papa Gillis killed a 79-pound turtle. Mama Gillis made a life-like artificial turtle body to fill the shell.

Hunting with the Guys

As I come across some Venison recipes, this story of my deer hunting days creeps to mind.

We were lucky enough to have been raised on deer meat. That's what I call it. I love it. Like Papa, my daddy likes to hunt. He had his own cuber, and boy did we enjoy the cube steak. Me and Daddy would sit at the table with a platter of venison cube steak and finish it off like nobody's business.

As I got older, I wanted to try my hand at hunting and living on a plantation, had its advantages. It seemed that every time I was taken to a deer stand, I was given the deer stand (the only deer stand) that was made out of a couple of 2 x 4s. Not only could I barely sit on the stand, it also seemed that I was put on the same stand every time I went hunting. I can just about bet that they (all of the men that were responsible) made that deer stand just for me. I never saw a living thing. I'm not so sure that the stand may have been put in a field that was freshly plowed, which means no FOOD for "BAMBI" and that meant I would never see a deer.

One morning when they picked me up at the deer stand, all of the hunters were crammed in the cab of the truck. They usually would let me have the cab of the truck where it was warm; but on this morning, it was different. They motioned for me to get in the back of the pick-up truck. They were too quiet for comfort. They usually would be joking and cutting up with me. I didn't say anything to them and I started towards the back of the truck. I didn't want them to think I was a sissy, even though I was freezing to death.

No sooner than when I got to the back of the truck and swung one leg over the tailgate, that leg of mine went tearing back into the woods and I was screaming bloody murder. They had killed a coyote and placed the coyote sitting upright as if it were ready to lunge at me. That was it for my deer hunting with the guys.

Note: As you know, deer meat is somewhat of a tough meat, so you need to use moist heat for the cooking process for the most part. Stewing and Pot Roasts are examples of using the moist heat. The tender cuts of the deer meat, such as the loins, chops, and steaks are delicious pan fried or baked.

Sketch by Ruthie Gillis

Venison Marinade

(For 5 pounds of meat)

3	cups red wine vinegar
½	cup olive oil
2	cloves of garlic, minced
2	whole cloves
4	whole peppercorns, crushed
2	bay leaves
3	thick slices of lemon
	Several slices onion
2	Celery tops

Season venison with salt and pepper. Place all ingredients, including the venison, in a 2-gallon zip-top bag. Marinate in the bag for at least 12 to 24 hours, turning meat several times.

Venison Cube Steak

2	pounds venison steaks, cubed (no thicker than ¾-inch thick)
	Salt and Pepper to taste
	Worcestershire sauce
1	cup all-purpose flour
	Oil to fry the steaks

Heat the skillet to 350-degrees with ¼-inch of oil in the skillet, until sizzling hot. Season the steaks with salt and pepper. Sprinkle with Worcestershire sauce and dip the steaks in the flour. Sear on medium heat on both sides until golden brown. Cover and simmer until done.

Note: You can always make gravy with this recipe and serve it with rice or mashed potatoes. Good eating!

Yields: 6 servings

Deer Burgers

2	pounds ground venison
¼	pound ground beef fat or you may use mild sausage
1	small onion, chopped
4	slices bread, broken up in pieces
1	egg, beaten
¼	teaspoon thyme
	Seasoned salt
	Dash of pepper
4	tablespoon shortening to fry

Mix the venison, fat or sausage, onion, bread, egg and seasonings, mixing well. Make into patties and fry.

Yields: 6 servings

Venison Meat Loaf

2	eggs, beaten
2	tablespoons Worcestershire sauce
1	(8-ounce) can tomato sauce
1	onion, finely chopped
1½	cups dry bread crumbs
1½	teaspoons salt
1	teaspoon pepper
1½	pounds ground venison

Topping:
4	tablespoons brown sugar
4	tablespoons prepared mustard
4	tablespoons vinegar

In a large bowl, combine the beaten eggs, Worcestershire sauce, tomato sauce, onion, crumbs, salt and pepper. Add the meat and mix well. Press into a 9 x 5 x 3-inch loaf pan. Bake, uncovered at 350-degrees for 1 hour. During the last 30 minutes of the cooking time, mix the topping ingredients in a small bowl and pour the topping mixture on the meat loaf. Continue to cook the required amount of time.

Yields: 5 to 6 servings

Grilled Marinated Back Strap (Tenderloin)

1	venison back strap
1	bottle Italian dressing
	Strips of bacon

Marinate the back strap in the Italian dressing by soaking in a large zip-top bag. Let marinate several hours or overnight. Wrap in bacon, securing the bacon with toothpicks. Grill until desired doneness.

If you choose to roast in your oven, do so in a 325-degrees oven for 20 minutes per pound. My mouth is watering right now. *(But this is so good, it's hard to share.)*

Yields: 4 servings

Venison Roast

1   (4 to 5 pounds) venison roast

Marinade:
1½   cups red wine vinegar
½   cup olive oil
½   cup apple cider vinegar
2   celery tops
1   large onion, sliced
4   slices lemon
1   large carrot, scraped and sliced
1   tablespoon salt
10   whole black peppercorns
2   bay leaves
2   cloves of garlic, minced

Cooking ingredients:
¼   cup all-purpose flour
6   slices bacon, thick sliced
1   envelope dry onion soup mix
2   (10.75-ounce) cans cream of mushroom or cream of celery soup
1   soup can water

Combine all of the marinade ingredients and place in a 2-gallon zip-top bag. This liquid is the marinade and later, you will discard. Place roast in the bag with the ingredients. Put in the fridge for at least 12 hours, no longer than 24 hours. After marinating, take the roast out of the bag, wipe with paper toweling and coat with the flour. Wrap the roast well with the bacon. Place the roast in a baking dish and sprinkle with the dry onion soup mix. Carefully, pour the soup and the water around the roast. Cover and bake in a preheated oven at 250-degrees for 4 to 5 hours, depending on pounds. Venison roast needs a moist heat, so you need to be sure to cover.

Yields: 6 servings

I cooked this roast for one of my husband's friends at work. It was fork tender and no wild gamey taste was present.

Venison Chili

2	pounds venison, ground
½	cup olive or vegetable oil
1	cup onions, chopped
2	cloves of garlic, minced
1	large green pepper, chopped
3	tablespoons chili powder
2	teaspoons sugar
1	teaspoon salt
½	teaspoon cumin
1	(6-ounce) can tomato paste
1	(28-ounce) can stewed or whole tomatoes
1	(10-ounce) can Rotel diced tomatoes and green chiles
2	(15-ounce) cans kidney or chili beans

In a large saucepan, brown the venison in the oil, adding the onions, garlic, and green pepper. Cook until the onions and pepper are tender. Add the chili powder, sugar, salt, cumin, tomato paste, tomatoes, and Rotel. Bring to a boil on medium high heat, stirring often to prevent from sticking. Add the beans last, blending well. Simmer on low heat for 1½-hours. If the chili cooks down and you like it a little thinner, just add 1 cup of water.

Yields: 6 to 8 servings

Stan Gambrel, creator of Georgia's Big Pig Jig in Vienna, Georgia

BBQ Queen

Little did my Papa know that when I was a little girl and watching him late into the night BBQing and smelling those wonderful clouds, that I would grow up and become a Certified Judge for the most prestigious BBQ competitions in the world.

Yes, I have been privileged to judge the Memphis in May BBQ competition in Memphis, Tennessee, the Big Pig Jig in Vienna, Georgia, as well as other Memphis in May sanctioned contests. I have judged the Big Pig Jig for over 20 years now. This, in addition to my cooking, is my passion. I have also been chosen to judge the final round of competitions on several occasions, which is the ultimate. Believe me, I'm not just whistling Dixie. I know great BBQ!

I am very serious minded when judging. These folks work hard to compete and earn every red cent of their winnings.

Everyone asked me when I moved to snow country if I would continue my judging. I just looked at them like they had lost their minds. Judging still remains a part of me and always will.

BBQ ranks right up there with chocolate fudge. Now you know!

Always cook your pork low and slow. You can't get in a hurry! You know, maybe that's why it originated in the South. We don't get in a hurry and we enjoy life. At least I do.

I like dry rub marinades. For those who don't know, that is a thick layer of seasonings on the outside of the meat with no sauce. But the wet marinades you can't beat either.

I still don't have a preference in the types of wood used for cooking. Apple wood is excellent as well as Oak and Hickory, but I also like the taste of Pecan wood, for it has a unique taste all its own.

Mama Gillis made one heck of a BBQ sauce. My sauce will hit the market soon.

Kathryn's BBQ Boston Butt
Transformed into Pulled Pork Sandwiches

1   (4-pounds) Pork shoulder roast
Texas Toast
Melted Butter
Favorite BBQ Sauce or go to my section on sauces and find one and make it your favorite.

Sweet and spicy Dry Rub:
You may increase these measures to fit ribs, tenderloins, etc.

- ¼ cup brown sugar
- 1½ teaspoons onion powder
- ½ teaspoon cinnamon
- ½ teaspoon black pepper
- 1 teaspoon salt
- ¼ teaspoon paprika
- ½ teaspoon garlic powder
- Pinch of cayenne pepper

You may want to adjust these to your taste.

Mix together. Wearing gloves, rub on the roast and put in the fridge overnight. I enclose my meat in a zip-top bag.

Basting and Mopping Ingredients:
- 1 cup apple juice
- ¼ cup apple cider vinegar
- 2 teaspoons Worcestershire sauce

Combine these ingredients and mop (baste) this solution while cooking. Again, I cook my pork low and slow whether on the indirect gas grill, oven or smoker. Place the roast on a rack, skin side up, do not cover. If you are cooking this on a gas grill or oven, cook on 325-degrees until internal temperature reaches 190-195-degrees. If you cook the roast to this temperature, it will be easily pulled for sandwiches. You may have to put a sheet of aluminum foil on top to prevent excessive browning. After temperature is reached, let the meat sit 15-20 minutes to rest. Wear gloves for the meat will be hot and literally tear the meat to pieces. You may use a fork to shred the meat. Smear the melted butter on the outside of the bread. Fill the bread up with about 1 cup of this wonderful meat. Slather the meat down with extra BBQ sauce. Place the other piece of toast on the meat and toast the bread on a hot griddle or frying pan in order grill both sides. Serves 8. Go to my Sauce section for the BBQ Slather and Sop Sauce and "sop" away with this sauce.

Jack's Old South

I am Myron Mixon, Chief cook of Jack's Old South Competition Bar-B-Que Team. I started Jack's Old South in 1996 as a way to promote our family Bar-B-Que sauce that was made by my mother and father, Gaye and Jack Mixon. We competed in our first competition in Augusta, Georgia, where we took 1st place in Whole Hog, 1st place in Pork Ribs and 3rd in Pork Shoulder. Since the beginning, we have won 140 plus grand championships resulting in over 1400 total trophies, 30 state championships including wins in Georgia, Florida, Alabama, Virginia, Arkansas, Mississippi, Kentucky, Illinois, South Carolina, and Tennessee, team of the year six times, and 7 national championships. In addition we have been the Grand Champion at the World Championship in Memphis three times, 2001, 2004 and 2007. We have also taken a first place in the Whole Hog category at the World Championship in 2001, 2003, 2004 and 2007. Jack's Old South has been the Memphis in May Team of the Year with the highest number of points for the 6 years in a row. We are also the only team to win Grand Championships in Memphis in May, Kansas City BBQ Society and Florida BBQ Association in the same year. As a result of all of our success on the various BBQ circuits we have been featured on several television shows including Food Network, Discovery Channel, the History Channel, Travel Channel and the BBQ All Stars on the Versus Network. Mastering the art of Bar-B-Queing has lead to the development of our own line of Jack's Old South Grills and Smokers as well as instructor for the Ultimate Bar-B-Que Cooking School. My website is www.jacksoldsouth.com. Turn the page for my Rib Recipe.

Here's a recipe for ribs...

I like to use meaty baby-back ribs. I remove the membrane and trim any excess fat from the top of the ribs. Then I apply my Jack's Old South rub to the top and bottom and let them set for 3 hours. Place on a pit at 250-degrees and cook for 1½ hours. Remove and put brown sugar and butter on bottom of rib. Place back on pit for 1 hour top of rib down. Take back off and repeat to the top of the ribs. Take off again and apply your favorite sauce to the bottom of the ribs and place back on the rack, top down. About 45 minutes later, take off and do the same to the top for 45 more minutes. This gives you almost a 5 hour cook time and great competition ribs.

The Grand Finale!

Finally, here it is! I have told you over and over about Mama Gillis' 14-layer cakes. Here is the recipe for the 14-layer Chocolate Fudge Layer cake. It is absolutely wonderful. The layers are teeny-tiny with cooked chocolate fudge icing between them. It gets even better after the first day of baking it. How many times have you had 2 and 3 layer cakes with just a "smidgen" of icing on them? All cake and no goody. With this cake, you bite down and taste chocolate in every bite.

Writing this book has helped me in so many ways. Realizing, that I was one lucky gal to have experienced the life with two wonderful individuals, who loved and accepted me for who I was.

There are a lot of folks in this world that would say, why give out all of your good recipes? Well, Mama Gillis did not mind sharing and she lived a full rewarding life.

I was torn between using the spelling of DIVA versus DEVA in this book. DIVA means Prima Dona and DEVA means "good in spirit". Now you know why I chose the spelling DEVA. I always wanted to be like Mama Gillis and she was and still is the DEVA of all time.

Ron Krueger, Food Editor of The Flint Journal, wrote an article on Mama Gillis and me titled, "Spirit of Christmas Past." The jest of the article is about my invisible assistant in the kitchen while preparing meals. By now you know who that invisible assistant is. Mama Gillis was with me while preparing this cake for you.

I know she would be proud of this book.

Mama Gillis' 14-Layer Cake,
Chocolate Fudge Layer Cake

Mama Gillis' 14-Layer Chocolate Fudge Layer Cake

Normally, I make my icing while my cake layers are cooling, but with this cake, I make the icing first thing. The icing takes 45 minutes to cool and is just right to spread onto the cooked layers.

Chocolate Cooked Icing:
- 4 cups granulated sugar
- 2 sticks butter
- ⅔ cup cocoa
- 1 cup evaporated milk
- 1 teaspoon vanilla extract
- 1-1½ cups powdered sugar (if needed)

Using a heavy saucepan, mix all of the ingredients, except for the vanilla extract. Stir constantly on medium heat until the mixture comes to a full boil. Turn the heat back to low heat and boil for 4 minutes. Take off heat. Don't stir. Cool for 45 minutes and add the extract after the cooling process. While the icing is cooling, make the cake layers.

Note: Just before icing the cake layers, you may need to beat the icing with a wooden spoon, just enough for the icing to hold shape or to coat a spoon. You want it to be able to spread easily, almost to a dripping point. Normally, you beat cooked icing till it loses its gloss. But you can not do that with this icing, since you have 14 layers to ice.

As you near the 14th layer, you may need to add 1 to 1½-cups sifted powdered sugar with a little evaporated milk to the icing for spreading consistency. You should have enough icing to ice between the layers and the top and sides of the cake.

You do not need to put a whole lot of icing between the layers of the cake. Remember there are 14 layers and a little icing goes a long way.

Cake Layers:

4	sticks butter, softened to room temperature
4	cups granulated sugar
10	eggs, room temperature
2	tablespoons vanilla extract
4	cups cake flour, sifted

Preheat oven to 400-degrees. You will be using 8-inch round cake pans. Grease and line pans each time you bake a layer. I cook three cake layers at a time. Cut 14 circles of wax paper liners and have them ready to place them in the pans. Set aside.

I was raised by Mama Gillis to use a griddle (or "spida") to cook the layers on; however, I find the cake pans work as well as the griddle.

Using a heavy duty mixer, cream butter while adding the sugar gradually and beat until light and fluffy. Add the eggs, one at a time, beating well after each addition, add in the vanilla. Lastly, add the flour small amounts at a time, beating on medium speed, scraping bowl often.

Place 4 tablespoons of batter into each cake pan. Bake 2 to 3 minutes, just until lightly browned. The layers will be very thin. After you have cooked the first three cake layers, then grease and line those same cake pans with the circles of wax paper. Turn the first layer out on a cake plate and the other two cake layers, place on a cake rack which has been sprayed with baking spray. After the third layer has been cooked, start spreading the icing. This works fast. As you continue to bake the layers, stack them and spread the icing between the layers.

Southern Cuisine with a Touch of Class

WATCH FOR OUR OPENING IN THE SPRING 2008!

The Divine Dixie Deva's Bed 'N' Breakfast

It will feature a full-scale Southern breakfast with Southern sausage, ham and all the trimmings. A supper time meal will be available featuring The Deva's delectable homemade desserts.

www.dixiedeva.com   www.thedivinedixiedeva.com.

Resources
Great Southern Sausage

When you come to The Divine Dixie Deva's Bed and Breakfast, you will experience the true taste of Southern smoked sausage from Abbott's Food Center.

Abbott's Food Center
Specializing In Country Smoked Sausage, Beef or Pork, in addition to fresh pecans— Abbott's is a supplier of all your needs. WE WILL SHIP YOUR ORDERS!
Leary Highway at Old Pretoria Road / Albany, Georgia 31721
Phone (229) 883-9102 / Fax (229) 883-9244
Also open Sundays 8:00 a.m. to 7:30 p.m.
BP Gas / Deer Processing Also Available

Located in Albany, Georgia, or better yet in the Deep South, we have been in business for over 33 years. Mr. Ray Abbott, Sr. has perfected the art of making good ole-fashion country sausage, just like your grandparents made many years ago.

Our most popular sausage are our mild and hot smoked (all pork) sausage. We also smoke a beef and pork sausage and an all beef sausage.

The Divine Dixie Deva has been using our sausage for over 25 years. Her favorite in addition to the smoked all pork sausage, is the fresh link sausage which comes in pan or patty fry.

If you like country sausage at its best, then try us. We guarantee our sausage.

The Divine Dixie Deva says, "Try Abbott's Grocery in Albany, Georgia, located right down the road from where I grew up."

Mr. Ray Abbott, Sr. and Mr. Philip Abbott

Mayhaw Jelly

Remember this is the Cadillac of all jellies! If you want to try it here's the location of where you can purchase it and you can see for yourself.

Wilkins IGA
P.O. Box 175
212 W. Main Street
Colquitt, Georgia 39827
(229) 758-3371

Hot Dogs

Never had a jam up Hot Dog until I came here in the North. When I make Calvin's Confederate Coney Sauce, I use Koegel Hot Dogs. Here is a source for Hot Dogs that you can't beat.

Koegel Meats, Inc.
3400 W. Bristol Rd.
Flint, MI 48507
www.koegelmeats.com

Michigan Apples

Montrose Orchards
12473 Seymour Road
Montrose, Michigan 48457
Kitchen phone – (810) 639-6971 or fax (810) 639-2533
Dan and Debbie Hill-Proprietors

Cooking Measures and Equivalents

4 quarts	1 gallon
4 cups	1 quart
2 pints	1 quart
2 cups	1 pint
1 pint	2 cups
1 cup	8-ounces or ½ pint
1 gallon	4 quarts

16 tablespoons	1 cup
12 tablespoons	¾ cup
10 tablespoons plus 2 teaspoons	⅔ cup
8 tablespoons	½ cup
5⅓ tablespoons	⅓ cup
4 tablespoons	¼ cup
2 tablespoons	⅛ cup or 1-ounce
1 tablespoon	3 teaspoons
48 teaspoons	1 cup

Baking Equivalents

½ cup butter	4-ounces
2 cups butter	1 pound
4 cups all-purpose flour	1 pound
4½ to 5 cups cake flour, sifted	1 pound
1 square chocolate	1-ounce
1 cup semisweet chocolate chips	6-ounces
4 cups marshmallows	1 pound
2¼ cups brown sugar, firmly packed	1 pound
4 cups confectioners' sugar	1 pound
2 cups granulated sugar	1 pound

Cereal and Bread Equivalents

Note: There could be slight variations in these equivalents, due to different brands of products used. Be sure to measure accurately before mixing into recipes.

1 cup dry bread crumbs, crumbled fine .... 4 to 5 slices
1 cup soft bread crumbs .... 2 slices
1 cup bread cubes, cut into small cubes....................... 2 slices
1 cup cracker crumbs, crushed fine .... 28 saltines
1 cup vanilla wafer crumbs........................... 22 vanilla wafers
1 cup cornflakes, crushed .... 3 cups uncrushed
4 cups cooked macaroni........................... 8-ounces, uncooked
3½ cups cooked rice .... 1 cup uncooked

Dairy Products

1 cup cheese, shredded.. 4-ounces
1 cup cottage cheese 8-ounces
1 cup sour cream 8-ounces
1 cup whipping cream .... ½-cup heavy cream
⅔ cup evaporated milk .... 1 small can
1⅔ cups evaporated milk .... 1 (13-ounce) can

Fruit Products

4 cups apples, sliced or chopped	4 medium
1 cup bananas, mashed	3 medium
3 cups coconut	8-ounces
4 cups cranberries	1 pound
1 cup dates, pitted	1 (8-ounce) package
1 cup candied fruit	1 (8-ounce) package
3 to 4 tablespoons lemon juice with 1 tablespoon lemon rind, grated	1 large lemon
⅓-cup orange juice with 2 teaspoons orange rind, grated	1 orange
4 cups peaches, sliced	8 medium
3 cups raisins	1 (15-ounce) package

Nuts

1 cup nuts, chopped	4-ounces, shelled
1 cup nuts, chopped	1 pound, unshelled

Vegetable Products

2 cups canned tomatoes	1 (16-ounce) can
1 cup onion, chopped	1 large onion
8-ounce fresh mushrooms	1 (4-ounce) can
4 cups potatoes, sliced or chopped	4 medium
1 cup carrot, grated	1 large carrot
4 cups cabbage, shredded	1 pound

Meat products

2 cups chicken, cooked and chopped	1 (2½-pounds) chicken
2 cups ground beef, round or chuck	1 pound, cooked

A

APPETIZERS:
A Man's Man Appetizer	40
Apple Cheese Crescents	38
Apple Nut Biscuit Treat	55
Baby Pizzas	53
Baked Oysters	41
Cheese Crackers	37
Cheesy Apple Spread	34
Chicken Salad Puffs	46
Chicken Wings with Wing Ding Sauce	45
Corned Beef Balls	39
Crabmeat and Spinach Appetizer	44
Cute Coconut Toasties	56
Deviled Eggs with Shrimp	42
Deviled Ham Balls	44
Edna Lane's Baby Quiches	54
Herb Dip	51
Holiday Cheese Ball	32
Jezebel Cheese Ball	32
Kathryn's Favorite Cheese Ring	33
Kicker Cheese Ring	33
Lemon Curd Tassies	58
Marinated Shrimp	42
Nacho Waffle Bites	55
Ole Timey Cheese Straws	36
Orange Cheese Spread	35
Party Shrimp Mold	43
Peanut Butter Cheese Ball	38
Peanut Butter Pork Balls	50
Pecan Cheese Ball	34
Porky Balls with Dipping Sauce	50
Riblet Nibblers	51
Rice Crispy Cheese Wafers	37
Salmon Log	40
Sausage Bites	47
Sausage Stuffed Mushrooms	47
Scotch Eggs	48
Shrimp Spread	41
Smoked Fish Spread	39
Spiced Pecans	53
Spicy Cheese Loaf	35
Swedish Meatballs	49
Tipsy Grapes	57
Apples, Onions & Beer	356
Apples Stuffed With Sweet Potatoes	357
Asa's Blueberry Salad	311

B

Baby Pizzas	53
Bacon Spread	352
Baked Pears and Pineapple	372
Baked Stuffed Tomatoes	391

BARBECUE:
Kathryn's BBQ Boston Butt	472
Ribs	474

BEVERAGES:
Almond Fruit Punch	70
Apple Cider Nog	68
A Swig of Sweet Tea	80
Banana Milk Shake	73
Bridal Shower Punch	64
Cheap and Easy Kool-Aid Punch	71
Chocolate Mint Milkshake	74
Cranberry Lemon Supreme	77
Eggnog	66
Fruity Health Shake	72
Georgia Peach Brain Freeze	75
Good Morning Shake	72
Hawaiian Slurp Drink	70
Honey Bee Banana Booster	73
Hot Cranberry Punch	78
Hot Lemon Spiced Tea	78
Ice Ring	62
Kool-Aid Fruit Punch	61
Lime Orange Freeze Drink	64
Maple Milkshake	73
Melon Breeze	77
Mocha Eggnog Punch	63
Mocha Punch	62
Non-Alcoholic Georgia Peach Brain Freeze	75
Orange Lemonade	79
Party Punch	68
Peppermint Eggnog	67
Rainbow Punch	65
Southern Sea Breeze Smoothie	76
Sparkling Fruit Punch	69
Steaming Hot Cocoa	69
Strawberry Lemonade	77
Strawberry Lemon Punch	63
Vanilla Milk	71
Yellow Fruit Punch	61
Blackberry Cough Cordial	178

INDEX

BREADS:
Angel Biscuits	88
Apple Brown Betty	222
Apple Cheese Crescents	38
Apple Nut Biscuit Treat	55
Baked French Toast	255
Corn Bread Sticks	83
Cracklin' Sticks	83
Crackling Bread	84
Cranberry Glazed Rolls	86
Hot and Spicy Biscuits	91
Hot Chili Cornbread	92
Hot Dog Bun Bread Sticks	82
Hush Puppies	93
Loaf Bread	85
Mama Gillis's Buttermilk Biscuits	89
Mini Cheese Biscuits	90
Poppy Seed Yeast Bread	84
Quick 'n' Easy Buttermilk Rolls	87
Quick Bread Sticks	82
Sour Cream Biscuits	87

SWEET BREADS:
Apple Bread	105
Apple Carrot Muffins	100
Apple Coffee Tea Bread	106
Apple Date Nut Bread	104
Banana Walnut Bread	101
Blueberry Muffins	99
Carrot Bread	108
Cherry Surprise Muffins	95
Coconut Muffins	96
Homemade Cinnamon Sweet Rolls	102
No Knead Raisin Bread	109
Orange Nut Muffins	100
Pecan Caramel Muffins	94
Pineapple Muffins	97
Pumpkin Bread	110
Raisin Bran Muffins	96
Zucchini Carrot Muffins	98
Zucchini Tea Bread	110
Breakfast Scramble	258
Brown Rice	387
Buttermilk Pancakes	251

C

CASSEROLES:
Any Meat Casserole	302
Broccoli and Cauliflower Casserole	362
Butternut Squash Casserole	388
Cranberry Apple Pineapple	395
Hilda's Broccoli Casserole	361
Hominy Hot Pot	302
Hot Turkey Casserole	305
Italian Sausage and Black-Eyed Pea Casserole	301
Macaroni and Cheese Ham Casserole	306
Ole Favorite Squash Casserole	389
Saturday Night Lasagna	299
Sausage and Hash Brown Casserole	260
Sausage Rice Casserole	301
Scalloped Corn Casserole	364
Sour Cream and Green Bean Casserole	359
Snappy Spinach Casserole	400
Swedish Green Potato Casserole	383
Taco Bake	303
Tomato Casserole	394
Turkey and Wild Rice Casserole	304

Cheese Grits	257
Cheese Onions with a Hint of Sherry	370
Cheese Potato Soufflé	381
Chicken Gravy	290
Cocktail Sauce	417
Coconut Crust	225
Coconut Macaroons	181
Coconut Muffins	96
Coconut Pound Cake	160
Coconut Washboard Cookies	192
Coffee Chiffon Dessert	117
Cooked Apple Wedges	356
Cooked Pear Wedges	372
Almond Crescent Cookies	187
Corn and Okra Side Dish	366
Corned Beef and Cabbage Dinner	272
Corned Beef Balls	39
Cornish Hens with Wild Rice	297
Crabmeat and Spinach Appetizer	44
Cranberry Cheese Sandwich Spread	349
Cranberry Congealed Salad	312
Cranberry Cruncher	219
Cranberry Glazed Rolls	86
Cranberry Lemon Supreme	77
Cranberry Orange Tea Cake	168
Cranberry Relish	354
Cranberry Sauce	411
Cream Cheese Pastry Crust	225
Cream Cheese Pudding Pie	211
Cream of Bacon and Potato Soup	340
Cream of Mushroom Soup	332
Creamy Bacon, Lettuce, Tomato Salad	328
Creamy Broccoli Soup	335
Creamy Butterscotch Sauce	406
Creamy Cauliflower Dish	364

INDEX

Creamy Corn Chowder	338
Creamy Ham N Cheese Sandwich Spread	346
Cube Steak Dinner	278
Cute Coconut Toasties	56

D

Date Nut Balls	180
Decorating Cream Icing	175
Decorating Icing	174
Deep Fried Fish	456
Deep South Peanut Butter Cake	152
Deer Burgers	467

DESSERTS:

Cakes

Ann Gambrell's No Name Cake	151
Autumn Spice Cake	159
Banana Split Dessert Cake	116
Butter Cream Yellow Layer Cake	149
Coconut Pound Cake	160
Cranberry Orange Tea Cake	168
Deep South Peanut Butter Cake	152
Georgia Peach Shortcake	158
Heavenly Pecan Cake	136
Japanese Fruit Cake	170
Lemon Cheese Cake	134
Lemon Coconut Sheet Cake	167
Luscious Lime Cake	166
Mama Gillis' 14-Layer Chocolate Fudge Layer Cake	477
Michigan Apple Cake with Caramel Glaze	153
Milky Way Cake	145
My Hubby's Groom's Cake	164
One Bowl Pineapple Cake	141
Peter Paul Mound Cake	146
Pineapple Pound Cake	133
Red Velvet Ganache Cheesecake	156
Sour Cream Pound Cake	142
Strawberry Cake	163
Strawberry Delight Cake	138
The Divine Dixie Deva's Favorite Cake	169
The Fastest Chocolate Cake in Town	144
Upside-Down Apple Cake	161
White Butter Cake	150
Willie Kirk's Coconut Cake	154
Yellow Sheet Cake	148

Candies

Ambrosia Candy	243
Banana Bars	199
Baked Apples	114
Buttermilk Fudge	234
Butterscotch Haystacks	246
Candied Apples	248
Chocolate Peanut Clusters	241
Divinity	246
Easy-to-Make Marshmallow Popcorn Balls	240
Georgia Pecan Pralines	235
Kathryn's Blonde Fudge	237
Maple Pecan Buttermilk Candy	234
Mints	241
Mocha Cream Pralines	236
Mocha Fudge	242
Old Time Chocolate Fudge	236
Peanut Brittle	245
Peanut Butter Fudge	237
Pecan Brittle	244
Peter Pan's Cornflake Candy	245
Popcorn Balls	239
Rocky Road Candy	247
Southern Pecan Logs	240
Truffles	242
Two–Toned Georgia Crackers	243
Banana Pudding	113
Banana Split Ice Cream	123
Butter Pecan Ice Cream	122
Chocolate Bread Pudding	126
Chocolate Ice Cream	122
Chocolate Pudding Torte	112
Cinnamon Apple Sticks	425
Coffee Chiffon Dessert	117
Easy Egg Custard	119
Fudge Cake Pudding	127
Homemade Ice Cream	120
Homemade Peach Ice Cream	121
Lemon Ice Cream	120
Mama Gillis' Bread Pudding	128
Peach Custard Dessert	115
Peach Peeling-Peach Seed Jelly	425
Pineapple Pudding	114
Pumpkin Custard	130
Strawberry Surprise	118
The Deva's Chocolate Mousse	125
Vanilla Custard Ice Cream	124

Cobblers and Pies

Apple Cobbler	216
Autumn Sweet Potato Pie	203
Banana Cream Pie	206
Blackberry Cobbler	218
Blueberry Buckle	223
Brown Paper Bag Apple Pie	209
Buttermilk Pie	210

INDEX

Cheesecake Deluxe with Raspberry Glaze	162
Cream Cheese Pudding Pie	211
Easy Apple Pie	215
Elvis Pie	205
Fresh Blueberry Pie	213
Gerb's Peanut Butter Pie	204
Holiday Cranberry Raisin Pie	208
Lemon Chess Pie	215
Mocha Ice Cream Pie	212
Ole Fashion Egg Custard Pie	214
Peach Cobbler	217
Pecan Pie	210
Raspberry and Lemon Lush Pie	207

Cookies

Almond Crescent Cookies	187
Banana Bars	199
Brown Sugar Cut-Outs	191
Butter Cookies	182
Cinnamon Apple Sticks	425
Coconut Macaroons	181
Coconut Washboard Cookies	192
Date Nut Balls	180
Elaine's Last Minute Drop Cookies	198
Fruitcake Cookies	189
Gingerbread Bars with Lemon Glaze Icing	197
Greenville Tea Cakes	185
Jumbo P-nut Butter M & M Cookies	193
Kathryn's Favorite Cereal Cookie Recipe	196
Kathryn's Sugar Cookie Recipe	186
Oatmeal Raisin Cookie	183
Peanut Butter Brownies	181
Peanut Butter Fingers with Chocolate Icing	194
Peanut Butter Pecan Cookies	183
Reese's Cup Chocolate Cookies	200
Snickerdoodles	182
Sweet Molasses Cookies	184
The Good Ole Faithful Blondie Bar Cookie	188
The Redhead's Favorite Peanut Butter Cookies	195
War Tack	190

Custards and Puddings

Chocolate Bread Pudding	126
Chocolate Pudding Torte	112
Easy Egg Custard	119
Fudge Cake Pudding	127
Mama Gillis' Bread Pudding	128
Peach Custard Dessert	115
Pineapple Pudding	114
Pumpkin Custard	130
Strawberry Surprise	118
The Deva's Chocolate Mousse	125
Deviled Egg Spread	347
Deviled Eggs with Shrimp	42
Deviled Ham Balls	44
Deviled Ham Spread	353
Divinity	246
Don's Grilled Eye Round Roast	271
Down Home Country Fried Steak	277

E

Easy-to-Make Marshmallow Popcorn Balls	240
Easy Apple Pie	215
Easy Egg Custard	119
Edna Lane's Baby Quiches	54
Egg Drop Soup	339
Eggnog	66
Egg Salad Sandwich in a Hot Dog Bun	348
Elaine's Last Minute Drop Cookies	198
Elegant Prime Rib Roast	273
Elvis Pie	205
English Peas and Dumplings	377
English Peas and New Irish Potatoes with Cream Sauce	374
English Peas with Cream Sauce	373

F

Flavored Nut Butter	413
Freezing Bananas	198
Fresh Blueberry Pie	213
Fresh Country Cream Corn	365
Fresh Tomato Garden Pie	393
Fresh Tomato Salsa	442
Fried Eggplant with Parmesan Cheese	366
Fried Florida Scallops	452
Fried Frog Legs	453
Fried Green Tomatoes	394
Fried Okra	363
Fried Oysters	449
Fried Quail	463
Fried Red Tomatoes	392
Fried Shrimp	450

FROSTINGS, FILLINGS AND ICINGS:

Butter Cream Frosting	173
Chocolate Seven Minute Frosting	176

INDEX

Decorating Cream Icing	175
Decorating Icing	174
Hawaiian Cake Filling	177
Lemon Cheese Filling	175
Ole Fashioned Cooked Chocolate Icing	177
Orange Drizzle	172
Royal Icing	174
Seven Minute Frosting	176
Snow-Capped Icing	135
Sour Cream Coconut Frosting	173
Fruit and Nut Salad	310
Fruit Bowl Salad with Fruit Dressing	329
Fruitcake Cookies	189
Fruity Health Shake	72
Fudge Cake Pudding	127

G

Georgia Peach Brain Freeze	75
Georgia Peach Chutney	433
Georgia Peach Dumplings	220
Georgia Peach Shortcake	158
Georgia Peach Spread	345
Georgia Praline Sauce	407
Gingerbread Bars with Lemon Glaze Icing	197
Gingerbread with Lemon Sauce	140

GLAZES, GRAVIES, SAUCES, SYRUPS AND TOPPINGS:

Apple Dapple Topping	403
Apricot Honey Glaze	410
Basic Recipe for White Sauce	418
BBQ Slather and Sop Sauce	419
Blueberry Sauce	402
Brandy Sauce	411
Brown Sugar Butter Sauce	406
Brown Sugar Hard Sauce	406
Cal's Confederate Hot Dog Coney Sauce	285
Cheesy Cheese Sauce	412
Chicken Gravy	290
Chocolate Sauce	405
Cinnamon Apple Topping	403
Cocktail Sauce	417
Cranberry Sauce	411
Creamy Butterscotch Sauce	406
Flavored Nut Butter	413
Game Bird Orange Sauce	459
Georgia Praline Sauce	407
Gooey Caramel Pecan Sauce	404
Hog Sauce	420
Homemade Tartar Sauce	417
Honeybee Syrup	414
Honey Butter	414
Hop Sopping Syrup	413
Hot Fudge Topping	40
Hot Pepper Sauce	436
Mama Gillis' Red-Eye Gravy	416
Mama Gillis' Sawmill Gravy	416
Maple Syrup Cream	413
Marshmallow Sauce for Sundaes	408
Onion Gravy	415
Peach Blueberry Sauce	402
Pineapple Glaze for Ham	410
Pineapple Raisin Sauce	409
Pineapple Sauce	407
Plantation Hard Sauce	410
Powdered Sugar Drizzle	104
Raisin Sauce	409
Raspberry Sauce	403
Rum Sauce	404
Sour Cream Dill Gravy	267
Sour Cream Gravy	414
Stroganoff Gravy	415
Sweet Strawberry Sauce	402
Zippy Meatloaf Topping	412
Zippy Pineapple Sauce	408
Good Morning Shake	72
Good Ole Southern Cornbread Dressing With Giblet Gravy	398
Good Ole Southern Pimento Cheese Spread	352
Gooey Caramel Pecan Sauce	404
Greenville Tea Cakes	185
Grilled Marinated Back Strap (Tenderloin)	468
Grits	256

H

Ham and Cheese Quiche	253
Hamburger and Onion Pie	269
Ham Salad Spread	345
Hawaiian Cake Filling	177
Hawaiian Slurp Drink	70
Heavenly Pecan Cake	136
Herb Dip	51
Hilda's Broccoli Casserole	361
Hog Sauce	420
Holiday Cranberry Raisin Pie	208
Holiday Fruit Salad	308
Homemade Chicken Soup	341
Homemade Cinnamon Sweet Rolls	102
Homemade Tartar Sauce	417
Homemade Waffles	252

INDEX

Hominy Hot Pot	302
Honey Bee Banana Booster	73
Honeybee Syrup	414
Honey Butter	414
Honey Raisin Spread	353
Hop Sopping Syrup	413
Hot and Spicy Apricot Spread	344
Hot and Spicy Biscuits	91
Hot Chili Cornbread	92
Hot Cranberry Punch	78
Hot Dog Bun Bread Sticks	82
Hot Fudge Topping	405
Hot Ham Brunch Casserole	259
Hot Lemon Spiced Tea	78
Hot Pepper Sauce	436
Hot Turkey Casserole	305
Humongous Hamburgers	281
Hush Puppies	93

I

ICE CREAM AND SHERBETS:

Banana Split Ice Cream	123
Butter Pecan Ice Cream	122
Chocolate Ice Cream	122
Homemade Ice Cream	120
Homemade Peach Ice Cream	121
Vanilla Custard Ice Cream	52
Ice Ring	62
Italian Sandwich Spread	352

J

JAMS, JELLIES, PICKLES AND PRESERVES:

Bernice's Cherry Pear Preserves	424
Bernice's Peach Preserves	424
Blueberry Peach Jam	430
Bounty Fresh Vegetable Beef Soup for Supper	437
Canned Peach Chutney	434
Fresh Tomato Salsa	442
Georgia Peach Chutney	433
Mama's Pickled Peaches	435
Mama Gillis' 9-Day Pickle	438
Mayhaw Jelly Recipe	427
Ole Fashion Apple Butter	443
Peach Peeling-Peach Seed Jelly	425
Pear Chutney	434
Pear Honey	428
Pepper Sauce	436
Quick and Easy Sweet Pickles	441
Red Pepper Relish	442
Squash Pickles	444
Strawberry Fig Preserves	429
Strawberry Rhubarb Jam	429
Sweet Red Pepper Sauce Syrup	436
Vidalia Onion Relish	431
Winter Cranberry Chutney	432
Japanese Fruit Cake	170
Johnny Appleseed's Apple Dumpling	221
Judy's Bean Salad	323
Jumbo P-nut Butter M & M Cookies	193

K

Kathryn's BBQ Boston Butt	472
Kathryn's Blonde Fudge	237
Kathryn's Citrus Salad	314
Kathryn's Favorite Cereal Cookie Recipe	196
Kathryn's Favorite Cheese Ring	33
Kathryn's Manicotti Meal	298
Kathryn's Stuffed Cheese Burgers with Salsa	282
Kathryn's Sugar Cookie Recipe	186
Kathryn and Bernice's Vegetable Soup Base	437
Kicker Cheese Ring	33
Kool-Aid Fruit Punch	61

L

Lamb Salad with Vinaigrette Salad Dressing	325
Layered Fresh Fruit Nut Salad	316
Lemon Cheese Cake	134
Lemon Cheese Filling	175
Lemon Chess Pie	215
Lemon Coconut Sheet Cake	167
Lemon Curd Tassies	58
Lemon Ice Cream	120
Lime Orange Freeze Drink	64
Loaf Bread	85
Luncheon Shrimp Salad With French Dressing	320
Luscious Lime Cake	166

M

Macaroni and Cheese Ham Casserole	306
Mama's Christmas Fruit Salad	313
Mama's Pickled Peaches	435
Mama Gillis' 14-Layer Chocolate Fudge Layer Cake	477

INDEX

Mama Gillis' 9-Day Pickle	438
Mama Gillis' Baked Macaroni N' Cheese	397
Mama Gillis' Bread Pudding	128
Mama Gillis' Fried Chicken	288
Mama Gillis' Fried Squirrel	464
Mama Gillis' Fried Sweet Potatoes	384
Mama Gillis' Red-Eye Gravy	416
Mama Gillis' Sawmill Gravy	416
Mama Gillis's Buttermilk Biscuits	89
Mandarin Orange Delight	309
Maple Milkshake	73
Maple Pecan Buttermilk Candy	234
Maple Syrup Cream	413
Marinated Black-Eyed Peas	376
Marinated Shrimp	42
Marinated Tomato Salad	318
Marshmallow Sauce for Sundaes, Cakes	408
Mashed Potato Meringues	379
Mayhaw Jelly Recipe	427

MEATS:

Beef

All Beef Meatball Recipe	277
Beefaroni	283
Beef Brisket	284
Beef Stew in a Skillet	268
Beef Stroganoff	270
Beefy Noodle Supper Dish	269
Chuck Wagon Dinner	272
Corned Beef and Cabbage Dinner	272
Cube Steak Dinner	278
Don's Grilled Eye Round Roast	271
Down Home Country Fried Steak	277
Elegant Prime Rib Roast	273
Hamburger and Onion Pie	269
Humongous Hamburgers	281
Kathryn's Stuffed Cheese Burgers with Salsa	282
Meat Balls with Dill Sour Cream Gravy	267
Round Steak Supper Dish	276
Stuffed Cabbage Rolls	274
Swiss Steak Dinner	279
The Divine Dixie Deva's Hamburgers	281
Tonight's Meatloaf	275

Fish

Baked Bluefish	457
Baked Fish	455
Basic Recipe for Broiling Fish	458
Broiling Fish	458
Deep Fried Fish	456
Pan-Fried Fish	454
Pan-Fried Walleye	452
Fried Frog Legs	453

Pork

Pork, Cabbage and Apple Skillet	266
Pork Chop and Spanish Rice Dish	266
Pork Chop Skillet Supreme	265
Southern Baked Pork Loin	262
Stuffed Pork Chops with Apple	264

Poultry

Chicken and Dumplings	292
Chicken Herb Dinner with Sweet Tators and White Tators	287
Chicken on a Shoe String Budget	293
Chicken or Turkey A La King	296
Chicken Pie	294
Chicken Supreme	295
Chicken Wings with Wing Ding Sauce	45
Cornish Hens with Wild Rice	297
Mama Gillis' Fried Chicken	288
Quick Supper of Oven Fried Chicken with Dressing	291

Seafood

Baked Oysters	41
Fried Florida Scallops	452
Fried Oysters	449
Fried Shrimp	450
Salmon Log	40
Scalloped Oysters	450
Scalloped Oysters with Corn	451
Shrimp Spread	41

Wild Game

Deer Burgers	467
Fried Quail	463
Game Bird Orange Sauce	459
Grilled Marinated Back Strap	468
Mama Gillis' Fried Squirrel	464
Papa's Oyster Stew	448
Plantation Smothered Quail Rice n' Gravy	462
Roasted Goose Glazed with Currant Sauce	460
Venison Chili	470
Venison Cube Steak	467
Venison Marinade	466
Venison Meat Loaf	468
Venison Roast	469
Kathryn's Manicotti Meal	298

INDEX

Melon Breeze	77
Mexican Macaroni	396
Michigan Apple Cake with Caramel Glaze	153
Milky Way Cake	145
Mini Cheese Biscuits	90
Mints	241
Mixed Bean and Bacon Salad	321
Mocha Cream Pralines	236
Mocha Eggnog Punch	63
Mocha Fudge	242
Mocha Ice Cream Pie	212
Mocha Punch	62
My Hubby's Groom's Cake	164
My Secret Little Side Dish	369
Roasted Leg of Lamb	286
Saturday Night Lasagna	299
Super Easy Taco Filling	280
Vegetarian Pie	300
Weenies N' Crescents	283

N

Nacho Waffle Bites	55
No Knead Raisin Bread	109
Non-Alcoholic Georgia Peach Brain Freeze	75

O

Oatmeal Raisin Cookie	183
Okra, Corn, and Tomatoes Side	368
Old Time Chocolate Fudge	236
Ole Fashion Apple Butter	443
Ole Fashioned Cooked Chocolate Icing	177
Ole Fashion Egg Custard Pie	214
Ole Favorite Squash Casserole	389
Ole Timey Cheese Straws	36
One Bowl Pineapple Cake	141
Onion Gravy	415
Onion Soup	336
Orange Cheese Salad	311
Orange Cheese Spread	35
Orange Drizzle	172
Orange Glazed Carrots	363
Orange Lemonade	79
Orange Mandarin Salad	309
Orange Nut Muffins	100
Orange Pineapple Spread	351
Orange Sherbet Gelatin Salad	313
Orange Vanilla Crust	227
Out-of-Season Cream Corn	367

P

Pan-Fried Fish	454
Pan-Fried Walleye	452

PANCAKES AND WAFFLES:

Buttermilk Pancakes	251
Homemade Waffles	252
Papa's Oyster Stew	448
Party Punch	68
Party Shrimp Mold	43
Peach Blueberry Sauce	402
Peach Cobbler	217
Peach Custard Dessert	115
Peach Peeling-Peach Seed Jelly	425
Peanut Brittle	245
Peanut Butter Brownies	181
Peanut Butter Cheese Ball	38
Peanut Butter Fingers with Chocolate Icing	194
Peanut Butter Fudge	237
Peanut Butter Pecan Cookies	183
Peanut Butter Pork Balls	50
Pear Chutney	434
Pear Honey	428
Pecan Brittle	244
Pecan Caramel Muffins	94
Pecan Cheese Ball	34
Pecan Pie	210
Peppermint Eggnog	67
Pepper Sauce	436
Perpetual Vanilla Extract	330
Peter Pan's Cornflake Candy	245
Peter Paul Mound Cake	146
Pickled Peach Salad	315

PIE CRUSTS:

Boiling Water Pie Crust	228
Butter Pecan Coconut Crust	224
Chocolate Coconut Crust	224
Chocolate Cookie Dough Pie Crust	227
Coconut Crust	225
Cream Cheese Pastry Crust	225
Orange Vanilla Crust	227
Pecan Crust	226
Plain Pastry Dough	229
Walnut Graham Cracker Pie Shell	225
Pineapple Casserole	378
Pineapple Cheesy Nut Spread	344
Pineapple Glaze for Ham	410
Pineapple Muffins	97
Pineapple Pound Cake	133

Pineapple Pudding	114
Pineapple Raisin Sauce	409
Pineapple Sandwiches	350
Pineapple Sauce	407
Pineapple Spread	343
Pizza Dogs	349
Plain Pastry Dough	229
Plantation Hard Sauce	410
Plantation Smothered Quail Rice n' Gravy	462
Pole Beans and New Potatoes	360
Popcorn Balls	239
Poppy Seed Yeast Bread	84
Pork Chop and Spanish Rice Dish	266
Pork Chop Skillet Supreme	265
Porky Balls with Dipping Sauce	50
Potato Balls	380
Potato Chip Sandwich	350
Powdered Sugar Drizzle	104
Pumpkin Bread	110
Pumpkin Butter	351
Pumpkin Custard	130

Q

Quick 'n' Easy Buttermilk Rolls	87
Quick and Easy Sweet Pickles	441
Quick Bread Sticks	82
Quick Supper of Oven Fried Chicken with Dressing	291

R

Rainbow Punch	65
Raisin Bran Muffins	96
Raisin Sauce	409
Raspberry and Lemon Lush Pie	207
Raspberry Sauce	403
Red Pepper Relish	442
Red Velvet Ganache Cheesecake	156
Reese's Cup Chocolate Cookies	200
Riblet Nibblers	51
Ribs	474
Rice Crispy Cheese Wafers	37
Roasted Goose Glazed with Currant Sauce	460
Roasted Leg of Lamb	286
Roasted Potatoes	382
Rocky Road Candy	247
Round Steak Supper Dish	276
Royal Icing	174
Rudolph's Breakfast Casserole	254
Rum Sauce	404

S

SALADS:

Apple Salad	317
Asa's Blueberry Salad	311
Bing Cherry Salad	312
Cranberry Congealed Salad	312
Creamy Bacon, Lettuce, Tomato Salad	328
Fruit and Nut Salad	310
Fruit Bowl Salad with Fruit Dressing	329
Holiday Fruit Salad	308
Judy's Bean Salad	323
Kathryn's Citrus Salad	314
Lamb Salad with Vinaigrette Salad Dressing	325
Layered Fresh Fruit Nut Salad	316
Luncheon Shrimp Salad with French Dressing	320
Mama's Christmas Fruit Salad	313
Mandarin Orange Delight	309
Marinated Tomato Salad	318
Mixed Bean and Bacon Salad	321
Orange Cheese Salad	311
Orange Mandarin Salad	309
Orange Sherbet Gelatin Salad	313
Pickled Peach Salad	315
Simply Southern Pear Salad	315
Slaw	327
Sour Cream Potato Salad	326
Southern Snowflake Ambrosia	324
Southwest Georgia Grape Salad	318
Supreme Egg Salad	322
Sweet Potato Salad	319
Taco Salad	329
Tomato Soup Mold Salad	328
Tutti-Fruity Salad	310

SANDWICHES AND SPREADS:

Bacon Spread	352
Bologna and Cheese Sandwich Spread	346
Cheesy Apple Spread	34
Chilly Cheese Spread	344
Cranberry Cheese Sandwich Spread	349
Cranberry Relish	354
Creamy Ham N Cheese Sandwich Spread	346
Deviled Egg Spread	347
Deviled Ham Spread	353
Egg Salad Sandwich in a Hot Dog Bun	348
Georgia Peach Spread	345
Good Ole Southern Pimento Cheese Spread	352
Ham Salad Spread	345

INDEX

Honey Raisin Spread	353
Hot and Spicy Apricot Spread	344
Italian Sandwich Spread	352
Orange Pineapple Spread	351
Pineapple Cheesy Nut Spread	344
Pineapple Sandwiches	350
Pineapple Spread	343
Pizza Dogs	349
Potato Chip Sandwich	350
Pumpkin Butter	351
Sassy, Saucy Ham Spread	52
Strawberry Cream Cheese Spread	353
Tuna Sandwich in a Hot Dog Bun	348
Sausage Bites	47
Sausage Stuffed Mushrooms	47
Sauted Onions	370
Scalloped Oysters	450
Scalloped Oysters with Corn	451
Scotch Eggs	48
Seven Minute Frosting	176
Simply Southern Pear Salad	315
Slaw	327
Smoked Fish Spread	39
Snickerdoodles	182
Snow-Capped Icing	135

SOUPS AND STEWS:

Beef Stew in a Skillet	268
Bounty Fresh Vegetable Beef Soup for Supper	437
Cheddar Cheese Soup	334
Chicken and Dumplings	292
Cream of Bacon and Potato Soup	340
Cream of Mushroom Soup	332
Creamy Broccoli Soup	335
Creamy Corn Chowder	338
Egg Drop Soup	339
Homemade Chicken Soup	341
Kathryn and Bernice's Vegetable Soup Base	437
Onion Soup	336
Taco Soup	336
Turkey Soup	337
Zucchini Soup	333
Sour Cream Biscuits	87
Sour Cream Coconut Frosting	173
Sour Cream Dill Gravy	267
Sour Cream Gravy	414
Sour Cream Potato Salad	326
Sour Cream Pound Cake	142
Southern Baked Pork Loin with Sausage Stuffing and Mushroom Sauce	262
Southern Concoction	56

Southern Pecan Logs	240
Southern Sea Breeze Smoothie	76
Southern Snowflake Ambrosia	324
Southwest Georgia Grape Salad	318
Spanish Rice	387
Sparkling Fruit Punch	69
Spiced Pecans	53
Spicy Cheese Loaf	35
Squash Pickles	444
Steaming Hot Cocoa	69
Strawberry Cake	163
Strawberry Cream Cheese Spread	353
Strawberry Delight Cake	138
Strawberry Fig Preserves	429
Strawberry Lemonade	77
Strawberry Lemon Punch	63
Strawberry Rhubarb Jam	429
Strawberry Surprise	118
Stroganoff Gravy	415
Stuffed Cabbage Rolls	274
Stuffed Pork Chops with Apple	264
Stuffed Vidalia Onions	371
Summer Squash Patties	390
Super Easy Taco Filling	280
Supreme Egg Salad	322
Swedish Meatballs	49
Sweet and Glazy Peanuts	54
Sweet Molasses Cookies	184
Sweet Potato Bread	385
Sweet Potato Crunch	386
Sweet Potato Salad	319
Sweet Red Pepper Sauce Syrup Recipe	436
Sweet Strawberry Sauce	402
Swiss Steak Dinner	279

T

Taco Bake	303
Taco Salad	329
Taco Soup	336
The Deva's Chocolate Mousse	125
The Divine Dixie Deva's Favorite Cake	169
The Divine Dixie Deva's Hamburgers	281
The Fastest Chocolate Cake in Town	144
The Good Ole Faithful Blondie Bar Cookie	188
The Old Favorite of Broccoli Rice and Cheese Dish	361
The Redhead's Favorite Peanut Butter Cookies	195
Tipsy Grapes	57
Tomato Casserole	394
Tomato Soup Mold Salad	328

INDEX

Tonight's Meatloaf	275
Top of the Stove Popcorn	238
Truffles	242
Tuna Sandwich in a Hot Dog Bun	348
Turkey and Wild Rice Casserole	304
Turkey Soup	337
Tutti-Fruity Salad	310
Two–Toned Georgia Crackers	243

U

Upside-Down Apple Cake	161

V

Vanilla Custard Ice Cream	124
Vanilla Milk	71
Vanilla Extract, Perpetual	330

VEGETABLES:

Apples Stuffed With Sweet Potatoes	357
Asparagus and Pea Casserole	358
Baked Pears and Pineapple	372
Baked Stuffed Tomatoes	391
Broccoli and Cauliflower Casserole	362
Brown Rice	387
Butternut Squash Casserole	388
Cheese Onions with a Hint of Sherry	370
Cheese Potato Soufflé	381
Corn and Okra Side Dish	366
Creamy Cauliflower Dish	364
English Peas and Dumplings	377
English Peas and New Irish Potatoes with Cream Sauce	374
English Peas with Cream Sauce	373
Fresh Country Cream Corn	365
Fresh Tomato Garden Pie	393
Fried Eggplant with Parmesan Cheese	366
Fried Green Tomatoes	394
Fried Okra	363
Fried Red Tomatoes	392
Mama Gillis' Baked Macaroni N' Cheese	397
Mama Gillis' Fried Sweet Potatoes	384
Marinated Black-Eyed Peas	376
Mashed Potato Meringues	379
Mexican Macaroni	396
Okra, Corn, and Tomatoes Side	368
Orange Glazed Carrots	363
Out-of-Season Cream Corn	367
Pole Beans and New Potatoes	360
Potato Balls	380
Roasted Potatoes	382
Sauted Onions	370
Spanish Rice	387
Stuffed Vidalia Onions	371
Summer Squash Patties	390
Sweet Potato Bread	385
Sweet Potato Crunch	386
The Old Favorite of Broccoli Rice and Cheese Dish	361
Vegetable Trio Bake	392
Vegetarian Pie	300

Venison Chili	470
Venison Cube Steak	467
Venison Marinade	466
Venison Meat Loaf	468
Venison Roast	469
Vidalia Onion Relish	431

W

Walnut Graham Cracker Pie Shell	225
Weenies N' Crescents	283
White Butter Cake	150
Willie Kirk's Coconut Cake	154
Winter Cranberry Chutney	432

Y

Yellow Fruit Punch	61
Yellow Sheet Cake	148

Z

Zippy Meatloaf Topping	412
Zippy Pineapple Sauce	408
Zucchini Carrot Muffins	98
Zucchini Soup	333
Zucchini Tea Bread	110